NEW COUNTRIES

NEW
COUNTRIES

Capitalism, Revolutions, and Nations
in the Americas, 1750–1870

JOHN TUTINO, EDITOR

―――

Duke University Press　Durham and London　2016

© 2016 Duke University Press
All rights reserved

Designed by Courtney Leigh Baker
Typeset in Garamond Premier Pro by Westchester Publishing Services

Library of Congress Cataloging-in-Publication Data
Names: Tutino, John, [date] author.
Title: New countries : capitalism, revolutions, and nations in the Americas,
1750–1870 / John Tutino.
Description: Durham : Duke University Press, 2016.
Includes bibliographical references and index.
Identifiers: LCCN 2016022709 (print) | LCCN 2016024859 (ebook)
ISBN 9780822361145 (hardcover : alk. paper)
ISBN 9780822361336 (pbk. : alk. paper)
ISBN 9780822374305 (e-book)
Subjects: LCSH: Industrial revolution—Europe. | Industrialization—
Latin America—History—19th century. | Industrialization—United States—
History—19th century. | Latin America—History—Autonomy and independence
movements. | Latin America—Foreign economic relations.
Classification: LCC HC240 .T826 2016 (print) | LCC HC240 (ebook)
DDC 330.97/004—dc23
LC record available at https://lccn.loc.gov/2016022709

To the
community of scholars
who worked together to build this new vision,
and to the families and communities
that sustain them.

CONTENTS

ACKNOWLEDGMENTS

A project that aims to rethink the origins of New World nations in a context of global transformations and that mobilizes diverse scholars over several years creates great debts that can never be fully recognized and acknowledged. My deepest debt, as stated in the dedication, is to the participant authors. In addition, Jonathan Brown joined us in our conversations at Georgetown and LASA San Francisco, sharing an economic perspective and a view from Buenos Aires that broadened our thinking. John McNeill was a key discussant at Georgetown—and read so many versions of my introduction and chapter 1 that I worry that he deserves coauthor credit. He made me become clearer—even when he does not share all my emphases.

Among our authors, David Sartorius began as a discussant at Georgetown and the strength of his understanding led the group to decide we needed him to write a chapter on Cuba. Jordana Dym argued that we needed to balance my opening emphasis on economic change with a chapter on transatlantic Hispanic politics—leading to the recruitment of Roberto Breña to join our community and write chapter 2. Adam Rothman read my contributions from a U.S. perspective, helping me see across borders and making me get clearer. Erick Langer generated the key ideas that we developed together in the epilogue—helping our volume look beyond 1870.

At Georgetown, the sponsorship and support of the Americas Initiative has been crucial. It was founded and funded by Dean of College Jane McAuliffe, who challenged us to look at key questions across borders and across the hemisphere. Dean Chet Gillis has kept us going through sometimes trying times. Evan Chernack, a student of Latin America in the world, volunteered to help finalize the manuscript. Most essentially, Kathy Gallagher has managed the initiative from its founding in 2006. She organized our gatherings and worked through funding challenges that made this project possible from first imagining to final publication. It is fitting that I write this on the same day that my wife Jane and I take Kathy to dinner to lament and celebrate her retirement. The Americas Initiative flourished for a decade thanks to her effective efforts and constant cheer; it will not be the same without her—though we will find a way to carry on.

Once again, Bill Nelson has produced maps with skill (and his good cheer)— this time with the added challenge of working with multiple chapter authors. His work makes our books better.

And it has been a pleasure to work again with Duke University Press. My first inquiry about *New Countries* proved to be my last formal correspondence with Valerie Milholland, on the eve of her retirement. She wisely passed the project on to Gisela Fosado, who saw potential in the volume, found readers that made us get better in many ways, and now leads us into production. I and many of the chapter authors previously worked with Valerie and Duke; we are pleased and honored to join Gisela as she keeps Duke's innovative and critical vision of the Americas alive.

REVOLUTIONS, NATIONS, AND
A NEW INDUSTRIAL WORLD

JOHN TUTINO

From 1500 to 1800, the Americas were a key part of a world of empires and global trades.[1] In the 1780s, New Spain drove silver production to new heights, concentrating wealth in Mexico City, by far the hemisphere's leading center of population and power. In the same decade, French Saint Domingue led the Atlantic world in sugar production and the concentration of enslaved laborers. Meanwhile, a fledgling United States was escaping British rule, building a republican polity, and searching for commercial prosperity—its free people enjoying solid well-being while a large enslaved minority saw bondage confirmed in a new constitution.

By 1850, the United States, having just claimed in war vast territories long tied to New Spain and then Mexico, was driving toward continental hegemony: southern cotton growers worked slave laborers to supply British mills that ruled a new industrial world economy; New England mills competed to profit in that economy; and free settlers drove commercial farming across a vast Mississippi basin into lands taken from displaced native peoples. At the same time, Mexico, its once dynamic silver economy fallen in the face of war and insurgency after 1810, faced endemic political conflicts while it searched for a new economy in a shrunken territory. And Haiti, built by revolutionary slaves in once rich Saint Domingue, consolidated a society of family cultivation and limited exports—excluded from the new global industrial economy. All would face political conflicts in the decades to come. But in the United States, Civil War led to an expansive prosperity; for Mexico, Reform Wars led to growing dependence on U.S. capital and markets; and in Haiti, internal conflicts came with continuing poverty and commercial exclusion.

The dramatic changes that marked the emergence of the United States, Mexico, and Haiti as nations only begin to illustrate the depth and complexity of the larger and more diverse transformations that created new countries across the Americas during the decades after 1770. After centuries in which European monarchs claimed sovereignty, diverse Christianities shaped the lives of the powerful, the colonized, and the enslaved, and dynamic trades led by Spanish American silver and Atlantic sugar and slavery made the hemisphere central to global trades—everything seemed to change, creatively for some, destructively for others.

During the century after 1750 people across the Americas fought and negotiated, traded and labored to forge new polities and new economies—thus new countries. In some regions, insurrectionary movements forced new social relations: in Haiti, where revolutionary slaves ended slavery and took the land; in core regions of Mexico, where insurgent communities took new control of production; in diverse other places where indigenous peoples found new autonomies as nations struggled to find political stability and commercial prosperity. Elsewhere, old social relations endured: in expansions of slave labor in Brazil, Cuba, and the U.S. South; in continuing political exclusions of many native peoples across the hemisphere. Diverse peoples came out of old empires in unimagined ways. They built states with new boundaries, new citizenships, new social relationships, and new ways of production.

While making new countries, the people of the Americas saw their histories diverge in many ways. Many founded republics, yet Brazil became an empire and Cuba remained a colony. Some former colonies joined together to become United States; others fragmented into small nations, as in Central America. And while forging such diversity, the new countries of the Americas stayed tied to a rapidly changing world economy. They emerged during the rise of a new industrial capitalism forged in England after 1800 and soon replicated in the northeastern United States. The rest of the Americas adapted. Some prospered while many struggled.

The aims and uncertainties of nation making are central concerns of every national history.[2] In this volume we analyze the emergence of nations (and Cuba's colonial persistence) across the hemisphere in the light of changing global relationships. Too often, the conflicts that led to the new American nations and the innovations that generated the British industrial revolution appear as simultaneous but separate—the definition of historical coincidence. We see them as simultaneous and inseparable. The Americas played key roles in the Atlantic conflicts that led to new nations and in the global transformation that led to industrial capitalism. We explore how New World peoples both joined in and adapted to key changes in the world economy after 1780, how they engaged in forging liberal and republican polities, and how eight new countries navigated times of conflictive change: four coming out of Atlantic slave colonies—the United States, Haiti, Cuba (a new country even as it remained a colony), and Brazil; four built in Spanish American societies with indigenous majorities—Mexico, Guatemala, Peru, and Bolivia. We aim to understand how new countries emerged and how they diverged while industrial capitalism rose to shape the nineteenth-century world.

In Search of an Integrated History

Too often, all this has been studied separately. Yet the founding dynamism of the early American silver and sugar economies, the late eighteenth-century challenges of war and political innovation, the revolutionary destruction of key colonies,[3] and the struggles to build nations in a changing global economy demand integrated analysis if we are to understand the transformation of the Americas after 1750—and how conflicts there contributed to the rise of British and later U.S. industrial capitalism.[4]

It is a tall order, of course, to integrate the global and the local, the economic and the political, along with social conflicts and cultural debates and innovations—across a diverse hemisphere. There have been illuminating attempts: In his classic study of *The Spanish American Revolutions, 1808–1826*, John Lynch linked hemispheric political processes and local conflicts in a work that included most of the continent and the majority of its peoples—those subject to Spanish sovereignty in 1800.[5] Robin Blackburn soon followed with the *Overthrow of Colonial Slavery, 1776–1848*, analyzing one pervasive conflict central to the era of independence across the continent.[6] Lester Langley took on the entire hemisphere in his ambitious *The Americas in the Age of Revolution,*

1750–1850.[7] Recently, in *Empires of the Atlantic World*, J. H. Elliott compared key regions of Spanish and British America from their colonial origins through independence,[8] and Jeremy Adelman offered *Sovereignty and Revolution in the Iberian Atlantic,* engaging Spanish and Portuguese South America from Cartagena to Buenos Aires.[9] All make important contributions: Lynch by emphasizing the local complexities of the Spanish American conflicts; Blackburn by focusing us on the breadth and complexity of the problem of slavery; Langley by demonstrating the necessity of a hemispheric analysis; Elliott by insisting on a comparative vision set in a long historical perspective; Adelman by emphasizing that within Spanish and Portuguese domains imperial breakdown preceded the contested emergence of national goals and states.

Still, all remain limited: Lynch brought his regionally grounded and mostly political vision only to Spanish America; Blackburn emphasized the demise of slavery, downplaying its powerful expansions in nineteenth-century Brazil, Cuba, and the United States; Langley understood Spanish American economic systems and political processes but partially; Elliott compared the mainland colonies of Spanish and British America—the former pivotal, the latter secondary to the eighteenth-century world—leaving key Caribbean plantation regions aside; and Adelman remained in Atlantic South America, leaving others to integrate the often-conflictive Caribbean, Andean, and Mexican–Central American sequences. The search for an integrated vision of the transformation the Americas from 1750 to 1870 remains a challenge.

In recent years, the challenge has become more complex. Three key historical advances have illuminated and complicated analysis of an era too long seen either as an Age of Revolution or the Era of Independence: First, a turn to a global view of history combined with a rethinking of the trajectory of the global economy have combined to emphasize the centrality of Asia around 1500, the importance of the Americas in global trades from the sixteenth century, and the late rise of a European hegemony that only consolidated after 1800. Second, new understandings of the Haitian Revolution and of insurgent roles in Mexican independence have brought popular demands and the changes they forced to the center of key conflicts in the age of revolutions. Third, a new appreciation of the interplay of war, political conflict, and liberal innovation in the Hispanic world after 1808 has brought Spain and its Americas to the center of new analyses of the origins of regimes of popular sovereignty. Recognition of each innovation underscores the importance and the difficulty of the larger analytical challenge.

Through most of the twentieth century, economic history offered a clear and too simple vision: the industrial capitalism that shaped the world after

1800 was a natural, almost inevitable result of Anglo-European-Protestant culture and institutions. England, Western Europe, and the United States led—and the world followed. Then, in the context of the shift to globalization in the 1990s, new studies challenged the presumptive reign of Anglo-European primacy in global economic history. A series of studies, led by Kenneth Pomeranz's *The Great Divergence: China, Europe, and the Making of the Modern World Economy*, have shown that China led the world economically around 1500 and that European industrial eminence came after 1770—precisely during the decades of New World transformation.[10] Then economists Ronald Findlay and Kevin O'Rourke gave us *Power and Plenty: Trade, War, and the World Economy in the Second Millennium*, confirming the early dominance of China and India, the late rise of industrial Europe—and the importance of New World silver in linking and stimulating Asian and European economies after 1550. They, too, confirm the late rise of Europe—and emphasize the importance of the Euro-Atlantic wars of 1750–1830 in the rise of Anglo-American industrial hegemony.[11] And now Sven Beckert's *Empire of Cotton* details the rise of industrial capitalism during the same pivotal decades as a transatlantic process tying a long developing "war capitalism" built on empire and slavery to a rising industrial system in England, in the process transforming the world.[12]

Our analyses will suggest that to begin to grasp the radical reconstruction of the world from 1750 to 1850, we must see the collapse of the silver capitalism that was grounded in Spanish America and integrated the Americas, Asia, and Europe from 1550 to 1810.[13] We must also recognized the challenges to and persistence of the war capitalism of slave-based production and trades that continued to supply essential cotton and complementary sugar and coffee to industrializing Europe and North America past 1850. And we must see all that as linked to the technological innovations and capital accumulations that drove the industrial revolution beginning in western Britain.[14]

Meanwhile, scholars have also been rethinking the historical importance and impact of popular revolutionary movements in Saint Domingue (as it became Haiti) and New Spain (as it became Mexico). Carolyn Fick began the process in *The Making of Haiti*, showing that armed ex-slaves forced not only the abolition of slavery, but also the collapse of the plantation economy so pivotal to French participation in Atlantic trade and European power politics.[15] In *Avengers of the New World* Laurent Dubois broadened and confirmed the emphasis that adamant and armed former slaves ended Saint Domingue's role as the largest and most profitable producer of sugar and the greatest purchaser of slaves in the Atlantic world.[16] Meanwhile, I began to understand that the silver economy of New Spain continued to soar at historic levels, stimulating global trades (and funding wars) to 1810—when the Bajío, the leading New World center of silver mining, textile manufacturing, and irrigated commercial cultivation, exploded in a popular rising that lasted a decade. Insurgents undermined silver production and turned a commercial economy to family production (as did the slaves in Haiti).[17] Now, in *En el espejo haitiano*, Luis Fernando Granados has detailed how the popular power first forged in revolutionary Haiti proliferated across diverse American regions to culminate in the insurgencies that transformed the Bajío beginning in 1810.[18]

It is now clear that by 1804 Haitian revolutionaries had destroyed war capitalism in Saint Domingue and crippled France's chances to join in the early rise of industrial capitalism. The same revolution drove war capitalists working slave laborers to expand sugar production in Cuba, sugar and coffee in Brazil, and cotton cultivation across the U.S. South—the latter an essential component of the industrial revolution. Soon after, beginning in 1810, Bajío revolutionaries took down the silver capitalism that had long integrated global trades, bringing China to crisis and opening the way for the rise of the industrialism so celebrated for its British innovations—while so many try not to see its role in expanding slavery. On a global scale, silver capitalism and war capitalism rose together from the sixteenth century to shape early global commercial capitalism. Then when silver capitalism collapsed and industrial capitalism rose in the early nineteenth century, the war capitalism grounded in slave labor persisted to enable the transition. In the process, the economies of Spanish America saw global importance give way to the marginalities later called underdevelopment. Haitians grappled with new autonomies that locked them into poverty. Cuba and Brazil found new prosperities in expanding slave production for industrializing markets. And the United States mixed the expanded war capitalism of a South built on slavery with the emerging industries of an industrial North and a westward expansion of commercial cultivation into lands taken from natives and Mexicans to become the New World hegemon of a new global industrial capitalism.

While these fundamental socioeconomic conflicts and changes were under way, political movements, conflicts, and revolutions moved the Americas and the Atlantic world toward new polities. Empires of divine right faced challenges; nations proclaiming popular sovereignties rose to reshape the Americas after 1810. A vast scholarship on Europe and the Americas between 1765 and 1830 has focused on these important developments.[19] Yet too often, analysts imagine a derivative and imitative process in which political innovations forged in Anglo-American domains and reenergized in French revolutionary worlds imposed themselves on Iberian Americans when they came late to nation making.

Since the 1990s, scholars have reanalyzed the histories of independence in Iberia and the Americas with new studies of the Hispanic political revolution that led to the Cádiz Constitution of 1812. That charter aimed to hold Spain and its Americas together in opposition to Napoleon's 1808 invasion and occupation of Spain. Mostly implemented in the Americas (most of Spain was occupied by the French), it contributed in complex and conflictive ways to the eventual rise of new republics. And while including some parallels with Anglo-American and French developments, the Cádiz process had deep roots in Hispanic traditions of popular sovereignty as old as those in England and France.

The new scholarship about Ibero-American independence began with François-Xavier Guerra's *Modernidades e independencias*[20] and culminated in Roberto Breña's *El primer liberalismo español y los procesos de emancipación de América, 1808–1824*.[21] The work came just in time to shape an explosion of studies focused on the celebrations of independence in the bicentennials of 1810. A vision of Cádiz liberalism as pivotal to Spanish American independence marked conferences often funded by national states implementing neoliberalism. At times, war and trade, strongmen and insurgents faded from view. Still, the scholarship on the rise of a deeply Hispanic liberalism within the conflicts that led to Spanish American independence was mostly positive—and further fueled the need to rethink the transformation of the Americas between 1750 and 1850.

From the sixteenth century, peoples across the Americas lived within European empires while tied to trades that spanned the globe. After 1760, they joined in unprecedented political conflicts shaped by new visions of popular sovereignty and electoral participation. Many broke with empires and built new polities—while an unprecedented industrial concentration rose in Britain and reshaped the world economy. Nation builders claimed different resources, engaged distinct indigenous and colonial traditions, and found uncertain opportunities in a world facing rapid economic change. Economic, political, and social outcomes diverged everywhere. How did broad hemispheric participation in shared economic and political challenges and opportunities lead to new countries with diverging trajectories in a nineteenth-century world driven by industrial capitalism? No one scholar is ready to take on that pivotal analytical challenge.

To accelerate the conversation a group of scholars who had already written deep studies of key regions and questions illuminating the era of independence across the Americas met at Georgetown University under the auspices of the

Americas Initiative. We began with a challenge: without losing sight of the political, social, and cultural dynamics of the nation making we knew so well, how had each region experienced the changing economic dynamics of the era? The chapters that follow emerged from a process of sharing, discussion, and revision. We engage common questions, but we offer no single thesis to explain the emergence of new countries across the Americas after 1750 and their diverse roles in the nineteenth-century world.

Common themes do link our studies: Imperial legacies shaped conflicts and debates everywhere. In Atlantic plantation colonies, slavery was always a key question: would it end, persist, change, or expand? In highland Spanish America, the role of the indigenous republics that gave native majorities land and limited self-rule, and held them in subordination, focused pivotal debates. And of course, imperial rule itself was debated. That it ended almost everywhere should not mask the enduring strength of groups that preferred to stay in the empires: Tories in the United States fled to Canada; Mexico's 1821 Plan de Iguala mobilized a coalition that led to independence by calling Spanish king Fernando to Mexico; Brazil, home to Portuguese regent and then king João from 1808 to 1821, became independent in 1822 by proclaiming his heir, Prince Pedro, emperor of Brazil. And Cuba remained the "most loyal" of Spain's American colonies.

Old regimes did not fall without a fight; wars were everywhere. They were international and internal, often at the same time. They were political and social, with popular risings sometimes furthering political leaders' agendas, sometimes limiting the fighters and resources available for state making. The U.S. war for independence was an international war; its rebels were backed by France and funded by Spain (with pesos from New Spain). The Wars of 1793 to 1815 set off by the French Revolution and Napoleonic expansion were inseparable from the Haitian Revolution, the U.S. acquisition of Louisiana, the flight of the Portuguese court to Brazil, the opening conflicts of the Spanish American wars for Independence, and the consolidation of U.S. independence in the War of 1812. Within the wars, popular insurgencies were most powerful in Haiti, Spain, and New Spain—yet they played roles nearly everywhere.

New visions of republican government and liberal institutions were also everywhere—discussed, debated, and fought about while variously defined. Famously, the first New World war for independence was fought to end British rule and forge republican governance in the United States. The Haitian Revolution began amid a search to bring constitutional order and universal rights to a French monarchy facing bankruptcy while deeply dependent on its hugely profitable and exploitative slave colony in Saint Domingue. And when

8—John Tutino

Napoleon's 1807–1808 invasion of Iberia sent the Portuguese court to Rio de Janeiro and deposed the Spanish Bourbons, guerrilla conflicts across Spain and debates about sovereignty there and in the Americas energized a traditional Spanish process of seeking sovereignty grounded in the pueblos (the towns). The resulting Cortes of Cádiz wrote the liberal charter of 1812; it was endlessly debated while it helped remake politics and governance in Spain, Portugal, and their Americas.

International and political wars mixed with insurgencies, all laced with movements for popular sovereignty in government, which stimulated demands for popular rights—freedom from slavery, access to land, and more. And all that combined in complex ways to promote a changing world economy—sometimes to force, sometimes to facilitate, sometimes to limit adaptations to an emerging industrial capitalism. The Haitian and Bajío revolutions took down the two American engines of eighteenth-century global trades. Haitians turned to family production and faced exclusion from the Atlantic economy; Mexicans tried to forge a nation while searching for a new economy—newly grounded in family production. Meanwhile, Cuba and Brazil took advantage of the commercial withdrawal and then exclusion of Haiti to expand production of coffee and sugar, importing more slaves to do the work. The United States drove the planting of slave-grown cotton across an expanding South to supply the rising industrial economy of England—and soon New England. Meanwhile, Spanish Americans from Mexico through the Andes struggled to make nations and find prosperity in a new world economy.

The common theme of our studies is divergence—on three different levels. Most obvious is the divergence that created more than a dozen new American nations out of lands long integrated into four European empires. And we must not forget that while the United States claimed independence, Canada and the British Caribbean did not; while slaves forced emancipation and independence in Haiti, Guadalupe and Martinique remained French and returned to slavery. While most of Spanish America broke away to become diverse nations, Cuba, Puerto Rico, and the Philippines, which had delivered New World silver to Asia, did not. And if all of Portuguese America became a Brazilian empire, it separated from Angola and other regions of Portuguese Africa that sustained the slave trade—while the trade carried on. National independence was neither universal nor inevitable. It led to diverse new nations while it left diverse other regions within old empires that had to change. Thus Cuba could both remain a colony and become a new country.

The second level of divergence was the rise of diversity—and sometimes of powerful separatist movements—within emerging American nations. Examples are legion. The historic integration of the Andean highland core under Inca rule and Spanish colonialism broke apart to create Peru and Bolivia. The colonial Kingdom of Guatemala that ranged from the Isthmus of Tehuantepec to the Isthmus of Panama took independence as one—and then in decades of conflict broke into five nations and the Mexican state of Chiapas. The Guatemala that remained struggled to integrate three distinct social, cultural, and economic regions. The fragmentation of Spanish America is legendary, furthered by the economic challenges of the era. Brazil famously held together, but not without strong forces for separation in the Northeast and South—strong attempts suppressed by military force backed by British naval power. And it is worth remembering that Texas's secession from Mexico spurred the war that took the vast Mexican North and its assertive indigenous peoples into the United States, in time leading the United States to split into two nations in 1860—only reunited by a devastating and deadly Civil War.

While nations struggled to consolidate and often fragmented, many indigenous peoples found new independence. The Comanche rose to become the dominant power for decades in western North America.[22] Once-colonized communities found new autonomies across Spanish American highlands. Our studies of the emergence of new countries detail how local innovation and enduring differences emerged from shared historical challenges. Against dreams of *E Pluribus Unum*, we found the opposite: from a hemisphere of four empires came a proliferation of diverse countries marked by divergences—and often by conflicts—within.

Their creation, with all their conflicts and diversities, contributed in fundamental ways to the third divergence we emphasize: the "great divergence" that brought the demise of China and South Asia; the collapse of the global trade in silver and new challenges to the sugar and slave economies that had long linked Europe, the Americas, Africa, and Asia; and the rise of a new industrial capitalism in which production and power concentrated in northwestern Europe and the northeastern United States, while the rest of the world was pressed to supply staples—pivotally, cotton grown by slaves in the U.S. South—and to buy manufactures—cotton cloth central among them. The creation of diverse new countries across the Americas was a foundational part of the history of the rise of the North Atlantic, Anglo-American axis that shaped the world in the century after 1800. The new countries of the Americas were born within— as both cause and consequence of—the great divergence that brought a new era of global history.[23]

Shared Challenges, Diverging Outcomes

To analyze the emergence of diverging new countries across the Americas, we present ten studies. Part I offers two chapters on processes that impacted histories across the Americas. In "The Americas in the Rise of Industrial Capitalism" I outline how the silver economies of Spanish America and the sugar and slave economies of Atlantic plantation colonies became pivotal to global commerce after 1550. Silver, centered in the Andes from 1550 to 1650 and then soaring in New Spain from 1700 to 1810, made Spain's Americas essential to trades linking China, India, the Islamic world, and Europe. Sugar and slavery, pioneered in the Spanish Caribbean, consolidated between 1570 and 1640 in Brazil, and dominating the British and French Caribbean after 1680 drove trades tying Europe and Africa to the Americas. Eighteenth-century competition led to wars and revolutions that began to destabilize the global economy around 1780. Revolutions in Haiti and the Bajío saw popular forces destroy the leading engines of New World economic dynamism after 1790. Meanwhile England, while fighting long wars to claim European, Atlantic, and global hegemony from France and Spain, built mechanized industries that took off and forced every New World region to adapt in the nineteenth century. Chapter 1 offers a framework to understand how diverse regions of the Americas lived that complex global economic transformation.

Amid the transformations driven by wars and revolutions, political actors and ideologues worked to design new polities based on rising notions of popular sovereignty and electoral participations. These designs and debates were essential to the Thirteen Colonies' break with British rule to become United States; they were central to the French Revolution, which set the stage for the Haitian Revolution—which focused on more fundamental liberations. Coming out of European political debates since the seventeenth century and recent decades of enlightenment thinking, republican projects in Britain, the United States, and France are deeply studied and well recognized.[24] Less recognized and studied only recently are the parallel seventeenth-century roots of a Hispanic popular sovereignty that mixed with enlightenment innovations and revolutionary adaptations to generate the world's first self-defined liberalism in Cádiz between 1810 and 1812—and to influence the debates of nation making across Iberia, Latin America, and beyond.[25]

Because most readers are familiar with the rise of regimes of popular sovereignty in Anglo-Atlantic and French domains (or can easily gain access to key studies), yet few will know the pivotal role of Cádiz liberalism in Spain, Portugal, and the Americas, we present Roberto Breña's chapter 2, "The Cádiz Liberal Revolution and Spanish American Independence." It explores the deep and complex historic roots of Hispanic liberalism, its consolidation amid the struggle against Napoleon from 1808 to 1814, its limited role in Spain under French occupation, its wide if uneven implementation across Spain's Americas, its abrogation in 1814, and its return in 1820 in both Spain and its Americas. Designed to create a constitutional monarchy to hold Spain's empire together, Cádiz liberalism fueled debates about sovereignty that generated movements for regional autonomy. Many evolved into conflicts that led to national independence, in the process often limiting the sway of liberal ways as men on horseback took power. Breña's study of Cádiz liberalism underlines its transatlantic importance and contradictory reverberations to help frame our analyses of Cuba, Brazil, Mexico, Guatemala, and the Andes.

Part II presents four chapters analyzing the emergence of new countries in the slave societies of Atlantic America. We begin with Adam Rothman's study "Union, Capitalism, and Slavery in the 'Rising Empire' of the United States" because the mainland British colonies from New England to Georgia were the first to break colonial bonds, and because after decades of expansion and conflict culminating in the deadly war of 1860–1865, the United States held together to become the New World country that adapted most profitably to the world of industrial capitalism. Rothman brings a new hemispheric vision to the intensely studied and still debated process that forged the United States.

The war for independence that created the United States was most innovative in proclaiming popular sovereignty and opening electoral rights—rights limited by expanding slavery and enduring racist exclusions. Emerging from marginality in the first world economy, the United States latched onto British industrialization; southern states became key providers of cotton (raised by slaves while Britons proclaimed opposition to slavery). During Napoleonic wars (including the War of 1812 against Britain), northern states turned reluctantly to industry. To gain land to expand cotton and slavery, from the 1820s southerners colonized Mexican Texas. Texans seceded from Mexico in 1836, helping provoke the war that took the lands from Texas to California in the 1840s. The challenge of balancing slave states and free states in regions taken from Mexico led to the Civil War that kept the union together, ended slavery, and opened a diverse continent to rapid agro-industrial expansion—while deferring questions of justice for freed blacks, invaded Native Americans, and expropriated Mexicans. The making of the United States both opened and culminated hemispheric processes with global ramifications.

Carolyn Fick's "From Slave Colony to Black Nation: Haiti's Revolutionary Inversion" analyzes the second American society to break with imperial rule. Haiti did not copy the United States, but in many ways inverted its trajectory. French Saint Domingue was the driving engine of the Atlantic sugar and slave economy after 1770. Its expansion led to extreme polarizations; its population included a huge majority of recently arrived African slaves, when in 1790 promises of popular sovereignty arrived from revolutionary Paris and set off conflicts among the few people of European, mixed, and African ancestry who were free and might claim rights proclaimed as universal and granted to Frenchmen. Fick details how slaves took arms to control the outcomes of years of debate and conflict—by 1804 ending slavery, French rule, and most plantation production. She goes on to offer an essential new analysis of how early national rulers committed to sustaining a state and military capable of surviving in a world of hostile powers faced a populace committed to household production and staunch in refusing plantation labor. The result was a nation of military rule, family self-sufficiency, and commercial poverty. Haitians rejected slavery, enabled family autonomy, and faced deep and enduring difficulties in a world shaped by rising industrial capitalism.

Cuba appears the antithesis of Haiti. David Sartorius's "Cuban Counterpoint: Colonialism and Continuity in the Atlantic World" shows how Cuba became new while remaining Spanish. It did not become a nation in our era of transformation, yet became a new country. It turned to sugar and slavery in the late eighteenth century. The Haitian Revolution opened new markets for Cuban planters and new access to slaves, including some brought from Haiti by fleeing planters. When Napoleon invaded Spain in 1808, Spanish Cubans remained loyal to the Cádiz liberal regime, gaining new rights and participations (which Cádiz liberals carefully denied to people of African ancestry). When mainland Spanish America turned to independence in the 1820s, Cuba held loyal to Spain—a reenergized slave country in a transatlantic Spanish nation. Sartorius shows that Cuban loyalty, strategic to planters' defense of sugar and slavery in a world of British antislavery, also came with deep engagements in debates about liberal rights and monarchical legacies. Cubans, at least free Cubans, joined the free peoples of the United States in prospering by expanding slavery between 1800 and 1860. The contrasts with Haiti—and the similarities with Brazil—are striking.

Brazil perhaps experienced the least conflict and the most seamless change of all the regions that broke with colonial rule before 1825. Yet it too became a new country, facing the conflicts and uncertainties of creating politics while facing changing links to the world economy. In "Atlantic Transformations and Brazil's Imperial Independence" Kirsten Schultz explores how Portuguese colonies that had proven the global possibilities of sugar and slavery in the sixteenth and seventeenth centuries became leading producers of gold and diamonds after 1700 (still relying on slave labor). Portuguese rule rested ever more on Brazilian production linked to British markets—and through the eighteenth century, Lisbon aimed to prosper by both limiting and taxing those links. When revolution cut Haitian exports of sugar and coffee and imports of slaves, sugar and slavery revived in Brazil's Northeast, while coffee and slavery began to remake Rio de Janeiro's hinterland. Rising Brazilian trades sustained Portugal and Britain in times of war after 1793. When Napoleon took Lisbon in 1807, the British navy helped ferry the Portuguese monarchy to Rio, tightening ties with England. With Napoleon gone in 1814, King João stayed in Rio—until Lisbon liberals turned to the Cádiz model seeking new ways to restore their transatlantic power. They began conflicts that drew João back to Portugal— and to Brazil's separation in 1822 as an empire under Prince Pedro, who would rule as Pedro I. Regional separatist movements faced military forces funded by strong export earnings and backed by British navies. Vast Portuguese colonies—and claims to a larger Amazon—held together within a Brazilian empire. By 1830 Brazil was an expanding continental country sustained by coffee and slavery, which were tied to rising British industry. Like the U.S. republic and still-colonial Cuba, imperial Brazil expanded slavery to prosper in the new world of industrial capitalism.

The former colonies that expanded slave-made exports after 1800 found commercial prosperity and relative political stability until the 1860s. Then all faced conflicts over slavery—none more destructive than the U.S. Civil War. In contrast, Haitian slaves claimed liberty and land in revolution; from 1800 they faced continuous challenges of state making and exclusion from the world economy—while former slaves and their families lived better for generations. The new countries made out of Atlantic slave colonies lived enduring contradictions.

Part II looks at nation making in Mesoamerica and the Andes. Before Europeans came, these were regions of strong indigenous states sustained by cultivating communities. After 1500 they were reshaped by disease and demographic collapse, Spanish rule and silver economies. The Andes led the mining that drove global trades from 1550 to 1650; New Spain, including Mesoamerica and regions north, dominated silver production after 1700. Across mainland Spanish America, the era of independence brought the fall of the silver economies and difficult searches for new ways to prosper in the emerging world of industrial capitalism, while elites sought new political systems and many communities, indigenous and mixed, pursued local autonomies. Social, political, and economic challenges and conflicts shaped diverse new countries across

Spanish America—countries that struggled for decades to find stable polities and prosperous places in the new industrial world economy.

In "Becoming Mexico: The Conflictive Search for a North American Nation" Alfredo Ávila and I explore the most radical economic transformation and one of the most complex and conflictive political transitions in Spain's Americas. New Spain remained economically dynamic and socially stable to 1810; strong silver production stimulated global trades and funded European wars during the era of U.S. independence and the French and Haitian Revolutions. Napoleon's 1808 invasion of Spain broke sovereignty across the empire, setting off political conflicts in New Spain, leading to popular insurgency there in 1810. From 1812 to 1814, authorities implemented Cádiz liberalism's participatory openings aiming to counter insurgency; they offered local autonomy to regional elites and indigenous republics, aiming to hold loyalty to Spain in the fight against France. Scattered political insurgents refused the offer, fighting for greater autonomy and even independence until 1815. Popular insurgents in the key mining, manufacturing, and cultivating region of the Bajío remained in arms to 1820; pacification came with a collapse of mining and a turn to family production reminiscent of Haiti.

When Spain returned to liberalism the same year, men who had fought insurgents and independence for a decade led an alliance of the powerful calling Fernando VII to New Spain (unsuccessfully) and then proclaiming a Mexican monarchy in 1821. They imagined a continental empire reaching from Costa Rica to Texas and California. But the collapse of the silver economy left the imagined Mexico to search for both a polity (republican from 1824) and a new economy. The result was a mix of creative and conflictive politics (often rooted in Cádiz legacies), economic uncertainty, empty treasuries, political wars, and social instability—combining to favor independence in the provinces, the autonomy indigenous villages, and the prosperity of family cultivators. Texas seceded in 1836 to preserve slavery for waves of Euro-American immigrants growing cotton on rich coastal plains, aiming to profit by supplying British industry. Decades of conflict culminated in the 1840s when the United States invaded to take Mexico's North, including California, where gold drew a westward rush and gave new capital to a newly continental United States. Mexico was left to search for a polity with shrunken economic potential; the United States (after the Civil War) found unprecedented hemispheric hegemony.

The colonial Kingdom of Guatemala extended from highland Chiapas to lowland Costa Rica. Far from centers of silver production, the Maya peoples of Chiapas and Guatemala held onto land and local autonomies in indigenous republics; more mixed peoples to the south mostly lived by ranching. The one important eighteenth-century export was indigo, raised in Pacific lowlands around San Salvador and sent to Atlantic markets by Guatemala City merchants. As Jordana Dym details in "The Republic of Guatemala: Stitching Together a New Country," the kingdom enjoyed limited prosperity and general stability to 1808. It engaged Napoleon's incursion and the Cádiz experiment with only a few conflicts, political and social. Mexico's turn to an imperial independence in 1821, which aimed to include the Kingdom of Guatemala and sent an army to press the point, brought the break with Spain—and then from Mexico in 1822.

Decades of political experiment followed. A Central American federation was possible (minus Chiapas, which stayed in Mexico) while many regional leaders pursued local interests. The indigo economy around San Salvador gave way to cochineal, a red dye raised by *ladino* (mixed) growers in eastern Guatemala. By the 1840s Guatemala began to consolidate, combining Maya western highlands, central valleys around the capital where merchants, landlords, and professionals concentrated, and the ladino eastern uplands that produced the nation's only export. El Salvador separated—as did Honduras, Nicaragua, and Costa Rica (while dreams of federation lived). Guatemala emerged from the kingdom of the same name, a new and smaller country with a Maya majority and great internal diversity, linked to industrial Britain by one valuable dye. Only the late nineteenth-century rise of coffee in Pacific hills and bananas in Atlantic lowlands built a Guatemalan state with the power to rule assertive Maya communities.

The Spanish Andes led the first global silver economy, centered at Potosí from 1550 to 1640, by mobilizing and commercializing indigenous ways of rule, production, and work. Silver revived in limited ways in the eighteenth century, while the Spanish regime took growing exactions in times of war and global competition. Social conflict escalated from the 1740s, culminating in the great risings led by Túpac Amaru and others in the 1780s. They were contained, yet left those who ruled wary of indigenous rights and participations for decades to come.

To explore independence and nation making in the Andes we offer two chapters, one on political processes, one on indigenous assertions. In "From One Patria, Two Nations in the Andean Heartland," Sarah Chambers emphasizes that new countries were neither inevitable nor always grounded in traditional unities. As capital of the Inca empire, Cuzco had dominated and integrated the highland regions that are now Peru and Bolivia. When Potosí became the leading center of global silver production in the sixteenth century, Cuzco and the nearby highlands became key sources of supplies and labor. When Madrid reformers kept Cuzco tied to Lima while assigning Potosí to a new viceroyalty at Buenos Aires in 1776, the separation inhibited the response to the 1780s uprisings that spanned the region. After pacification, while the formal split continued, the Andean heartland remained integrated in many ways.

The Napoleonic incursion and the Cádiz experiment set off local conflicts in the Andes, but no adamant risings, political or social. The powerful preferred stability—and feared another rising of the native majority. Yet the question of independence could not be avoided. Amid the liberal revival in Spain, San Martín led armies from Buenos Aires and Chile to liberate Lima in 1821; Bolívar came in 1822 with forces from Caracas and Bogotá to lead battles that finalized independence in Upper Peru in 1824—founding Bolivia. Chambers shows how during that process and for decades after, the separation of Peru and Bolivia was contested. A union of the heartland linking Cuzco and Potosí held possible. The ultimate division of Peru, ruled by more Spanish Lima, and Bolivia, with an indigenous majority in search of an economy, came out of uncertain conflicts. Peru eventually found political stability in an economy of wool and nitrate exports. Bolivia struggled to revive mining and lost the chance of coastal export development in war with Chile. It remains a nation with an indigenous majority searching for a role in the world.

Erick Langer's concluding chapter, "Indigenous Independence in Spanish South America," focuses on native peoples in the Andes and nearby lowlands. It explores an outcome also noted in Ávila and Tutino's analysis of Mexico and emphasized in recent studies of Comanche power in North America: while empires fell and new countries struggled, native peoples often claimed new independence in local rule, production, and trade—at times finding more effective independence than young nations facing industrial powers. Langer details how natives across Andean highlands took new control of local production and trade, and how people in eastern lowlands found a greater independence parallel to the Comanche and others in the North American West. He shows how they used that autonomy to their benefit for decades, until export economies tied to industrial capitalism solidified national regimes after midcentury. Then, native peoples faced rising threats to political autonomies and the lands essential to their economic independence. National consolidations under export economies ended indigenous independence. Still, for generations after 1820, native peoples across the Americas found relief from political powers and economic impositions. Deep contradictions shaped decades of transforming divergence.

In an epilogue, Langer and I outline how the rise of export economies after 1860 brought the consolidation of politically oligarchic and commercially liberal republics across Spanish America along with the decline of indigenous independence there (and in the U.S. West)—while the longer flourishing Atlantic export economies faced the conflicts (most intense in the United States and Cuba) that ended slavery. New countries built in conflicts and contradictions from 1750 to 1870 finally consolidated—retaining polarities within, divergences across the hemisphere, and limited roles in the world of industrial capitalism. Only the United States claimed power in that world—and it concentrated in the Northeast. Many in the South, Midwest, and West saw themselves as struggling in export economies ruled by an industrial-financial core in a nation that was also a continental empire. The United States thus replicated within its expanding boundaries the larger relationships (including indigenous subordination and Spanish American dependence) that tied all of the Americas to the North Atlantic core of industrial capitalism after 1870.

Our histories link global processes, regional challenges, and local conflicts to understand the hemispheric divergences that created new countries. Across Atlantic America, we emphasize the close link between the expansion of export economies grounded in slavery and early political stability—often seen as "success" in the world of early nations. Brazil and the United States held together to expand as continental nations; Cuba remained in the Spanish empire. All expanded slavery to prosper as exporters tied to a rising industrial capitalism; all later faced difficult conflicts to end slavery—and deal with racial inequities. The contrast with Haiti is striking: there, armed slaves ended slavery and most export production; they lived better for generations while their insistence on farming for sustenance led to commercial "failure" and national poverty.

Across highland Spanish America, the collapse of once dynamic silver economies during the wars set off by Napoleon's occupation of Spain and the opportunities of Cádiz liberalism led to republics that began in the 1820s. They faced openings to new polities while struggling to find new economies. Political conflicts persisted while the dimensions of new nations were contested and native peoples claimed new independence. Spanish Central America and the Andes broke into nations searching for coherence and new roles in an industrializing world. They consolidated after 1860, as they found export economies sending staples to England, Europe, and the United States.

Mexico held together (after losing Central America), experimented with industry in the 1830s, and then lost its North in war to an expanding United States—a conflict that also sealed the fate of the Comanche empire. Both North American nations faced civil wars in 1860s. It was only after Union victory held the nation together and ended slavery that the United States rose to continental and later global industrial hegemony. In Mexico, liberals triumphed in the

War of Reform and outlasted French occupation in the 1860s to rule a struggling nation increasingly tied to U.S. expansion in a new industrial world. The new countries of the Americas faced many challenges in the internal, national, and global divergences that came with their conflictive origins. Amid the rise of popular sovereignty, politically, socially, and culturally complex nations (and enduring colonies) became part in a new industrial world. Long marginal mainland colonies of British North America become a hegemonic continental nation. The once pivotal silver economies of Spanish America and sugar and slave colonies of Atlantic America became uncertain and often contested nations searching for new futures. There are many histories in this history of new countries.

Notes

1. The importance of sugar and slavery is the subject of a huge literature, best synthesized in Robin Blackburn, *The Making of New World Slavery* (London: Verso, 1997). The earlier and larger role of the silver economies of Spanish America is emphasized in Henry Kamen, *Empire: How Spain Became a World Power, 1492–1763* (New York: HarperCollins, 2003), and John Tutino, *Making a New World: Founding Capitalism in the Bajío and Spanish North America* (Durham, NC: Duke University Press, 2011).

2. Spain's war for independence against Napoleon and the importance of Cádiz liberalism have received their due in studies beginning with François Xavier-Guerra, *Modernidades e independencies: Ensayos sobre las revoluciones hispánicas* (Mexico City: Fondo de Cultura Económica, 1993), and culminating in José Gregorio Cayuela Fernández and José Ángel Gallego Palomares, *La guerra de independencia: Historia bélica—pueblo y nación en España, 1808–1814* (Salamanca: Ediciones Universidad de Salamanca, 2008), and Roberto Breña, *El primer liberalismo español y los procesos de emancipación de América, 1808–1824* (Mexico City: El Colegio de México, 2006).

3. The new history of the Haitian Revolution began with Carolyn Fick, *The Making of Haiti: The Saint Domingue Revolution from Below* (Knoxville: University of Tennessee Press, 1990), and culminated with Laurent Dubois, *Avengers of the New World: The Story of the Haitian Revolution* (Cambridge, MA: Harvard University Press, 2005).

4. This wave was ably synthesized in C. H. Bayly, *The Birth of the Modern World, 1780–1914* (Oxford: Blackwell, 2004).

5. John Lynch, *The Spanish American Revolutions, 1808–1826*, 2nd ed. (New York: Norton, 1986).

6. Robin Blackburn, *The Overthrow of Colonial Slavery: 1776–1848* (London: Verso, 1990).

7. Lester Langley, *The Americas in the Age of Revolution, 1750–1850* (New Haven, CT: Yale University Press, 1996).

8   J. H. Elliott, *Empires of the Atlantic World: Britain and Spain in America, 1492–1830* (New Haven, CT: Yale University Press, 2007).

9   Jeremy Adelman, *Sovereignty and Revolution in the Iberian Atlantic* (Princeton, NJ: Princeton University Press, 2006).

10 Kenneth Pomeranz, *The Great Divergence: China, Europe, and the Making of the Modern World Economy* (Princeton, NJ: Princeton University Press, 2000).

11 Ronald Findlay and Kevin O'Rourke, *Power and Plenty: Trade, War, and the World Economy in the Second Millennium* (Princeton, NJ: Princeton University Press, 2007).

12 Sven Beckert, *Empire of Cotton: A Global History* (New York: Knopf, 2014).

13 See Tutino, *Making a New World*, in the context of Man Huang Lin, *China Upside Down: Currency, Society, and Ideologies, 1808–1856* (Cambridge, MA: Harvard University Press, 2007).

14 On war capitalism and industrial capitalism, see Beckert, *Empire of Cotton*.

15 Fick, *The Making of Haiti*.

16 Dubois, *Avengers of the New World*.

17 On the Bajío and New Spain's silver in the world economy, see Tutino, *Making a New World*; on collapse after 1810, Tutino, "The Revolution in Mexican Independence: Insurgency and the Renegotiation of Property, Production, and Patriarchy in the Bajío, 1800–1855," *Hispanic American Historical Review* 78:3 (1998), 367–418.

18 Luis Fernando Granados, *En el espejo haitiano: Los indios del Bajío y el colapso del orden colonial en América Latina* (Mexico City: Ediciones Era, 2016).

19 On the politics of U.S. independence, Gordon Wood, *The Creation of the American Republic, 1776–1787* (Chapel Hill: University of North Carolina Press, 1969), remains the classic; on the transatlantic rise of popular sovereignty, see Edmund Morgan, *Inventing the People: The Rise of Popular Sovereignty in England and America* (New York: Norton, 1989); and on the inseparability of slavery and nation making, see Edmund Morgan, *American Slavery, American Freedom: The Ordeal of Colonial Virginia* (New York: Norton, 1975). On the French Revolution, see François Furet, *Revolutionary France, 1770–1810* (Oxford: Blackwell, 1992); on Haitian interactions with revolutionary France, see Dubois, *Avengers of the New World*.

20 Guerra, *Modernidades e independencies*, built on the pioneering work of Nettie Lee Benson, *The Provincial Deputation in Mexico: Harbinger of Provincial Autonomy, Independence, and Federalism* (published in Spanish, 1955; reprint, Austin: University of Texas Press, 1992).

21 Breña, *El primer liberalismo español*; on the complex mix of war and insurgency against Napoleón in Spain, see Cayuela Fernández and Gallego Palomares, *La guerra de independencia: Historia bélica*.

22 Pekka Hämäläinen, *The Comanche Empire* (New Haven, CT: Yale University Press, 2008), and John Tutino, "Globalizing the Comanche Empire," *History and Theory* 52:1 (February 2013), 67–74.

23 To add another divergence to integrated global processes, if Europe and the Americas forged nations at the foundations of industrial capitalism in order to spread that capitalism, the European powers later forged a second generation of empires

spanning the Middle East, Africa, and South Asia. See Bayly, *Birth of the Modern World.*

24 Again, see Morgan, *Inventing the People*, and Dubois, *Avengers of the New World.*

25 The last work of the great historian of Russia Richard Stites details the impact of Cádiz liberalism from Spain to Naples, Greece, and Russia. See *The Four Horsemen: Riding to Liberty in Post-Napoleonic Europe* (New York: Oxford University Press, 2013).

PART I

HEMISPHERIC CHALLENGES

I

THE AMERICAS IN THE RISE OF
INDUSTRIAL CAPITALISM

JOHN TUTINO

In 1500, the Americas were home to powerful states concentrated in western highlands, cultivating communities along Atlantic coasts and in eastern wood-lands, and diverse hunting, gathering, and farming peoples in vast interiors. The peoples of the hemisphere faced war and trade, production and migration—yet lived in a world of their own. They were only connected to Europe, Africa, and Asia after Iberians arrived in the 1490s, an accident of Europeans' search for new routes to trade with Asia. China produced silks and porcelains, South Asia made printed cotton cloth, and Southeast Asia provided pepper, cinnamon, and other spices—all coveted by European consumers. Asians sought little made by Europeans; rather, they demanded payment in money, gold and silver, for their fine manufactures and rare commodities. China and South Asia were economic powers around 1500. Europe could charitably be called an emerging region.[1]

Trade between Asia and Europe had a long history. Overland excursions departed Krakow and other towns in Eastern Europe with silver to swap for silks and other luxuries. Traders from Venice and Genoa sailed through the Bosporus and across the Black Sea to meet overland caravans heading east. Others landed in the eastern Mediterranean to deal with Muslim merchants who moved money and goods across the Levant and on to South Asia and China. The old trades were limited in two ways: Europe produced little gold and limited silver, the latter mostly in Germanic lands; and land routes and sea-lanes required traders to deal with intermediaries aiming to profit and states demanding revenue for protection. Still, trade flourished for centuries.

When fifteenth-century Portuguese mariners, often funded by Genoese bankers, aimed to sail around Africa to trade directly with South Asia, their goal was to enter established trades while limiting the involvement of merchants and monarchs along the way. When Columbus, a Genoese mariner sailing for Castile, headed west across the Atlantic, his goal was the same—however poor his global geography. For a time, the Americas became an obstacle in the search for direct trade with Asia (while Columbus insisted he had already arrived there). Soon enough, however, the hemisphere, long a world to itself, became a key producer of commodities that accelerated trades that for the first time were truly global. Spanish American gold and especially silver stimulated trade everywhere. Meanwhile, the Atlantic Americas produced rising quantities of sugar, sending the sweet that was also a preservative and in time became a staple to Europeans in exchange for growing numbers of enslaved Africans—people who were made commodities of trade, drawing their continent ever deeper into global circuits of profit and degradation.

The incorporation of the Americas into four European empires—first Spanish and Portuguese, later British, and French—grounded the first world economy. The empires spread European ways of rule and promises of justice; they promoted Christianity (with diverse emphases), and promised salvation to those who embraced new truths. They also aimed to subordinate native American majorities—while the smallpox and other diseases that came as fellow travelers from the Old World decimated indigenous numbers. Then, to replace the dying and replenish laboring populations, Europeans turned to buying young African men (and women too), setting them to work in pursuit of profit—justifying their enslavement with racial and religious legitimations.

The taking of the Americas into the European empires inserted the hemisphere in global trades—the founding moment of the world economy. In the sixteenth century and long after, the pivotal exchange was Asian manufactures for bullion—drawing Asian wares to Europe. The gold and silver that stimulated expanded trades came primarily from Spanish America. Most went to Spain, passed through Western Europe and Mediterranean cities, often sent to Muslim ports, and then on to South Asia and China—drawing Asian goods in return flow. After 1570, an important second flow sailed from Acapulco to Manila, where a Chinese merchant community assembled wares from across Asia—Chinese silks and porcelains, Indian cottons, Island spices—for shipment across the Pacific to Spain's America, which thanks to booming silver economies had means to buy them. After 1600, transpacific trade took up to a third of American silver for the next century—evidence of a truly global commercial economy. Meanwhile, sugar made by slaves sold out of Africa shaped Brazil in the seventeenth century, the greater Caribbean in the eighteenth. Silver, sugar, and slaves made the Americas pivotal to a new world economy for centuries—until everything changed around 1800.[2]

The Americas in the World Economy: The Challenge

A new and more global understanding of the economic history of the world has emerged in recent decades. Through the twentieth century, the rise of European—or, better, Western European and North American—hegemony was presumed, and mostly explained by cultural characteristics and innovative efforts within European domains in analyses ranging from Max Weber's *The Protestant Ethic and the Spirit of Capitalism*[3] to the works of Douglass North, beginning with *The Rise of the Western World* (with Robert Paul Thomas)[4] and culminating in *Understanding the Process of Economic Change*.[5] The rise of China in the 1990s opened scholars to new visions. Asia was rediscovered, and the era of European hegemony was recognized as relatively brief—beginning about 1800 and of uncertain longevity as the twenty-first century began. The new understanding began with recognition of the long historic primacy of Asia in Andre Gunder Frank's *ReOrient*[6] and Kenneth Pomeranz's *The Great Divergence*.[7] In different ways, they emphasized the economic dominance of Asia in the sixteenth century and the late rise of Europe as the nineteenth began. The new challenge focuses on explaining, not presuming, the rise of Europe—a task begun by Pomeranz and continued by many, including Prasannan Parthasarathi in his bluntly titled *Why Europe Grew Rich and Asia Did Not*.[8] The new vision gained powerful synthesis in Ronald Findlay and Kevin O'Rourke, *Power and Plenty: Trade, War, and the World Economy in the Second Millennium*.[9]

The Americas are everywhere in the new vision: the stimulus of New World silver from the sixteenth century; the Atlantic economy of sugar, slavery, and more from the seventeenth. Pomeranz explains the rise of British hegemony around 1800 by two factors: access to local coal for energy and to American lands for raw materials and markets. Still, the place of the Americas in global economic history comes late in Pomeranz and remains limited in most syntheses. They focus on a shifting balance between China and Western Europe, with the Islamic world and South Asia as essential participants and intermediaries. The Americas appear often as suppliers of silver and sugar, but rarely as major participants in the world economy—until the rise of the United States toward industrial hegemony in the late nineteenth century.

Here, I sketch an emerging understanding of global economic history after 1500—pointing to ways that the Americas were pivotal participants. I then turn to the two great economies tying the Americas to global production and trade—silver; and sugar and slavery—and to the links integrating them. With that foundation, I explore the ways that wars and shifting trades rooted in global strategic-economic changes helped set off the conflicts that led to new countries across the Americas after 1760 and how those conflicts were pivotal to accelerating the global turn that consolidated the British-ruled industrial capitalism that shaped the nineteenth century. I conclude by surveying the very different opportunities and challenges faced by the emerging countries of the Americas in the new industrial world. Brazil, Cuba, and the United States prospered for decades supplying staples raised mostly by slaves; all ended slavery after 1860—but only the United States found industrial power in late nineteenth century. In contrast, the silver economies of Spanish America collapsed as Mexico, Peru, and Bolivia became nations. They struggled for decades. So did Haiti—where slave revolution led to withdrawal and then exclusion from global trades—and Guatemala, which had never lived the stimulus of silver and contributed only dyestuffs to the new economy of the early nineteenth century.

The transformation of the global economy and the rise of new countries across the Americas between 1750 and 1870 were inseparable processes. Yet their integration is little understood, in good part because scholars of New World nation-making focus insistently on internal (and sometimes transatlantic) social and political developments while globally oriented analysts of economic history attend minimally to the Americas. This essay aims to deepen understanding of—and expand conversations about—the integration of the Americas in the world in a key era of global change.

The Americas in the World Economy: An Emerging Vision

It is a truism that a global economy could only develop in the sixteenth century when European empires began to incorporate the Americas into trade networks linking Europe, Africa, and Asia. Still, it is important to recognize the importance of long-distance trade before 1500. For centuries, trade linked Western Europe and East Asia, sometimes passing overland, sometimes taking mostly water routes from the Middle East via South Asia to China. Luxuries such as spices and silks generally traveled west, exchanged for silver or furs or other primary goods. Those trades also touched Africa via the Indian Ocean and across the Sahara. Luxury goods of high value to low weight ruled early commerce, generating wealth for traders, revenue for rulers, and prestige for rich consumers. Different ports and centers of trade, diverse producers and consumers, were favored or prejudiced over time. Throughout, Europe mostly produced primary goods and bought luxuries; centers of innovative production and trade moved around the Islamic world, South Asia, and China, while trade linked diverse Eurasian societies.[10]

A second "world economy" integrated much of the Americas before 1500. Dependence on archaeology has left knowledge of the hemisphere focused on sites of power and symbols of rule and religion along with material products from crops to pottery. We lack the travel and trade narratives that tell so much of what we know about early Eurasian exchanges. Still, recent studies show that during the first millennium (CE) trade linked diverse peoples from the highland basins of central Mexico ruled by the great city of Teotihuacan, through Gulf lowlands where Olmecs had earlier ruled, highland Oaxaca led by Monte Albán, to the Maya zones of Yucatán and Guatemala. Imperial centers rose and fell—as in Eurasia—but trade persisted, as did war. War and trade shaped both Eurasia and Mesoamerica through the first millennium.[11]

Commercial integration drove north from Mesoamerica in the second millennium. After the fall of Teotihuacan, Tula and its Toltec rulers consolidated power in central Mexico, keeping trade alive with Mayas far to the southeast while pressing northward. Centers of power and enclaves of cultivation reached the upper Río Grande Valley (now greater New Mexico), linked by trade and cultural exchange to central Mexico. Waterborne trade followed the Gulf Coast and went up the Mississippi to bring Mesoamerican trade, goods, and cultural contacts to Cahokia—a state emerging near the confluence of the Ohio, Missouri, and Mississippi Rivers. The spread of maize, Mesoamerica's great contribution to the Americas and the world, across North America to coastal New England long before 1500 reveals very wide exchanges.[12]

While trades within Mesoamerica and linking that region to North America are best known, there is evidence of ties to South America as well. Maize became a major crop in Andean valleys in the first millennium; the Tarascan regime of western Mesoamerica resisted Mexica (Aztec) expansion in the fifteenth century in part thanks to copper metallurgy gained from Andean contacts.[13] In the Andes, the Inca state remains famous for pressing power and exchange outward from Cuzco, integrating regions now highland and coastal Peru, Ecuador, and Bolivia and reaching southern Columbia and northern Chile and Argentina. Scholars insist that exchange was not trade inside the Inca domain and that it operated through hierarchies of reciprocity organized by local, regional, and imperial lords. Still, exchange was everywhere, tied to military power and regime rule, and legitimated by claims of reciprocity (that masked and perhaps limited inequities). Seen in its larger function, Inca exchange was not radically different from Eurasian trades, where military power was always a factor, state sanction essential, and claims of mutual benefit constant. The Inca perhaps took the fusion of regime and exchange to an extreme, but the integration was far from unique.[14]

Before 1500—and long after—the Eurasian and American "world economies" were what Findlay and O'Rourke call polycentric. No single city, regime, or region of power dominated. Places of rule might be pivots of trade; often they were separate—as when inland capitals dealt with coastal ports of trade. Over time, political regimes rose and fell; commercial nodes and trade routes shifted too. Still, trade persisted, stimulating production of luxury goods, precious metals, and more; profiting merchants and funding regimes and their militaries on land and sea. Because of high transport costs, long-distance trade focused on goods of high value and low weight. Trade thus stimulated production, generated wealth, and sustained powerful states; yet every center of power and trade in the early world economies had to be supplied with food, cloth, combustibles, and building materials by local and regional producers.

While trade promoted continuing exchanges and constant wars, the local economies that supplied trades and sustained regimes varied widely. Production might depend on small growers and artisans, large-scale producers, or a mix; labor could be bound, drafted, or negotiated, paid well, poorly, or not at all. Cities and ports might draw sustenance by trade, tributes, or taxes. Local markets might be vibrant or limited. Concentrations of profit and power could be great or limited; inequities and exploitations could be limited or deeply debilitating. The key is that in polycentric commercial economies, trade linked centers of power and production across long distances, over time favoring some, weakening others. Commerce stimulated and sustained local and regional diversities of power and production—while all interacted in war and trade.

Polycentrism continued to mark the larger world economy that began when Europeans linked the Americas, Eurasia, and Africa after 1500. The inclusion of the Americas brought rising flows of silver after 1550, of sugar after 1600—and the growing trade in slaves they stimulated. American silver paid for Chinese silks and porcelains, Southeast Asian spices, and Indian cottons; sugar and silver stimulated the soaring demand for slaves. And in the profitable process, European and Euro-American merchants found newly pivotal roles while demanding and funding protection by newly powerful European regimes becoming oceanic empires.

Europeans were not suddenly dominant, as too many histories suggest. But they shifted from struggling as marginal participants often subject to Islamic and other intermediaries to gain Asian wares, to become traders in control of key commodities and linking American, Asian, African, and European markets and producers. Portuguese, Dutch, and English traders sailed directly to South and East Asian ports; Spanish American merchants delivered silver to Chinese merchants entrenched at Manila, exchanging it for wares from China, the islands, and South Asia. Into the eighteenth century, industrial primacy in silks and porcelains remained with China; South Asia made cotton goods coveted in Africa, Europe, and the Americas. Europeans became traders of rising importance thanks to control of the world's primary sources of silver, the profits of Atlantic sugar and slave trades, innovations in sailing technology, and rising naval power.

Competition among Europeans, and between Europeans and Asians, set off escalating conflicts that became a crisis in the late eighteenth century. From that time of conflict and crisis came a new British industrial, commercial, and imperial hegemony that ended the long era of polycentric economic interactions. In what Findlay and O'Rourke call a new era of global specialization, the industrial capitalism that developed in England after 1780 led to a new world economy: power and industrial production concentrated in one pivotal region, in time spreading to a very few others; the rest of the world provided raw materials, foodstuffs, stimulants—and markets. The era of conflict and transformation from 1750 to 1870 was more than the rise of British power grounded in new techniques of production. It was the end of a long era of wide competition for power and profit in a polycentric world economy and the rise of a new industrial-commercial-imperial hegemony based in England, Western Europe, and the northeastern United States.

The rest of the world was not left out; most of the Americas, Africa, and much of Asia were locked into roles as dependent suppliers of primary products, raw materials and foodstuffs that were mostly land and labor intensive. The importance of a commodity to industry, or to feeding industrial populations, the quality and extent of land or mineral deposits, the plenty and mobility of labor all varied. Some regions—and many regimes and traders—prospered supplying industrial inputs and sustenance. Few beyond the North Atlantic axis of industrial concentration contended for power and primacy in the world of nineteenth-century industrial capitalism.

The global shift from polycentric commercial competition and integration to Anglo-centric industrial capitalism shaped the possibilities and constraints facing new countries across Americas after 1800. Most analysts see a global transformation driven by events in Europe—powered by the intersection of war, revolution, and technological innovation there. The conflicts that broke the dominance of the European empires in the Americas and led to the birth of diverse new nations appear as simultaneous, yet largely separate, developments. As the new countries of the Americas emerged in the 1820s, British dominance of a new industrial world seemed set. People and nascent states across the Americas had no choice but to respond.

Analyses that see the rise of industrial capitalism as external to the Americas tend to exclude the Americas from the analysis of that pivotal transformation—an unfortunate deficit in the generally persuasive synthesis of Findlay and O'Rourke in *Power and Plenty*. New World silver, so pivotal in studies of world trade after 1550, disappears from their discussions of conflict and trade after 1770—even as New Spain's silver output reached historic peaks.[15] The sugar and slave trades so central to studies of the eighteenth-century Atlantic too often become marginal to analyses of the years after 1800, especially when the goal is to explain industrialism in Europe and its global impact. Yet we know that Atlantic sugar and slave trades were radically disrupted by the Haitian Revolution in the 1790s and that silver collapsed as a New World stimulus to world trade after 1810, undermined by insurgency in the Bajío region of New Spain. Popular risings abruptly destroyed the two leading engines of American participation in world trade.[16]

The two New World risings and their economic consequences are the most obvious evidence that the global economic transformation and the emergence of new countries across the Americas were not separate processes. The rise of industrial capitalism usually appears a European triumph; the emergence of new American nations too often seems a tragedy—with the celebrated exception of the United States. An integrated analysis of the Americas from 1750 to 1870 will show that triumph and tragedy were inseparable—across the Americas and around the world.

American Silver and the First World Economy

Two primary economies tied the Americas to the world in the eighteenth century: a silver economy based in mainland Spanish America and the sugar and slave economy in Atlantic colonies from Brazil through the Caribbean. Regions not directly shaped by these core trades often supplied one, the other, or both. There were exceptions: the gold (and slave) economy of the early eighteenth century in southern Brazil and the fur trade of inland North America. The latter reminds us that many peoples remained independent, uncolonized, in American interiors, yet they too joined rising trades. Still, the silver of Spanish America and the sugar and slavery of Atlantic America powerfully shaped global trades and defined the hemisphere's place in the world in the eighteenth century.

Silver rose first. In the wake of the early sixteenth-century incursions that destabilized Mesoamerican and Andean states and brought diseases that set off devastating depopulations, the great mountains of silver encountered at Potosí and Zacatecas in the 1540s fed China's soaring demand for silver (decreed the only specie for taxation and large-scale and international trade there in the 1550s). The profits of silver stimulated new ways of production and consolidated European rule across Spain's Americas. Taxco near Mexico City pioneered silver mining from the 1530s; Potosí and the Andes led the mining that fueled world trade between 1550 and 1650; Zacatecas and northern New Spain took off around 1600. After a slowdown during the second half of the seventeenth century, Zacatecas and Guanajuato led New Spain to global leadership in the eighteenth century, while Potosí and the Andes struggled to regain earlier dynamism.[17]

In the process, three variants of silver societies developed in Spanish America. In the Andes, the Inca led the largest and most consolidated state in the Americas in 1500. After Inca rule collapsed and during the years that Old World diseases devastated native communities, regional native powers carried on as silver rose. Perhaps because of long wars and a slow consolidation of Spanish rule while native population fell by more than 80 percent, regional native lords (*kurakas*, sometimes renamed caciques) remained pivotal to colonial rule and the silver economy. So did the *mitá*, the Inca labor draft adapted to

Boston
St. Louis
New York
VIRGINIA
San Francisco
Santa Fé
Charleston
BRITISH
NORTH
AMERICA
San Antonio
New Orleans
Zacatecas
Guanaiuato
Havana
Mexico City
CUBA
SAINT DOMINGUE
SANTO DOMINGO
ATLANTIC
OCEAN

VICEROYALTY
OF NEW SPAIN
CAPTAINCY
OF GUATEMALA
Caracas

Bogatá
VICEROYALTY
OF NEW GRANADA
Quito

PORTUGUESE BRAZIL
Recife

Lima
Cuzco
Salvador

VICEROYALTY
OF PERU
Potosí

PACIFIC
OCEAN
Rio de Janeiro

Santiago

Buenos Aires
VICEROYALTY
OF RIO DE LA PLATA

N

0   500   1000   1500 mi
0   1000   2000 km

MAP 1.1. The Americas, ca. 1780

send workers to Potosí. Yet as the city of silver high in the Andes rose to global eminence—its population reaching 150,000 after 1600 while the wider Andes fell to less than a million—Europeans seeking wealth and natives seeking chances together forged (unequally, of course) new commercial ways around mines that drove global trade.

The silver economy of Andean Potosí built on—and commercialized—indigenous precedents more than other regions of Spanish America. Lima became the Andean center of government, finance, religion, and education, while nearby Callao sent silver into world trade; in Ecuador, Guayaquil built ships for Pacific trade while Quito made cloth sold across the Andes; regions now in northwestern Argentina sent livestock to Potosí; Chile provided a European diet of wheat, wine, and olive oil to those who ruled the Andean boom in Lima and Potosí. All that prospered to 1650, laden with exploitations and cultural conflicts, then collapsed and struggled to revive in the eighteenth century. The limits of the revival and rising Spanish revenue demands made the Andes a region of escalating conflict from 1740 to the 1780s.[18]

New Spain developed two distinct silver societies before 1650. Warring Mexica, Tarasco, Zapotec, Maya, and other states contested rule in Mesoamerica around 1500. Conquest proved more rapid there, thanks to deep local divisions and the disease-driven depopulation that devastated the region from the 1520s. When silver mining rose near Mexico City at Taxco in the 1530s and Pachuca in the 1550s, indigenous ways of rule and work faced challenges. By 1600, few native lords still held roles parallel to those claimed by Andean kurakas. The *repartimiento* labor draft, built on the Mexica's *cuatequil* levy, was fragmented and less pivotal than the mitá, declining rapidly around Mexico City from the 1630s. Still, the silver economy there depended on the hundreds of native communities reconsolidated after 1550 as indigenous republics—ruled by councils of native notables and holding lands that sustained local governance, religion, and family production. After 1600, as population fell to 10 percent of precontact levels, increasingly commercial market and labor relations linked communities, silver mines, and the city together—and to rising global trades.[19]

North of Mesoamerica, commercial dynamism shaped everything. Before 1520, Mesoamerican states had faced fiercely independent hunting, gathering, and sometimes cultivating Chichimecas in the region called the Bajío. When Europeans arrived, the fertile basin was a conflict zone; neither states nor communities accustomed to sustain them ruled there or in regions north. After silver was found at Zacatecas in 1546 and Guanajuato in 1555, a flood of migrants—Europeans seeking profit, Mesoamericans looking for opportunity, and Africans bound to work—set off decades of conflict with Chichimecas struggling to stay independent. After pacification in the 1590s, the Bajío and the North saw the construction of a thoroughly commercial social order (few communities gained rights as republics). With Chichimecas devastated by war and disease, and marginalized in missions and mountain enclaves by the 1590s, Spanish North America grew as a thoroughly commercial domain of mines, cities of trade and textiles, irrigated estates, and grazing properties.

New Spain, which integrated Spanish Mesoamerica and North America through its capital city of Mexico, remained second to the Andes in silver before 1650; but as production collapsed at Potosí, it revived at Parral, far north of Zacatecas, in the 1640s. Spanish North America ruled world silver production during the eighteenth century, led again by Zacatecas and Guanajuato. The Bajío, mixing mining at Guanajuato, trade, textile, and tobacco production at Querétaro, and irrigated commercial cultivation across rich bottomlands, became the most dynamic capitalist region of the Americas. Facing a brief decline of Chinese demand for silver and rising Spanish revenue demands in the 1760s, Guanajuato mine workers protested new taxes and militia recruitment. They were crushed in 1767. Then, silver drove to new heights in the Bajío and regions north from 1770 to 1810. Thanks to Bourbon trade policies and rising demand, most of that silver went first to Europe, funding wars and commercial expansion there. But ultimately the production of silver that peaked in New Spain after 1770 responded to record demand and purchases in China from 1775 to 1808.[20]

Mexico City replaced a shrunken Potosí as the largest New World city, passing 130,000 around 1800. (Other leading cities—New York, Guanajuato, and Querétaro in North America, and Lima, Rio de Janeiro, and Buenos Aires in South America—hovered around 50,000–60,000.) The principal center of government, finance, and trade in the Americas, Mexico City integrated the silver economies of Spanish Mesoamerica and Spanish North America, linking them to Spain, Europe, and China. The cities and the mines along New Spain's silver routes—from the Gulf port of Veracruz through Puebla to Mexico City (with an extension to Acapulco on the Pacific), then north through Querétaro and Guanajuato, Zacatecas, and San Luis Potosí to regions from Texas to California (after 1770)—generated the most dynamic economy in the Americas, sustaining with grains, sugar, cloth, tobacco, and livestock the production of silver that drove global trade.

In contrast, southern Mesoamerica, less tied to the stimulus of silver, remained a region of small and scattered Spanish towns surrounded by indigenous communities that sustained themselves and sought commercial gain when they could. In highland Oaxaca, Mixtec villagers made cochineal dye sent to native weavers, colonial cloth makers, and European industries. Farther south, in the

FIGURE 1.1. In the heights of silver capitalism: The Rayas Mine and Mellado Church, Guanajuato, Mexico. Author photo

Kingdom of Guatemala, growers around San Salvador raised indigo, another dye sent to cloth makers in worlds old and new. In warm basins and coastal lowlands, native growers raised cotton for artisans across New Spain. Offshore, Havana built ships and provided military protection against European interlopers. The soaring revenues of New Spain's silver economy paid for Spanish rule from Yucatán to California, in Manila where Chinese merchants traded Asian wares for American silver, and in Havana and New Orleans—with surpluses sent to the always-strained treasury in Spain.[21]

While the silver economy of the Andes struggled and faced resistance that culminated in the great rebellions of the 1780s, followed by years of repression and reconstruction, the silver economy of New Spain soared through the eighteenth century—and peaked after 1770.[22] Social pressures mounted there too. But across Mesoamerica, they were negotiated by enduring indigenous republics and mediated by colonial judges—keeping most conflict in the courts and workers in mines and fields.[23] In northerly regions of Spanish North America, social pressures were moderated before 1750 by persistent population scarcities that favored workers and tenants, forcing mine entrepreneurs and estate operators to offer fair remunerations and solid securities. After 1770, population pressures in the pivotal Bajío allowed entrepreneurs in mining and commercial cultivation to press new exploitations in a region where community rights and lands were scarce and judicial mediation less accessible. Social pressures deepened, exacerbated by cultural conflicts provoked by enlightened elites who increasingly maligned popular religious ways. Still, Chinese demand drove an economic boom that sustained social peace and soaring production in the Bajío to 1810—when everything collapsed in a revolutionary conflagration.[24]

The Atlantic Economy: Sugar and Slavery

The Atlantic sugar and slave economy developed in parallel with the Spanish-global silver economy. There were early experiments in sugar and slavery in Spanish Santo Domingo, but once silver flourished, capital flowed to the mainland. Enclaves of sugar and slavery emerged along New Spain's Gulf Coast, in lowland basins south of Mexico City, and later on the coast of Peru, but they were adjuncts to silver economies.[25] Sugar became the primary product, and enslaved Africans essential laborers, in Atlantic America. Starting in Portuguese Brazil, Europeans turned to sugar to compete with the power silver generated in Spain's America.

Sugar and slavery had a long history. The pairing began to help fund the Crusades in the eastern Mediterranean. Profitable, the combination migrated west across the inland sea and took hold on eastern Atlantic islands in the fifteenth century. Africans became the primary slaves—and a growing commodity in trade. Still, sugar production, the African slave trade, and the European markets and profits they stimulated remained limited. The great expansion came when the complex crossed the Atlantic in the sixteenth century. After experiments in the Spanish Caribbean, Brazil led the rise of sugar production in the Americas—and the shift to bound African labor on a mass scale.[26]

After 1550, the Portuguese regime's drive for revenues, settlers' search for profit, and Genoese financiers' readiness to invest made the northeast coast of Brazil home to an expanding sugar industry. The climate was perfect; coastal lands were ample, fertile, and well watered. The challenge was labor. At first, planters used few enslaved Africans—usually skilled craftsmen purchased in the Atlantic islands to oversee planting and refining. Most permanent workers were bound Tupí and other natives taken in raids into the interior; harvest labor came from free natives congregated in Jesuit mission villages. The combination provided flexible labor at low cost; it built the industry and showed its profitability. But the early labor system proved short-lived; natives drawn into regular contact with Europeans suffered the same diseases that devastated people across Spain's Americas. As the profitability of sugar was proven, the first labor system that sustained it in Brazil collapsed. The Portuguese with Genoese financing turned to the African slave trade, escalating its numbers to sustain a promising second Atlantic economy.[27]

In the decades after 1600, Portuguese Brazil (under Spanish sovereignty 1580–1640) proved the potential of sugar and slavery. The Dutch, at war with Spain's Hapsburgs, invaded to claim the rich coasts around Recife in the 1620s. With ample capital and maritime capacity, once the Dutch mastered sugar production and the slave trade, they helped transfer the combination to the Caribbean, where the British and French learned quickly. Sugar (not unlike silver) lives cycles of boom and decline; the crop exhausts the nutrients in once-rich soils after eighty to one hundred years. Brazil made the industry a staple of Atlantic America from 1570 to 1650 (coinciding with the Andean silver cycle at Potosí). Brazil's decline helped British Barbados rise after 1640, soon followed by Jamaica. As European markets widened, French Saint Domingue expanded sugar and slavery after 1720. When British Islands began to falter in the 1760s, Spanish Cuba found new openings.[28] As colonies rose and decayed, sugar production moved to fill demand in Europe—drawing growing numbers of slaves from Africa. After 1750, Saint Domingue became the leading Atlantic sugar and slave economy. Production along with planter and slave trader profits soared; so did slave numbers as degradations deepened.[29]

Like silver, sugar and slavery stimulated widespread commerce. Early on, the Brazilian interior provided sugar plantations with staples and livestock. From the seventeenth century, the farming, fishing, timbering, and shipbuilding of New England sustained British sugar and slave colonies.[30] Before 1765, Louisiana supported French Saint Domingue; then under Spanish rule it took a similar role sustaining sugar and slavery in Cuba. Sugar islands might be small—but their dynamic industry stimulated the slave trade that took millions of people out of Africa and promoted linked economic activities across far regions of Atlantic America.

Sugar—which found expanding European markets as a sweet, a preservative, and later as a quick energy substitute for protein in popular diets—made the slave trade possible and profitable on a large scale.[31] The trade made slaves available to other colonial producers. Southern Brazil boomed with an economy of gold, diamonds, and slavery from 1695 to 1750, stimulating a frontier of settlement and staples production based in São Paulo, driving west, and also grounded in slave labor.[32] In Atlantic North America, environments too cold for sugar saw the rise of rice, indigo, and slavery in South Carolina, and tobacco and slavery around the Chesapeake. Slaves labored on Hudson Valley estates and Long Island farms, producing staples often exported to the Caribbean. The plains around Caracas built an economy of cacao and slavery. Planters found profit and regimes took revenues.[33] Slave labor spread across Atlantic America while sugar and slavery, profit and degradation, peaked in Saint Domingue. When Paris revolutionaries proclaimed liberty and equality and shook colonial rule, slaves in Saint Domingue rose after 1790 and took freedom and justice as they saw them.

Silver and Sugar and Slavery: Global Integration

The silver economies of Spanish America and the sugar and slave economies of Atlantic America often appear separate. They developed in different regions of the Americas, under different empires, with different ways of production, labor relations, and cultural conversations. Yet they developed in parallel: both had beginnings before 1550; both rose to global importance between 1570 and 1650; both faced lulls from 1650 to 1700—and both soared to unprecedented heights during the eighteenth century. While the leading centers of production shifted from the Andes and Brazil between 1550 and 1650 to New Spain and the Caribbean from 1700 to 1800, the parallel trajectories held. More than parallel: the two New World economies were linked.

Most obviously, the two great early American economies were linked in the competition for geopolitical economic primacy among European powers. Early on, the bullion of Spanish America favored Hapsburg power. When Phillip II claimed the Crown of Portugal in 1580, he vastly enlarged Hapsburg domains and trades by adding the emerging sugar economy of Brazil and trading ports in Africa and Asia. The original Potosí silver and Brazilian sugar booms not only came simultaneously from 1570 to 1640—they peaked under a common Spanish sovereignty that in the early 1600s ruled all of Europe's Americas (but for a few marginal British and Dutch settlements). That unprecedented accumulation of American domains and wealth in global trades set Dutch republicans (who rebelled against Hapsburg rule in 1564), British and French monarchs, and merchants everywhere in search of parallel domains and trades. Without gaining revenues and riches in the new global economy they could not compete in a transformed world of power.[34] The Dutch became key intermediaries in the rise of competing British and French Atlantic empires in the seventeenth century. With no access to silver, the latecomers settled on sugar and slavery.

The larger ties linking the silver and sugar and slave economies become clear when we see them in global context. It has finally become commonplace to emphasize the centrality of New World silver to Europeans' ability to trade in Asia—to buy Chinese silks and porcelains, island spices, and Indian cottons.[35] Now Prasannan Parthasarathi has focused analysis on the key link tying sugar and slavery to silver. Fine printed cotton cloths from India were the leading products demanded in Africa as the price of slaves—and Europeans only gained those cloths with silver from Spain's Americas.[36] In the era of the foundation of the New World economies, common sovereignty facilitated Portuguese traders' access to Andean silver, delivered to India to purchase cloth taken to Africa to buy slaves shipped to Brazil and Spanish America from 1580 to 1640. After 1700, British merchants of the monopoly East India Company took growing quantities of Indian cotton goods, paid with rising flows of New Spain's silver (gained through the *asiento* contract to supply slaves to Spain's Americas), to purchase people bound as slaves to labor in Atlantic sugar production and related enterprises.[37] Spanish American silver also funded allied French merchants' ability to sell Africans in Saint Domingue. We now see why British and French merchants and regimes did all they could in war and trade, legally and illegally, in open and clandestine transactions, to gain New Spain's silver. They worked through factors in Seville and Cádiz; they smuggled in Caribbean ports and Buenos Aires. And we understand why Spain insisted that its ships and merchants must monopolize silver, ensuring that silver would profit Spaniards and Spanish revenues in the Americas and Europe—while allowing loopholes large enough to enable silver to find its way to pivotal global trades.[38]

New Challenges, 1750–1790

Wars escalated across the Atlantic world in the eighteenth century. European empires fought for hegemony at home and wealth in the Americas and around the world. Our new understanding of the linked importance of the two New World economies to European power and global trade places that time of conflict and its escalation after 1750 in new light—light essential to understanding the role of the Americas in the conflicts of 1790 to 1825 that accelerated the global transformation to industrial capitalism.

The War of Spanish Succession begun in 1700 set Bourbons on the Spanish throne, cementing a dynastic and commercial alliance between Spain and France and giving the latter favored access to Spain's American trade and silver. The Methuen Treaty of 1703 tied Portugal to Britain, assuring the latter privileged access to the gold beginning to flow from southern Brazil. Then the Treaty of Utrecht that ended the war in 1713 compensated Britain with a monopoly of the slave trade to Spain's Americas, tightening the linkage of New Spain's silver, Indian cottons, and African slaving as English traders supplied both British and Spanish America.

The first half of the eighteenth century proved an era of rising global trades. New Spain's silver and Brazil's gold soared simultaneously, the former stimulating the world and especially China, the latter notably benefiting Britain. Only a strong expansion of trade could sustain booms in both metals. Then around 1750, Brazilian gold production dropped as Chinese demand for silver fell. Gold production declined through the rest of the century. Silver revived in the 1770s, flowing more fully toward Europe, then on to India to buy cottons to trade for African slaves, and finally on to China.[39] With less Brazilian gold after 1750, British merchants and their regime backers sought greater access to Spanish American silver in their drive toward global commercial hegemony. Wars came quickly.

The Seven Years' War of 1757 to 1763 is perhaps better named the First World War, as it was fought in Europe and across the Americas, India, and the Philippines, and the sea-lanes that linked them. Early on Britain mobilized North American colonials to claim Canada from France—a conquest of much cost and little immediate economic value. More revealing, British forces took Havana and Manila in 1762 and 1763, demonstrating the military vulnerability of Spain and the strategic-commercial importance of New Spain's silver. Silver regularly accumulated in Havana before sailing west to Europe; the Pacific flow landed in Manila to be traded with Chinese merchants for Asian wares. Taking the ports was possible, claiming the silver a challenge—the precious commodity could be held in New Spain to the end of the war or diverted to other channels. By the Treaty of Paris, Britain kept Canada and gained Florida, consolidating rule in eastern North America. It returned Havana and Manila to Spain, which also gained Louisiana—reinforcing its control of the silver economy of New Spain and North America west of the Mississippi. From a war often imagined a great British victory Britain gained little in the Americas, where Spanish power was reinforced. Britain did win European recognition of its rising hegemony in India.[40]

In the near term, the primary result was that all the empires faced great debts. Their first response was to make colonials pay. Spain's Bourbons demanded new taxes, militia recruitment, and administrative controls beginning in 1764, provoking riotous resistance in and around the mines of Guanajuato and regions north in New Spain. There, colonial entrepreneurs quickly backed the regime in a mix of repression and accommodation. Peace was reestablished in 1767 and silver production rose to hold at historic peaks from 1770 to 1810 thanks to renewed Chinese demand. Parallel demands for revenues and power struck the colonies of British North America from Massachusetts to Virginia in the 1760s. There, however, key colonial merchants and planters saw no reason to pay; they led resistance demanding limited taxation and self-rule that culminated in U.S. independence—declared in 1776 and accomplished in 1783.[41]

Simply stated, the silver economy made the link between Spain and New Spain so valuable to Bourbon rulers and colonial entrepreneurs that they colluded to maintain the colonial relationship. In contrast, the mainland colonies of British America were a costly burden to imperial officials while the revenue demands of the 1760s and 1770s made imperial rule unacceptable to many colonial merchants and planters. New Spain remained Spanish because its silver economy was uniquely valuable; the United States became the first New World nation in good part because its economy was a peripheral adjunct to Caribbean sugar and slave economies, where planters and merchants continued to profit and proved slow to imagine independence.[42]

Still, the war that enabled U.S. independence had global ramifications. France sent troops and a navy, the latter pivotal to Washington's victory at Yorktown—generating debts that led to calling the Estates General in 1789 and the outbreak of revolution in Paris. Spain provided British American rebels with sustenance and funds—mostly silver pesos from New Spain (which became the basis of the U.S. dollar). Amid the conflict, with Spain distracted and backing Anglo-American independence, 1780 saw the outbreak of the great risings led by Túpac Amaru and the Kataris in the Andean heartland (where the silver economy struggled). Mass violent demands for native rights and social justice were contained only when colonial elites again rallied to Spanish colonial rule in devastated uplands. Britain lost its mainland colonies south of Canada; Jamaica, its leading Caribbean sugar and slave colony, lost dynamism. Meanwhile, French Saint Domingue soared to new heights of sugar, coffee, indigo, and slavery.

The First Great Transformation

It is often said that U.S. independence turned Britain's imperial attention to India. It is now clear that Britain, in an unplanned shift in which merchants, manufacturers, and regime officials both competed and colluded without set goals, transformed cotton manufacturing, global trades, and capitalism. From 1780 to 1820, while wars and revolutions raged across Europe and the Americas, a new world economy dominated by Britain rose. Every region of the Americas and the world had to adapt—sooner in the new countries of the Americas and old empires of Asia, later in regions less tied to global trade around 1800.[43]

The rise of Britain to global industrial hegemony has been honored as a triumph of British entrepreneurship and technological innovation—and it was both in pivotally important ways.[44] The development of water- and steam-powered ways of spinning cotton thread during the late eighteenth century transformed production and work in ways that would go on to transform the world. The achievement is clear—and well emphasized. The goals at the beginning are now equally clear—thanks to Parthasarathi. A group of British inventors and manufacturers backed by merchants outside the East India Company aimed to displace Indian cotton goods in the world economy. Why? British-produced cotton cloth would not require silver. Success after 1780 required technological innovation and new sources of cotton, which first came from Brazil and then increasingly from the newly independent United States. As Beckert shows in *Empire of Cotton*, early industrialism linked British industry and U.S. plantations to compete with the EOC and Indian producers in world cotton markets. Still, British and Indian-EOC production held strong past 1810, until silver production collapsed—favoring British industries and U.S. planters as the Napoleonic wars ended in British triumph. In time, British power in India used taxes and prohibitions to inhibit South Asian cloth from competing with British manufactures.[45] The rise of British industrial hegemony was both a technological triumph and an unplanned outcome of complex global-imperial wars, insurgencies, and trades. They were simultaneous, essential, and inseparable.[46]

In the process, the balance of economic power in the Americas and the world shifted. British manufacturers and traders aimed to mechanize production of cotton wares in England in order to replace Indian cloths in markets in Europe, Africa, and the Americas. With success thanks to mechanical innovation and imperial power, they reduced the need for New Spain's silver to purchase the South Asian cloth much in demand in European and American markets, and essential to buying African slaves. The detailed ramifications await careful study, but key developments seem clear.

Chinese demand for silver had dropped briefly after 1750, and then rose to new heights in the 1770s.[47] With the growth of British cotton production and the displacement of Indian cloth in British trade, British traders might spend less silver in India and send more directly to China. We know that the value in pesos (identical to U.S. dollars after 1780) of silver production in New Spain rose into the 1750s, fell in the 1760s, then soared to new heights from 1770 to the mid-1780s—to dip slightly, stabilize, and fluctuate at historically high levels from 1795 to 1810.⁴⁸ During the era of escalating European warfare after 1793, Britain and France competed for access to New Spain's rising flows of silver.⁴⁹ To the extent that British merchants needed less silver to buy South Asian cotton goods to trade for African slaves, they could seek direct trade with China where demand held strong. While the French monarchy faced the debts created by supporting U.S. independence, French merchants still needed New Spain's silver to access the cloth needed to send rising numbers of Africans to Saint Domingue in the 1780s. While debt crisis led to political revolution in Paris, the flood of recently arrived Africans, often young men enslaved after fighting as soldiers, fed the extreme polarities of Saint Domingue—extreme even compared with other Caribbean slave colonies—that exploded in revolution in the 1790s.

Crucible of Conflict, 1790–1825

There was, of course, no direct and simple causal line from the rapid expansion of slavery in Saint Domingue to the Haitian Revolution, nor from deepening pressures on Bajío producers to insurgency in 1810. War and politics inevitably intervened. Better, the decades from 1780 to 1820 proved the inextricable linkages among global trades, geopolitical conflicts, regional economies, social relations of production, popular risings, Euro-American monarchies, and Asian regimes as old empires fragmented, new nations rose, and popular communities pressed gains when they could. The challenge—and necessity—is to seek an integrated history of the Americas while the polycentric global economy of 1500 to 1800 gave way to the industrial concentration that shaped the nineteenth century. British industrial innovation, French political revolution, Haitian total revolution, Bajío popular insurgency (an apolitical revolution?), Indian economic demise and Chinese collapse—all caught up in decades of geopolitical conflict and shifting global trades—were all essential elements of the transformation that reshaped the world as the nineteenth century began.

The peace that ended the War of U.S. Independence in 1783 proved brief. The French monarchy faced debts it could not pay, in large part resulting from its support of British American rebels. Seeing no other recourse, Louis XVI called long-dormant Estates General, and that assembly became the site and source of a French Revolution that promised new liberties and participations to French people—who, now proclaimed citizens, deposed and killed the king—and eventually led to Napoleon's rule, first in France, then across Europe. Early proclamations of citizenship and liberty set off debates and armed conflicts in Saint Domingue, leading to slave risings that ended slavery, broke with France, and in 1804 founded the second nation in the Americas—Haiti.[50] In the process, armed ex-slaves took the land for family production and destroyed the leading sugar and slave economy of Atlantic America. By the mid-1790s, Saint Domingue no longer sent sugar or profits to France, nor did it buy slaves.

The collapse of Saint Domingue did not end the importance of sugar and slavery in the Atlantic world. Production quickly revived in Brazil, as did demand for slaves in Portuguese colonies still tied to Britain. Sugar and slavery also rose in Cuba, still a Spanish colony, yet in times of war dependent on British acquiescence and U.S. neutral shipping to sell sugar and buy slaves. War and revolutions in France and Haiti shifted the focus of sugar and slavery in the Americas, sustaining continuing conflicts over trade and revenues. Silver production in New Spain, after dipping in the late 1780s, rose to new heights in the early 1790s and held near those peaks to 1810 thanks to Atlantic war and Chinese demand.[51] Saint Domingue lost its leading role—and ended slavery. In the early 1800s, France lost power in the Americas as it expanded in Europe. Spain struggled in the geopolitics of Europe—but New Spain flourished; Cuba rose as a sugar and slave colony; and Buenos Aires found new trade supporting revived Brazilian plantations.

From the 1790s, U.S. merchants had profited as the only seafaring neutrals in the Atlantic in times of shifting conflicts—while cotton production rose across an expanding South to supply British mills. Able to increase the number of slaves without imports, southern planters developed a growing cotton and slave economy—without dependence on New Spain's silver to obtain labor. Britain, favored by industrial innovation, maritime power, and insular location faced constant conflicts, always away from home, that brought gains at the intersection of war, trade, and industrial development. In the Americas, the leading role of New Spain's silver economy and the dynamism of sugar and slavery (away from Haiti) persisted to 1810. The polycentric world economy held on.

In 1793, on the pretext of defending monarchy after the killing of the Louis XVI, the European powers led by Britain and including Spanish Bourbons and Austrian Hapsburgs turned to war against revolutionary France. With Paris in disarray and Saint Domingue in flames, it was a chance for the remaining old regimes to crush a struggling contender for Atlantic power. The attempt to restore monarchy failed (until 1815), however, thanks to the revolutionary regime's ability to mix nationalist visions, new participations, and the end of feudal taxes and fees and successfully call a *levée en masse* that mobilized vast armies to defend the revolution. In 1802, when the Peace of Amiens brought a respite from war, Britain ruled the seas and global trade, and continued to industrialize; France dominated its continental neighbors, having lost the trade and revenues of Saint Domingue; and Spain still held New Spain, the source of silver that still fueled global trades and funded European regimes. Carlos Marichal has shown how France and Britain disputed the peak silver flows from 1796 to 1810—a conflict as pivotal as any battle. By deals among regimes, merchants, and financiers, far from the public eye, about two-thirds of New Spain's record production benefited a renewed French-Spanish alliance. An important third funded British war and trade.[52] Still, nearly all eventually passed in trade to China—and British merchants increasingly ruled that profitable commerce. The world had changed enormously since the 1550s, but Spanish American silver remained pivotal to the global geopolitical economy in 1808, even as industrial innovation and threats to the slave trade eroded its role.

With the loss of Saint Domingue to ex-slave soldiers backed by yellow fever and malaria that devastated European troops sent to the tropics,[53] Napoleon faced embarrassment in the world of European armies and a loss of trade and the revenues it made. That marginalization was completed in 1805 when the British navy destroyed the combined French and Spanish fleets at Trafalgar. New Spain's silver could only reach Europe via deals brokered by British foes. It still came, as every power needed funds in times of war—but France's reliance on its primary foe for access to key specie created a debilitating dependence.

From 1805, Britain ruled Atlantic sea-lanes, thus Europe's access to the Americas, New Spain's silver, and the profits of still flourishing China trades. Attempting to counter by controlling continental Europe, Napoleon took the gamble of invading Iberia in 1807, taking Lisbon, then turning on Madrid early in 1808. The Portuguese monarchy escaped to Brazil, escorted by a British fleet, ensuring that plantations there (booming again after the collapse of Saint Domingue) would benefit Britain's trade and revenues.[54] So Napoleon turned to invade his Spanish ally, provoking divisions in the monarchy—until he captured both contenders to rule and in May 1808 saw the people of Madrid rise to challenge his armies, setting off wars for independence in Spain and diverging responses across the Americas.[55]

In Spain, resistance to Napoleon concentrated in Seville and then Cádiz, leading to the liberal constitution of 1812 that offered new but limited rights to colonials, hoping they would remain in the empire.[56] In New Spain, two years of debates focused in Mexico City from 1808 created deep rifts, dividing those loyal to the regime emerging in Seville from others who preferred to claim regional autonomy awaiting the resolution of the conflicts in Europe.[57] Those divisions led to the revolt led by Miguel Hidalgo in the Bajío in September 1810. The rising mobilized regional elites, Guanajuato mine laborers, and rural workers and tenants to take control of the Bajío in the fall of 1810. Early in 1811, the political movement collapsed, Hidalgo and other leaders were captured, and most mine workers returned to the mines. But the rural majority returned home to the Bajío to press a popular, redistributive insurgency from early in 1811. In a decade of conflict, they took the land from the commercial estates that had ruled their lives and sustained the silver economy for centuries, turning to family production. The parallels with Haiti are clear.

The Bajío insurgency strangled silver mining by raising the costs of supplies and transport and breaking the integration of the Bajío with Mexico City and the larger economy of Spanish North America.[58] Popular insurgency, civil war, and economic disruption led to a decade without investment in the mines that made the world's money. Infrastructure and production both collapsed. From 1795 to 1810, New Spain sent over 20 million pesos of silver yearly into the world economy. From 1811, silver production was cut in half, and with limited fluctuations held at 10–12 million pesos yearly to 1840. It was a devastating collapse for the economy of New Spain as it became Mexico in 1821. The fall of silver at the hands of Bajío insurgents also transformed global trades.[59]

Since the 1780s, the rise of British industrial textiles had begun to limit the need for New Spain's silver to buy Indian cotton cloth to pay for African slaves. But war, rising Atlantic trade, and Chinese demand had kept demand for silver high. When from 1811 the silver flowing from New Spain fell by half, the global reverberations proved extensive and enduring.

For two and a half centuries, silver was a key commodity and money in an expanding polycentric world economy. Its sudden scarcity after 1810 struck trades already challenged by constant war from 1750 to 1815. Fernand Braudel dated the end of eighteenth-century global economic growth to 1812—without seeing the link to the collapse of New Spain's silver mines.[60] Now, Man-Houng Lin has shown that the sudden fall of Chinese production and participation in global trade resulted directly from the dearth of silver. She sees Latin American independence wars as the cause; within those wars, it was the decade of popular insurgency in the Bajío that undermined New Spain's silver production and the global trades it fueled.

The sudden scarcity of silver, amid war and commercial disruption, both stimulated and enabled Britain's acceleration of textile industrialization, limiting its need for silver to buy Indian cottons, replacing them in global markets with cloth made in British mills. In a radical reorientation of Asian trade, British merchants began to sell South Asian opium in China, extracting silver in payment. The silver that had flowed into China for centuries began to flow out, demonetizing the economy, inhibiting commercial life, cutting state revenues, stimulating political instability—and spreading all the liabilities of a proliferating opium culture among the Chinese. China became the "silver mine" that met India's demand for silver as the new Mexican nation learned its mines would not recover for decades. And China lost economic dynamism as it exported raw silk (rather than fine silk cloth) and tea, along with its stores of silver—in exchange for opium. Once a dynamic engine in a polycentric world economy, China became a commodity exporter, a society Europeans would later see as "underdeveloped"—ignoring their own profitable role in creating that underdevelopment.

Meanwhile, Britain protected itself at home by shifting to gold as primary money. It had relied increasingly on gold since gaining favored access to Brazil after 1700. Amid the wars of 1790–1815 it turned to a de facto gold standard, tied to developing paper monies. After the wars it shifted explicitly to a gold standard in the 1820s, insulating its industrializing economy from the difficulties linked to continuing scarcities of silver.[61]

While revolutionary slaves destroyed the plantation economy of Haiti, popular insurgents undermined the silver economy of the New Spain, and Britain rose to industrial eminence between 1790 and 1820, other regions of the Americas adapted as they could. The rise of sugar and slavery in Cuba, and of sugar and coffee and slavery in Brazil, are widely recognized. Both experienced relatively stable adaptations to the new world of British power after 1820. The young United States lived more complex and conflictive adaptations during the decades of war and global transformation.

In the 1790s, deep debates divided the new republic. One vision, promoted by Thomas Jefferson, saw an agrarian and export-driven future, honoring yeoman farmers while presuming slave production on southern plantations (despite Jefferson's dreams of emancipation and deportation). The alternative pressed by Alexander Hamilton preferred commercial ways focused in northern trading cities. Both were sustained after 1793 by northern traders' ability to prosper as neutrals in Atlantic wars. They sold farmers' grains to diverse Europeans and planters' cotton to British industries; they traded in New Spain to keep silver flowing into global commerce. Jefferson's taking the presidency in 1800 suggested a triumph of his vision—though the election was very close and contested.

War soon proved decisive to the adaptive rise of the U.S. economy. With the end of the Peace of Amiens in 1804 and British victory at Trafalgar in 1805, Britain aimed to monopolize Atlantic commerce while France consolidated power on mainland Europe. U.S. merchants saw opportunity in trading between the Americas and Europe—an opportunity Britain aimed to stop with embargoes and naval power. Rising conflict at sea led Jefferson to impose his own embargo in 1808—hoping to stop costly naval contests, and perhaps to consolidate a republic grounded in cultivation. Of course farmers could easily continue to feed themselves and the residents of small port towns, but planters committed to cotton lost outlets in Britain.

While merchants and planters protested the embargo, New Englanders invested in mechanized cotton mills, using the southern slave-grown staple earlier sold to Britain. Under the embargo from 1808 to 1812 and war with England from 1812 to 1814, the Northeast became an industrial producer. After the peace, new industrialists demanded tariff protection against British imports. The wars of 1790 to 1825 were as pivotal to the rise of U.S. power as they were to the Haitian Revolution, which destroyed France's role in the Atlantic economy, and to the Bajío insurgency, which brought down New Spain's silver economy. As the 1820s began, the United States balanced southern and northern interests in the Missouri Compromise, enabling the expansion of a continental economy now grounded in northern commerce and industry and southern cotton and slavery; speculators and settlers pressed a westward expansion that displaced native peoples to generate staples in the Ohio basin and cotton (and slavery) in a new Southwest focused on Louisiana.[62]

Of course, the greatest economic transformation of the age was under way in Britain between 1790 and 1820. The one pivotal participant in three decades of war that never saw destructive conflicts at home, Britain kept trade alive while entrepreneurs accelerated industrial innovation. Meanwhile, wars on the European mainland inhibited industry in France while counterinsurgency in Spain from 1808 to 1814, fought by Spaniards backed by Britain, destroyed the mechanized cotton industry that had begun in Calatuña in the 1780s.[63] When the era of war closed in the 1820s, Britain was positioned to rule a world economy dominated by industrial textile production and supplied by slave-grown U.S. cotton, taking soaring profits from the trades they stimulated.

Breaking Away

In 1820 in the Americas, only the United States and Haiti were independent; in Spanish America, only Buenos Aires and Caracas were committed to independence. The political future of the hemisphere was far from set. But the first global economy had fallen, leaving people everywhere searching for new futures. And 1820 brought new uncertainty to questions of sovereignty in the Spanish empire when military forces in Spain forced Fernando VII to reinstate the liberal Constitution of 1812. As economic change accelerated, Spanish Americans faced new debates that led to five years of renewed conflict and the emergence of new polities. By 1824 all Iberian America had claimed independence, except Cuba and Puerto Rico in the Caribbean. Brazil held together as a constitutional monarchy, while Spain's domains fragmented into diverse republics.

Buenos Aires and Caracas consolidated independence by sending armies led by José de San Martín and Simón Bolívar, respectively, to break Spanish rule in the Andes. Bolívar finished the work by creating the republic of Bolivia, including Potosí, long ago the heart of the global silver economy, in 1824. Loyalists in New Spain were pacifying the last popular insurgents in the Bajío in 1820, when Spain's return to liberal rule set Agustín de Iturbide, who had fought to defend Spain for a decade, to forging an alliance of the powerful that founded Mexico in 1821 as an empire that quickly collapsed and became a federal republic in 1824. Portuguese King João remained in Rio de Janeiro into 1821, then returned to Lisbon to deal with a Cádiz-inspired liberal movement aiming to return Brazil to colonial status. His son Pedro broke with Portugal in 1822, crowned emperor of a Brazil that remained a monarchy until 1889.

Spanish America turned to building republican nations between 1821 and 1824; Brazil worked to forge a constitutional monarchy. All joined the political processes of the age, grounding new regimes in variants of popular sovereignty and offering new electoral participations. Across the Americas, diverse new countries converged in turning to the politics of popular sovereignty, opening processes that proved long, conflictive, and repeatedly coercive—including in the United States, where the war of 1860–1865 proved the bloodiest conflict of all. Yet history repeatedly reports the United States as a most creative and successful republic, while seeing Latin Americans as incapable, repeatedly turning to military-authoritarian rule. The dichotomy was never so clear. To understand the diverging trajectories of the new countries that emerged across the Americas in the first half of the nineteenth century, we must see their different possibilities and responses in new times of industrial capitalism. The new countries of the Americas converged—and never simply copied, as Roberto Breña emphasizes—in pursuing politics of popular sovereignty. They diverged as regions with diverse resources and populations adapted to a rapidly and radically changing world economy. The result was mostly divergence.

Divergence in Atlantic America

Haiti diverged most. The armed slaves' assault on sugar and slavery transformed its economy; withdrawal and exclusion from trade led to economic isolation. Haitians struggled on, committed to personal liberty and family production while facing exclusion in the world of nations and trade. Limited coffee exports earned some revenues, minimally funding regimes decried as too military— yet that acquiesced in the turn to family sustenance that was the first interest of the emancipated populace. The revolutionary fall of sugar and slavery in Haiti did not end that long-profitable relationship in the greater Caribbean. It expanded in Cuba, on smaller islands, and in mainland zones such as British Demerara, where in 1823 slaves attempted to follow Haitian's example in a rising that did hasten the end of slavery in Britain's empire.[64] Older British and French islands saw sugar production and profits wane as soils exhausted and slavery ended between 1830 and 1850. They remained colonies (even if officially part of a French nation) searching for economies. Ironically, people of African ancestry across the British and French Caribbean, long enslaved, lived by economies of sustenance through most of the nineteenth century. By different means, they ended where Haitians had fought to get. The parallels were limited, however. Haitians often held their own land, yet faced international exclusions aimed to punish black revolutionaries; islanders under British and French rule usually lived as tenants, while gaining some access to education and trade: the small rewards of not being revolutionary.[65]

Cuba was different, not because it was Spanish and remained a colony, but because its expansion of sugar and slavery came on fresh soils after 1750, to accelerate in the 1790s when the Haitian Revolution opened markets. Into the nineteenth century Cuba was economically prosperous for local planters and merchants in Havana, Spain, Britain, and the United States. Many of the latter profited by delivering growing numbers of slaves, despite proclaimed opposition and the illegality of the trade in Britain and the United States after 1807. Slaves paid for Cuba's rise during and after the conflicts that led to Haitian and Latin American independence. Masters and merchants profited while ideologues worried about Haitian precedents; together they aimed to keep slaves less than a majority. Cuba's sugar and slave boom, the last of the cycles that shaped Atlantic America, generated limited resistance during decades of expansion. Deepening conflicts came in the 1860s, ending slavery in 1886 and Spanish rule in 1898.[66]

Brazil, where sugar and slavery first flourished in the Americas, lived important continuities as it diverged from other former slave colonies after 1820. Its sugar, gold, and diamond economy had linked to Britain (via Portugal) in the early eighteenth century. Exports fell after 1750, despite the Marquis de Pombal's enlightened policies. The economy struggled through the 1780s, until the Haitian Revolution opened markets for a revival of northeastern sugar and slavery and the beginning of coffee and slavery around Rio. The 1808 arrival of

MAP 1.2. The Americas, ca. 1850

the royal court in Rio definitively linked a revitalized slave economy to British merchants and markets.[67]

Brazil avoided a long, destructive war for independence. When the regime broke with Portugal in 1822, it fought regional conflicts to expel the last Portuguese forces, to hold northeastern and southern regions in the empire based in Rio, and to block limited slave resistance.[68] Thanks to export profits and British naval support, Brazil held together as a monarchy (with new constitutional participations) committed to slavery (in this it was like Cuba, in a Spanish empire struggling toward constitutional ways). Sugar declined in the face of Cuban expansion in the 1820s, but coffee and slavery grew to sustain a Brazilian empire linked to Britain. Slave imports held strong to 1850, when British opposition turned from rhetorical to naval. The empire of coffee and slavery promised popular sovereignty and electoral competition in a regime shaped by entrepreneurial power and patronage politics. Facing political uncertainties and periodic conflicts into the 1840s, Brazil proved the most stable regime in the Americas until slavery and empire collapsed together in 1888–1889. Throughout, Brazil sustained British power and prosperity.[69]

The same can be said of the southern United States to 1860. Slavery was long established around the Chesapeake and near Charleston, serving tobacco, indigo, and rice growers. A war for independence and early national politics led by slaveholding planters guaranteed the endurance of slavery, facilitating the rise of cotton and slavery to supply British industry from the 1790s. Slavery expanded numerically and geographically, making cotton to sustain British production. The United States proved the rare region where slave populations grew without imports, assuaging British opposition to the oceanic slave trade while its industry, power, and prosperity depended on slave-grown cotton.[70]

Still, the rise of the United States was more complex. As noted, trade embargo and war between 1808 and 1814 brought a reluctant turn to industry in the North. New England became a consumer of slave-grown cotton and an emerging competitor to British manufacturers. New Englanders depended on the slave South while promoting wage labor in industries at home. Contradiction was everywhere. After the Missouri Compromise of 1820 an economy of continental contradictions drove west, taking land from independent natives to expand cotton grown by slaves and staples raised by free farmers. In 1835 southerners facilitated the secession of Mexican Texas to expand cotton and slavery. From 1846 to 1848 they pressed a war begun to take Texas into the Union—and ended by taking a vast new West, including California's gold.[71]

The United States claimed a continent of unparalleled resources—a republic of popular sovereignty, committed to slavery, slowly opening electoral rights for free white men. Its expansive prosperity generated conflicts that deepened after war with Mexico brought vast new lands into the Union—Texas, grounded in cotton and slavery; California, producing vast riches in gold; and all the lands between. A devastating and not very civil war ended slavery in 1865, confirmed the triumph of northern industry, and set the reunited continental nation on course to become Britain's great competitor for global hegemony.[72]

Britain ruled the world of concentrated economic power that shaped the nineteenth century by building industry at home, drawing resources and selling cloth in markets across the globe, and emerging unchallenged from the wars of 1790–1825. The United States later built a parallel power, concentrating industry in its Northeast, while drawing resources and selling in markets across a continent taken into a huge nation populated by people fleeing Europe—at the cost of slaves, Mexicans, and native Americans. Both the enormity and the fragility of Britain's rise became clear as it faced the competition of a United States with continental foundations after 1880.[73]

The Atlantic America created by sugar and slavery—Beckert would call it war capitalism—found diverse adaptations in the nineteenth-century world of concentrated industrial power. Haitians withdrew for their own very good reasons—and paid with poverty. Brazil deepened its ties with Britain and prospered as a key commodity producer—while growing numbers labored in slavery. Cuba remained a colony to become the last sugar and slave economy of the Americas. The United States took advantage of early independence to prosper from trade and then industry during the wars of 1790–1820, sustaining British power with expanding cotton and slavery to 1865, while northeastern mills competed with British industry. Haitians made a revolutionary choice to end slavery and exports. Brazil, Cuba, and the United States, in contrast, expanded slavery, found commercial success, and after 1860 faced conflicts grounded in the contradictions of their slave-based export successes.

Inversions in Spanish and Indigenous America

The continental regions of Spanish America broke ties with Spain after 1820 and quickly broke apart to create more than a dozen new countries. Following three centuries of pivotal global importance thanks to the silver, no region of Spanish America would contend for power, and few found prosperity in the era of North Atlantic industrial capitalism. Spanish America and China had been linked for centuries in silver-fueled global trades. The fall of silver left both to grapple with economic challenges and political conflicts—in inevitably different ways.

THE COTTON PRESS.

RATION DAY.

SOWING.

THE CALL TO LABOR.

HOEING.

ARWaud

PLANTATION GRAVEYARD

SATURDAY EVENING DANCE.

SCENES ON A COTTON PLANTATION

FIGURES 1.2 AND 1.3. At the base of industrial capitalism:
Scenes on a cotton plantation

THE COTTON GIN.

PLOUGHING.

THE PLANTER AND HIS OVERSEER.

PICKING.

PRAYER-MEETING.

The Andean silver economy had stimulated global trade as it commercialized social relations still grounded in Inca and indigenous ways from 1550 to 1650, also stimulating a broad commercial integration linking regions that would become northern Argentina, central Chile, and Ecuador to Lima, Potosí, and the Andean heartland. As New Spain became the center of silver production and global trades in the eighteenth century, Andeans struggled as rising state demands provoked social conflicts that culminated in the 1780s. Madrid tried a cure by shifting Andean silver toward the Atlantic via Buenos Aires in 1776, helping set off the risings of the 1780s and contributing to disruptions that continued through a repressive aftermath. Most of the powerful in the Andean heartland resisted independence until the 1820s; then, caught between Spanish liberalism and armies from Buenos Aires and Caracas, they built fragmented republics—Peru and Bolivia in the heartland; Chile, Ecuador, Colombia, and Venezuela in outlying regions. All searched for new economies and polities; none succeeded until they found export links to the industrial world after 1850: Chile stabilized first when it provided foodstuffs to gold rush California; coastal Peru and Chile (in regions taken by war from Bolivia) profited when they sent guano and nitrates to fertilize commercial fields in Cuba and elsewhere; Colombia and Venezuela prospered late when they joined the stimulant economy of coffee exports later in the century.[74]

Buenos Aires and the Río de la Plata provide a revealing history of a region that was geographically Atlantic, not grounded in sugar and slavery, but instead long linked to the Andean silver economy in peripheral ways. The area faced complex changes from 1790 to 1825 and endured deep political conflicts long after. Still, while struggling to become nations, the ports and peoples of the Plata and the Pampas found prosperity sustaining the rising power of Britain.

Buenos Aires was founded in the late sixteenth century to block Potosí silver from trading outside preferred imperial channels; the name of the estuary, the River of Silver, shows that silver found its way to the Atlantic there. For two centuries, the city survived by smuggling just enough silver to profit those sent to limit smuggling. The opening of the port in 1776 and the new viceroyalty set there with jurisdiction over Potosí aimed to promote silver production and ease its arrival in Atlantic trade (as eighteenth-century flows were drawn increasingly east toward Europe before heading to India and China). But the risings that rocked the Andean heartland in the 1780s guaranteed that Buenos Aires would never become a great silver exporter.

Instead, the South Atlantic port found new opportunity during Haiti's revolution and the shifting production and trade it opened. As Brazil revived sugar and slavery in the Northeast and began coffee and slavery in the South, the

Pampas became a source of salted beef and other foodstuffs to sustain growing numbers of slaves. Buenos Aires became a center of trade, shipping, and processing; its population grew toward sixty thousand around 1800—including large numbers of African slaves made available and affordable by the closure of Saint Domingue. In his transforming study *Workshop of Revolution: Plebian Buenos Aires and the Atlantic World, 1776–1810*, Lyman Johnson details how the city became a center of production and social tension that fended off British invasion in 1806 and quickly turned to seeking independence when Napoleon invaded Spain in 1808. The merchants and artisans, growers and grazers of greater Buenos Aires sought access to the world to continue to prosper.[75]

Decades of war—first within and then against the Spanish empire, later among neighbors along the Río de Plata—followed as a region facing new economic prospects struggled to consolidate states and political systems. Buenos Aires eventually became the center of an emerging Argentina that prospered first by sustaining slaves in Brazil and Cuba, then by sending wool, leather, wheat, and beef to Britain. Uruguay became a small replica of Argentina, set up by Britain to create a buffer with Brazil.[76] Paraguay turned inward to become a mostly Guaraní nation, rejecting trade to preserve economic autonomy and indigenous ways—until a deadly war funded by Britain set an alliance of Argentina, Brazil, and Uruguay against Paraguay, forcing it open to the world in the 1860s, consolidating a nation of enduring Guaraní poverty.[77]

Paraguay's creation as a Guaraní nation was the extreme case of a common outcome of the conflicts and transformations of 1790 to 1825 in South America. As new nations struggled to build polities and new economies, indigenous peoples often found new autonomies that endured for decades. In regions once at the heart of the silver economy, indigenous republics found economic openings while facing fragile and contested national political powers. Other native peoples who had lived free at the margins of empires, yet dealt with traders for the horses, arms, tools, and other goods that enabled independence, found new ways of assertion as new states struggled after 1810. The spread of indigenous independence across the Andes and adjacent lowlands frustrated those who presumed native subordination. But that independence was real—if, outside Paraguay, never recognized in the world of nations—long into the nineteenth century.[78] Only the consolidation of export economies tied to British hegemony and rising U.S. demand after 1860 enabled South American states to solidify and then curtail native independence—and crush Paraguay.

The transformation of the Viceroyalty of New Spain, which in its largest sense stretched from Costa Rica to California, followed a different path. Still, it too ended with disintegrations, struggles to create new polities, searches for new economies, and indigenous independence—all facilitating the rising power of the United States. What made New Spain different was the strength of its silver economy to 1810—and the depth of the insurgent-driven collapse that followed. The fall of silver was clear in 1811, and entrenched by 1820 when Spain returned to liberal rule, setting off a movement that aimed to draw Fernando VII to Mexico City to rule all New Spain—including the Kingdom of Guatemala (Central America) and Cuba in a North American Bourbon monarchy. Fernando refused, Cuba never joined, and Guatemala broke away.

Cuba remained a prosperous Atlantic colony of sugar and slavery; had it joined Mexico, a mostly mainland nation would have gained the profits of sugar, the problem of slavery (which it later faced in Texas), and the merchant and naval power they sustained. The Kingdom of Guatemala had gained little from the silver economy. It was linked to the world in the eighteenth century mostly by the indigo raised around San Salvador and sent into trade by Guatemala City merchants. The region had little incentive to become subordinate to a regime based in Mexico City. Guatemala led the kingdom away in 1822, to soon face conflict and fragmentation into five Central American states. As cochineal from the highlands east of Guatemala City replaced indigo as the region's primary trade commodity, El Salvador broke with Guatemala. Guatemala then reconstituted as a union of indigenous western highlands, ladino (mixed/Hispanic) eastern uplands, and a capital region that concentrated power.[79] None of the Central American nations built solid states until they found commodities to sell in the new economy of the late nineteenth century: coffee in Pacific hills from the 1850s; bananas in Caribbean lowlands from the 1890s.

In Mexico, Agustín Iturbide, a commander noted for hard campaigns against political rebels and Bajío insurgents, became emperor on Fernando's refusal to take a New World throne. When New Spain began to fragment as silver collapsed, the empire gave way to a federal republic in 1824. Its central powers faced an empty treasury as mine revenues plummeted and silver and internal taxes went to the states. British lenders funded the regime for a few years, opened Mexico to British cloth, and created debts that plagued the nation for decades. To 1810 New Spain had exported revenue and capital; after 1820, the Mexican state and entrepreneurs turned to British investors for capital and new technologies. They sustained the state and drained some mines—but generated few profits as silver production held low. Once the world's source of money,

Mexico became an importer of capital and technology—a debtor with an uncertain future.

Across central and southern regions the residents of indigenous republics, earlier granted land and self-rule to sustain the silver economy, found new autonomies as the nation and commercial ways floundered. Families that had led the decade of insurgency in the Bajío, taking down the silver economy, kept control of often-irrigated lands, feeding themselves, supplying local markets, enjoying autonomies that extended to new roles for women heads of rural households.[80] Popular gains held amid national troubles.

Decades of economic challenge and political conflict followed. Amid debates over centralism and federalism, liberalism and conservatism, Zacatecas's mines came back to life in the 1820s; Guanajuato revived in the 1840s—when silver production finally began to rise. British investors had left facing bankruptcies; they also left steam pumps and other technologies that, adapted by Mexican entrepreneurs to Mexican ways of production, began to revive mining. Meanwhile, in the early 1830s, a government seeking a new economy set tariffs on cloth imports to fund a national development bank that underwrote mechanized industries in the 1830s and 1840s. Could Mexico combine revived silver mining with mechanized industry to find new prosperity and political consolidation? As the 1840s began, it seemed imaginable.[81]

Any consolidation, however, faced two threats from the north. The Comanche, like many South American natives, had lived on the margins of the Spanish world, adopting horses and firearms to assert independent power. With the fall of the silver economy and the instability of the Mexican republic, a Comanche empire rose after 1810 on the lands between New Mexico, Texas, and the United States. Mexican northward expansion ended as Comanche drove south.[82] Meanwhile, migrants from the United States expanded cotton and slavery in Texas. In 1836 they took Texas out of Mexico, deepening Mexican political conflicts.[83] In 1846, expansionist U.S. southerners won incorporation of secessionist Texas as a slave state, knowing the act would provoke war with Mexico and allow the U.S to claim the land from Texas through California. The war also helped end Comanche independence. Defeat and the loss of northern territories renewed political and social conflicts in Mexico, inhibiting economic revival for decades.[84]

The collapse of New Spain's silver economy brought a difficult birth to Mexico and favored the expansive power of the United States. When gold revived an economy of bullion, irrigated cultivation, and commercial grazing in the 1850s, it came in California, stimulating the economic growth and westward expansion of the United States. Yet the challenge of dealing with the expansion of slavery into the lands claimed from Mexico led directly to the Civil War.[85] Only after 1865 did the United States consolidate as a nation under northern leadership, accelerating a westward expansion that often replicated the bullion economy of Spanish North America in lands recently taken under U.S. rule and increasingly emptied of long-resistant native peoples.[86]

Mexico did not find a political settlement or a new economy until the 1870s—in a liberal authoritarian regime that pressed against small producers, favored capitalist agriculture, and welcomed U.S. capital to revive mines, build railroads, and energize an economy increasingly tied to U.S. markets. In a great North American inversion, the regions of New Spain that had driven global trade via a flourishing silver economy before 1810, by 1870 were dependencies of a rising United States. Irony upon irony: much of the "U.S." capital that came to profit in Mexico was generated in California, Colorado, and Arizona mining booms. After 1848, lands once Mexican prospered by replicating the silver economy of Spanish North America; they benefited from the work of Mexicans, some long-established residents, others migrants newly arrived on well-trodden trails or newly built rails.[87] The United States that challenged Britain for global hegemony around 1900 was favored by the collapse of New Spain's silver economy; it prospered by incorporating its northern lands, its dynamic ways, and many of its industrious peoples.

The world of concentrated industrial capitalism persisted into the early twentieth century. After 1870, Britain shared and disputed hegemony with industries and empires rising in the United States and Germany. Both competitors joined Britain on the gold standard in the 1870s, ending the long sway of that metal-money—and ultimately prejudicing any revival of the silver economies that once had made the Andes and New Spain central to global trades. A North Atlantic axis of geopolitical economic power ruled militarily and industrially, drawing commodities from and selling wares to an expanding and often colonized "rest of the world," until the competitors for hegemony fell into brutal war from 1914 to 1918, while key outliers—Mexico, Russia, and China—turned to revolutions that became crucibles for imagining different ways of global and national development.

Still, the world created between 1770 and 1830 limped forward to 1930—when the Great Depression completed the collapse of the first global industrial economy. Then, nations across the Americas turned to programs promising to bring the benefits of industrialism home in projects of national development. The attempt proved difficult, often impossible, in a mid-twentieth-century era of wars, revolutions, and technological innovation—this time bringing population explosion, unprecedented urbanization, and a new postindustrial globalization.[88]

Notes

1　These sketches of global trends are grounded in innumerable studies, synthesized ably in Ronald Findlay and Kevin O'Rourke, *Power and Plenty: Trade, War, and the World Economy in the Second Millennium* (Princeton, NJ: Princeton University Press, 2007).

2　Again, there are many sources. For a synthesis of Spanish America and the silver economies, see Henry Kamen, *Empire: How Spain Became a World Power, 1492–1769* (New York: HarperCollins, 2003); on the slave colonies, the best synthesis remains Robin Blackburn, *The Making of New World Slavery* (London: Verso, 1997).

3　There are many editions. See Max Weber, *The Protestant Ethic and the Spirit of Capitalism and Other Writings on the Rise of the West*, trans. and introduction by Stephen Kalberg (New York: Oxford University Press, 2008).

4　Douglass North and Robert Paul Thomas, *The Rise of the Western World: A New Economic History* (Cambridge: Cambridge University Press, 1970).

5　Douglass North, *Understanding the Process of Economic Change* (Princeton, NJ: Princeton University Press, 2005).

6　Andre Gunder Frank, *ReOrient: Global Economy in the Asian Age* (Berkeley: University of California Press, 1998).

7　Kenneth Pomeranz, *The Great Divergence: China, Europe, and the Making of the Modern World Economy* (Princeton, NJ: Princeton University Press, 2000).

8　Prasannan Parthasarathi, *Why Europe Grew Rich and Asia Did Not: Global Economic Divergence, 1600–1850* (Cambridge: Cambridge University Press, 2011).

9　See Findlay and O'Rourke, *Power and Plenty*.

10　For a detailed summary, see Findlay and O'Rourke, *Power and Plenty*, 43–142. On early European marginality and the importance of trade between the Islamic world with South and East Asia, the key work is Janet Abu-Lughod, *Before European Hegemony: The World System, AD 1250–1350* (New York: Oxford University Press, 1989).

11　For different views converging on the same understanding, see William Sanders and Barbara Price, *Mesoamerica: The Evolution of a Civilization* (New York: Random House, 1968), and Ross Hassig, *War and Society in Ancient Mesoamerica* (Berkeley: University of California Press, 1992).

12　This Mesoamerican–North American commercial integration is emphasized in Francis Jennings, *The Founders of America from the Earliest Migrations to the Present* (New York: Norton, 1993), and Alfredo López Austin and Leonardo López Lujan, *El pasado indígena*, 2nd ed. (Mexico City: Fondo de Cultura Económica, 2001).

13   See López and López, *El pasado indígena*. On Mexica political economy around
     1500, see Ross Hassig, *Trade, Tribute, and Transportation: The Sixteenth-Century
     Political Economy of the Valley of Mexico* (Norman: University of Oklahoma Press,
     1993).

14   See Thomas Patterson, *The Inca Empire: The Formation and Disintegration of a
     Pre-Capitalist State* (New York: Berg, 1997). For a comparison of the Aztec and
     Inca regimes, focused on religion but sustaining the emphasis on power and trade
     offered here, see Geoffrey Conrad and Arthur Demarest, *Religion and Empire:
     The Dynamics of Aztec and Inca Expansionism* (Cambridge: Cambridge University
     Press, 1984).

15   This is a focus of John Tutino, *Making a New World: Founding Capitalism in the
     Bajío and Spanish North America* (Durham, NC: Duke University Press, 2011).

16   Again, I emphasize the importance of Carolyn Fick, *The Making of Haiti: The
     Saint Domingue Revolution from Below* (Knoxville: University of Tennessee Press,
     1990), and Laurent Dubois, *Avengers of the New World: The Story of the Haitian Revo-
     lution* (Cambridge, MA: Harvard University Press, 2005), in the context of Tutino,
     "The Revolution in Mexican Independence: Insurgency and the Renegotiation of
     Property, Production, and Patriarchy in the Bajío, 1800–1855," *Hispanic American
     Historical Review* 78:3 (1998), 367–418.

17   On American silver and global trade, see Dennis Flynn and Arturo Giráldez,
     "Born with a 'Silver Spoon': The Origins of World Trade in 1571," *Journal of World
     History* 6:2 (1995), 201–221, and "Cycles of Silver: Global Unity through the Mid-
     Eighteenth Century," *Journal of World History* 13:2 (2002), 291–427. More recently,
     my understanding of the changing role of silver in China has been been revised
     thanks to Man-Houng Lin, *China Upside Down: Currency, Society, and Ideology,
     1808* (Cambridge, MA: Harvard University Press, 2006).

18   On the Andean silver economy, see Carlos Sempat Assadourian, *El sistema de la
     economía colonial: El mercado interior, regiones y espacio económica* (Lima: Instituto
     de Estudios Peruanos, 1982), and Enrique Tandeter, *Coercion and Mining: Silver
     Mining in Colonial Potosí, 1692–1826* (Albuquerque: University of New Mexico
     Press, 1993). On Potosí, see Peter Bakewell, *Miners of the Red Mountain: Indian
     Labor in Colonial Potosí* (Albuquerque: University of New Mexico Press, 1984),
     and Jane Mangan, *Trading Roles: Gender, Ethnicity, and the Urban Economy in
     Colonial Potosí* (Durham, NC: Duke University Press, 2005). On outlying regions,
     see Karen Spalding, *Huarochirí: An Andean Society under Inca and Spanish Rule*
     (Stanford, CA: Stanford University Press, 1983); Brooke Larson, *Cochabamba:
     Colonialism and Agrarian Transformation in Bolivia, 1550–1900*, rev. ed. (Durham,
     NC: Duke University Press, 1998); and Ann Zulawski, *They Eat from Their
     Labor: Work and Social Change in Colonial Bolivia* (Pittsburgh: University of
     Pittsburgh Press, 1995). On eighteenth-century conflicts see Ward Stavig, *The World
     of Tupac Amaru: Conflict, Community, and Identity in Colonial Peru* (Lincoln:
     University of Nebraska Press, 1999); Charles Walker, *Smoldering Ashes: Cuzco and
     the Creation of the Peruvian Republic, 1780–1840* (Durham, NC: Duke University
     Press, 1999); Sergio Serulnikov, *Subverting Colonial Authority: Challenges to Spanish*

Rule in the Eighteenth-Century Southern Andes (Durham, NC: Duke University Press, 2003); and Sinclair Thomson, *We Alone Will Rule: Native Andean Politics in the Age of Insurgency* (Madison: University of Wisconsin Press, 2003).

19 On early commercialization of production and community life in the regions around Mexico City, see José Enciso Contreras, *Taxco en el siglo XVI: Sociedad y normatividad en un real de minas novohispano* (Zacatecas: Universidad Autónoma de Zacatecas, 1999); Sarah Cline, *Colonial Culhuacan, 1580–1600: A Social History of an Aztec Town* (Albuquerque: University of New Mexico Press, 1986); and Gilda Cubillo Moreno, *Los dominios de la plata: El precio del auge, el peso del pode; los reales de minas de Pachuca a Zimapán, 1552–1620* (Mexico City: INAH, 2006). My synthesis reflects those works and the classic studies of the Mesoamerican core from Charles Gibson, *The Aztecs under Spanish Rule* (Stanford, CA: Stanford University Press, 1964), to James Lockhart, *The Nahuas after the Conquest* (Stanford, CA: Stanford University Press, 1992).

20 On Spanish North America, see Peter Bakewell, *Silver Mining and Society in Colonial Mexico: Zacatecas, 1546–1700* (Cambridge: Cambridge University Press, 1971); D. A. Brading, *Miners and Merchants in Bourbon Mexico, 1763–1810* (Cambridge: Cambridge University Press, 1971); and Tutino, *Making a New World*.

21 The key study of New Spain's late colonial revenues is Carlos Marichal, *La bancarrota del virreinato, Nueva España y las finanzas del imperio español, 1780–1810* (Mexico City: Fondo de Cultura Económica, 1999), now complemented by Barbara Stein and Stanley Stein, *Edge of Crisis: Wars and Trade in the Spanish Atlantic, 1789–1808* (Baltimore: Johns Hopkins University Press, 2009).

22 On Chinese demand for American silver and its demise around 1750, see Flynn and Giráldez, "Cycles of Silver." On peaking Chinese demand after 1770, increasingly via British traders, see Lin, *China Upside Down*.

23 See William Taylor, *Drinking, Homicide, and Rebellion in Colonial Mexican Villages* (Stanford, CA: Stanford University Press, 1979), and Brian Owensby, *Empire of Law and Indian Justice in Colonial Mexico* (Stanford, CA: Stanford University Press, 1979).

24 Tutino, *Making a New World*.

25 See Antonio García de León, *Tierra adentro, mar en fuera: El Puerto de Veracruz y su litoral a Sotavento, 1519–1821* (Mexico City: Fondo de Cultura Económica, 2011).

26 On early sugar and slave colonies: Stuart Schwartz, ed., *Tropical Babylons: Sugar and the Making of the Atlantic World* (Chapel Hill: University of North Carolina Press, 2004).

27 The key study of Brazil is Stuart Schwartz, *Sugar Plantations and the Formation of Brazilian Society, Bahia, 1550–1835* (Cambridge: Cambridge University Press, 1985).

28 For an overview of the sugar colonies: Blackburn, *The Making of New World Slavery*. On the early British Caribbean: Richard Dunn, *Sugar and Slaves: The Rise of the Planter Class in the British West Indies, 1624–1713* (New York: Norton, 1972); on Jamaica: Michael Craton, *Searching for the Invisible Man: Slaves and Plantation Life in Jamaica* (Cambridge, MA: Harvard University Press, 1978).

29　On Saint Domingue, I rely on Fick, *The Making of Haiti*, and Dubois, *Avengers of the New World*.

30　See John McCusker and Russell Menard, *The Economy of British America, 1607–1789* (Chapel Hill: University of North Carolina Press, 1991).

31　See Sidney Mintz, *Sweetness and Power: The Place of Sugar in Modern History* (New York: Viking, 1985).

32　Kathleen Higgins, *Licentious Liberty in a Brazilian Gold Mining Region: Slavery, Gender, and Social Control in Eighteenth-Century Sabará, Minas Gerais* (State College: Pennsylvania State University Press, 1999), and Alida Metcalf, *Family and Frontier in Colonial Brazil: Santana do Parnaíba, 1580–1822* (Berkeley: University of California Press, 1992).

33　Again, see McCusker and Menard, *The Economy of British America*.

34　See Kamen, *Empire*, and Findlay and O'Rourke, *Power and Plenty*.

35　See K. N. Chaudhuri, *Trade and Civilization in the Indian Ocean: An Economic History from the Rise of Islam to 1750* (Cambridge: Cambridge University Press, 1985), and Findlay and O'Rourke, *Power and Plenty*.

36　This understanding depends on the essential analysis in Parthasarathi, *Why Europe Grew Rich*. On silver, textiles, and slaves, see pp. 21–50.

37　Parthasarathi, *Why Europe Grew Rich*, tables 2.1 and 2.2, p. 25.

38　On French and British penetrations of Spanish trade, see Stanley Stein and Barbara Stein, *Silver, War, and Trade: Spain and America in the Making of Early Modern Europe* (Baltimore: Johns Hopkins University Press, 2000).

39　See Pierre Vilar, *A History of Gold and Money, 1450–1920* (London: Verso, 1984), 222–231 and appendix II, p. 351; and Flynn and Giráldez, "Cycles of Silver." On gold, its relations with silver, their linked importance, and how the decline of Brazilian gold led to the conflicts after 1750, see Alfredo Castillero Calvo, *Los metales preciosos y la primera globalización* (Panama City: Editora Novo Arte, 2008).

40　For studies of the war that emphasize British success, see Fred Anderson, *Crucible of War: The Seven Years' War and the Fate of Empire in British North America* (New York: Knopf, 2000), and Brendan Simms, *Three Victories and a Defeat: The Rise and Fall of the First British Empire* (New York: Basic Books, 2009).

41　Edward Countryman, *The American Revolution* (New York: Hill and Wang, 2003).

42　This comparison is developed in Tutino, *Making a New World*, chap. 4.

43　I aim to bring the Americas to the center of the transformation analyzed well by Findlay and O'Rourke in *Power and Plenty*—except for an inability to see the Americas outside the United States. The global adaptations that followed are synthesized well by C. A. Bayly in *The Birth of the Modern World, 1780–1914* (Oxford: Blackwell, 2003)—except for his difficulty seeing the Americas—including the United States.

44　See David Landes's classic, *The Unbound Prometheus: Technological Change and Industrial Development in Western Europe from 1750 to the Present* (Cambridge: Cambridge University Press, 1969), and Robert Allen, *The British Industrial Revolution in Global Perspective* (Cambridge: Cambridge University Press, 2009).

45 Parthsarathi, *Why Europe Grew Rich*, 89–262. The more complex understanding I sketch here emerges from that work; Sven Beckert *Empire of Cotton: A Global History* (New York: Knopf, 2014); and the timing of the triumph of industry after 1810 detailed in Allen, *British Industrial Revolution.* The fall of silver is clear in Tutino, *Making a New World,* and Lin, *China Upside Down.*

46 And thus it is time to end the endless debates about which mattered most.

47 On the Manila trade, see Carmén Yuste López, *Emporios transpacíficos: Comerciantes mexicanos en Manila, 1710–1815* (Mexico City: UNAM, 2007).

48 Tutino, *Making a New World,* table D.1, p. 550.

49 Stanley Stein and Barbara Stein, *Apogee of Empire: Spain and New Spain in the Age of Charles III, 1759–1789* (Baltimore: Johns Hopkins University Press, 2003).

50 Again see Fick, *The Making of Haiti,* and Dubois, *Avengers of the New World.*

51 Tutino, *Making a New World,* table D.1, p. 550.

52 Marichal, *La bancarrota del virreinato.*

53 On tropical lowlanders immunological advantages in war against European newcomers or American highlanders, see J. R. McNeill, *Mosquito Empires: Ecology and War in the Greater Caribbean, 1620–1914* (New York: Cambridge University Press, 2010).

54 On the shift of Portuguese rule to Rio and the consequences for Brazil, see Kirsten Schultz, *Tropical Versailles: Empire, Monarchy, and the Portuguese Royal Court in Rio de Janeiro, 1808–1821* (London: Routledge, 2001).

55 Nicholas Fraser, *Napoleon's Cursed War: Spanish Popular Resistance in the Peninsular War, 1808–1814* (London: Verso, 2009), and José Gregorio Cayuela Fernández and José Ángel Gallego Palomares, *La guerra de independencia: Historia bélica; pueblo y nación en España, 1808–1814* (Salamanca: Ediciones Universidad, 2008).

56 The rise of liberalism in Spain is detailed in chapter 2, "The Cádiz Liberal Revolution," by Roberto Breña; the conflicts of 1808 to 1810 and the emergence of the Hidalgo revolt are detailed in chapter 7, "Becoming Mexico," by Alfredo Ávila and John Tutino.

57 That the conflicts that began in New Spain in 1808 were not seeking independence from Spain is the focus of Jaime Rodríguez, *"We Are Now the True Spaniards": Sovereignty, Revolution, Independence, and the Emergence of the Federal Republic of Mexico, 1808–1824* (Stanford, CA: Stanford University Press, 2012).

58 See Tutino, "The Revolution in Mexican Independence."

59 Miguel Lerdo de Tejada, *Comercio exterior de México* (1853; rpt. Mexico City: Banco Nacional de Comercio Exterior, 1967).

60 Fernand Braudel, *Civilization and Capitalism, 15th–18th Century,* vol. 3, *The Perspective of the World,* trans. Sian Reynolds (New York: Harper and Row, 1984), 77–79.

61 See Vilar, *History of Gold and Money,* 211–231, 309–319. For China and opium, see Lin, *China Upside Down.*

62 See Stanley Elkins and Eric McKittrick, *The Age of Federalism: The Early American Republic, 1788–1800* (New York: Oxford University Press, 1993); Drew McCoy, *The Elusive Republic: Political Economy in Jeffersonian America* (Chapel Hill: University of North Carolina Press, 1980); and Charles Sellers, *The Market Revolution:*

Jacksonian America, 1815–1846 (New York: Oxford University Press, 1992). None shares my global emphasis; the War of 1812 remains minimized or viewed in national perspective. See the classic study of Roger Brown, *The Republic in Peril: 1812* (New York: Norton, 1971), and the recent work of Alan Taylor, *The Civil War of 1812: American Citizens, British Subjects, Irish Rebels and Indian Allies* (New York: Knopf, 2010). My understanding of this era is deeply influenced by Adam Rothman's *Slave Country: American Expansion and the Origins of the Deep South* (Cambridge, MA: Harvard University Press, 2005).

63 See Fraser, *Napoleon's Cursed War,* and Cayuela Fernández and Gallego Palomares, *La guerra de la independencia.*

64 Emilia Viotti da Costa, *Crowns of Glory, Tears of Blood: The Demerara Slave Rebellion of 1823* (New York: Oxford University Press, 1994).

65 On postrevolutionary Haiti, see Laurent Dubois, *Haiti: The Aftershocks of History* (New York: Metropolitan Books, 2012); on the end of British and French Caribbean slave regimes, see Robin Blackburn, *The Overthrow of Colonial Slavery, 1776–1848,* new ed. (London: Verso, 2011).

66 On sugar and slavery in Cuba, the classic history is Manuel Moreno Fraginals, *El ingenio: Complejo económico social cubano del azúcar* (reprint, Barcelona: Editorial Crítica, 2001); analysis in English begins with Franklin Knight, *Slave Society in Cuba during the Nineteenth Century* (Madison: University of Wisconsin Press, 1970). On challenges to slavery and the persistence of sugar, see Robert Paquette, *Sugar Is Made with Blood: The Conspiracy of La Escalera and the Conflict between Empires over Slavery in Cuba* (Middletown, CT: Wesleyan University Press, 1990); Ada Ferrer, *Insurgent Cuba: Race, Nation, and Revolution, 1868–1898* (Chapel Hill: University of North Carolina Press, 1999); and Gillian MacGillivray, *Blazing Cane: Sugar Communities, Class, and State Formation in Cuba, 1868–1959* (Durham, NC: Duke University Press, 2009).

67 See Kenneth Maxwell, *Conflicts and Conspiracies: Brazil and Portugal, 1750–1808* (Cambridge: Cambridge University Press, 1973); Schultz, *Tropical Versailles*; Richard Graham, *Britain and the Onset of Modernization in Brazil, 1850–1914* (Cambridge: Cambridge University Press, 1972); Stanley Stein, *Vassouras: A Brazilian Coffee County, 1850–1900* (Cambridge, MA: Harvard University Press, 1957); Emilia Viotti da Costa, *The Brazilian Empire: Myths and Histories,* rev. ed. (Chapel Hill: University of North Carolina Press, 2000).

68 See Richard Graham, *Feeding the City: From Street Market to Liberal Reform in Salvador, Brazil, 1780–1860* (Austin: University of Texas Press, 2010), and João José Reis, *Slave Rebellion in Brazil: The Muslim Uprising of 1835 in Bahia* (Baltimore: Johns Hopkins University Press, 1995).

69 On imperial politics, see Viotti da Costa, *The Brazilian Empire,* and Richard Graham, *Patronage and Politics in Nineteenth-Century Brazil* (Stanford, CA: Stanford University Press, 1990). On ties to Britain, see Graham, *Britain and the Onset of Modernization.*

70 See Sellers, *The Market Revolution.* Studies of slavery's expansion begin with Eugene Genovese, *The Political Economy of Slavery* (New York: Vintage, 1965), and lead to

Adam Rothman, *Slave Country*. The inseparable integration of southern cotton and slavery and British industry is now the focus of Beckert, *Empire of Cotton*.

71 Sellers, *The Market Revolution*, remains essential: see also Paul Lack, *The Texas Revolutionary Experience: A Political and Social History, 1835–1836* (College Station: Texas A&M University Press, 1995); Pekka Hämäläinen, *The Comanche Empire* (New Haven, CT: Yale University Press, 2008); Brian Delay, *The War of a Thousand Deserts: Indian Raids and the U.S.-Mexican War* (New Haven, CT: Yale University Press, 2008).

72 On how war with Mexico led to Civil War, see John Ashworth, *The Republic in Crisis, 1848–1861* (Cambridge: Cambridge University Press, 2012); that the Civil War was fought over slavery, see Chandra Manning, *What This Cruel War Was Over* (New York: Knopf, 2007); understanding the postwar United States begins with Eric Foner, *Reconstruction: America's Unfinished Revolution, 1863–1877* (New York: Harper and Row, 1988).

73 This links this volume and Findlay and O'Rourke, *Power and Plenty*. After 1880 Britain built a new empire in Asia and Africa, while the United States expanded beyond the continent, beginning in Cuba. France, Germany, Japan, and Russia joined the scramble.

74 On Andean independence, see Walker, *Smoldering Ashes*, and Sarah Chambers, *From Subjects to Citizens: Honor, Gender, and Politics in Arequipa, Peru, 1780–1854* (University Park: Pennsylvania State University Press, 1999).

75 Lyman Johnson, *Workshop of Revolution: Plebian Buenos Aires and the Atlantic World, 1776–1810* (Durham, NC: Duke University Press, 2011).

76 New studies of independence in the Río de la Plata began with Jonathan Brown, *A Socioeconomic History of Argentina, 1776–1860* (Cambridge: Cambridge University Press, 1979); Ricardo Salvatore pioneered new visions of the postindependence era in *Wandering Paysanos: State Order and Subaltern Experience in Buenos Aires during the Rosas Era* (Durham, NC: Duke University Press, 2003), and now Lyman Johnson has delivered *Workshop of Revolution* on developments before 1810.

77 For analysis placing Paraguay at the center of a history focused on those who rejected British hegemony, see Bradford Burns, *The Poverty of Progress: Latin America in the Nineteenth Century* (Berkeley: University of California Press, 1981).

78 See Erick Langer, *Expecting Pears from an Elm Tree: Franciscan Missions on the Chiriguano Frontier in the Heart of South America, 1830–1949* (Durham, NC: Duke University Press, 2009).

79 The conflicts that led to Mexico are synthesized in Alfredo Avila, *En nombre de la nación* (Mexico City: Taurus, 2002); Jordana Dym, *From Sovereign Villages to National States: City, State, and Federation on Central America, 1759–1839* (Albuquerque: University of New Mexico Press, 2006), brings new depth to understanding independence and fragmentation in the former Kingdom of Guatemala.

80 On assertive indigenous communities after independence, see John Tutino, *From Insurrection to Revolution in Mexico: Social Bases of Agrarian Violence, 1750–1940* (Princeton, NJ: Princeton University Press, 1986); on Bajío families after insurgency, see Tutino, "The Revolution in Mexican Independence."

81 See Araceli Ibarra Bellón, *El comercio y el poder en México, 1821–1864* (Mexico City: Fondo de Cultura Económica, 1998).

82 Hämäläinen, *The Comanche Empire*; Delay, *The War of a Thousand Deserts.*

83 Lack, *The Texas Revolutionary Experience.*

84 This synthesizes John Tutino, "Capitalist Foundations: Spanish North America, Mexico, and the United States," in *Mexico and Mexicans in the Making of the United States*, ed. John Tutino (Austin: University of Texas Press, 2012).

85 John Ashworth, *Slavery, Capitalism, and Politics in the Antebellum Republic*, 2 vols. (1995; reprint, Cambridge: Cambridge University Press, 1995).

86 See Tutino, *Mexico and Mexicans in the Making of the United States.*

87 Tutino, *Mexico and Mexicans in the Making of the United States.* For a detailed case history, see Katherine Benton-Cohen, *Borderline Americans: Racial Division and Labor War in the Arizona Borderlands* (Cambridge, MA: Harvard University Press, 2009).

88 I explore twentieth-century national projects, urbanization, and globalization in John Tutino, "The Americas in the Twentieth-Century World," chap. 1 in John Tutino and Martin Melosi, "New World Cities," in progress.

2
———

THE CÁDIZ LIBERAL REVOLUTION
AND SPANISH AMERICAN INDEPENDENCE

ROBERTO BREÑA

Preamble

The new countries that came to define the modern Americas emerged within the "Age of Revolution," a historical period widely recognized, yet open to diverse periodizations. Many focus on the half century from 1775 to 1825, emphasizing the revolution of the Thirteen Colonies (1776–1783), the French Revolution (1789–1799), the Haitian revolt and independence (1791–1804), and the Spanish American independence movements (1810–1824).[1] Another common vision sees the chronological span of the Age of Revolution as the century that goes from 1750 to 1850.[2] From a political perspective some historians go as far back as 1688 (to include England's "Glorious Revolution"); some are more "selective," like Jacques Solé, who circumscribes this revolutionary era to the period from 1773 to 1804,[3] some like David Armitage and Sanjay Subrahmanyam prefer a "global" Age of Revolution from 1760 to 1840,[4] and, finally, others have no problem extending this age to include the 1848 revolutions.[5]

In this essay, I focus my analysis on the political revolution that took place in the Spanish-speaking world from 1808 to 1824. My main interest is to show the decisive influence that the Cádiz liberal experience had on the Spanish American independence movements. Without understanding this experience it is almost impossible to grasp what went on politically and intellectually in Spanish America during those sixteen years (with variations, of course, depending on the region and the years in which we focus our attention). While the Spanish American independence processes can be considered an integral part of the Atlantic revolutions, their Atlantic character stems mainly from the peninsular political revolution focused on Cádiz. This is not to say that the revolution in the *mundo hispánico* did not share broad political principles, selected ideas, and some debates with the other Atlantic revolutions; in this essay, however, I emphasize the many particular, at times unique, visions, and programs that defined political debates in the mundo hispánico between 1808 and 1824. They make it clear that no revolutionary sequence, no "revolutionary wave," began in Boston, flowed to Paris, crashed in Port-au-Prince, and then flooded Mexico City, Caracas, and Buenos Aires.

The Spanish American independence movements are unintelligible from a political and intellectual perspective without understanding the events and innovations that began in Spain in 1808. After decades of wars and trade conflicts, with France usually as an ally and Britain normally as an enemy, the uprisings in several Spanish cities against Napoleon's army in the spring of 1808 started the political crisis that turned the mundo hispánico upside down. In the following years, peninsular Spaniards and Spanish Americans shaped a new political vision that can be defined, albeit with varying emphases and connotations, as "liberal" and that can be encapsulated, *within the sociohistoric context of the time*, in the term "liberalism." More precisely, I define it as *liberalismo hispánico*. In the end, the crisis of 1808 led to the loss of all of Spain's continental territories in the New World; a loss suffered by an empire that had faced political and military decay for more than a century (even as New Spain, Cuba, and the Río de la Plata lived economic revivals); that had become increasingly dependent on France; and that, as the battle of Trafalgar definitively showed in 1805, had lost the military confrontation against England that had characterized European-Atlantic history since at least the War of Austrian Succession (1740–1748). However, no conflict of the eighteenth century was as important as the Seven Years' War (1756–1763) in showing the Spanish Crown the need to overhaul its full military, fiscal, and administrative structure in the New World. The British occupation of the strategic port of La Habana in 1762 revealed worrisome vulnerabilities.[6] Yet Spain's empire carried on. Its demise in America during the first quarter of the nineteenth century was a protracted process, with military and administrative weakness countered by economic resiliency. Social upheavals also marked the second half of the Spanish American eighteenth century, as shown by the Quito insurrection of 1765 and the Túpac Amaru rebellion of 1780 and related risings. Still—and despite the search by so many "nationalist" historians to find precursors everywhere—the conflicts and debates that began in Spain in 1808 and by diverse routes led to Spanish American nations in the 1820s surprised everybody. The wars of independence were completely unexpected (as many of its protagonists recognized).

The political crisis of the mundo hispánico began in 1808 with the Napoleonic invasion and occupation of most of Spain. Two years later, the futures of Spain and Spanish America became inextricably linked to the city of Cádiz. The reasons were mostly military: its geographical location on an isolated peninsula with a very narrow access by land ensured that French armies could not capture Cádiz—while British and Spanish ships could guard and supply it from the sea. Safe from invading forces, Cádiz became the meeting place of the approximately 260 delegates from the Peninsula and overseas (all from Spanish America, but two from the Philippines) who gathered from September 1810 onward in the famous Cortes of Cádiz. From a political perspective, this Parliament radically transformed the Spanish monarchy; first through a series of decrees and then with its culminating work: the Constitution of Cádiz or 1812 Constitution, sanctioned in March of that year.[7] In January 1814 the Cortes moved from Cádiz to Madrid, only to be dissolved by the recently restored Fernando VII in May of that same year. The dissolution of the Cortes ended the liberal revolution in the Peninsula and returned absolutism to Spain and its empire. It did not end, however, the influence of Cádiz liberalism in the mundo hispánico.

In the first section of this chapter I offer an overview of the Spanish liberal revolution and its main intellectual sources. In the second I consider how the revolution affected the Spanish American emancipation processes—which gradually turned into "independence movements."[8] Finally, I explore the recent historiography dealing with the mundo hispánico and the Spanish American independence movements to emphasize that a more profound understanding of Cádiz liberalism and the *revoluciones hispánicas* should lead to a more complex understanding of the "Age of Revolution."

The political and social turmoil that began in Spain in 1808 and soon spread to its Americas began in the face of the invasion of the Iberian Peninsula by Napoleon's army in the fall of 1807. Officially, this was not an "invasion" because the Spanish Crown had signed the Treaty of Fontainebleau in October, permitting French troops to enter Spanish territory on their way to invade Portugal. Soon, however, the supposed transit became an occupation: a tense calm lasted for several months, until the people of Madrid revolted against the French garrison on May 2, 1808. Three weeks later, when the *Gazeta de Madrid* spread the news to several other Spanish cities of the so-called "abdications" of Bayonne, a general insurrection began.[9] The presence of Napoleon's army in Spanish territory then became a full-fledged occupation. From that moment, the traditional alliance between Spain and France that had persisted during almost all of the eighteenth century, formalized through several Bourbon *pactos de familia*, came to an end. For the next six years the Peninsula was the scene of a war so harrowing that Goya's famous depiction of it (*Los desastres de la guerra*) became an enduring symbol of the senseless and inexhaustible violence of all wars.

The war with France meant that the Spanish army and people had to face the most powerful army of the time. Yet in an unexpected and unique way, the military conflict became a political revolution. During the first two years the revolution was led by a variety of local juntas, later coordinated with much difficulty by a Junta Central that suddenly dissolved in January 1810 in the face of political adversities and defeats against the French army. To that point, the events taking place in the Peninsula did not have a political label. That changed during 1810 when the political group with the upper hand in the Cortes that gathered in Cádiz became known as *liberales*. The extent and depth of the changes that the Cortes designed for Spain and Spanish America are so vast that it is difficult to detail them in a few pages. I will first outline important elements of the political situation in the Peninsula between 1808 and 1814, then proceed to engage the main political tenets of the "first Spanish liberalism," and finally explore key doctrinal and intellectual sources.[10] Together, these three elements should give a clear idea of the revolutionary character of first Spanish liberalism while revealing of some of its tensions and ambiguities.

The liberal revolution of 1808 to 1814 derived some of its main traits from key aspects of Spanish society at the beginning of the nineteenth century. The extraordinary power wielded by the *valido* Manuel Godoy (Carlos IV's first minister for fifteen years) was increasingly resented; in fact, the Spanish Crown's legitimacy and power declined markedly during Godoy's tenure. Legitimacy plummeted for two main reasons. The first one was the Crown's increasing

MAP 2.1. The Cádiz Constitution and Spanish America, ca. 1812–1814

dependence on Napoleon. The second one was the all too public confrontation between Carlos IV, king since 1789, and his eldest son, Fernando. These confrontations led to the abdication by Carlos to his son after the so-called *motín* (riot) of Aranjuez in March 1808 (a rising planned by Fernando's supporters).[11] The Spanish monarchy was losing respect and legitimacy at the very moment when the French army was occupying almost all of Spain's peninsular territory.

This uncertain legitimacy opened the way for the *dos años cruciales* (two crucial years), as François-Xavier Guerra called 1808 and 1809. A profound ideological transformation affecting the whole mundo hispánico began in the biennium that preceded the Cortes of Cádiz and the beginning of the Spanish American emancipation processes.[12] Militarily, the years 1808–1810 brought a long list of French victories on Spanish battlefields (notwithstanding the famous Spanish victory at Bailén in July 1808). In the political realm the Junta Central had a difficult time constituting itself as the head of the numerous local juntas while Fernando was a prisoner of Napoleon at Bayonne.[13]

For a long time, Spanish historiography presented these local juntas, that organized the fighting against the French, as "popular," that is, formed by members of all levels of society, including the least advantaged. It is now clear that the vast majority of them were formed by the notables of each city or town. Still, the crisis of 1808 started as a popular revolt against the French and, in the context of the moment, most juntas could not work without popular support. At the same time, the Spanish war against French occupation made the term "guerrilla" synonymous with armed popular resistance.[14] This pivotal period of Spanish history was therefore shaped in important ways by social movements of popular origin. Such foundations were reflected, explicitly or implicitly, in the ideology the liberals developed from 1808 through 1814; they were a central element of Spanish patriotism during the war—and of an enduring Spanish nationalism.

In January 1810, the Junta Central, overwhelmed by military defeats, without economic resources, and facing a campaign of discredit by internal enemies, dissolved itself. In the process, it first made its most important decision: to summon the election of Cortes. The institution was no novelty: Cortes had existed in several Spanish kingdoms since the Middle Ages, gathering representatives of cities and towns to discuss, sanction, or limit royal decisions. But there was novelty in the Cortes that gathered in Cádiz in 1810: the vast majority of the members would be elected by much of the adult male population, something unprecedented in Spain (or in any other part of the world). No less important, the Americas were included in the new representative body (though the method of electing them was different, to ensure that deputies from the peninsula would hold a strong majority). As mentioned and although numbers vary depending on the date and the issue under discussion, in total around 260 deputies participated in the extraordinary Cortes that opened in Cádiz in September 1810. Of them, about sixty were Spanish Americans—though Spanish America's population was larger than Spain's.[15]

The participation of the American representatives in the debates was very important; several topics would not have been discussed at all or would have been debated very differently without the Americans' presence. But they were a minority, and they were defeated at every turn when votes came on the most important economic or political issues (i.e., free trade or political autonomy for their territories). Despite their active participation in several of the most important debates, the *direct* contributions of Spanish American deputies to the 384 articles of the final version of the Cádiz Constitution were limited. We will return to the document later. At this point, it is important to look at Cádiz, the city that became the head and the heart of the Spanish liberal revolution.

As mentioned, Cádiz was the seat of the Spanish government from 1810 to 1814 for purely geo-military reasons. Still, it is important to recognize the exceptionality of the city within Spain. It was a port and by far the most important point of contact of the Peninsula with Spain's Americas. This brought a constant circulation of goods, persons, and ideas from across the world, and the presence of merchants, bankers, intellectuals, and politicians of diverse nationalities. Cádiz was a cosmopolitan city, a place used to "other" ways of thinking, with the vitality of any port where business is vibrant—and in the eyes of many visitors a very beautiful city. Lord Byron, for example, wrote in 1809: "Cadiz, sweet Cadiz!—it is the first spot in the Creation. The beauty of its streets and mansions are only excelled by the loveliness of its inhabitants."[16] Cádiz was not a "traditional" Spanish city. How "untraditional" it was can be inferred by the revolution it hosted and by the reaction of the majority of Spaniards when Fernando VII returned to the Peninsula from his captivity in France and destroyed all that the Cortes had done. In fact, in May 1814 the king issued a decree stating that Spaniards should behave as if the Cortes had never existed.[17] Most Spaniards, exhausted by six years of war and skeptical about the liberals' political innovations, acquiesced in the fall of liberalism (until 1820, when liberals returned to power and the 1812 Constitution was reinstated).

Still, what happened in Cádiz between 1810 and 1814 cannot be explained mainly by the characteristics of the city, unorthodox as it was within the Spain of 1810. What went on in the port has to be explained first by the men who shaped the liberal revolution. They were, by any standard, a small group—in fact, a very small group of men. Any list can be extended to include dozens of names, but the main protagonists of the Spanish liberal revolution in Cádiz were few: among the *peninsulares*, I would mention Manuel José Quintana, Agustín de Argüelles, José María Queipo de Llano (better known as the count of Toreno), Diego Muñoz Torrero, Álvaro Florez Estrada, and, with hindsight and from a distance (for he left Spain for England in 1810), José María Blanco White. Among the Spanish American representatives with unequivocal liberal perspectives, I would highlight José Mejía Lequerica, José Miguel Ramos Arizpe, José Miguel Guridi, and Joaquín Fernández de Leiva. On this short list, all but Quintana, Flórez Estrada, and Blanco White were deputies in the Cortes. Four were priests (Muñoz Torrero, Blanco White, Ramos Arizpe, and Guridi), five had studied law (Quintana, Flórez Estrada, Argüelles, Mejía Lequerica, and Fernández de Leiva) and one was a noble (Toreno). Such a list, revealing in some respects (for example, the weight of churchmen in the Spanish liberal revolution), is clearly insufficient. It ignores the hundreds of other men who enabled key achievements and spread important ideas. Many deputies contributed proposals, arguments, and votes to shape Cádiz liberalism, although most did so in "selective" ways, depending on the issue under discussion. On questions concerning Spanish America, Peninsulars and Americans were often on different sides.

The men listed above could not have led the Cádiz liberal revolution without the unprecedented situation created by the 1808 crisis. The absence of the king, the occupation of most Spanish territory by the French army, the popular turmoil provoked by the war against Napoleon, the British economic and military support, the de facto freedom of the press that existed in the Peninsula since the beginning of the *crisis hispánica*, and last but not least, the widespread discontent with Godoy and the way he handled the monarchy for years, all combined to create an exceptional "breeding ground." Among these elements, the liberty to publish political texts was paramount: from the spring of 1808 the Spanish press became an open and vibrant political forum.[18]

Liberal leaders quickly established a direct link between the war against Napoleon and the political revolution they were trying to forge—*nuestra revolución* (our revolution). A major political crisis, popular participation in uprisings all over the Peninsula, the religious character of the war against the French (considered atheists by many Spaniards), and freedom of the press became an explosive combination. If we add the unlimited devotion of the Spanish people to the absent king Fernando (known as El Deseado, "the Desired One"), the concentration in the city of Cádiz of Spaniards looking for a political change, and the fact that for the first time in Spanish history elected Cortes were in permanent session working on a new constitution, we can get an idea of life in "sweet Cadiz" during the liberal revolution.

In any case, while this revolution was the result of the participation of many people, at its core was the small number of deputies identified as liberales. For the first time, the term "liberal" defined a political group. From Cádiz, the term extended to Spanish America, then across Europe and, eventually, to the rest of world.[19]

The first Spanish liberalism mixed traditional and revolutionary elements. In new historical circumstances, traditional elements gained strong reformist connotations and led to revolutionary consequences. Karl Marx saw the ambiguous nature of the Cádiz Constitution as a combination of the old and the new in which the latter prevailed. For him, the document was a compromise between the "liberal ideas of the eighteenth century" and "the obscure traditions of theocracy"; the fusion made him wonder how such a radical document came out "of the old monastic and absolutist Spain."[20]

The main tenets of the first Spanish liberalism are centered in the following constitutional articles: national sovereignty (art. 3), protection of individual rights (art. 4), purpose of government ("the happiness of the Nation and the well-being of the individuals that compose it," art. 13), division of powers (arts. 15–17), national representation (art. 27), indirect electoral system in three levels (arts. 34–103), inviolability of individual liberty by the king (art. 172, section 11), fair administration of criminal justice (arts. 286–308), inviolability of each person's home (art. 306), general taxation (art. 339), national education (arts. 366–370), and, last but not least, freedom of the press (art. 371). Many of these stipulations may not seem new, to the extent they had precedents in the British legislation emanating mainly from the "Glorious Revolution" (1688–1689), the Constitution of the United States (1787), or the French constitutions that came out of the revolution of 1789.

Still, some provisions of the Cádiz Constitution were revolutionary from any perspective: for example, the wide extension of the franchise and the inclusion of the Americas' indigenous peoples as citizens. Ultimately, the revolutionary character of any constitution comes from the prevailing sociopolitical conditions in which it sees light. The Cádiz Charter came out of a global monarchy (including the Philippines) that had worked for time immemorial under principles of divine right. In that context, the Constitution of 1812 brought a revolutionary rebalancing of the power of God, the rights of the pueblos in Cortes, and a people suddenly in arms against ungodly French usurpers. The core political, social, and cultural values that sustained the Antiguo Régimen in Spain and its empire for centuries were reworked in transforming ways.

Marx's perception of the radicalism of the Cádiz Constitution was right; its novelty built on traditional elements that explain the ideological ambiguity he read in the document. The main argument against the constitution's revolutionary character has focused on article 12, establishing Catholicism as the exclusive religion and forbidding any other. Other articles in the charter point in the same direction: articles 35–58 on the organization of elections at the parish level (thus overseen by local priests) and article 249, maintaining the legal privileges of the clergy. If simple claims of divine right ended with the declaration of national sovereignty the Cortes made on its first day (September 24, 1810), the recognition of God's ultimate power and of Catholic rights held strong.

Many historians have focused on article 12 to question the depth of the first Spanish liberalism. But if Spanish political traditions and new historical circumstances are taken into consideration, this position is untenable. It ignores Spanish history since at least the end of the fifteenth century. Limiting the power of the monarch with a written constitution was a radical turn that did not require a denial of God's rights or the Church's roles. And the Realpolitik of re-creating government in the face of a foreign invasion and broad popular mobilization also inhibited any explicit turn against the Church. As leading liberals like Argüelles and Toreno argued years later to justify their less than radical position regarding the Church, many of the changes pressed by the constitution were going to face adversity within Spanish society (as was the case); a proclamation of religious tolerance would have undermined the whole liberal project.[21]

Still, many decrees issued by the Cortes before the constitution was sanctioned in March 1812 did diminish the power of the Church, seeking to reduce its size and limit its power. The abolition of the Inquisition was a major liberal accomplishment. The six articles of title IX (arts. 366–371) are equally important: education at all levels became the responsibility of the government and a "General Direction of Studies" was created to review and control public education (art. 369). Education came under the oversight of continuing Cortes that will "legislate on everything that has to do with [this] important object" (art. 370). Article 371 also guaranteed freedom of the press, ending Church censorship. It is difficult to exaggerate the importance of these articles in promoting a secularization that can be considered timid only by those blind to the role the Church and the power of Catholicism in Spanish society—historically and still in 1810. Taking education from the Church was an indispensable step toward the kind of society the liberales wanted for Spain and its overseas territories.[22] The 1812 Cádiz Constitution maintained Catholicism, but simultaneously ended the exclusive role of the Church in education, the press, and public discourse.

A good way to gauge what national sovereignty, political equality, separation of powers, individual rights, elections, and a national system of education meant in peninsular Spain and its territories in America and Asia is the reaction of the Church to the Cádiz Constitution. Clerical opposition could not have been more adamant or more vocal. It is impossible to explain the reception of Fernando VII on his return to Spain in 1814 and the ease with which he reinstalled absolutism without the total support of the clerical hierarchy. (The same applies to the army; in fact, in the heat of the moment its support was even more decisive for the return of absolutism.) It should be remembered, however, that several priests played central roles in the Cortes, either designing many liberal measures or supporting them wholeheartedly. Their participation contrasts with the staunch and permanent antiliberal position of the Church hierarchy in every domain of political and social life (an opposition that continued throughout the nineteenth century, and beyond).

The actions of Fernando VII when he returned and reinstated absolutism in 1814 also give a good measure of the radical significance of the Cádiz Constitution. Much has been written about the alliance between "the Throne and the Altar" in eighteenth-century Spain. The alliance was tested by the "regalist" reforms of Carlos III; but after his death in 1788 and then in reaction to the French Revolution, the Spanish Crown and Church grew closer under Carlos IV. If we add the widespread belief among the Spanish people that the French were anti-Catholic and the profound Catholicism of Fernando VII, it is no surprise that the defeat of the French in 1814 brought a renewal of an intimate alliance between king and Church in Spain.

This exploration of the complex relationship among Cádiz liberals, Catholicism, and the Church highlights the role of the 1812 Constitution as revolutionary—within Spanish history and Spanish tradition. Analysts coming from other traditions cannot claim that Cádiz liberalism copied Anglo-American and French precedents—and malign it for not copying their anticlerical examples. In this and many other ways, Hispanic liberalism was uniquely revolutionary.

What were the main intellectual sources of the first Spanish liberalism? The most important are scholasticism, the modern school of Natural Law, Spanish historic nationalism (*nacionalismo histórico*), the Spanish Enlightenment, and finally French constitutional thought (especially the Constitution of 1791).[23] These currents reveal the eclecticism of Spanish liberalism. Let us briefly outline the importance of each.

On scholasticism, during the crisis hispánica of the early nineteenth century it is better to refer to "neoscholasticism." The main neoscholastic authors "present" in the Cádiz Cortes were Francisco de Vitoria (1485–1546), Juan de Mariana (1536–1624), and Francisco Suárez (1548–1617), thinkers often identified with the School of Salamanca. As Quentin Skinner has shown, these authors led a revival of Thomism that made very important contributions to the development of modern political thought. They laid the foundations of social contract theory and took the notion of consent to new levels of development.[24] However, if Vitoria, Mariana, and Suárez were present in Cádiz, it was not mainly because of the idea of consent, but regarding four related questions that were on the Cortes's agenda due to the French occupation: the ultimate locus of power, the sovereignty of the pueblos (cities, towns, and other communities), the subsequent limits of kingly power, and the consequent right of the pueblos to resist any usurpation of sovereignty. The neoscholastics gave these topics different connotations, but all insisted on the preeminence of the community as the foundation of political legitimacy.[25] Their presence in the debates of the Cortes was in a certain way inevitable; Vitoria, Mariana, and Suárez were essential to the curricula of every Spanish and Spanish American university. They were, in other words, part of the "intellectual baggage" of the vast majority of the Cádiz deputies. The sovereignty of the pueblos, derived ultimately from God, was an enduring and very much debated Spanish tradition; it did not have to be imported or copied from anywhere.

The important exponents of modern Natural Law were many; the best-known in Spain during the second half of the eighteenth century were Grotius (1583–1645), Pufendorf (1632–1694), Barbeyrac (1644–1744), and Vattel (1714–1767). The neo-Thomists rigorously maintained the traditional scholastic hierarchy of Eternal, Divine, Natural and human law. For them, Natural Law was a reflection of Eternal Law—an "implant" in men to understand the designs of God.[26] This understanding of Natural Law began to change when Grotius saw it as a dictate of reason, of the rational nature of man; for him, the key was not conformity with nature, but conformity with *rational* nature.[27]

Several proponents of modern Natural Law were introduced into Spanish universities in the 1770s, shaping the visions of many political thinkers as the nineteenth century began. In the Cádiz Cortes, two of the most important theses of what Joaquín Varela Suanzes calls *iusnaturalismo racionalista* came up in several debates, especially regarding the state of nature and the social contract.[28] Closely linked to rationalist Natural Law is another important source of the first Spanish liberalism: the constitutional thought contained, implicitly or explicitly, in the works of French thinkers like Montesquieu, Rousseau, and Sieyès. These authors were also present in the Cádiz debates, albeit in varied disguises. In the case of Rousseau, contemporary historiography is cautious when calibrating his influence on Spanish liberalism. His literary and peda-gogic ideas influenced the Spanish Enlightenment, no doubt; but his politics were challenged, and become hard to discuss and assess since the French Revo-lution and even more after the occupation by Napoleon's army in 1808.

In this regard, the relative openness of the Spanish Crown to the books and ideas coming from its Bourbon ally and neighbor came to a drastic halt in 1789. The count of Floridablanca, one of the most important ministers of the pe-riod, closed the border to stop revolutionary material from entering Spain. The closure was not fully effective, but the political reaction of the Spanish gov-ernment and its increasingly conservative stance toward revolutionary France are evident. Between 1790 and 1792 the most "progressive" members of the Spanish government lost their posts: Cabarrús, Jovellanos, Campomanes, and Aranda. The French Revolution thus fortified the ideology, the interests, and the political position of the Church and of the most conservative sectors of Spanish society.

As Emilio La Parra showed in his biography of Godoy, it is true that on questions of regalism and some economic goals there was no rupture of the Spanish Enlightenment between Carlos III and Carlos IV. However, there is no denying that in other aspects the arrival of Godoy to power in 1790 stulti-fied winds of change that had flourished under Carlos III.[29] As Antonio de Maravall and Antonio Elorza showed long ago, some Spanish authors made enlightened and advanced political proposals in the 1780s (León del Arroyal, Manuel de Aguirre, and Valentín de Foronda among them). Still, the limited diffusion of their work and the notion, present in all of them, that the king had to be the center and arbiter of political reforms, make it difficult to see a direct link between the Spanish Enlightenment and the Cádiz Cortes, that were so adamant in limiting the king's power.[30] The links between the Spanish Enlight-enment, a rationalist movement focused on socioeconomic (i.e., nonpolitical) reform, and the Cádiz political revolution are not as easy to establish as schol-ars suggested for a long time, and some historians still do. The Enlightenment was primarily a protracted intellectual process focused on administrative and economic reforms that aimed to bolster the monarchy; Cádiz was first and foremost a political revolution that aimed to limit the monarchy, turn it into a constitutional regime, expel the French, and hold the empire together.

A lot of ink has been spilled on the purported influence of the French Con-stitution of 1791 on the Spanish Charter of 1812. Was the Cádiz text an imita-tion of the 1791 document? The French text had clear influences on the Cádiz Constitution, but there were also blatant differences regarding certain aspects of government, political values, and ideological visions. Most notably, a deep

Spanish historical perspective—the *historicismo nacionalista* discussed in what follows—justifies the Cádiz text, while a tabula rasa mentality prevails in all the French constitutions drafted in the shadow of the revolution of 1789. The Cádiz Charter permits popular participation in elections and devotes a lot of space to electoral issues, but includes no Declaration of Rights. And as noted, the Cádiz document remained firmly grounded in Spanish Catholicism, much in contrast with the areligious character of French revolutionary texts. Influence, yes; copying, no.

We arrive at arguably the most important doctrinal and ideological source of the first Spanish liberalism: Spanish nationalist historicism or *historicismo nacionalista*. The notion of Spain's "historic constitution" was one of the most debated issues in Cádiz. The concept had been discussed in Spanish intellectual circles since 1780, when Jovellanos presented his discourse of admission to the Royal Academy of History titled *Sobre la necesidad de unir al estudio de nuestra legislación el de nuestra historia* ("On the need to join the study of our legislation to the study of our history").[31] He argued that the political liberty individuals enjoyed in Spanish medieval kingdoms was lost under the Habsburg dynasty at the beginning of the sixteenth century. The liberty assured until that moment by Cortes that existed in several Spanish kingdoms had kept the power of kings within certain limits. The situation changed with the Hapsburgs—especially the first two, Carlos I and Felipe II. For Jovellanos civil liberty was progressively lost (thus the notion of "liberty recovered," so important for first Spanish liberalism). Therefore, Jovellanos argued that the primary task was to end three hundred years of despotism; his practical recommendations, however, were less critical.[32] Without ignoring his historical inaccuracies regarding the real power of the medieval Cortes, Jovellanos's idea of a liberty reclaimed or recovered became, in the hands of the *liberales doceañistas*, one of the most powerful ideological devices at work in Cádiz.

The same can be said of the vision of Spain's history presented by the second most important author of "historical nationalism": Francisco Martínez Marina. He wrote *Teoría de las Cortes*, the most complete text of this current of thought; this book was a historical interpretation and an ideological construct that became a political device.[33] Martínez Marina's life and work reflected the ambiguities and inconsistencies of the first Spanish liberalism—to such an extent that it is difficult to locate him in the ideological spectrum of the age. He first collaborated with the Napoleonic government of José I, but his *afrancesado* past did not prevent his ideas from being read and discussed widely, nor block his election as a deputy in the revived Cortes of 1820.[34] Martínez Marina began to develop Jovellanos's ideas in his *Ensayo histórico-crítico sobre la legis-*

lación y principales cuerpos legales de los reinos de León y Castilla (1808), but it was his later *Teoría de las Cortes* (1813) that gave him notoriety. He extended Jovellanos's thesis insisting on the despotism of the Habsburg and Bourbon dynasties. In the aftermath of the 1808 crisis, Martínez Marina's argument was recovered, modified, and developed by Cádiz liberals who found in it Spanish precedents for popular sovereignty, the rejection of absolutism, and the recovery of individual and municipal liberties.[35]

The third key text of Spanish historic nationalism, following Jovellanos and Martínez Marina, is the "Preliminary Discourse" that prefaced the Cádiz Constitution. Its authorship is traditionally attributed to Argüelles, the deputy considered by friends and foes alike as the leader of the liberal group at the Cádiz Cortes. Although he was responsible for most of its content, other members of the constitutional commission contributed to the "Discourse." This text became the most important synthesis of the doctrine and program of early Spanish liberalism. Its opening words have been cited repeatedly. I present them here again because they show the level of complexity and tension of the relationship that Spanish liberals established with their past:

> The Commission does not propose anything that cannot be found in authentic and solemn form in the various legislative bodies of Spain, but rather the novelty lies in the way in which the duties of government have been distributed. Said duties have been ordered and classified such that they might form a system of foundational and constitutional law that was in accordance with the fundamental laws of Aragon, Navarre, and Castile with regard to national liberty and independence, to the privileges and obligations of citizens, to the dignity and authority of the King and the judicial system, to the establishment and use of the armed forces, and to the economic and administrative methods to be employed in the provinces.[36]

In these lines, the revival of Spanish monarchical traditions could not be stated more clearly. Yet as María Luisa Sánchez-Mejía emphasizes, the constitution also contained articles that were pure "revolutionary liberalism": sovereignty of the nation, a one chamber parliament, individual liberties, clear limits to the king's power, division of powers, and the responsibility of ministers to the Parliament.[37] The insistence of key liberals on the traditional character of their enterprise may thus seem odd. However, with the Spanish people immersed in a brutal war against Napoleon, this insistence gains intelligibility as another example of their political ability. Let us read some lines from the end of the "Discourse":

The Constitution will never be in greater danger than from the moment it is announced until, following the proposal that the Constitution will put into place [that it cannot be modified in eight years, article 375], the document begins to more firmly establish itself and thereby reduce the aversion and repugnance that work against it. Feelings of resentment, revenge, worries, diverse interests, and even habit and tradition, will conspire against the Constitution.[38]

Regarding those authors who still question the liberal character of the Constitution and the Spanish revolution of 1808–1814, it should be mentioned that there is no one model or archetype of liberalism. Instead, diverse historical liberalisms have existed in the Western world during the last two hundred years. It is useful to cite more of the "Discourse" to show to what extent the Cádiz enterprise belongs among them:

The Government must ensure that our laws are upheld. This must be its primary concern; but in order to preserve the peace and tranquility of the people, the government does not need to determine the interests of private citizens by means of court rulings and political decisions. *The harmful insistence on controlling all areas of civilian life by means of the regulations and mandates of political authorities have brought about similar and even greater ills than those that were supposed to be prevented by such control.*

A few lines ahead:

True progress means protecting liberty in each individual's exercise of his physical and moral authority according to his needs and preferences. There is nothing more appropriate for the achievement of this objective than the entities that established under the proposed system. This system rests on two principles: to preserve the role of government so that it might be able to perform all its obligations and *to grant freedom to the nation's private citizens so that personal interest might be, in the case of each and every individual, the agent that drives their efforts toward well-being and advancement.*[39]

These liberal elements in the "Discourse" were partially grounded in some of the central tenets of historic nationalism: the adherence to the historic legislation of Spain, the utmost admiration for the Spanish medieval Cortes, the decadence of Spain attributed to kingly despotism, and the progressive loss of the limiting power that the Cortes supposedly wielded. The mixture was unstable, due to the prescriptive role given to history by nacionalismo histórico. Still, in the political situation created by the crisis of 1808, this historical, ideological, and political "cocktail" proved to be very effective. In the final analysis, historic nationalism was the most original element of the first Spanish liberalism—a history and a nationalism that could not be imported, yet could be exported and adapted to Spanish America.

Cádiz Liberalism and Spanish America

In the "Preliminary Discourse" of the Cádiz Constitution there is only one mention of the wars that by March 1812, when the charter was sanctioned, had been going on for more than a year and a half in several parts of Spanish America. The reference points to the liberal decrees that the Cortes adopted on the administration of justice, which the "Discourse" stated "will obviously begin to heal the wounds that the rejection of the motherland's revolution, together with the disorder and arbitrariness of the previous Government, have opened unfortunately in some of Spain's overseas provinces."[40] These words evince an idea cherished by peninsular liberals: that the text, almost by itself, would pacify the American insurrections. Regarding the "disorder and arbitrariness of the previous Government," the drafters of the "Discourse" surely referred to the Junta Central. The reference reveals a lack of self-criticism. The Junta Central had disappeared in January 1810, and the Cortes that gathered in Cádiz in September of that year not only failed to offer any proposal to pacify the Americas; on the contrary, it sent more soldiers to fight American "rebels."[41]

If one goal of the Cádiz project was to hold Spain's Americas in the empire and in the fight against Napoleon, it succeeded despite insurgencies in New Spain and resistance in Caracas and Buenos Aires during its first years of implementation. Yet the 1812 Constitution contributed to transatlantic political debates that led most of the Americas to break away—during the charter's second implementation (with a new anticlerical edge), after 1820. Cádiz liberalism alone could not hold Spain's domains together, nor did it alone create Spanish American republics. But it did create liberties that helped keep the empire together in the face of insurgencies to 1814—and fueled divisions that contributed to its fall after 1820.

It should not be forgotten that reactions in Spanish America to Napoleon's 1808 invasion of the Peninsula unanimously supported the motherland (*madre patria*), and specifically Fernando VII. During 1809 there were confrontations in Chuquisaca, La Paz, and Quito between Americans and the peninsular authorities regarding the way the king's sovereignty was to be kept while he was a prisoner in France. Overt conflict between the metropolis and its colonies in America began in April 1810, when the Junta of Caracas decided not to recognize the legitimacy of the Regency that had succeeded the Junta Central in January of that year as the highest entity representing the deposed king. This conflict turned into an open war for separation in July 1811, when a Caracas junta declared Venezuela independent.[42] Separation had become an option.

At Cádiz, the empire was reconceived as a constitutional monarchy that would guide the destiny of a transatlantic Spanish nation united under shared liberal principles and institutions. While many in the Americas saw gain, they also saw the limits of Cádiz when dealing with some of their most cherished goals: commercial freedom and local self-rule. Paradoxically, the Cádiz liberalism designed to forge transatlantic unity increasingly became a language and a tool that fostered divisiveness between *españoles peninsulares* and *españoles americanos*.

Beginning in the summer of 1808 new political ideas coming from the Peninsula were discussed and debated with growing intensity across Spanish America. Newspapers, pamphlets, and leaflets published in Madrid, Seville, and Cádiz arrived in the American ports and reached all the important cities. Inevitably, there was a lapse of months between events in the Peninsula and the time they were known in America. More important, the news of several months often arrived at once in American ports (creating uncertainty, limiting understanding of peninsular events, and inhibiting possibilities of reacting effectively). Finally, the enormous distances and the time ships took to make the journey (especially to distant ports in South America) often made measures taken by the Junta Central, the Regency, or the Cortes obsolete on arrival. Such delays can be more or less harmless in "normal" times, but more than once they proved to be crucial as the mundo hispánico lived critical months.

By the time the Cortes gathered on September 24, 1810, Juntas of Caracas, Buenos Aires, and Bogotá had decided not to recognize the executive power claimed by the Regency. And although the new Cortes could not know it, a few days earlier a popular rebellion against Spanish authorities had begun in New Spain, the richest and most populated territory of the Spanish America. The rising, headed by the priest Miguel Hidalgo, was crushed after only four months; still, it shook established powers, devastated the silver economy (so important to the fight against Napoleon), and set off continuing conflicts— political and popular—that would change the face of the viceroyalty permanently. Less violent movements that would nonetheless also end up in independence several years after, also started in September 1810 in two South American cities, Santiago and Quito.

Meanwhile, the Spanish American deputies at Cádiz faced possibilities and limits.[43] As noted, the American minority was always defeated when their most important political and economic demands came to a vote. This was perhaps inevitable: peninsular liberals never recognized the distinctive nature of the American territories and the different needs of its inhabitants. This "centralizing" perspective prevailed in the Cádiz Cortes from the very beginning (the same can be said of the Madrid Cortes during the Trienio Liberal of 1820–1823). However, it is important to put this issue in historical perspective. During the eighteenth century, the Spanish American territories had been treated increasingly as colonies, though Spanish legal tradition considered them kingdoms. Between 1810 and 1814 the American territories did obtain many things from the Cortes: among them, the end of tributes paid by indigenous and mixed peoples, limited representative institutions, freedom of cultivation, some commercial openings, new rights to justice and education, and legislation that softened social hierarchies. In contrast with the numerous constitutional documents drafted in Spanish America during these years, the goal of the Cádiz Constitution was to keep the transatlantic Spanish nation together. Article 18 granted full citizenship to indigenous Americans—a radical inclusionary step taken by Spanish liberals, far beyond anything contemplated by the men who turned thirteen colonies into the United States thirty years earlier.[44]

The 1812 Constitution aimed to keep the transatlantic nation together through "unitary" rule. It centralized political power in the hands of new *jefes políticos* or *jefes superiores* appointed by the king in each Spanish American jurisdiction. The political chiefs would rule over two local entities created by the constitution—the *diputaciones provinciales* (Provincial Deputations) and *ayuntamientos* (city and town councils) that were given only administrative prerogatives. However, once in place the ayuntamientos progressively acquired capacities that were both administrative and political. In this, some of the most prescient peninsular liberals were proven right in their fears that due to the enormous distance from the center of political power, any political autonomy allowed to Spanish Americans would lead sooner than later to federalism and, in the long run, to the dissolution of the monarchy. In this and other ways, rights given by a charter seeking to forge unity worked to facilitate autonomy—and, in time, division.

The Cádiz Constitution did not operate in the whole of Spanish America during its first period of application (1812 to 1814); it ruled less widely when it was reinstalled during the Trienio. During its first phase, it was implemented in the Viceroyalty of New Spain (except in the Bajío and other regions mired in insurgency), the Captaincy of Guatemala, the Viceroyalty of Peru, and some cities in the Captaincy of Venezuela and the Viceroyalty of New Granada, as well as the city of Montevideo. Provincial deputations appeared in regional capitals, leading cities elected constitutional councils, old indigenous republics experimented with liberal municipalities—via parish elections that included all Hispanic and indigenous men, and excluded those of African ancestry, until selections moved up to electors who ensured that only the notables gained office. The influence of first Spanish liberalism was direct in some cases, important in many others, but always debated, due to the conflictive circumstances.

Liberalismo hispánico also exerted influence in discussions and debates in territories where the constitution was not implemented.[45] Recent studies show that the Cádiz Constitution and the first Spanish liberalism had considerable influence even in the Río de la Plata region. While pursuing local autonomies, leaders kept informed of constitutional debates and constitutional offerings, responding in their own way to peninsular liberalism and at the same time promoting independence from the metropolis.[46] A leading Argentine scholar of the political history of the Río de la Plata in the independence period, Marcela Ternavasio, concluded that the Cádiz experience "had a strong presence in the *rioplatense* revolutionary process."[47]

The first Spanish liberalism came to an abrupt end in the Peninsula, and formally in the Americas, with the return of Fernando VII in 1814. Six years later liberals returned to power in Spain and forced the Cádiz Constitution on Fernando. In the interim, movements toward independence had advanced in South America. In Peru loyalty still held, thanks to the political and military abilities of Viceroy José Fernando de Abascal and a creole elite who feared any experiment with popular sovereignty as the memories of the devastating risings of the 1780s held strong. In New Spain, political insurgency had declined since 1815, yet was never vanquished—and the popular insurgency that had devastated the Bajío was just ending in 1820.

Yet, while much had changed in the Americas since 1814, the Trienio Liberal (1820–1823) did not alter the attitudes and actions of the peninsular deputies in dealing with America. They remained committed to the limited representation and central control that had prevailed in the Cortes of Cádiz. A new approach to the *problema americano* might have been politically wise, as several territories, notably Buenos Aires and Caracas, were far along the road to independence, and many elsewhere were actively debating its benefits. Yet Spanish liberals still refused significant concessions to Americans regarding political autonomy and commercial openings. When peninsular deputies began to attend to American requests, it was too late. In September 1821 Mexico declared independence and New Spain's deputies, the largest American delegation at the

Madrid Cortes, returned to their homeland. Three years later, in December 1824, the battle of Ayacucho meant that the whole of continental America was irretrievably lost to Spanish rule.

The triumph of the Spanish American emancipation movements after 1820 should not obscure the importance of the Trienio Liberal for Spanish history and Spanish American independence. It was the first time that liberalism was implemented in all of peninsular Spain. More important, this time the liberales came to power by themselves, not in response to invasion and occupation—but by a rising of military forces about to be sent to fight for the monarchy in South America. During the Trienio liberalism was not a cloistered anomaly in a city under siege. Operating across Spain, in 1820 liberals known as *exaltados* began to press radical antiaristocratic and anticlerical measures. Most of the revolutionaries remaining from the 1812 experience, the *doceañistas*, became *liberales moderados*—rivals of the exaltados. The second coming of Spanish liberalism was laden with contradictions; among them, military leaders forced a constitution grounded in popular sovereignty on a reluctant monarch in 1820 and new anticlerical and antiaristocratic energies turned powerful defenders of Spanish rule in New Spain to lead a monarchical Mexican independence in 1821. In the metropolis, the rise of radical anticlericalism, divisions and conflicts among liberals, and the hard political and ideological turn toward absolutism across Europe after Napoleon's defeat contributed to the short life of the second Spanish liberal experience: in 1823 an army of the Holy Alliance reinstalled Fernando VII as an absolutist king.

From a chronological perspective, the foundational Spanish liberalism of 1810–1814 and 1820–1823 appears as a brief experiment that failed. However, its values, visions, and goals would remain part of a polarized Spanish polity throughout the nineteenth century as its radicalism progressively softened.[48] The implementation of the constitution on American soil was always selective: elections and freedom of the press were allowed as those in power thought warranted. In New Spain, the war and insurgency of 1810 to 1815 limited its application. In Guatemala, tendencies to localism were strong and economic conditions too adverse to enable full implementation. In Peru, Abascal modified or varied the enforcement of the constitution, yet it was applied in several aspects.[49] Still, even with its limits and variations, the implementation of the Cádiz Constitution meant that for the first time millions of Americans experienced individual rights, elections, freedom of the press, and the social dynamism they entailed.

The Cádiz Constitution was in force in almost all of the Spanish American territories considered in this book, among them the core regions of the silver economies and those with the strongest, most enduring bases in indigenous republics—which Cádiz would replace with constitutional municipalities. As Erick Langer's chapter will show, debates over preferences for indigenous republics and liberal municipalities and the potential gains and losses for native peoples would mark the nineteenth century in Mexico and Guatemala, Peru and Bolivia, and to a lesser degree elsewhere.

The Viceroyalties of New Granada and Río de la Plata, as well as the Captaincy General of Venezuela and the "Kingdom" of Chile, although much less populated than the territories where the constitution was in force, were roughly equivalent in size to the territories considered in this book. Those four administrative entities were less central to the silver economies, less grounded in indigenous majorities, less organized in indigenous republics. But their commercial importance had risen in the late eighteenth century; they felt increasingly constrained by imperial trade restrictions. These long peripheral territories also received, read, and discussed the hundreds of publications that arrived from the Peninsula from 1808 onward. While Cádiz liberals, like their monarchical predecessors, focused on holding the rich silver economies in the empire and favoring Cuban sugar growers with restrictions on Afro-Americans' citizenship, they did not open trade possibilities for commodity exporters in Caracas and Buenos Aires. These territories did not send delegates to Cádiz and rejected the constitution. They formed their own juntas and pursued autonomous routes. Cádiz liberalism clearly led to diverse responses: while the capitals of the Captaincy General of Venezuela and the Viceroyalties of New Granada and Río de la Plata ignored Cádiz, some cities within these entities stayed loyal to Fernando VII and accepted the constitution.[50]

The intellectual, ideological, and political transformations that took place in the mundo hispánico between 1808 and 1824 were complex and laden with ambiguities and contradictions. That almost three hundred years of Spanish rule was often not perceived as domination by many españoles americanos help explain why so many years, so many qualms, so many hesitations, and so many battles had to take place before several territories broke from the metropolis. In general, loyalty did not shift from Spain to the new patria in a direct and unequivocal manner. On the key viceroyalties of New Spain and Peru, Brian Hamnett, a leading analyst of the period, suggests that the erosion of the "middle position" allowing autonomy within the monarchy was "the main characteristic of the period 1808–1821."[51]

Amid the complex imperial and local conflicts that marked Spanish America after 1808, the Cádiz revolution was never determining in a simple way. It was influential in political ideas, political debates, and constitutional proposals, but it was always limited by peninsular and regional economic interests, and by international wars, local events, internal insurgencies, and military leaders. While Cádiz and its constitution shaped liberal political visions in the whole mundo hispánico, powerful men on horseback at the head of diverse armies were equally important—and often pivotal in determining political outcomes between 1810 and 1830. Bolívar, San Martín, and Iturbide may be the first to come to mind, but many others played pivotal political and/or military roles in Spanish America at key moments during those two decades: among them, Moreno, Morelos, Rodríguez de Francia, Artigas, Santander, Sucre, Belgrano, O'Higgins, and Monteagudo; in Spain, Rafael del Riego forced liberalism onto King Fernando in 1820.

The Cádiz revolution was a hope, a promise, and a possibility for many Spaniards and Spanish Americans. However, the vast distances and geo-economic differences between the *madre patria* and its American territories, the political divergences that began with the French invasion of the Peninsula, the opposition of *americanos* who did not want to continue under Spanish rule, the war against the Spanish American territories (which the Cortes never really dealt with politically), and the refusal of peninsular deputies in Cádiz and Madrid to attend to the diverse needs of these territories made that possibility vanish.[52] Still, in one way or another Cádiz marked everything in the vast Hispanic world for a pivotal decade and, in certain respects, long after.

Liberalism and the Mundo Hispánico in the Age of Revolution
The ambitious project that peninsular liberals tried to put in place between 1810 and 1814 failed; it did not result in an enduring constitutional regime limiting monarchical rule; the political and social forces opposed to liberalism proved to be stronger. The king led the opposition, but support for the monarch in the top echelons of the army and the Church was decisive. Important opposition also came from conservative deputies who showed political muscle in the elections for the ordinary Cortes that opened in October 1813. Less than a month before the return of the king, these deputies drafted a document, known as the Manifiesto de los Persas, condemning the preceding extraordinary Cortes that had written the constitution. If we add a peasantry that saw little change emerging from liberal proclamations (inevitable, as the constitution could not be implemented in most of Spain before it was abrogated in 1814) and a society exhausted by six years of war, the delirious welcome that Spanish towns and cities gave Fernando VII on his way to Madrid in the spring of 1814 come as no surprise.[53]

In the end, a coalition of conservative forces and interests defeated Spain's liberals. Many of them suffered the king's repression; some died because of it, but some were able to participate in the comeback of liberalism in 1820 and, with it, the reinstatement of the Cádiz Constitution. This time, however, Spanish liberals had to share power with a "constitutional" monarch who was not captive in another country, but very much present and had been working with international allies to bring down the liberal government and the Cádiz Constitution since the beginning of its reinstallation. Thus the revival of liberalism in Spain was short-lived.[54] Absolutism returned in 1823 without the liberals being able to put up a real fight. The king would stay in power another decade, until his death in 1833.

The reactions and responses to peninsular liberalism in Spanish America were varied, complex, ambiguous, and thus much more difficult to follow, among other reasons because there was no "liberal" political group identified as such. The size and greater social diversity of Spain's American domains also help to explain this complexity. In any case, the core principles of liberalism— national sovereignty, political equality, individual liberties, division of powers, representative government—were pursued almost everywhere. The challenge is to distinguish between liberal principles and complex and often-contested sociopolitical practices.

From 1811 onward a constitutional "explosion" took place in Spanish America. Between that year and 1816 more than thirty constitutional documents were drafted in the region (especially in New Granada). However, given the state of war that prevailed in many regions, liberalism proved to have limited social reach during the independence period in Spanish America. Constitutions and formal political structures did not lead societies to adopt liberal values, attitudes, and behaviors. Very slowly and not without countermarches, this adoption would take place during the nineteenth century. In that long process, different segments of Spanish American societies would adapt and use liberalism for differing purposes. Facing that diversity, scholars have used the term "popular liberalism" to label many of the varied instances when rural communities mobilized liberal rhetoric to demand rights from the powerful. Whether those communities had become committed to central tenets of liberalism such as individual rights and electoral rule, or primarily pursued local political advantage, is much debated.

The search for popular liberalism in large part emerged as part of the search for subaltern contributions, participations "from below" in the political development of independence movements and also of republicanism in some Spanish American countries (during the independence period and beyond). In some cases, these contributions have opened new and more complex understandings of early national conflicts and political challenges.[55] In others, we remain far from an integrated and convincing understanding of the diverse interactions among liberalism, republicanism, and popular participation in the complex processes of nation making in nineteenth-century Spanish America.[56]

The relationship between liberalism and republicanism during the era of Spanish American independence also remain subject to debate. The institutional and constitutional coincidences between the two ideologies far outweigh, in my view, the contrasts in the political language that some historians have privileged. Some of liberalism's deepest goals—popular sovereignty, electoral rule, freedom of the press—remained honored goals in most Spanish American republics throughout the nineteenth century. Though too often abrogated, they were proclaimed constantly and practiced more often than sometimes recognized. Parliamentary practice and liberal principles, some of them rooted in Cádiz, played roles that were far more than perfunctory. Political and intellectual history should recognize these facts and pursue studies aiming to understand the enduring limits to the realization of liberal goals in the history of Spanish America.

After more than 150 years of ignoring and sometimes denigrating the political history of the region during the first half of the nineteenth century, Western historiography recently began to recuperate topics such as elections, citizenship, sociabilities, the press, and public opinion. The change, provoked a quarter of a century ago by François-Xavier Guerra, is most welcome. Scholars began to see that not everything was chaos and caudillos in the origin and formation of Spanish American nations. Too often, however, historiographic reactions become overreactions. Studying aspects of the political and social life of the new nations that were neglected or ignored is positive; suggesting that life in the emerging nations was infused with liberalism, republicanism, and citizenship is another matter.[57] One aim of the chapters that follow is to explore the interplay of the economic transformations analyzed by Tutino in chapter 1, with the political and ideological innovations engaged here, and with the hard domains where power faced participation of different kinds in diverse American societies.

In the wake of Guerra's oeuvre, the Hispanic world of the first quarter of the nineteenth century has become a vibrant field of inquiry for political and intellectual history.[58] New circumstances and new analyses have contributed to a renewed interest in the "Age of Revolution."[59] I conclude by considering critically some of the ways Atlantic history has viewed the revoluciones hispánicas within the Age of Revolution.

The Atlantic approach has become the dominant prism through which the anglophone academy views and studies the independence movements of Latin America. Too often, proponents of that approach assume that commonalities and sequences prevailed over the complex specifics of the several revolutionary processes that shaped this pivotal age.[60] Lurking behind this assumption is another one: that the first Atlantic revolutions (the independence of the thirteen colonies and the French Revolution) became "models" followed in Spanish America from 1808 onward.

The Atlantic perspective on Spanish American independence is an enormous step forward vis-à-vis the nationalistic approaches that prevailed for too long. Such approaches were parochial and limited. Put simply: it is impossible to understand Spanish American independence from a political and intellectual perspective by studying separate national processes. The Spanish American nations came out of a single empire. In the last twenty-five years, nationalist histories of Spanish American independence have given way to broader perspectives. They recognize the influence of general political principles and constitutional architectures in part originating in the North American and French revolutions (with important British antecedents). But studies of Hispanic American independence have forged a new prism that is mainly Hispanic—or, better, Hispanic Atlantic. Rather than presume an inevitable sequence of innovation that began in the United States and France, the Hispanic-Atlantic perspective emphasizes that Spain and Spanish America began, negotiated, and ended their revolutionary processes in deeply Hispanic ways.

Atlantic history has proven its fertility in topics like migration, commercial exchanges, and slavery—notably when it focuses within the British empire. Too often, however, the innovations of Atlantic history have not extended to questioning much older presumptions of Anglo-American primacy in the making of the modern world. The enduring tendency to expect that Anglo-American innovations, mediated by French revolutionary aspirations, shaped independence movement in the mundo hispánico leads, in my view, to fundamental misunderstandings of the Age of Revolution.[61]

Global and Atlantic processes, economic, political, and ideological, affected the independence of Spanish America, no doubt—but local historical circumstances, an ideological arsenal of great complexity, and a series of regional conflicts inextricably linked to Hispanic politics led to the new countries that emerged in Spanish America between 1810 and 1830. There is a clear link between the French Revolution and the events that shook Saint Domingue between 1791 and 1804, but it was a link of reverberations that led to oppositions, as Carolyn Fick shows in chapter 4. There were also conflictive reverberations of the French Revolution, through Napoleon, on the 1808 invasion of Spain, on Cádiz liberalism, and on the Spanish American conflicts that led to independence, but none of them were imitations.[62] The presumptive assertion of imitative Atlantic revolutions diminishes the complexity of the Age of Revolutions—and the creativity of Hispanic revolutionaries, intellectuals, and state makers.[63]

The causal chain often suggested by Atlantic historians mainly refers to *ideas* or constitutional principles (in their most general expression). Such links are often found by intellectual historians who exalt ideas and tend to downplay political and social conflicts and practices.[64] The revoluciones hispánicas did not begin in the light of historical or political "forces" emanating from the United States or revolutionary France (and the Hispanic American elites who started these revolutions and declared the independence of new countries saw nothing positive in Haiti). The revolutionary movements in Spanish America began as a reaction against Napoleon's invasion and occupation of the Iberian Peninsula. French revolutionary ideology was rejected outright for a very simple reason: the invading army came from the land of Rousseau, Marat, and Robespierre.[65]

In Spanish America, at the beginning of the crisis hispánica public declarations were not *against* the king, but *for* the king—and most Spanish Americans, including indigenous peoples, remained devoted to the king throughout. The oft-repeated claim that an accumulation of hatred among Spanish American *criollos* against peninsular Spaniards was one of the main causes of the independence movements is clearly wanting as an explanation of events after 1810. Why did such "disaffected" elites in New Spain and Peru remain loyal to the Spanish Crown for more than a decade after 1810?

Spanish America included a diversity of racial and social groups with no parallel in British North America, making the challenges of independence and nation making radically different. Careful analysis of Spanish America between 1808 and 1824 cannot suggest, much less conclude, that its independence processes were last "episodes" of a single Atlantic Revolution—as chapters 7 to 10 of this volume will show.

At the same time, however, no historical process is absolutely original. The revoluciones hispánicas developed within the broad economic and imperial, political, and intellectual events that shaped the second half of the eighteenth century. There is no reason to deny the resonance of important aspects of North American and French political thought and constitutional thinking. Still, Cádiz liberalism and the revoluciones hispánicas emerged as independent creations, that must be taken seriously to understand the Age of Revolution. Understandings emphasizing transatlantic interactions must remain; presumptions of Anglo-American primacy and Hispanic imitation must end.

The Hispanic revolutions must not be presumed isolated or self-generating. They engaged and revised many of the broad political principles that played decisive roles in the birth of the United States and in revolutionary France. The chronological precedence and geographical proximity of these conflicts made these influences inevitable. The general political principles that were the basis of the Spanish American revolutions—national sovereignty, political equality, individual liberties, division of powers, representative systems—were also paramount in the American and French Revolutions, *but with different connotations and emphases in each case.* Since the Middle Ages, the Spanish world was part of a European debate on monarchical power and popular participation. A unique Hispanic emphasis on the rights of the pueblos enabled Spanish monarchs to allow local republics for indigenous peoples across its American domains since the sixteenth century and helps explain why the Cádiz Constitution recognized these same peoples as part of the citizenry.

When the mundo hispánico was turned upside down by Napoleon's occupation of the Iberian Peninsula in 1808, Spanish and Spanish Americans became active and innovative participants in political, intellectual, social, and economic debates and conflicts. The revoluciones hispánicas inscribed themselves within the Age of Revolution in ways far more creative than too many histories allow. To fully understand Atlantic processes in the formation of the modern world, we must recognize the creative complexity and the ambiguous originality of the Hispanic revolutions—the political and social movements that culminated the Age of Revolution.[66]

Notes

I want to thank the anonymous readers for Duke University Press for their critical comments. Although I did not always agree with their views, this essay benefited significantly from their attentive reading. I also want to thank John Tutino for the hours he devoted to my essay and the recommendations he made to improve it. Needless to say, all of its shortcomings are my responsibility.

1   These are the four "classic" *Atlantic Revolutions*, therefore in this case we could talk of certain identification between the *Age of Revolution* and the *Atlantic Revolutions*.

2   Some options to study the *mundo hispánico* with this chronology are Kenneth J. Andrien and Lyman Johnson, eds., *The Political Economy of Spanish America in the Age of Revolution, 1750–1850* (Albuquerque: University of New Mexico Press, 1994), and Victor M. Uribe-Uran, ed., *State and Society in Spanish America during the Age of Revolution* (Wilmington, DE: SR Books, 2001). On the whole continent, see Lester D. Langley, *The Americas in the Age of Revolution, 1750–1850* (New Haven, CT: Yale University Press, 1996).

3　*Les révolutions de la fin du XVIIIe siècle aux Amériques et en Europe, 1773–1804* (Paris: Éditions du Seuil, 2005). Solé's final chapter on Latin America uses very limited sources.

4　David Armitage and Sanjay Subrahmanyam, eds., *The Age of Revolutions in Global Context, c. 1760–1840* (Basingstoke: Palgrave Macmillan, 2010).

5　Following a classic written more than fifty years ago: Eric Hobsbawm's *The Age of Revolution: Europe 1789–1848* (London: Abacus, 1962).

6　As I will suggest, the reforms of Charles III's reign (1759–1788) influenced Cádiz's liberalism in a limited way.

7　The promulgation of the 1812 Constitution is why the Spanish liberals of this period are also known as *doceañistas*, and *doceañismo* is sometimes used to label their ideological, political, and social project—a project that, it may be added, resonated not only in Spanish America, but also in Portugal, Italy, Norway, and even Russia. On the three first cases, see Ignacio Fernández Sarasola, "La proyección europea e iberoamericana de la Constitución de 1812," in *La Constitución de Cádiz (Origen, contenido y proyección internacional)* (Madrid: CEPC, 2011), 292–308. On the Russian case, see Richard Stites, "Decembrists with a Spanish Accent," *Kritika* 12:1 (winter 2011).

8　Some ideas in the first section of this essay appeared in my book *El primer liberalismo español y los procesos de emancipación de América (Una revisión historiográfica del liberalismo hispánico)* (Mexico: El Colegio de México, 2006). Some arguments presented in the second and third sections appeared in *El imperio de las circunstancias (Las independencias hispanoamericanas y la revolución liberal española)* (Madrid: Marcial Pons/El Colegio de México, 2012).

9　See Emilio La Parra, ed., *La guerra de Napoleón en España* (Alicante: Universidad de Alicante/Casa de Velázquez, 2010). The contributions by Fraser, Hocquellet, and Álvarez Junco in this volume show the decisive role played by the diffusion of the Bayonne abdications and not the uprisings in Madrid in igniting the general insurrection of 1808. In strict legal terms, the only "abdication" was the one in which Carlos IV ceded the crown to his son Fernando in March 1808. Two months later, Fernando VII returned the crown back to his father, who gave it to Napoleon the day after. A month later, he awarded the crown to his brother Joseph, who became José I "rey de España e Indias."

10　I use the term "first Spanish liberalism" to refer to the political revolution in the Peninsula between 1808 and 1814. However, the expression can also include the Trienio Liberal (1820–1823), and some authors extend it to the end of the 1830s.

11　It is impossible to deal here with Godoy and his power from 1792 to 1808. See Emilio La Parra, *Manuel Godoy (La aventura del poder)* (Barcelona: Tusquets, 2002).

12　See Guerra's article "Dos años cruciales (1808–1809)," in *Modernidad e independencias (Ensayos sobre las revoluciones hispánicas)* (Madrid: Mapfre, 1992), 115–148. The use of the word *hispánicas* in the subtitle reflects that for Guerra the first quarter of the nineteenth century had to be understood from a *Hispanic* perspective (including Spain and Spanish America). For him, the two years were "crucial" mainly because peninsular newspapers and other publications spread the ideas, principles, and values of the political revolution taking place in the Peninsula to Spanish America.

13 It was also in this city that in June 1808 Napoleon gathered a series of Spanish and Spanish American notables to discuss and approve a constitutional document that his advisors had drafted. This Constitution or Statute of Bayonne was never applied in Spanish America (in the Peninsula its application was minimal). Its influence on the Cádiz Constitution is hard to determine, but it is clear that the concessions offered by the Statute to the Spanish Americans in political and commercial terms could not be ignored by the deputies who gathered in Cádiz more than two years later.

14 The role of the guerrillas has been exaggerated in Spanish historiography; a tendency that diminishes the importance of the British army and the Duke of Wellington, the commander of allied British, Spanish, and Portuguese troops. A balanced view suggests that guerrillas were very important in harassing the French army day in and day out throughout the war, but did not determine the military outcome.

15 Almost thirty of them were substitute deputies chosen in Cádiz among the American residents. This limited the legitimacy of the Spanish American delegates; more so in the regions that never sent proprietary deputies. This was the case across South America, except for the Viceroyalty of Peru and the cities of Maracaibo and Montevideo.

16 Thomas Moore, *Letters and Journals of Lord Byron with Notices of His Life* (London: John Murray, 1830), 195.

17 This is exactly what the king established in the decree that he issued on his return to Spain. The document is dated May 4, but became known only days later to avoid reactions against it: http://www.cervantesvirtual.com/obra/real-decreto -de-fernando-vii-derogando-la-constitucion-valencia-4-mayo-1814/, Biblioteca Virtual Miguel de Cervantes (www.cervantes virtual.com), accessed 13 April 2015.

18 Up to that time, most output of Spanish presses had been religious. On freedom of the press, see Elisabel Larriba and Fernando Durán, eds., *El nacimiento de la libertad de imprenta* (Madrid: Sílex Ediciones, 2012). The Cortes first sanctioned this freedom in December 1810, then confirmed it in article 371 of the constitution.

19 Of course, the word existed for centuries in Spanish, English, French, and Italian, meaning "generous"; I refer here to its use as an adjective labeling a political group with a shared ideology.

20 Marx expressed these ideas in a series of articles in the *New York Daily Tribune* in 1854. Karl Marx and Friedrich Engels, *Escritos sobre España*, ed. Pedro Ribas (Valladolid: Editorial Trotta, 1998), 131, 139; my translation.

21 The intensity of the opposition to the liberales and the measures they proposed can be surmised by some paragraphs of the "Preliminary Discourse" of the constitution, discussed at the end of this section.

22 The articles on education in the Cádiz Constitution have not received the attention they deserve, even by historians inclined to underline the liberal character of the document.

23 With a couple of minor changes, this is the classification given by Joaquín Varela Suanzes, in his article "La Constitución de Cádiz y el liberalismo español del siglo

XIX," in *Política y Constitución en España (1808–1978)* (1987; reprint, Madrid: CEPC, 2007).

24 Quentin Skinner, *The Foundations of Modern Political Thought*, vol. 2: *The Age of Reformation* (Cambridge: Cambridge University Press, 1993), 159, 163. On page 174, Skinner underlines the influence of the Spanish neo-Thomists on John Locke and his *Two Treatises on Government*.

25 For Mariana political power rested essentially and permanently with the community, making the right of resistance a permanent option (a position Vitoria and Suárez rejected).

26 See Skinner, *The Foundations*, 148, and Howard P. Kainz, *Natural Law (An Introduction and Re-examination)* (Chicago: Open Court, 2004), 31.

27 "The idea that natural law might be valid and binding even if God did not exist was suggested before Grotius by Robert Bellarmine and other scholastics. But Grotius made this point more explicitly and forcibly, and is credited with the groundbreaking attempt to disengage natural law from the existence of a Divine Legislator." Kainz, *Natural Law*, 33.

28 *La teoría del Estado en las Cortes de Cádiz* (Madrid: CEPC, 2011), 42.

29 See La Parra, *Manuel Godoy*, chaps. 4 and 5.

30 Antonio de Maravall, "Las tendencias de reforma política en el siglo XVIII español," in *Estudios de historia del pensamiento español s. XVIII* (1967; reprint, Madrid: Mondadori, 1991); Antonio Elorza, *La ideología liberal en la ilustración española* (Madrid: Tecnos, 1970).

31 The discourse can be found in Jovellanos, *Obras en prosa*, ed. José Miguel Caso González (Madrid: Castalia, 1988), 71–102. On the political thought of Jovellanos, the most important thinker of the Spanish Enlightenment, see *Obras completes*, vol. 9: *Escritos políticos*, ed. Ignacio Fernández Sarasola (Oviedo: Ayuntamiento de Gijón/Instituto Feijoo de Estudios del Siglo XVIII, 2006).

32 Some Spanish American intellectuals and politicians favoring independence adopted the notion, making despots of all the Spanish authorities in America.

33 *Teoría de las Cortes* (Bilbao: Gestingraf, n.d.); this book, in three volumes, is number 9 of the collection "Clásicos Asturianos del Pensamiento Político," edited by the Junta General del Principado de Asturias. On Martínez Marina's political thought, see Joaquín Varela Suanzes, *Tradición y liberalismo en Martínez Marina* (Oviedo: Caja Rural Provincial de Asturias, 1983).

34 I have not paid any attention to the Spaniards that supported José I: the *afrancesados*. Long condemned as traitors, their historiographical rehabilitation started with *Los afrancesados* by Miguel Artola, published in 1953. By now it is clear that the motives of those who supported José were complex and that many of them were ideologically very close to the liberales, their sworn enemies.

35 Martínez Marina's main political and historical ideas can be found in a brief discourse on the Cortes he first published by itself, but then used to introduce *Teoría de las Cortes* in 1813. It has been read through this lens since then (see *Teoría de las Cortes*, 5–49).

36 There are many printed versions of the "Discourse"; an option is the one that accompanies *La Constitución de Cádiz (1812)* by Antonio Fernández García (Madrid: Editorial Castalia, 2002), 195–270. The English translation I use here is by Liberty Fund. Conference "Liberals and Liberty in 1812; Spain and Beyond," Eduardo Nolla, organizer, Santiago de Compostela, Spain, January–February 2013, 2.

37 "Tradición histórica e innovación política en el primer liberalismo español," *Revista de Estudios Políticos*, no. 97 (July–September 1997), 281.

38 Liberty Fund translation, 44.

39 Liberty Fund translation, 37, 38 (my emphasis in both cases).

40 Liberty Fund translation, 29.

41 Due to the war with Napoleon, its number was limited, but that is secondary to the point I make here.

42 The Spanish American wars of independence were civil wars, rarely setting *peninsulares* against *americanos*. The royalist armies were filled by Americans who for diverse motives did not seek separation from Spain—as the histories in this book show.

43 Marie Laure Rieu-Millan, *Los diputados americanos en las Cortes de Cádiz: Igualdad o independencia* (Madrid: CSIC, 1990).

44 On slavery, only two of the new countries on Spanish America abolished it quickly (Chile and Mexico); most maintained it until the middle of the nineteenth century.

45 On the two "variants" of the *liberalismo hispánico* (peninsular liberalism and Spanish American liberalism), they were so intermingled in the first quarter of the nineteenth century that one must be careful with the division. Once Spanish American countries achieved independence (often long after they *declared* it), we cannot refer any longer to *liberalismo hispánico* but to Spanish, Mexican, Chilean, Argentine, (etc.) liberalisms.

46 Venezuela declared independence in 1811, Paraguay in 1813, the Provincias Unidas del Río de la Plata (Argentina) in 1816, Chile in 1818, Peru in 1821 (and again in 1824), New Spain (Mexico), and the Capitanía General de Guatemala in 1821.

47 Marcela Ternavasio, *Gobernar la revolución (Poderes en disputa en el Río de la Plata, 1810–1816)* (Buenos Aires: Siglo XXI, 2007), 261. Ternavasio refers to Spanish American territories that for geographical and military reasons were never threatened by the Spanish Crown during the whole independence period.

48 See Varela Suanzes, "La Constitución de Cádiz y el liberalismo español del siglo XIX."

49 On New Spain, see Roberto Breña, "The Emancipation Process in New Spain and the Cádiz Constitution (New Historiographical Paths regarding the Revoluciones Hispánicas)," in *The Rise of Constitutional Government in the Iberian Atlantic World (The Impact of the Cádiz Constitution of 1812)*, ed. Scott Eastman and Natalia Sobrevilla Perea (Tuscaloosa: University of Alabama Press, 2015). For Guatemala, Mario Rodríguez, *The Cadiz Experiment in Central America, 1808–1826* (Berkeley: University of California Press, 1978), and Jordana Dym, "Central America and Cadiz: A Complex Relationship," in *The Rise of Constitutional Government in the Iberian Atlantic World*. On the Peruvian case, see Víctor Peralta, *En defensa de la autoridad:*

Política y cultura bajo el gobierno del virrey Abascal, 1806–1816 (Madrid: CSIC/ Instituto de Historia, 2002), and Natalia Sobrevilla Perea, "Loyalism and Liberalism in Peru," in *The Rise of Constitutional Government in the Iberian Atlantic World.*

50 At different times and facing different war situations, this was the case in cities like Coro, Maracaibo, and Valencia in Venezuela; Popayán, Santa Marta, and Cartagena in New Granada; and Montevideo in Río de la Plata.

51 Brian Hamnett, *Revolución y contrarrevolución en México y el Perú (Liberalismo, realeza y separatismo, 1800–1824)* (Mexico: FCE, 1978), 17. There is a new and updated version: *Liberales, realistas y separatistas, 1800–1824* (Mexico: FCE, 2011).

52 The return of Fernando VII in 1814 and of absolutism in 1823 sealed the fate of the first Spanish liberalism and the destiny of what he considered to be his *possessions* in America. He died in 1833, without ever recognizing them as independent countries.

53 To get an idea of this reception, see last pages of what still is the most complete and best-written history of this period of Spanish history: the count of Toreno's *Historia del levantamiento, guerra y revolución de España* (Pamplona: Urgoiti Editores, 2008), specifically, 1179 and 1182. This edition has an excellent introduction by the late French historian Richard Hocquellet. I survey the book and make a critique of Toreno's ideas on Spanish America in a long review I wrote for *Historia Constitucional*, no. 13 (2012): "La *Historia* de Toreno y la historia para Toreno: el pueblo, España y el sueño de un liberal": http://www.historiaconstitucional.com/index .php/historiaconstitucional/article/view/350.

54 On the end of the Trienio, see Emilio La Parra, *Los cien mil hijos de San Luis: El ocaso del primer impulso liberal en España* (Madrid: Editorial Síntesis, 2007), and Emmanuel Larroche, *L'expédition d'Espagne, 1823: De la guerre selon la Charte* (Rennes: Presses Universitaires de Rennes, 2013).

55 See Marixa Lasso, *Myths of Harmony: Race and Republicanism during the Age of Revolution, Colombia, 1795–1831* (Pittsburgh: University of Pittsburgh Press, 2007), and Véronique Hébrard and Geneviève Verdo, eds., *Las independencias hispano-americanas: Un objeto de historia* (Madrid: Casa de Velázquez, 2013).

56 See, for example, James Sanders, "Revolution and the Creation of an Atlantic Counter-Modernity: Popular and Elite Contestations of Republicanism and Progress in Mid–Nineteenth Century Latin America," in *L'Atlantique révolutionnaire: Une perspective ibéro-américaine*, ed. Clément Thibaud, Gabriel Entin, Alejandro Gómez, and Federica Morelli (Bécherel: Éditions Les Perséides, 2013), 233–257.

57 I do not see Mexico City and Lima as rich in civic culture and democratic practices as Carlos Forment does in his book *Democracy in Latin America, 1760–1900*, vol. 1: *Civic Selfhood and Public Life in Mexico and Peru* (Chicago: University of Chicago Press, 2003).

58 Besides Guerra, Jaime Rodríguez, Antonio Annino, and Brian Hamnett have played very important roles in these fields. To engage the politics and intellectual life of the *mundo hispánico* in the first quarter of the nineteenth century requires reading in Spanish, in order to keep up with some of the best historians working nowadays on the period, among them José María Portillo, Elías Palti, Javier Fernández Sebastián, Marta Lorente, José Antonio Aguilar Rivera, Marcela Ternavasio,

Ignacio Fernández Sarasola, Víctor Peralta Ruiz, Carlos Garriga, Rafael Rojas, and Noemí Goldman.

59 For contemporary political reasons that Cádiz has received so much attention in recent years, see Gabriel Paquette, "Cádiz y las fábulas de la historiografía occidental," in *Cádiz a debate (Actualidad, contexto y legado)*, ed. Roberto Breña (Mexico: El Colegio de México, 2014), 49–61.

60 However, as I will suggest and as the present book gives ample proof, in several aspects the Atlantic approach enriches our understanding of the Spanish American independence movements. Two very good examples are Jeremy Adelman's *Sovereignty and Revolution in the Iberian Atlantic* (Princeton, NJ: Princeton University Press, 2006) and J. H. Elliott's *Empires of the Atlantic World (Britain and Spain in America, 1492–1830)* (New Haven, CT: Yale University Press, 2006). I dealt briefly with the Atlantic approach in "Liberalism in the Spanish American World, 1808–1825," in *State and Nation Making in Latin America and Spain*, ed. Miguel A. Centeno and Agustín Ferraro (Cambridge: Cambridge University Press, 2013), 271–281.

61 In the words of Atlantic historian Wim Klooster: "Seismic waves travelled through the Atlantic world in the half century after 1775, linking uprisings on either side of the Atlantic." *Revolutions in the Atlantic World: A Comparative Perspective* (New York: New York University Press, 2009), 158.

62 In "Was There an Age of Revolution in Spanish America?" Eric Van Young shows why Latin American historians should be cautious with the assumptions that lie behind the expression "Age of Revolution." This essay is the conclusion of the book *State and Society in Spanish America during the Age of Revolution*, 219–246.

63 There is a recent trend to establish close connections between the Haitian Revolution and Spanish American independence movements. If among the Atlantic revolutions only Haiti achieved a radical social transformation, this in fact limited its influence on the revoluciones hispánicas, which were eminently *political* processes. In *Myths of Harmony*, 33, Marixa Lasso states that while Haiti entered the local popular imaginary, it is difficult to assess the influence of the Haitian Revolution in Cartagena, a Caribbean city with a large slave population.

64 I dealt with this topic in "Las conmemoraciones de los bicentenarios y el liberalismo hispánico: ¿Historia intelectual o historia intelectualizada?" *Revista Ayer*, no. 69 (2008), 189–219.

65 Napoleon in many ways inherited the spirit of 1789, while at the same time, in several ways he was the denial of that same spirit. In any case, from 1789 to 1814 revolutionary France was a political countermodel in the mundo hispánico.

66 The regionally focused chapters that follow seek an understanding not only of the Spanish American independence movements, but of how diverse regions of the Americas negotiate their way through the Age of Revolution in very different ways.

PART II
ATLANTIC
TRANSFORMATIONS

3

UNION, CAPITALISM, AND SLAVERY IN THE
"RISING EMPIRE" OF THE UNITED STATES

ADAM ROTHMAN

Writing as Publius in October 1787, Alexander Hamilton jumped headfirst into New York's raging debate over whether to ratify the newly proposed constitution for the United States. "The subject speaks its own importance," wrote Hamilton at the very beginning of the very first *Federalist*, "comprehending in its consequences nothing less than the existence of the UNION, the safety and welfare of the parts of which it is composed, the fate of an empire in many respects the most interesting in the world." And just what was interesting about this new American empire? "It has been frequently remarked," Hamilton continued, "that it seems to have been reserved to the people of this country, by their conduct and example, to decide the important question, whether societies of men are really capable or not of establishing good government from reflection and choice, or whether they are forever destined to depend for their political constitutions on accident and force."[1]

Hamilton's "important question" was really two questions: could men really choose their own form of government, and if so, would they choose wisely? In 1787, the answer to the first question seemed to be an emphatic yes. The citizens of the United States believed they were—perhaps for the first time in history— freely deliberating on the basic structure of their polity, rather than inheriting it or having it forced upon them. The motto of the new country, *Novus ordo seclorum*, indicated the collective sense of a fresh start to human affairs, even as it paradoxically hearkened back to ancient lore. Despite this sense of novelty, the slate of society was not wiped clean by the revolution; the heritage of the colonial era could not be erased. Nor were Hamilton and his countrymen de- liberating in blissful isolation from the rest of the world. Despite a successful war for independence, the new United States faced a treacherous international landscape, and to Hamilton and other Federalists, a stronger national govern- ment was required to meet the challenge of national survival.[2]

The answer to the second question remained in doubt. Hamilton was not at all sure that his fellow citizens would accept the proposed constitution, which he preferred to the existing Articles of Confederation. It "affects too many particular interests, innovates upon too many local institutions" not to arouse opposition. Reason would inevitably be clouded on all sides by "ambi- tion, avarice, personal animosity, party opposition, and many other motives not more laudable than these." Actual politics barely resembled the republican ideal of a rational quest for the common good. Some influential people might even prefer a "subdivision of the empire," Hamilton feared, to "union under one government." The fear of disunion was central to the constitutional politics of the early United States. Supporters of both a stronger and a weaker national government argued that their vision would be more likely to preserve the unity of a large and diverse country in a dangerous world.

Hamilton erred in posing a sharp dichotomy between reflection and choice on one hand, and accident and force on the other. These were two sides of the same historical coin, as inseparable as heads and tails. Choice was structured by force, and often, force was masked as choice. This essay argues that the ori- gins and development of the United States from the British imperial crisis of the 1760s to the end of the U.S. Civil War combined "reflection and choice" with "accident and force"—indeed, with a great deal more "accident and force" than many people in the United States care to remember today. As Marx wrote about another people, U.S. Americans made their own history, but they did not make it just as they pleased. How then did they make it?[3]

This essay focuses on three major aspects of the early history of the United States: the character of the polity forged out of the American Revolution; the growth and expansion of the country across the continent; and the contest over slavery that tore it apart. Hamilton signaled the first two aspects in his uses of the words "union" and "empire" in *Federalist* 1. By union, he meant the complex political arrangement by which several disparate states ("the parts") collected themselves under one overarching government without each losing its corporate integrity; by empire, he acknowledged the vast size and big expectations of this new republic. He did not mention slavery in that paper, but it cropped up in others and lurked perilously in the ratification debates. Although contained for sixty years by a long series of political compromises that were largely concessions to slave owners, arguments over slavery rooted in real socioeconomic changes would emerge in time as the chief cause of the "subdivision of the empire" that Hamilton and other founders feared above all other evils.

Divergence, a keyword of this volume, offers a handy frame for conceiving the history of the new United States in an international context and a comparative way. John Tutino's introduction suggests multiple meanings of divergence. Colonists throughout the Americas seceded from transatlantic empires in revolutionary processes of national state formation, diverging from those who remained within imperial polities. The new countries they founded then diverged from each other, taking different paths across the nineteenth century and sometimes colliding into each other, as the United States and Mexico did in 1846. Many new countries experienced internal fissures and fragmentation as well; divergence between North and South nearly wrecked the United States over the question of slavery. That internal divergence was intricately connected to the "great divergence" described by Kenneth Pomeranz.[4] The powerfully disruptive forces of the rise of industrial capitalism fundamentally reconfigured the Americas' economic prospects. Some prospered. Others suffered. The northern United States emerged as Britain's most successful imitator across the Atlantic, while the southern United States grew into the most formidable slave society in the world on the basis of white southerners' ability to harness slave labor to supply short-staple cotton to British textile manufacturers. Over time, the country became "half slave and half free," as Lincoln put it in 1858.[5] Considering the United States within this set of divergences provides an antidote to the dogma of exceptionalism without losing sight of the peculiar aspects of the United States' historical trajectory.

The Federal Union

"A more perfect Union"—that was the first aim of the constitution. But a union of what or whom, and on what terms? Answering that question requires a panorama of the British mainland North American colonies at the end of the Seven Years' War in 1763, and a tracing of the revolutionary dynamic from the origins of the imperial crisis to the ratification of the constitution and beyond. How thirteen diverse colonies managed to secede from the British empire, forge a durable framework of government, and survive the pressures of a war-torn Atlantic world is a story of successful divergence in the short term, even if Hamilton, who was killed by his political nemesis in a duel, did not live to taste the fruits of peace.

Relative latecomers to the early modern Atlantic world, the British mainland North American colonies were settler societies populated largely by free and quasi-free people of mostly British descent but harboring a substantial proportion of enslaved Africans and people of African descent as well, particularly in Virginia and South Carolina. The late colonial population numbered roughly 2 million on the mainland, of whom 15 percent were enslaved (compared to roughly 400,000 in Britain's Caribbean colonies, of whom 85 percent were enslaved). The zone of Euro-American settlement was fairly narrow, hugging the eastern seaboard and rivers that flowed into the Atlantic. Within the constricted zones of colonial settlement, indigenous people had mostly been annihilated or driven out, but the vast continental interior west of the Appalachian mountains remained populated almost entirely by indigenous and métis people, except for the lower Mississippi Valley, which had been penetrated by French settlements that from 1765 lived under Spanish rule. Unvanquished indigenous power in the continental interior was confirmed by the uprising known as Pontiac's War, which stretched across the southern Great Lakes region in 1763–1766.[6]

The seaboard colonies were fundamentally agricultural but economically diverse, ranging from the mixed farming societies of New England to the more plantation-oriented southern colonies, where slaves labored to grow tobacco and rice for export. Coastal towns—Boston, New York, Philadelphia, and Charleston—were nodes of artisanal production and Atlantic commerce, with ties to both Europe and the Caribbean. Hence, maritime trades were also important. The mainland colonies were closely tied to the lucrative Caribbean sugar islands, which they supplied with fish, grain, lumber, and other supplies. The mainland fueled the islands. To put the mainland colonies in a broader British colonial perspective, almost three-quarters of the value of exports to Great Britain from British America came from the West Indies; on the other hand, the value of British exports to the mainland colonies was more than double the value of exports to the West Indies.[7] The mainland American colonies provided ready markets for British goods and nurtured a thriving consumer culture, particularly in urban settings. Nothing represents the cosmopolitanism of British Americans' consumer habits as much as their taste for tea, which became famously politicized in the imperial crisis that led to revolution.[8]

The mainland colonies enjoyed considerable local political autonomy. Royal officials had to contend with strong colonial assemblies representing propertied men who insisted on their rights and privileges within the British empire. The colonies' strength derived from the fact that the empowered class of propertied men was relatively large, literate, and prosperous, and the metropolitan authorities were basically willing to leave them alone. They lacked the coercive power to do otherwise. Even in the commercial regulation of "external" trade, which had been the focus of metropolitan oversight, extensive smuggling made a mockery of restrictive policies.[9] Despite class stratification and cultural markers of status, most of the mainland colonies had a popular politics that embraced a wide swath of free men from the middling and lower ranks, while generally limiting free women to more circumscribed modes of participation, like petitioning, and excluding slaves from formal participation altogether. The presence of chattel slavery, however, made free people in the colonies hypersensitive about their own freedom, as Samuel Johnson observed in his famous quip "How is it we hear the loudest yelps for liberty from the drivers of negroes?" When the imperial crisis came, rebellious colonists loudly protested that the British wanted to "enslave" them.[10]

The religious diversity of the British North American colonial world was crucial to the formation of an independent and flourishing civil society. The colonies were deeply Protestant, but they also exhibited "a strange religious medley," in Crevecoeur's words. Widespread Protestant dissent challenged the established Anglican and Congregational churches. Non-Protestants, like Catholics in Maryland and Jews in Charleston, also carved out a sacred space for themselves. Not coffee houses but churches were the most important arena of colonial civil society, and religious associations provided the spark and the model for more secular voluntary organizations. Although Protestantism had begun to make inroads into the increasingly creole, or native-born, slave population, most African and African-descended slaves were probably Catholic, Muslim, or animist in their beliefs and practices.[11]

Historians have chipped away at the idea that a growing sense of a distinctively American national identity inexorably led to the revolution. Rather, colonists' concept of themselves as equal British subjects was at the core of the imperial crisis that spiraled into a colonial revolt. To make a long story short, metropolitan efforts to tighten Britain's grip over the colonies and shift some of the fiscal burden for security onto them in the wake of the costly Seven Years' War led many British American colonists to protest the violation of their rights, their lack of representation in Parliament, and ultimately, the collapse of the king's protection. South Carolinian Henry Laurens, who served as president of the Continental Congress in 1777–1778, put the case succinctly. Stung by a jibe from a British admiral, Laurens retorted, "I had once been a good British subject, but after Great Britain had refused to hear our petitions, and had thrown us out of her protection, I had endeavored to do my duty."[12]

The revolutionary dynamic from 1763 to 1783 precipitated an American nationalism, and not the other way around. Popular mobilization by local organizations like the Sons of Liberty, intercolonial communication and coordination through the Committees of Correspondence and Continental Congress, widely circulated propaganda like Paine's pungent *Common Sense* (which is as much an artifact of English radicalism as American nationalism), the shared hardship and blood sacrifice of soldiers in the Continental army and battered communities, the remembrance of the wartime struggle in culture and politics—all these created a new national or "patriot" sensibility among mainland British North Americans. Whether that new national sensibility was actually widely shared, deeply felt, and politically effective is a matter of lively debate. And we might wonder what would have happened to American nationalism if Great Britain had successfully quashed the rebellion. The long shadow of Confederate nationalism over the post–Civil War South might provide some clues.[13]

When the Declaration of Independence spoke for "one people" in 1776, its authors expressed a hope more than a reality. The colonists were internally divided; significant numbers of loyalists maintained their allegiance to the king. The revolution was simultaneously a civil war, especially in the southern colonies, where partisan and guerrilla warfare broke out as the war dragged on. Loyalists were harassed, punished, and dispossessed. Roughly sixty thousand loyalists fled to safer havens elsewhere in the British empire, reshaping Canada, Florida, and the Caribbean. Several hundred black loyalists founded the experimental antislavery colony of Sierra Leone, while a few others ended up in Australia. Often forgotten in recent histories celebrating the prospect of freedom for black loyalist refugees are the roughly fifteen thousand slaves whom loyalist owners carried with them into exile.[14]

The loyalist flight to Canada and the Caribbean illustrates the geographic limits to U.S. nationalism during the revolution. Just as not all colonists were patriots, not all the British colonies joined the revolution. Why not? Demographic differences, political concessions, and a stronger British military presence were crucial. The British won over Canada's large French population with the 1774 Quebec Act (which outraged patriots in the lower colonies), while

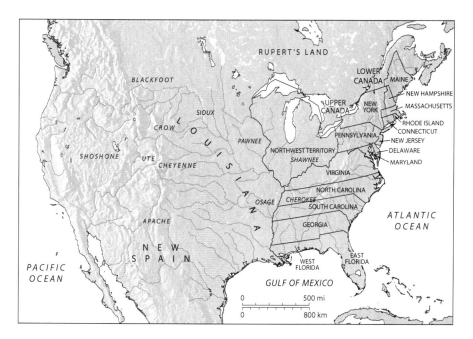

MAP 3.1. The United States in North America, ca. 1790

British West Indian planters' dependence on Britain and fear of slave rebellion made them cling to British power. The imperial crisis and revolution divided Britain's American empire but did not destroy it, and the new United States had to contend with an enduring British imperial presence in its vicinity even as the locus of Britain's empire shifted eastward. The British presence in Canada, as well as Spanish persistence beyond the new country's southern and western borders in Florida and Louisiana, gave rise to what might be called a *paracolonial* situation. However postcolonial the United States may have been, it was still ringed by other powers' colonies. Many in the new country optimistically expected that these neighboring territories would eventually turn republican and join the United States, but nobody knew exactly how and when that would happen. In the meantime, the postcolonial republic coexisted with a persistent colonial order.[15]

The patriots did not win the Revolutionary War by themselves. European imperial competition and American environmental conditions played into their hands. At the conclusive battle at Yorktown, they got timely help from the French navy and the malaria-bearing *Anopheles quadrimaculatus* mosquito. The French were no less self-interested than the mosquitoes, as the colonial revolt gave them a chance to exact some revenge upon the British for the Seven Years' War. French and also Spanish involvement turned an intraimperial war into an interimperial one that rippled beyond mainland North America and touched every inhabited continent. If the Minutemen at Lexington fired the "shot heard round the world," then the sound reverberated through the echo chamber of European imperial power.[16]

In the breakaway colonies, secession inevitably led to the central questions of who should rule at home and how. Nearly all agreed that the states should be part of a single Union, and the new government should be "republican," that is, ruled by the citizenry through their representatives and not by a monarch. In today's debates over the revolutionary nature of the American Revolution, the radical quality of the principle of republican self-government at the time should not be underestimated, despite the all-too-obvious limits on the definition of "we, the people" in actual practice. At the same time, consensus on the principle of republican self-government left plenty of room for diverse visions of who should be included and how they should govern themselves, and what to do about those who were left out.[17]

Much as in the newly independent countries of Latin America in the early nineteenth century, a fault line running through the postrevolutionary United States divided state-oriented elites who envisioned strong local autonomy within a loose federal system and nationally oriented elites who preferred a strong central government with plenary powers over the states. The former held sway under the Articles of Confederation, ratified in 1781, which a frustrated George Washington lampooned a few years later as a "half-starved, limping Government, that appears to be always moving upon crutches, and tottering at every step." Despite some important successes, including the Northwest and Land Ordinances that established a template for western expansion, the union under the Articles turned out to be a diplomatic and fiscal failure. It was unable to raise taxes, enforce treaties, maintain an army, or secure its commercial interests abroad. Some historians have emphasized the centralists' anxiety over populist politics in the states, but an equally powerful impetus for the overthrow of the Articles was the intensifying sense that the federal structure was inadequate to deal with a hostile and meddling outside world. Notable challenges included Britain's persistent military presence in the northwestern borderlands, and the failure of commercial diplomacy to crack open Caribbean markets to mainland merchants.[18]

Three famous sets of compromises secured the constitution. The first compromise balanced the interests of large and small states through the mechanism of a bicameral legislature. One chamber, the Senate, gave each state two representatives, while the other, the House, apportioned representation according to population (with the slave population counted in a three-fifths ratio). The second involved slavery. The three-fifths clause decided how much added representation slaveholders would enjoy in the House by virtue of owning slaves; the Fugitive Slave Clause prevented slaves from gaining their freedom by escaping to another state; the Slave Trade Clause barred Congress from prohibiting slave imports before 1808, a twenty-year window of opportunity for slavers. The third compromise, completed after ratification, led to a Bill of Rights, which gave suspicious anti-Federalists additional guarantees that the new national government would not overstep its bounds and infringe on individual liberty or state prerogatives. One recent historian argues that the constitution should be seen as a "peace pact" among the states, which kept the Union from fragmenting into regional confederacies or succumbing to anarchy (until it failed to do so).[19]

One mark of the new constitution's initial success was that the new Union successfully navigated the dangerous currents of international politics in the late eighteenth and early nineteenth centuries. The country held together, even thrived, in an era of almost unremitting European and Caribbean war from 1789 to 1815. Its population and territory doubled, and it began to pursue what might be called "self-strengthening" policies that placed the national state on a stronger footing. The first party system, a rivalry between Hamiltonian Federalists and Jeffersonian Republicans, was powerfully shaped by the French Revolution and its ripple effects. And as France warred with its enemies, the United States' active neutral carrying trade invited attacks from belligerent powers at sea. Although Washington's successors heeded his advice to avoid "entangling alliances" with foreign powers, they could not escape the global vortex.[20]

Hamiltonian Federalists admired Britain and hoped to emulate it. They deployed the national government to court European investment in domestic enterprise and accelerate capitalist development. Particularly important was Hamilton's fiscal program designed to shore up public credit. By contrast, the Jeffersonian opposition regarded Britain as an antimodel of concentrated power and inequality, and they were more sympathetic to the French Revolution until it careened toward terror. Most notably in the debate over the chartering of a national bank, Jeffersonian Republicans sought to keep the powers of the national government strictly limited by a narrow construction of the language of the constitution. During the Adams administration in the late 1790s, the Federalists overplayed their hand, and the Jeffersonian Republicans swept them aside in the election of 1800, which reasserted antifederalist principles of state sovereignty within the structure of the constitution. In power,

Jeffersonians sought to pry open European markets and secure the virtuous commercial-agrarian republic. They deployed the young navy against the Barbary pirates, and took advantage of Napoleon's plight in the Caribbean and Europe to purchase Louisiana—recently regained from Spain. The Republicans' trade policies of discrimination and embargo failed, but unintentionally stimulated "domestic manufactures" and industrial enterprise.[21]

The War of 1812 showed both the strains and the strength of the republican nation-state. James Madison's administration managed the war poorly. The United States failed to wrest Canada out of British hands, mocking Jefferson's rash prediction that the conquest of Canada would be "a mere matter of marching." The war antagonized New England's anglophilic, arch-Federalist merchant elite. At the Hartford Convention in 1814, New Englanders threatened to secede from the Union. Most embarrassing of all was the burning of public buildings in the nation's capital. Not all was disaster for the United States. Tecumseh's pan-Indian alliance collapsed in the Ohio Valley. Planter-general Andrew Jackson crushed the Red Stick Rebellion among the southern Indians and beat back a British invasion of New Orleans. The war spelled the doom of indigenous power east of the Mississippi River. Victories for the United States on the western and southern frontier stoked a heady nationalism and new imperial ambitions. An era of national consolidation, territorial expansion, and capitalist development would follow the War of 1812 in republican North America as much of Spanish America plunged into uncivil wars for independence.[22]

A Rising Empire

Hamilton was not alone when he referred to the United States as an "empire," but what he and others meant by that word is elusive. Its most regular usage simply denoted an extensive territory under a sovereign power. A 1789 dictionary published in Philadelphia defined empire as "imperial power; the region over which dominion is extended; command over anything." It was often used metaphorically, as Hamilton did in *Federalist* 6 to refer facetiously to the "happy empire of perfect wisdom and perfect virtue." However, there are several references in the *Early American Imprints* database to the United States as a "rising empire," one as early as 1776, suggesting that the concept of American empire was, from the very start, linked to the emergence of the United States as a power in the hemisphere if not the world.[23]

Recent scholars have effectively historicized the founders' idea of a "republican empire," their solution to the problem of preserving liberty and pursuing expansion at the same time. The political key was the principle of the equality of the states composing the Union. The Northwest Ordinance of 1787 enshrined the expectation that new territory would eventually be absorbed into the Union as states on an equal basis with the original states. Promising westerners equal political rights to local self-government was intended to prevent separatist and secessionist movements on the frontier, particularly those incited by meddling Spanish officials in the lower Mississippi Valley. And by endowing westerners with substantial responsibility for their own self-government and defense—in a word, citizenship—republicans attempted to limit a potential source of the growth and concentration of power in the national government: colonial administrative patronage and a standing army. Federalism thus blazed the way for a continental, if not infinitely expansible, "empire of liberty," to use Jefferson's famous phrase.[24]

Turning western "wilderness" into republican "civilization" offered a social basis for the empire of liberty. This transformation was accomplished through myriad policies on the federal and state levels that promoted migration, commercial development, and national integration, including the creation of a regulated land market, a postal network, and other infrastructural projects that eased the transportation of people, goods, and information back and forth between interior communities and the Atlantic world. The infiltration of civil society also assisted greatly in this transformation. Religious missions and churches, schools, debating societies, newspapers, and the national political parties formed a diffuse and highly effective lattice of infrastructural power that spread the nation across an "improved" western landscape. Federalist fears of frontier settlers' reversion to barbarism faded pretty quickly, or morphed into a new concern about the spread of slavery.[25]

In retrospect, the westward march of the United States across North America appears inexorable if not inevitable, but it was actually a sporadic process that depended heavily on "accident and force" and sparked enormous international and domestic conflict. Consider the windfall known as the Louisiana Purchase. Jefferson's main goal was to protect western farmers' access to foreign markets by keeping New Orleans out of the hands of the French after the secret Treaty of San Ildefonso, but St. Domingue's rebels and mosquitoes defeated Napoleon's ambitions to revive French empire in North America and the Caribbean, so Napoleon threw in the whole vast Louisiana territory as lagniappe. (That's what they call it in New Orleans.) In acquiring Louisiana, the United States not only played the Old World's game of imperial diplomacy but also benefited from the explosion of the ultimate contradiction between metropolitan liberty and colonial slavery in transatlantic imperialism. The shocks from that explosion would continue to reverberate in Louisiana and elsewhere for sixty years. The *New Orleans Daily Picayune* was still reeling in May 1861, when it charged that the "abolition party" in the North "would gloat to see the South made the scene of another massacre like that of St. Domingo." The fates of the United States and Haiti diverged in innumerable ways across the nineteenth century, but they were also deeply entwined.[26]

In acquiring Louisiana's roughly eight hundred thousand square miles, the United States gained more than enough land to perpetuate the agrarian republic for generations. It also acquired nominal dominion over at least fifty thousand people of European and African descent living in colonial settlements mostly on the lower Mississippi, and at least another hundred thousand Indians spread across the vast territory. Nobody knew exactly how many there were at the time, because of the autonomy of indigenous communities from imperial control—and census-takers—in the late eighteenth century. One hundred years later, the U.S. government officially counted 144,000 Indians living in the region of the Louisiana Purchase; whether relocation and reproduction made up for displacement and death is difficult to say.[27] Whether and how to integrate all these people into the United States posed a considerable array of challenges for the proponents of republican empire. It also posed a considerable array of challenges for those American Jonahs swallowed by the U.S. whale. Perhaps the most innovative new scholarship on America's continental empire focuses on the view from inside the belly of the beast.

Louisiana's white, largely francophone population descended from early French settlers in the Mississippi Valley, as well as later migrants such as the Acadian and Caribbean refugees. Many eastern Federalists expressed suspicion of their republican credentials and would have liked to place them under an indefinite political apprenticeship until they could learn the proper habits of citizenship, but after some debate and negotiation, they were admitted to the United States under similar rules as governed the Northwest and Southwest Territories. So their political equality with the rest of the country was ensured—at least in time. Thirteen states were eventually carved out of the Louisiana Purchase, ending with Oklahoma in 1907, which means that the process of folding Louisiana into the republican empire took more than a century. The political status of citizens living in so-called unorganized areas of the Purchase, or areas stuck in the territorial stage of government, was a subordinate one, reminiscent of those of us who live in Washington, D.C., today, who lack voting representation in Congress.[28]

Up and down the Mississippi Valley, Greater Louisiana's "creole" population soon found itself outnumbered by newcomers from the eastern United States and foreigners from abroad. According to the 1850 census, only 40 percent of the 1.2 million white people living in the four states then formed out of the Louisiana Purchase (Louisiana, Arkansas, Missouri, and Iowa) were native to the state they lived in, and 10 percent of the whole population of these states had been born abroad. New Orleans was second only to New York as a port of disembarkation for immigrants before the Civil War, most of whom headed up the Mississippi River into the continental heartland, where the U.S. government was selling federal lands for a minimum of $1.25 an acre. Immigrants populated the towns and cities of the Upper Mississippi to a remarkable extent; more than half the residents of St. Louis in 1860, for instance, were foreign-born.[29]

While the creoles were overrun, the Indians were pushed aside. Not only did the Louisiana Purchase bring many new Indian peoples under nominal U.S. sovereignty, but it occurred to a few U.S. policy makers (included Jefferson) that "uninhabited" Louisiana could serve as a potential receptacle for displaced eastern Indians. Mounting demographic and political pressure against the eastern Indians reached a critical juncture in the late 1820s with the election of Andrew Jackson as president. Jackson and his followers regarded the enduring Indian presence as an obstacle to democratic republicanism. They saw assertions of Indian sovereignty, most notably the Cherokee Constitution of 1827, as illegitimate assaults on the constitutional prerogatives of the states and unjust monopolies on valuable land. Indian removal truncated federal and evangelical efforts to "civilize" the eastern Indians through the provision of farm implements and the establishment of Christian schools and missions. Consequently, removal met with strong but ultimately unsuccessful opposition from the Indians' largely northeastern evangelical and anti-Jackson allies inside the United States, as well as fierce opposition from the Indians themselves.[30]

Jackson defended Indian removal as a benevolent alternative to physical annihilation or unwanted cultural and political assimilation, but it was in fact a vicious, deadly sham conducted with fealty to the outward forms of diplomacy and justice—force dressed up as choice. "To destroy human beings with greater respect for the laws of humanity would be impossible," observed Alexis de Tocqueville, who witnessed a miserable group of emigrant Choctaws crossing the Mississippi at Memphis. By 1845, roughly seventy-five thousand Sac, Fox, Kickapoo, Shawnee, Potawatomi, Miami, Cherokee, Chickasaw, Creek, Choctaw, and Seminole Indians had been compelled by fraud and violence to migrate to the so-called Indian Country, a reserve carved out of the Louisiana cession west of Missouri and Arkansas in what today is Oklahoma. Several thousand died along the way from starvation and disease (including newly arrived cholera); hundreds of others were killed in the wars of removal, including the Black

Hawk War in Illinois and Wisconsin and the protracted Seminole War (1835–1842) in Florida.[31]

Emigrant and relocated Indians tried to compose themselves in the Indian Country west of the Mississippi River, but their displacement created a whole new set of challenges. The new Indian settlements butted against the powerful Osage, Sioux, and Comanche Indian nations of the Plains, who were often hostile to them. Feckless U.S. Indian agents and army garrisons did not help. In the 1850s, another wave of Euro-Americans broke over them as the bloody saga of Indian annihilation, displacement, and confinement repeated itself on different terrain and with more lethal technology. "Bleeding Kansas," the infamous battleground between proslavery and antislavery settlers in the 1850s, was also the first theater of the thirty-year war between the Lakota Sioux and the U.S. Army. The heart of North America became a crossroads of conflict.[32]

A long chain of causation led from the Louisiana Purchase to war between the United States and Mexico, which resulted in the United States' next great territorial extension. As Ávila and Tutino's essay on Mexico in this volume makes clear, the origins of that pivotal war (perhaps it should be called "The War of Northern Aggression") must be viewed as much in the context of contests over state formation and market development on Mexico's northern margin as in the context of U.S. western expansion and rhetoric of Manifest Destiny. Texan secession and independence from Mexico was not only fueled by Anglo migrants from the United States, but also had deep roots in the clash between Mexican centralists and localists (into which Anglo migrants inserted themselves on the localist side), the expansion of plantation slavery and trade with New Orleans and St. Louis, Mexican abolition of slavery in 1829, and the failure of the Mexican government to protect northern Mexican communities against Indian raids.[33]

By itself, the rhetoric of Manifest Destiny explains little about the internal pressures behind U.S. expansion, which were shaped in crucial ways by partisan political competition between Democrats and Whigs, who had contrasting cross-sectional coalitions that led to different outlooks on war and territorial expansion. Polk and the southern-dominated Democrats coveted not just slave-based Texas, but also control of West Coast harbors that would fulfill a long-standing desire to push into Pacific and Asian markets. The more northern-dominated Whig Party had greater fears about the divisive sectional effects of expansion. That conflict over slavery shaped these divisions became apparent when South Carolina's John Calhoun, in his capacity as secretary of state, argued for the annexation of Texas as a bulwark against British abolitionism in North America, clinching northern antislavery opinion that Texas annexation, and the war that followed, was a proslavery plot. Whig and abolitionist opponents registered anguished objections to the war.[34]

The U.S. victory was not the cakewalk it has often seemed to be in the historiography. While its battlefield victories were often overwhelming and decisive—due in great measure to the professionalism of the United States' West Point–trained officer corps—occupying extensive Mexican territory proved far more challenging. (Sound familiar?) Local uprisings against the U.S. presence made Mexican territory hot to the touch. In the end, the United States grabbed as much Mexican territory with as few inhabitants as possible via the Treaty of Guadalupe Hidalgo. Even so, the acquisition of territory posed similar problems for the republican empire as had the Louisiana Purchase: how to incorporate Mexicans; what to do about Indians; whether the territory should be slave or free. But too much had changed for these problems to be solved in the same way as before.[35]

The discovery of gold at Sutter's Mill in 1848 put the U.S.-Mexican War in a whole new light. A massive influx of migrants from around the world quickened California, as well as the ports and passageways leading to it. Almost 40 percent of California's population in 1860 was foreign-born, including 35,000 Chinese, 33,000 Irish, and 22,000 Germans, as well as argonauts from Sonora, Peru, and Chile. The California gold rush inspired the equally great discovery of gold in Australia, and the infusion of massive quantities of gold from the Pacific World powerfully stimulated the American and global economies. Friedrich Engels ruefully admitted that the *Communist Manifesto* had not foreseen the "creation of large new markets out of nothing." The rapid development of California stirred schemes to tie the West Coast closer to the eastern United States through a transcontinental railroad, which in turn ignited the bitter sectional strife over slavery that led to the Civil War. But that next war remained hidden beyond the horizon when the nineteenth century reached its midpoint, and few people in the United States would have predicted it, despite their divisions. In the wake of the so-called Compromise of 1850, which appeared to soothe the tensions over slavery's expansion resulting from the war with Mexico, more would have been more apt to celebrate a new era of peace, prosperity, and power than to fear an impending crisis.[36]

An Irrepressible Conflict
All changed quickly. Just a decade after the conclusion of the Mexican-American War, William Seward—a leader of the new Republican Party that caught fire in the North—proclaimed the existence of an "irrepressible conflict" between two

political systems in the United States, one based on "servile, or slave labor" and the other on "voluntary labor of freemen."[37] Seward's irrepressible conflict soon became a vicious civil war that revolutionized the foundations of the Union by breaking up the "slave power." Why did the United States split apart? How was it remade? Answering these questions remains a challenge for historians, but the global turn in U.S. history has infused the study of the Civil War era with a new dimension. The nation's history must now be embedded in more global dynamics of capitalism, national state formation, imperial expansion, international diplomacy, and the clash of ideas about slavery and freedom.[38]

The North American slave regime changed in important ways between independence and Civil War. It became more sectional, more completely domesticated, and enmeshed in the transatlantic cotton economy. First more sectional: slavery disappeared from the northeastern states through a state-by-state process of gradual emancipation, and it was barred from the "old Northwest" by legal enactments (the Northwest Ordinance and the Missouri Compromise). A mix of revolutionary antislavery ideals, evangelical perfectionism, and emerging bourgeois norms of freedom motivated northern abolition, which was made feasible by the relative insignificance of slave labor in the northern economy. Free people of color in the North generally occupied the lowest rungs on the economic ladder, and they faced newly institutionalized forms of racism, but they also organized vigilance committees, mutual aid societies, schools, and (most importantly) churches that provided the bedrock of an African American civil society.[39]

As slavery disappeared in the northern states, the northern economy experienced a transformation that some historians have called a "transition to capitalism" and others a "market revolution." In crude summary, demographic growth and improvements in transportation led to an intensifying social division of labor and economic specialization, the commercialization of agriculture, the emergence of proto-industrial production, and the proliferation of towns and cities. Placing the so-called market revolution in a transatlantic context, it's clear that these developments mirrored similar developments in Britain and borrowed liberally from the British model. New England entrepreneurs smuggled industrial knowledge out of Britain, while skilled and semiskilled immigrants added their own technical know-how and ingenuity. A common language facilitated this transfer of human capital. British lenders helped to finance state-sponsored internal improvement projects in the 1830s and private railroad construction in the 1840s and 1850s. Throughout the era, British goods flooded American markets, providing standards of industry and fashion that domestic manufacturers struggled to imitate and improve upon behind a protective wall of tariffs.[40]

By midcentury, a broad array of northerners celebrated "free labor" as the just, progressive basis of their social order, while regarding southern slavery as cruel and backward. Free labor ideology did not necessarily lead to abolitionism, however, since distance, racism, property rights, and federalism all stood in the way. It took something more for the transformation of northern society to precipitate into a politically effective antislavery movement. Yet free labor ideology harbored a crucial tension. The concept encompassed both the independent farmer and artisan who worked for himself and commanded his own household, and the wage laborer, increasingly common in the North, who "voluntarily" worked for someone else under the compulsion of the labor market rather than the lash. Spokesmen for the northern white working class invoked the slogan of "wage slavery" to indict the swindle of free labor, and at times, they transmuted "wage slavery" into its doppleganger, "white slavery."[41]

In the southern states, by contrast, the "market revolution" traced a different, slavery-based path toward modernity. The well-known rise of the short-staple cotton production invigorated and extended North American slavery from the Carolina upcountry to Texas. A local crop used for home textile production in the eighteenth century, short-staple cotton became the favorite fiber of cotton textile manufacturers, the vanguard of the industrial revolution in the nineteenth century. Annual North American short-staple cotton exports increased from almost none in 1790 to 4 million bales by 1860. The United States produced two-thirds of the world's short-staple cotton on the eve of the Civil War, and three-quarters of the U.S. crop was exported, mostly to Great Britain. Cotton alone accounted for more than half the value of all U.S. exports throughout the pre–Civil War era. All this did not magically occur because of the cotton gin. That simple invention was less a cause than an effect of the new structure of opportunity in the transatlantic economy.[42]

Neither capitalism nor the market revolution (whichever one wants to call it) bypassed the southern states. Rather, the cotton plantation system at the core of the nineteenth-century South latched onto transatlantic industrial revolution and went along for the ride—an unnatural symbiosis in which the parasite feeds its host. Outside the cotton core were other slave-grown crops (tobacco and hemp in the Upper South, rice in the Carolina-Georgia low country, and sugar in lower Louisiana), upcountry enclaves where non–slave owners predominated, and an outer ring of towns and smaller cities from Baltimore to New Orleans where slavery took on a distinctive urban form. North

American masters weathered the revolutionary challenge and adapted slave labor to a wide range of environments and economies, much like their counterparts in Cuba and Brazil.[43]

Unlike Cuba and Brazil, the United States "domesticated" its slave population by (mostly) withdrawing from the Atlantic slave trade before 1820. Instead of imported Africans, biological reproduction and a massive internal slave trade sustained the expansion of cotton and sugar production in the Deep South in the decades before the Civil War. The routine buying and selling of people gave the nineteenth-century South its most brutally commercial aspect, notwithstanding slave owners' many strategies of denial and concealment. Those strategies were in fact crucial elements of proslavery ideology—a conceptual domestication. Proslavery was the antithesis of northern free labor ideology. Southern slave owners came to insist that slavery was natural, just, and even progressive in the classic sense. Most of all, they endorsed it as a sacred Christian arrangement and a bulwark against the dangerous isms of the modern world.[44]

The clash between northern antislavery and southern proslavery viewpoints crystallized within broader transatlantic debates over slavery and freedom, and it was paracolonial in that both sides drew lessons from the models of emancipation pioneered elsewhere in the Atlantic world. Both sides reacted to the British campaign against the slave trade, the Haitian Revolution and other foreign slave revolts, the various West Indian emancipations, and antislavery colonization projects in West Africa. Intellectuals on both sides of the slavery debate drew from European political economy, anthropology, and sociology to bolster their positions. U.S. abolitionists beginning in the 1830s allied with their British counterparts through personal correspondence, the travel and lecture circuit, and antislavery publishing and marketing. The transatlantic icon of abolitionism, a kneeling slave emblazoned with the slogan "Am I not a man and a brother?," illustrates this collaboration. The abolitionists' foreign connections could backfire, however, since it opened them to the potent charge of anglophilia.[45]

Southern slave owners looked on with increasing alarm at a spreading antislavery epidemic in the North. From the 1820s to the 1840s, they more or less successfully quarantined the national state from infection through their influence in the political parties, the suppression of debate via the "gag rule" in Congress, and an insistence on a narrow reading of the national government's constitutional powers with respect to slavery. But they had no such power over northern civil society, where antislavery flourished in churches and middle-class parlors. While the immediatist, antiracist stance of William Lloyd Garrison attracted many black northerners, his brand of radical abolitionism remained marginal among white northerners. A more diffuse and sentimental antislavery attitude made greater headway. Many subscribed to African colonization in the delusional hope that removing black people would pave the way for a gradual emancipation. That many white Americans thought an overseas colony could solve the problem of domestic slavery is, among other things, a good indication of just how much slavery—and the racism it spawned—unhinged republican principles.[46]

What translated northern antislavery opinion into an antislavery politics beginning in the 1840s? The trigger was the Mexican war and the emergence of free-soilism. Free soil fused an indictment of slavery with a defense of the rights of white northerners against infringement by the "slave power." Although the question of the status of slavery in the Mexican cession was resolved by the so-called Compromise of 1850 (which admitted California as a free state and shifted the burden of decision onto local communities in the rest of the cession through the mechanism of "popular sovereignty"), the debates over once-Mexican lands Mexico let the slavery genie out of its bottle. When Stephen Douglas's Kansas-Nebraska bill applied the principle of popular sovereignty to the newly organized Louisiana Purchase territories of Kansas and Nebraska in 1854, the bottle shattered. The operation of the new Fugitive Slave Law, filibusterism in Cuba and Nicaragua, and loud southern agitation to resume African slave importation all strengthened northern fears that southern slavery had aggressive national, and even international, ambitions—what Abraham Lincoln called "the high-road to a slave empire." By 1860, Whigs had virtually disappeared, Democrats had divided along sectional lines, and a new antislavery party calling itself Republican had reassembled the shards of northern politics into a winning electoral coalition.[47]

Lincoln, a western railroad lawyer mythologized as a rail splitter, won the presidency in 1860 without a single southern electoral vote. Even though Lincoln and the Republican platform disavowed abolitionism and pledged not to touch slavery in the states where it already existed, southern secessionists viewed the outcome as immensely dangerous to slavery. It placed the national government in the hands of a northern antislavery party. Once in control of the legislative and executive branches of the national government, they foresaw, Republicans would do more than simply contain slavery. They could legislate slavery out of existence by degrees. They could use patronage to build up a southern antislavery party starting in the northern tier of slave states and working its way down. Or worst of all, the Republican victory could breed more John Browns, the militant abolitionist who tried to spark a slave revolt at Harpers Ferry, Virginia, in 1859.[48]

MAP 3.2. The United States in North America, ca. 1860

At the same time, secessionists did more than react defensively against an existential antislavery threat. They also attempted to forge a popular nationalism based materially and ideologically on slavery. The secessionist campaign following Lincoln's election, the establishment of a new Confederate government, and the initial mobilization for war were politically effective, though not uncontested, articulations of proslavery nationalism in the South. (Four border slave states remained in the Union, and opposition to secession was quite strong in non-slave-owning pockets of the South.) Over time, however, the long slog of war exposed Confederate weaknesses relative to the Union: a smaller citizenry, an inferior industrial base, difficulties of communication and coordination, a deep-seated localism, and, as it turned out, slavery itself. Confederate nationalist hopes that dependence on southern cotton would compel European diplomatic recognition and support went unfulfilled. Unlike the breakaway colonies during the American Revolution, the Confederacy had to fend for itself in a new era of industrial warfare.[49]

By contrast, only a few northern voices defended the right of secession. Lincoln could neither concede to slave owners' demands for constitutional protections for slavery nor let the South go. Most northerners regarded secession as "the essence of anarchy," as Lincoln put it in his first inaugural address. It flaunted basic democratic principle. Time and again, Lincoln emphasized the world-historical significance of American democracy. In 1862 he called it "the last best hope of Earth." In the Gettysburg Address he implored his countrymen to resolve that "government of the people, by the people, for the people shall not perish from the earth." Union soldiers agreed. They fought for the Union and the abstract principle of democratic self-government that it symbolized. Over time, however, northern war aims shifted away from merely preserving the Union to overthrowing slavery. This momentous shift resulted from the tenacity of Confederate resistance. If they had given up sooner, they might have held on to slavery longer.[50]

From southern slave owners' perspective, the Civil War turned into the very catastrophe they had hoped to prevent through secession. It was Haiti all over again, the military road to emancipation. Masters' authority eroded. Thousands of slaves fled to the Union lines. Almost two hundred thousand black men joined the Union army and navy in the last two years of the war once Lincoln authorized black enlistment. But the military road to emancipation was not straight and narrow. Different rules applied in different places and to different people; freedom came sooner to some than others. Among the last to be freed were slaves in the Union slave states of Kentucky and Delaware, where emancipation did not generally apply until ratification of the Thirteenth Amendment to the U.S. Constitution in December 1865. The physical and environmental devastation of the war made life difficult for freed people struggling to eke out a living from a ruined landscape. The trauma of war scarred southern society. Many former Confederates refused to accept the legitimacy of emancipation, and their rage at defeat took the ritual form of lynching and murdering freedpeople. The Thirteenth Amendment abolished slavery in the United States but did not define what freedom meant for newly emancipated people. As in other postemancipation societies in the Americas, the meaning of their freedom was hammered out over subsequent decades of intense and often violent struggle, and fell so far short of full citizenship and economic independence that "freedom" is a misnomer.[51]

The United States came through its "fiery trial" at a steep price in blood and treasure. At least 750,000 people died, and the war cost an estimated $10 billion (approximately $32 trillion today). The protagonists struggled to make sense of the death and carnage. Some found meaning in emancipation, others in martial virtues like courage. Most ultimately attributed the war to God's inscrutable will. In hindsight, historians have endowed the Civil War with more secular significance, such as "the last capitalist revolution" or "the

FIGURE 3.1. Defending the Union and freedom: A soldier
guards cannon in Virginia, 1865

first modern war." Less reductively, this essay has argued that the Civil War
and emancipation resulted from the intricate dynamics of republican state-
formation, transatlantic capitalist development, and imperial expansion across
North America. Ultimately, the crisis of the 1860s answered Hamilton's important question—choice or force?—in terms revealed by a photograph taken in
City Point, Virginia, in 1865, showing a black soldier guarding a line of cannon.
As Lincoln had reminded the U.S. Congress earlier in the war, "We cannot
escape history."[52]

The Civil War ended one era of U.S. history and launched another, yet
there is never a clean break with the past. The war did more than restore the
Union; it strengthened the hand of the national government in its unending

contest with the states. Still, there were significant reassertions of state-level power through the late nineteenth century, including the return to home rule in the South and the formation of new states in the West. Industrial capitalist development was spurred by the war and accelerated afterward. With railroads as a leading sector, the U.S. economy steamed toward new accumulations and concentrations of wealth, sharper inequality, and fierce class conflict often articulated in the seemingly outdated language of Jeffersonian republicanism. Unprecedented numbers of immigrants flooded into the country, diversifying and populating swelling cities and manning its workshops, slaughterhouses, and factories. The United States overtook Great Britain as the world's largest manufacturer by the 1890s.

Untangled from slavery and infused with industrial might, the American empire grew into a more global force. Seasoned Union veterans of the Civil War, armed with powerful weaponry, stampeded the Plains Indians into meager reservations and intensified the crusade of civilization against them. It did not take long for the United States to flex its muscle abroad. In 1867, the United States annexed tiny Middlebrooks (Midway) atoll in the Pacific, and just over three decades later, it would claim far bigger prizes from Spain—Cuba and the Philippines. By the dawn of the twentieth century, the rising empire of Hamilton's ambitious generation had transformed into a great power and a linchpin of the modern world.[53]

Notes

1 Publius [Alexander Hamilton], *Federalist* 1, http://thomas.loc.gov/home/fedpapers /fed_01.html, accessed April 14, 2016.

2 Jack N. Rakove, *Original Meanings: Politics and Ideas in the Making of the Constitution* (New York: Alfred A. Knopf, 1997), 131–132. On the continuity between the colonial and early national eras, see Jack Greene, "Colonial History and National History: Reflections on a Continuing Problem," *William & Mary Quarterly*, 3d ser., 64:2 (April 2007), 235–250. On the importance of placing the history of the United States in transnational, international, and global contexts, see the essays in Thomas Bender, ed., *Rethinking American History in a Global Age* (Berkeley: University of California Press, 2002), and Thomas Bender, *A Nation among Nations: America's Place in World History* (New York: Hill & Wang, 2006). This historiography is rapidly growing. On the new nation's international obligations, see Eliga H. Gould, *Among the Powers of the Earth: The American Revolution and the Making of a New World Empire* (Cambridge, MA: Harvard University Press, 2012).

3 Karl Marx, *The 18th Brumaire of Louis Bonaparte* (1852), translated and online at the *Marx & Engels Internet Archive*, online at https://www.marxists.org/archive/marx /works/1852/18th-brumaire/, accessed April 14, 2016. I learned much about the false

dichotomy between force and choice from Perry Anderson, "The Antinomies of Antonio Gramsci," *New Left Review* 1:100 (November–December 1976), 5–78.

4   Kenneth Pomeranz, *The Great Divergence: China, Europe, and the Making of the Modern World Economy* (Princeton, NJ: Princeton University Press, 2000). For an argument linking the expansion of slavery in the southern United States to the Great Divergence, see Edward E. Baptist, *The Half Has Never Been Told: Slavery and the Making of American Capitalism* (New York: Basic Books, 2014), 78–83.

5   For a succinct analysis of Lincoln's famous "House Divided" speech in Springfield, Illinois, in 1858, see Eric Foner, *The Fiery Trial: Abraham Lincoln and American Slavery* (New York: Norton, 2010), 99–102.

6   The best delineation of the geography of colonial settlement in mainland British North America is D. W. Meinig, *Atlantic America, 1492–1800* (New Haven, CT: Yale University Press, 1986). The most influential interpretation of the enduring Indian presence in eastern North America is Richard White, *The Middle Ground: Indians, Empires, and Republics in the Great Lakes Region, 1650–1815* (New York: Cambridge University Press, 1991).

7   Nuala Zahedieh, "Economy," in *British Atlantic World, 1500–1800*, ed. David Armitage and Michael J. Braddick (New York: Palgrave Macmillan, 2002), 58, 62.

8   For an argument linking colonial Americans' consumerism and the revolution, see T. H. Breen, *The Marketplace of Revolution: How Consumer Politics Shaped American Independence* (New York: Oxford University Press, 2005).

9   That the American colonies were governed by negotiated consent is a hallmark of the work of Jack Greene. For a succinct statement, see his "The American Revolution," *American Historical Review* 105:1 (February 2000), 93–102.

10 My favorite example is from George Washington's General Orders, February 27, 1776: "It is a noble Cause we are engaged in, it is the Cause of virtue, and mankind, every temporal advantage and comfort to us, and our posterity, depends upon the Vigour of our exertions; in short, Freedom, or Slavery must be the result of our conduct, there can therefore be no greater Inducement to men to behave well:— But it may not be amiss for the Troops to know, that if any Man in action shall presume to skulk, hide himself, or retreat from the enemy, without the orders of his commanding Officer; he will be *instantly shot down*, as an example of cowardice;— Cowards having too frequently disconcerted the best form'd Troops, by their dastardly behaviour." Washington apparently thought the fear of enslavement needed reinforcements. This document can be found online through the George Washington Papers at the Library of Congress, 1741–1799, https://memory.loc.gov /ammem/gwhtml/gwhome.html, accessed April 14, 2016.

11 Hector St. John de Crevecoeur, *Letters from an American Farmer* (1782), Letter 3, online at http://xroads.virginia.edu/~hyper/crev/letter03.html, accessed April 14, 2016; for an overview of colonial American religious history, see Jon Butler, *Awash in a Sea of Faith: Christianizing the American People* (Cambridge, MA: Harvard University Press, 1990).

12 "A Narrative of the Capture of Henry Laurens, of His Confinement in the Tower of London, &c. 1780, 1781, 1782," *Collections of the South Carolina Historical Society*

(1857), 21–22; Greene, "American Revolution." Among the countless books on the revolution, see Richard Bushman, *King and People in Provincial Massachusetts* (Chapel Hill: University of North Carolina Press, 1985).

13 John Murrin, "A Roof without Walls: The Dilemma of American National Identity," in *Beyond Confederation: Origins of the Constitution and American National Identity*, ed. Richard Beeman, Stephen Botein, and Edward C. Carter II (Chapel Hill: University of North Carolina Press, 1987). For the war as a touchstone of nationalism, see Sarah Purcell, *Sealed with Blood: War, Sacrifice, and Memory in Revolutionary America* (Philadelphia: University of Pennsylvania Press, 2002), and David Waldstreicher, *In the Midst of Perpetual Fetes: The Making of American Nationalism, 1776–1820* (Chapel Hill: University of North Carolina Press, 1997).

14 An outpouring of scholarship on the loyalists has been recently capped by Maya Jasanoff, *Liberty's Exiles: American Loyalists in the Revolutionary World* (New York: Random House, 2011). These numbers are Jasanoff's.

15 For the Caribbean, see Andrew Jackson O'Shaughnessy, *An Empire Divided: The American Revolution and the British Caribbean* (Philadelphia: University of Pennsylvania Press, 2000). For Canada, see Alan Taylor, *The Divided Ground: Indians, Settlers, and the Northern Borderlands of the American Revolution* (New York: Alfred A. Knopf, 2006). For the early United States as paracolonial, see Sean X. Goudie, *Creole America: The West Indies and the Formation of Literature and Culture in the New Republic* (Philadelphia: University of Pennsylvania Press, 2006), and on paracolonial states in this era, see C. A. Bayly, *Imperial Meridian: The British Empire and the World, 1780–1830* (New York: Longman, 1989), 228–235, which argues that several independent states thrived outside Europe, particularly in the Ottoman world. For the early United States as *postcolonial*, see Greene, "Colonial History and National History," and the essays in the same volume responding to Greene; Kariann Akemi Yokota, *Unbecoming British: How Revolutionary America Became a Postcolonial Nation* (New York: Oxford University Press, 2011); Sam W. Haynes, *Unfinished Revolution: The Early American Republic in a British World* (Charlottesville: University of Virginia Press, 2010).

16 John McNeill, *Mosquito Empires: Ecology and War in the Greater Caribbean, 1620–1914* (New York: Cambridge University Press, 2010); Bender, *A Nation among Nations*, chap. 2, places the American Revolution in the context of the long-term Anglo-French rivalry. Ungrateful Americans still find mosquitoes and the French irritating.

17 The strongest recent statement of the American Revolution as a revolution, see Gordon Wood, *The Radicalism of the American Revolution* (New York: Alfred A. Knopf, 1991). Wood's critics emphasize the class, racial, and gender limits of republicanism, and they generally view the constitution as a backlash against revolution's more democratic tendencies.

18 Important recent works rethinking the origins of the constitution in the context of international relations are David Hendrickson, *Peace Pact: The Lost World of the American Founding* (Lawrence: University Press of Kansas, 2003), and Max Edling, *A Revolution in Favor of Government: Origins of the U.S. Constitution and*

the Making of the American State (New York: Oxford University Press, 2003). Quotation from George Washington to Benjamin Harrison, January 18, 1784, *George Washington Papers*, https://memory.loc.gov/ammem/gwhtml/gwhome .html, accessed April 14, 2016. To the extent that any social basis undergirded the political division between the localists and nationalists, it was the gap between backcountry provincials and more urbane cosmopolitans, but like most broad analytical dichotomies, this one is subject to caveats, exceptions, and outright contradictions. A more complete analysis of the mosaic of interests on each side of the debate over the constitution is beyond the scope of this essay. Sean Wilentz, *The Rise of American Democracy: Jefferson to Lincoln* (New York: Norton, 2005), chapter 1. Proving the class basis of the constitution is the progressive Holy Grail of U.S. historiography.

19 Henrickson, *Peace Pact*. On the constitution, see Rakove, *Original Meanings*; David Waldstreicher, *Slavery's Constitution: From Revolution to Ratification* (New York: Hill & Wang 2009); Gordon Wood, *Creation of the American Republic, 1776–1787* (Chapel Hill: University of North Carolina Press, 1969).

20 On the French Revolution and the first party system, see Stanley Elkins and Erik McKitrick, *The Age of Federalism* (New York: Oxford University Press, 1993).

21 Drew McCoy, *The Elusive Republic: Political Economy in Jeffersonian America* (Chapel Hill: University of North Carolina Press, 1980).

22 J. C. A. Stagg, *The War of 1812: Conflict for a Continent* (New York: Cambridge University Press, 2012), emphasizes the weaknesses of the U.S. effort in the War of 1812.

23 S.v. "empire," *A complete dictionary of the English language, both with regard to sound and meaning: one main object of which is, to establish a plain and permanent standard of pronunciation. To which is prefixed a rhetorical grammar. By Thomas Sheridan, A.M.* (Philadelphia: Printed by William Young, bookseller, the corner of Second and Chesnut-Street, 1789), n.p.; for "rising empire," see *Large additions to Common sense; addressed to the inhabitants of America, on several important subjects. Being divided into eleven parts . . .* (Salem, MA, 1776), title page.

24 Peter Onuf, *Jefferson's Empire: The Language of American Nationhood* (Charlottesville: University of Virginia Press, 2000), chap. 2; In his Second Inaugural Address, Jefferson asked rhetorically, "But who can limit the extent to which the federative principle may operate effectively?"

25 Richard John, *Spreading the News: The American Postal System from Franklin to Morse* (Cambridge, MA: Harvard University Press, 2005); John Lauritz Larson, *Internal Improvement: National Public Works and the Promise of Popular Government in the Early United States* (Chapel Hill: University of North Carolina Press, 2001); Sam Haselby, *The Origins of American Religious Nationalism* (New York: Oxford University Press, 2015). On infrastructural power, see Michael Mann, *Sources of Social Power,* vol. 1 (New York: Cambridge University Press, 1986).

26 *New Orleans Daily Picayune*, May 7, 1861. On the United States and Haiti, see Tim Matthewson, *A Proslavery Foreign Policy: Haitian-American Relations during the Early Republic* (Westport, CT: Praeger, 2003); Matthew Clavin, *Toussaint*

Louverture and the American Civil War: The Promise and Peril of a Second Haitian Revolution (Philadelphia: University of Pennsylvania Press, 2010).

27 Annual Report of the Commissioner of Indian Affairs (Washington, 1902), 52. U.S. policy makers' nearly total ignorance of the Indian people in the Louisiana territory is evident from the "Description of Louisiana" Jefferson transmitted to Congress in 1803. One goal of the Lewis & Clark Expedition was to determine who was actually living there.

28 Gary Lawson and Guy Seidman, The Constitution of Empire: Territorial Expansion and American Legal History (New Haven, CT: Yale University Press, 2004), argues that the promise of statehood is what makes territorial acquisition constitutionally permissible.

29 Census data from Seventh Census of the United States: 1850 (Washington: Robert Armstrong, 1853).

30 The vast literature on Indian removal mostly focuses on the southern Indians (Cherokee, Creek, Chickasaw, Choctaw, and Seminole). For an introduction, see Anthony F. C. Wallace, The Long, Bitter Trail: Andrew Jackson and the Indians (New York: Hill & Wang, 1993). For the northern Indians, see John P. Bowes, Exiles and Pioneers: Eastern Indians in the Trans-Mississippi West (New York: Cambridge University Press, 2007).

31 D. W. Meinig, Continental America, 1800–1867 (New Haven, CT: Yale University Press, 1992); William Unrah, The Rise and Fall of Indian Country, 1825–1855 (Lawrence: University Press of Kansas, 2007); Bowes, Exiles and Pioneers. Quotation from Alexis de Tocqueville, Democracy in America, trans. Arthur Goldhammer (New York: Library of America, 2004), 391.

32 Some of the most exciting new work in North American history illuminates the complex world of these western Indian nations and empires before the U.S. onslaught, including their often hostile relations with the emigrant Indians. See Ned Blackhawk, Violence over the Land: Indians and Empires in the Early American West (Cambridge, MA: Harvard University Press, 2006); Kathleen DuVal, The Native Ground: Indians and Colonists in the Heart of the Continent (Philadelphia: University of Pennsylvania Press, 2006); Pekka Hämäläinen, The Comanche Empire (New Haven, CT: Yale University Press, 2008). On slavery and Indians in Kansas, see Kristen Tegtmeier Oertel, Bleeding Borders: Race, Gender, and Violence in Pre–Civil War Kansas (Baton Rouge: Louisiana State University Press, 2009).

33 Recent U.S. scholarship on the struggles on Mexico's northern frontier include Brian Delay, War of a Thousand Deserts: Indian Raids and the US-Mexican War (New Haven, CT: Yale University Press, 2008); Andrés Reséndez, Changing National Identities at the Frontier: Texas and New Mexico, 1800–1850 (New York: Cambridge University Press, 2005). Albert Hurtado, John Sutter: A Life on the North American Frontier (Norman: Oklahoma University Press, 2006), puts Sutter and California in a transnational context.

34 The political struggles behind the Mexican War on the U.S. side are laid out in detail in Wilentz, Rise of American Democracy, and Daniel Walker Howe, What Hath God Wrought: The Transformation of America, 1815–1848 (New York: Oxford

University Press, 2007). Amy Greenberg emphasizes domestic opposition to the Mexican war in *A Wicked War: Polk, Clay, Lincoln, and the 1846 U.S. Invasion of Mexico* (New York: Alfred A. Knopf, 2012). See also Thomas Hietala, *Manifest Design: American Exceptionalism and Empire* (Ithaca, NY: Cornell University Press, 2003).

35 Wayne Wei-siang Hsieh, *West Pointers and the Civil War: The Old Army in War and Peace* (Chapel Hill: University of North Carolina Press, 2009), chap. 3; John S. D. Eisenhower, *So Far from God: The US War with Mexico, 1846–1848* (Norman: University of Oklahoma Press, 2000). On local unrest and resistance in the Mexican war, see Anne F. Hyde, *Empires, Nations, and Families: A New History of the North American West, 1800–1860* (Lincoln: University of Nebraska Press, 2011), chap. 6.

36 On the California and Australian gold rushes, see H. W. Brands, *The Age of Gold: The California Gold Rush and the New American Dream* (New York: Doubleday 2002); James Belich, *Replenishing the Earth: The Settler Revolution and the Rise of the Anglo-World, 1783–1939* (New York: Oxford University Press, 2009), chap. 9. For California and sectional crisis, see Leonard Richards, *The California Gold Rush and the Coming of the Civil War* (New York: Alfred A. Knopf, 2007). Quotation from Friedrich Engels to Karl Marx, August 24, 1852, *Marx and Engels Internet Archive*, online at http://marx.libcom.org/works/1852/letters/52_08_24.htm, accessed on April 14, 2016. "Impending crisis" is the title of a classic history of the road to the Civil War, David Potter, *The Impending Crisis, 1848–1861* (New York: Harper & Row, 1976), which in turn plays on Hinton Rowan Helper's *The Impending Crisis of the South* (New York, 1857).

37 For William Seward's "irrepressible conflict" speech in Rochester in 1858, see George E. Baker, ed., *The Works of William H. Seward* (Boston: Houghton, Mifflin and Company, 1884), 4:289–302.

38 See for instance Thomas Bender, *A Nation among Nations: America's Place in World History* (New York: Hill and Wang, 2006), chap. 3.

39 For an overview of gradual abolition and the emergence of free black society in the North, see Ira Berlin, *Many Thousands Gone: The First Two Centuries of Slavery in North America* (Cambridge, MA: Harvard University Press, 1998), chap. 9. We might compare gradual emancipation in the northern states to the demise of slavery in the newly independent Spanish American republics.

40 Charles Sellers, *The Market Revolution: Jacksonian America, 1815–1846* (New York: Oxford University Press, 1991), argues that these transformations were wrenching and catastrophic; Howe, *What Hath God Wrought*, takes a more benign view. On the transatlantic transfer of technology and knowledge, see Doron S. Ben-Atar, *Trade Secrets: Intellectual Piracy and the Origins of American Industrial Power* (New Haven, CT: Yale University Press, 2004).

41 For a summary of the rise of free labor ideology, see the new introduction to Eric Foner, *Free Soil, Free Labor, Free Men: The Ideology of the Republican Party Before the Civil War* (New York: Oxford University Press, 1995), ix–xlii. On "wage slavery" and "white slavery," see the controversial David Roediger, *The Wages of*

Whiteness: Race and the Making of the American Working Class (New York: Verso, 1991).

42 Statistics from Douglas A. Irwin, "Exports of Selected Commodities: 1790–1989," table Ee569–589 in *Historical Statistics of the United States, Earliest Times to the Present: Millennial Edition*, ed. Susan B. Carter, Scott Sigmund Gartner, Michael R. Haines, Alan L. Olmstead, Richard Sutch, and Gavin Wright (New York: Cambridge University Press, 2006). Three important recent books contend that the brutal expansion of the South's cotton kingdom was an integral part of a global capitalist endeavor: Baptist, *The Half Has Never Been Told*; Sven Beckert, *Empire of Cotton: A Global History* (New York: Alfred A. Knopf, 2014); Walter Johnson, *River of Dark Dreams: Slavery and Empire in the Cotton Kingdom* (Cambridge, MA: Harvard University Press, 2013).

43 Anthony E. Kaye, "The Second Slavery: Modernity in the Nineteenth-Century South and the Atlantic World," *Journal of Southern History* 75:3 (August 2009), 627–650. A cogent comparison is Laird Bergad, *The Comparative Histories of Slavery in Brazil, Cuba, and the United States* (New York: Cambridge University Press, 2007).

44 David Eltis summarizes recent findings on the dimensions of the slave trade to the United States in "The U.S. Transatlantic Slave Trade, 1644–1867: An Assessment," *Civil War History* 54:4 (December 2008), 347–378. There are several fine books on the internal slave trade within the United States, including Michael Tadman, *Speculators and Slaves: Masters, Traders, and Slaves in the Old South* (Madison: University of Wisconsin Press, 1989); Walter Johnson, *Soul by Soul: Life Inside the Antebellum Slave Market* (Cambridge, MA: Harvard University Press, 1999); Steve Deyle, *Carry Me Back: The Domestic Slave Trade in American Life* (New York: Oxford University Press, 2005). On proslavery ideology, see most recently Eugene Genovese and Elizabeth Fox-Genovese, *Slavery in White and Black: Class and Race in the Southern Slaveholders' New World Order* (New York: Cambridge University Press, 2008), and Michael O'Brien, *Conjunctures of Order: Intellectual Life and the American South, 1810–1860* (Chapel Hill: University of North Carolina Press, 2004).

45 Recent work that places the U.S. slavery debates in a transatlantic context include Edward Rugemer, *The Problem of Emancipation: The Caribbean Roots of the American Civil War* (Baton Rouge: Louisiana State University Press, 2008), and W. Caleb McDaniel, *The Problem of Democracy in the Age of Slavery: Garrisonian Abolitionists and Transatlantic Reform* (Baton Rouge: Louisiana State University Press, 2013). Two panoptic works on emancipation are Robin Blackburn, *Overthrow of Colonial Slavery, 1776–1848* (New York: Verso, 1988), and more recently, Seymour Drescher, *Abolition: A History of Slavery and Antislavery* (New York: Cambridge University Press, 2009).

46 At the end of Harriet Beecher Stowe's *Uncle Tom's Cabin*, George Harris and his family emigrate to Liberia. Southern slave owners' grip on national politics is documented in Leonard Richard, *The Slave Power: The Free North and Southern Domination, 1780–1860* (Baton Rouge: Louisiana State University Press, 2000),

and Don Fehrenbacher, *The Slaveholding Republic: An Account of the United States Government's Relation to Slavery* (New York: Oxford University Press, 2001).

47 Foner, *Free Soil, Free Labor, Free Men*; Wilentz, *Rise of American Democracy*. Michael Holt, *The Rise and Fall of the American Whig Party: Jacksonian Politics and the Onset of the Civil War* (New York: Oxford University Press, 1999), emphasizes the complexity of state politics and the salience of issues other than slavery. On filibustering, see Robert E. May, *Manifest Destiny's Underworld: Filibustering in Antebellum America* (Chapel Hill: University of North Carolina Press, 2002). Lincoln quotation from Foner, *The Fiery Trial*, 154.

48 William Freehling offers a detailed and provocative narrative of these events in *The Road to Disunion*, vol. 2: *Secessionists Triumphant, 1854–1861* (New York: Oxford University Press, 2007). For a fine-grained state study, I like Michael Johnson, *Toward a Patriarchal Republic: The Secession of Georgia* (Baton Rouge: Louisiana State University Press, 1977).

49 The most recent synthesis along traditional lines is Russell Frank Weigley, *A Great Civil War: A Military and Political History, 1861–1865* (Bloomington: Indiana University Press, 2000). On the strength and limits of Confederate nationalism, see Drew Gilpin Faust, *The Creation of Confederate Nationalism: Ideology and Identity in the Civil War South* (Baton Rouge: Louisiana State University Press, 1988); Gary Gallagher, *The Confederate War* (Cambridge, MA: Harvard University Press, 1997); Stephanie McCurry, *Confederate Reckoning: Power and Politics in the Civil War South* (Cambridge, MA: Harvard University Press, 2010).

50 Chandra Manning, *What This Cruel War Was Over: Soldiers, Slavery, and the Civil War* (New York: Alfred A. Knopf, 2007). For emancipation as war policy, see Mark Grimsley, *The Hard Hand of War: Union Military Policy toward Southern Civilians, 1861–1864* (New York: Cambridge University Press, 1995).

51 For the process of wartime emancipation in the United States, see Ira Berlin, Barbara J. Fields, Steven F. Miller, Joseph P. Reidy, and Leslie S. Rowland, *Slaves No More: Three Essays on Emancipation and the Civil War* (New York: Cambridge University Press, 1992), and the documentary volumes of the Freedmen and Southern Society Project, *Freedom, a Documentary History of Emancipation, 1861–1867* (New York: Cambridge University Press, 1985–). Michael Vorenberg traces the origins of the Thirteenth Amendment in *Final Freedom: The Civil War, the Abolition of Slavery, and the Thirteenth Amendment* (New York: Cambridge University Press, 2001). The best account of the politics of emancipation is now James Oakes, *Freedom National: The Destruction of Slavery in the United States, 1861–1865* (New York: Norton, 2012). Steven Hahn presses a provocative comparison between the Civil War and Haitian Revolution in his *Political Worlds of Slavery and Freedom* (Cambridge, MA: Harvard University Press, 2009). For the postwar struggle, see Eric Foner, *Reconstruction: America's Unfinished Revolution, 1863–1877* (New York: Harper & Row, 1988); Steven Hahn, *A Nation under Our Feet: Black Political Struggles in the Rural South, from Slavery to the Great Migration* (Cambridge, MA: Harvard University Press, 2003).

52   The Lincoln quotations at both ends of the paragraph come from the conclusion
     to his Second Annual Message to Congress, December 1, 1862. For the full text
     see *The American Presidency Project*, online at http://www.presidency.ucsb.edu
     /ws/index.php?pid=29503, accessed on April 14, 2016. A new estimate revises
     the number of Civil War dead upward from the traditional 620,000 to 752,000;
     see J. David Hacker, "A Census-Based Count of the Civil War Dead," *Civil War
     History* 75:4 (December 2011). The estimate of the war's cost is from Roger
     Ransom, "Economics of the Civil War," *EH.Net Encyclopedia*, ed. Robert Whaples,
     August 24, 2001, online at http://eh.net/encyclopedia/the-economics-of-the
     -civil-war/, accessed April 14, 2016. For the reckoning with death, see Drew Gilpin
     Faust, *This Republic of Suffering: Death and the American Civil War* (New York:
     Alfred A. Knopf, 2008). "Last capitalist revolution" is from Barrington Moore
     Jr., *Social Origins of Dictatorship and Democracy: Lord and Peasant in the Making
     of the Modern World* (Boston: Beacon, 1966), chap. 3; "first modern war" is from
     Bruce Catton, *The Civil War and Its Meaning in American Culture* (Middletown,
     CT: Wesleyan University Press, 1958). These are older works, but still classic, and
     their interpretive tendencies remain vital today. The photograph also echoes John
     Quincy Adams's prediction in 1831 that the controversy over the doctrine of nullifi-
     cation "can be settled only at the cannon's mouth." Calvin Colton, ed., *The Private
     Correspondence of Henry Clay* (Boston, 1856), 313. See Lacy Ford, "Reconfiguring
     the Old South: 'Solving' the Problem of Slavery, 1787–1838," *Journal of American
     History* 95:1 (2008), 122.

53   This paragraph condenses a vast scholarship. On the key themes of this essay, I will
     single out for special mention Richard Bensel, *Yankee Leviathan: The Origins of
     Central State Authority in America, 1859–1877* (New York: Cambridge Univer-
     sity Press, 1991); William Cronon, *Nature's Metropolis: Chicago and the Great
     West* (New York: Norton, 1991); and D. W. Meinig, *The Shaping of America: A
     Geographical Perspective on 500 Years of History*, vol. 3: *Transcontinental America,
     1850–1915* (New Haven, CT: Yale University Press, 1998).

4
———

FROM SLAVE COLONY TO BLACK NATION
Haiti's Revolutionary Inversion

CAROLYN FICK

By the late eighteenth century, the French slave colony of Saint Domingue was by far the most lucrative colony of the French empire and the entire Atlantic seaboard. Its trajectory from a slave colony to an independent nation led by former slaves and their descendants in the early nineteenth-century Atlantic defies idealization. Yet its existence as an independent black state, the challenges it posed to Eurocentric notions of liberty, and the fact that the emancipatory revolution was launched and sustained by the slaves themselves were extraordinary and unprecedented accomplishments. To most contemporaries (and until the last few decades for most historians), the capacity of enslaved Africans to envision freedom, develop strategies to achieve it, and establish an independent nation-state to defend it, was inconceivable. Simply put, a slave revolution, *understood on its own terms*, lay outside the conceptual framework of Western thought.[1]

Yet Haiti did exist in 1804—and has endured despite a history of difficulties and denigrations. Its existence as an independent country, founded on anti-slavery, anticolonialism, and racial equality, rather than conventional forms of political philosophy and constitutional theory, came riddled with complexities and posed almost insurmountable barriers to leaders committed to state formation—and to Haitian masses seeking a nation grounded in peasant landholding, household production, and local markets.

Saint Domingue: The Quintessential Slave Colony

On the eve of France's 1789 revolution, Saint Domingue was at its peak. It had 7,000 plantations: nearly 800 in sugar, more than 3,000 in indigo, some 2,500 in coffee, another 800 in cotton, and some 50 cocoa growers—worked by over half a million slaves, two-thirds of them born in Africa.[2] Yet there was very little in its early stages of settlement in the late seventeenth century, with the spurious activities of freebooters, buccaneers, and pirates, and only a small number of tobacco and cotton farms, to indicate that a century later the colony would become the jewel of the French colonial empire and the engine that fueled her international commerce, supplied her domestic industries, employed millions of French workers, and guaranteed enviable trade surpluses through reexportation of finished colonial imports to European markets.

Only at the turn of the seventeenth century, after France acquired the western portion of Hispaniola from Spain in the Treaty of Ryswick (1697), did Saint Domingue enter its sugar boom, with 120 sugar plantations by 1704, 100 built from 1700 to 1704.[3] Over the next eighty years Saint Domingue's economy soared to new heights not only in sugar, but, during the decades following the end of the Seven Years' War in 1763, in an emerging coffee sector as well. By 1789, the total property values in the colony were estimated to be over 1.6 billion livres.[4]

Such prosperity was not possible without slavery and the slave trade. The slave trade was a key component of economic expansion in both the metropolitan and the colonial economies, with over a million slaves imported into the French West Indies during the eighteenth century, approximately 800,000 going directly to Saint Domingue. By the eve of the revolution, the colony was importing between 37,000 and 40,000 slaves annually.[5]

Part of the reason for the insatiable demand for slaves lay in the labor-intensive nature of sugar production and the profit-driven motives of Saint Domingue's planters. Sugar, unlike most other colonial exports, required extensive cultivation and semi-industrial manufacturing. The planting and harvesting of cane;

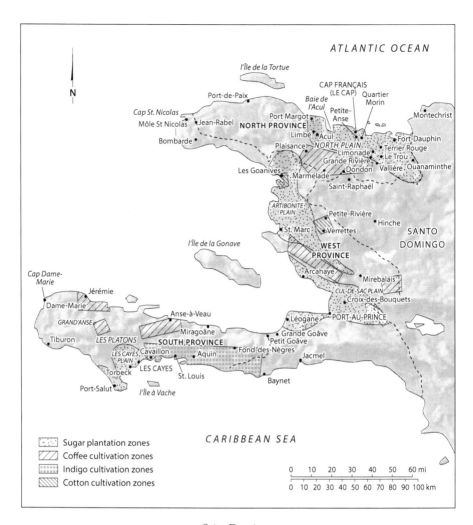

MAP 4.1. Saint Domingue, ca. 1790

the twenty-four-hour multistage process of hauling, milling, boiling the cane juice, crystallization, purging, and finally drying and packing the sugar, all required an inexhaustible, highly diversified, enslaved labor force. With mortality rates on the sugar plantations among newly arrived Africans reaching upward of 50 percent in their first five to eight years in the colony, planters continually purchased more slaves, not just to replenish their diminished stock of human labor, but to expand operations, increase profits, offset debts, and build personal wealth. The slave population never reproduced, and by 1789 well over two-thirds of Saint Domingue's slaves had been born in Africa.

FIGURE 4.1. Slaves milling cane in eighteenth-century Saint Domingue

As slave imports to Saint Domingue reached nearly forty thousand per year by 1791, most of the African-born, predominantly from the lower West African coast of Angola and the kingdom of Kongo, had arrived in the colony in the decade or two before the outbreak of the revolution.[6] On average, they were between the ages of fifteen and thirty-five on arrival. They had spent their formative youth and early adulthood acquiring knowledge and a worldview that embraced the politics, the languages, religious practices and cultural forms, kinship ties and obligations, as well as the landholding and agricultural practices of the African societies from which they came. Most had acquired a long experience in household production of food crops and local marketing, practices fundamentally at odds with the system of large-scale plantation production and commodity exports they were now forced to endure and sustain.

Slaves born in Saint Domingue, plus a few of the African-born who became acclimated to colonial slave society, generally occupied elite or supervisory positions in the slave hierarchy as domestics, coachmen, valets, skilled laborers, and artisans practicing trades in the towns or on plantations. Others held important roles as slave drivers, or *commandeurs*. Holding positions of responsibility and, as commandeurs, authority over other slaves, and with access to the outside world, some gained a knowledge of French and became aware of political and other events in the colony, as well as of the politics behind the events—which often originated in France. The core of the slave leadership that organized the massive slave insurrection of August 22, 1791, came from the ranks of the commandeurs, along with coachmen, domestics, and other elite slaves, who played key roles in its inception.[7] Toussaint Louverture, who would rise to the summit of power as a revolutionary black leader and statesman, had been born a slave, but was already free at the time of the revolution. The revolution, however, did not begin with slave revolt.

The Background to Slave Emancipation

To understand events in Saint Domingue, we must look to France on the eve of its revolution. An unprecedented financial crisis faced the Bourbon regime due in large part to debts incurred to fund the Seven Years' War (1756–1763) and military support of the British American war of independence. The resistance of the nobility and upper clergy to government tax reforms compounded the crisis—leaving the monarchy no alternative but to convoke the Estates General. In doing so, however, Louis XVI opened the floodgates to a revolutionary process beyond his capacity to control. In addition to dealing with taxation, representatives from each of France's three estates—clergy, nobles, and commoners—were to submit lists of grievances, or *cahiers de doléances*, to be considered by a deliberative assembly that had not met since 1614, yet with each estate meeting and voting separately. Finding themselves at a permanent two-to-one disadvantage with respect to the two privileged estates, the delegates of the Third Estate, which comprised close to 98 percent of the French population and included all classes of people—wealthy port merchants, slave traders, commercial agents, provincial lawyers, notaries, urban and rural artisans, and shopkeepers, as well as the peasantry—on June 17, 1789, boldly declared themselves a National Assembly, deliberating and speaking for the nation as a whole. Three days later, they swore not to adjourn until a written constitution was adopted for France. On August 26, they laid out foundational principles in the Declaration of the Rights of Man and Citizen: universal equality and the preservation of the natural rights to liberty, property, security, and resistance to oppression.

In the context of unfolding revolutionary events in France, sparked by the opening of the Estates General in 1789 and the egalitarian ideology put forward by the Third Estate, the colony's white planters and free coloreds (*affranchis*) mobilized—and fought against each other—to press their own grievances and obtain rights they believed to be theirs. The white planters wanted freedom from restrictive mercantilist policies, political autonomy within the colonial administration, and the maintenance of racial supremacy.

For the island's free coloreds, whose elite members were planters, and slave owners, coffee merchants, and militia officers, many educated in France, some having fought for British North American independence as volunteers in the French army, the goal was to gain access to the unfolding political process in France. They hoped to claim the rights of universal citizenship proclaimed in the Declaration of the Rights of Man and Citizen in France and thereby regain legal equality with their white counterparts, denied them because of their African heritage.[8]

They aimed to "regain legal equality" because initially, by Louis XIV's Code Noir of 1685, the affranchis were to enjoy "the same rights, privileges and liberties enjoyed by persons born free," which is to say, by all French subjects. This remained more or less the case until the Seven Years' War, after which Saint Domingue witnessed an influx of new French immigrants seeking fortune in the colony's expanding plantation economy. Facing competition from a rising class of free colored property owners for land, slaves, and employment, racial tensions became increasingly acute. From the late 1760s until the eve of the revolution, planters pressed racial exclusions. Colonial authorities passed legislation imposing racial segregation in public places, barring free coloreds from most "white" professions, restricting their ability to travel to France, and, to suppress feelings of social equality, imposed sumptuary regulations in the public sphere. By the early 1770s, free coloreds were required to renounce French surnames and adopt others suggesting African origins.[9] And they were prohibited from holding political office.

The revolutionary context of 1788–1791 suddenly opened the questions of political equality for free coloreds—of access to office and to the legislative and judicial processes of making, changing, and interpreting laws. The right to participate in the public domain took on special urgency. It became the battle-field on which not only the future of free coloreds, but the future of slavery itself would be fought and determined.

Free colored leaders like Vincent Ogé, a rich coffee merchant from the colony's North province, who was in Paris at the outset of the French Revolution, argued that only if they gained political equality by peaceful and constitutional means could a generalized slave revolt be averted. If free coloreds had to take to arms in defense of their rights, they could not be responsible for any actions the slaves might take. The white planters, for their part, argued that extending political rights to even one free colored in Saint Domingue would open the floodgate to demands for universal equality, including the colony's free blacks and ultimately their kin still in slavery. For the powerful white colonists, political and civil equality for free coloreds would inevitably lead to the end of slavery—and of their personal fortunes. In the end, both parties were proven right—for opposite reasons. A massive slave insurrection did break out in the colony's North province on August 22, 1791, a day after free coloreds in the West province announced taking recourse to arms to defend their cause and their lives from violent aggressions aimed against them across the colony, mostly by property-less "small white" and other déclassé elements. It would take another eight months of violent conflict among factions of white colonists—some wanting to secede from revolutionary France to defend racial supremacy; others embracing a counterrevolutionary royalist position; and still others who supported French revolutionary officials—and between these factions and the free coloreds, before the latter were granted universal rights of French citizenship by the Legislative Assembly in France on April 4, 1792.

With the new law, free coloreds were expected to aid French authorities in putting down the slave insurrections that had erupted throughout the colony, and in returning rebel slaves to their plantations. The task proved impossible. Those in the North, under the command of Jean-François and Biassou (with a small contingent of several hundred well-trained and hardened rebel slaves led by Toussaint Louverture), were fighting under the banner of Spain, defending monarchy, and occupying numerous parishes in the eastern part of the province. Slave insurgents in the West were close to forming alliances with the British, whose agents had begun to negotiate with secessionist planters to bring the colony under British domain. In the South, a massive slave rebellion was unfolding by the end of summer 1792 in the mountainous region around the capital of les Cayes; rebels formed a massive maroon community of ten to twelve thousand men, women, and children, with armed contingents and military outposts. By March 1793, France was at war with both Great Britain and Spain, and the threat of British invasion loomed.[10]

By late spring 1793, the two French civil commissioners, Léger Félicité Sonthonax and Étienne Polverel, having arrived in the colony in September 1792 with a mandate from the revolutionary government to restore order, enforce the April 4 decree, and suppress the slave insurrections, faced a near-hopeless situation. Amid threats of foreign occupation and agitations by secessionist and royalist factions, new conflicts broke out on June 22–23 in the northern capital of le Cap. The newly arrived governor-general, Thomas Galbaud, refused to recognize the superior authority of the civil commissioners, who dismissed him and issued deportation orders. Events escalated to rioting in the streets and the emptying of the prisons. Hundreds of disgruntled sailors aboard the governor's fleet in the harbor joined the fray, as did some ten thousand of the city's black slaves. By June 23, fires destroyed over two-thirds of the city. In the face of these events, and no longer able to rely upon the full support of free coloreds to save the colony from the revolution's domestic and foreign enemies, the commissioners turned to the rebel slave insurgents and their leaders, who had taken arms, torched plantations, and for two years maintained organized armies to defend their freedom: "It is with the natives of the country, that is, the Africans," the commissioners wrote to the French National Convention, "that we will save Saint-Domingue for France."[11] In desperation, and in the name of the French Republic, they offered legal manumission to any rebel slave who enrolled in the French army, with liberty soon extended to their wives and children. Yet not one of the major slave leaders, Toussaint included, rallied to the call, maintaining their professed allegiance to Spain in the struggle for freedom.

Nearly half of the slaves in the North province had deserted the plantations to join the rebel movements; those who remained, along with le Cap's white and free colored citizens fearing the power of slave insurgency, pressured Sonthonax to proclaim general emancipation. On August 29, 1793, the commissioner decreed slavery abolished in the North province, an act that was followed by Polverel in September and October for the West and South provinces, respectively. On February 4, 1794, the French National Convention ratified the abolition of slavery in all French territory and ostensibly extended the Rights of Man and Citizen to all colonial inhabitants, without regard to color or previous status. Unprecedented as this was in the history of slavery, the decree did not end colonial rule or the plantation regime of enforced labor and export commodity production.

From the moment the revolutionary commissioners abolished slavery, the problem of reconciling freedom, universal citizenship, and individual rights with coerced plantation labor and the large-scale production of exports that alone could generate commercial prosperity and strong government revenues, shaped defining debates and conflicts—and ultimately proved impossible to resolve. In the end, Haiti became a nation of peasant producers, as did the Bajío in Mexico after the popular insurgencies launched in 1810 brought the collapse of the silver economy there. For Haiti, the outcome appears inevitable, given the permanent rejection of plantation labor by the overwhelming majority of former slaves.

It was not the chosen path of those in power. In the transition from slavery to a postemancipation, and then to a postcolonial state and society based on universal freedom and legal equality, colonial administrators and independence rulers alike tried to maintain large-scale plantation production and commodity exports—and repeatedly faced the problem of replacing the social relations of slavery with the labor of free individuals. Every attempt failed. Barring coercion, military supervision or, at the very least, the suppression of individual rights, freed slaves refused to reconcile themselves to the plantation regime.

The labor regime first put in place in 1793–1794 by the civil commissioners after general emancipation served as a prototype for each successive regime of the revolutionary period and after, from Toussaint Louverture to Dessalines and Christophe long into the national period. The emancipation proclamations of Sonthonax and Polverel acknowledged that the plantation workers were free and that the rights of French citizenship extended to them. Freedom from chattel slavery, of course, was one thing; personal liberty and the right to land, quite another. Under the first emancipation regime, plantations would remain intact as productive units, as would the collective labor force. To assure a stable transition from slavery to "free labor," workers were ordered to remain on the plantations of their former owners, where they would labor at the same tasks as under slavery.[12] They would, however, gain a small wage for their labor, but only on fulfilling a six-day work week, as under slavery. Under this arrangement (*le système portionnaire*) one-third of the plantation revenues (or one-quarter after deduction of government taxes) were reserved for workers, to be divided among them in unequal portions according to rank, occupation, sex, and age; the other two-thirds belonged to the owner as profit and investment capital. Theoretically, the more the ex-slaves worked and the greater the output, the greater their collective portion of the crop revenues. Their only rights were those derived from their labor and confined to the plantation regimen. The August 29 emancipation proclamation issued by Sonthonax in the North province, followed by more a detailed document promulgated by Polverel in February 1794 for the West and South provinces, were the first of their kind in the history of slavery and abolition. While proclaiming universal emancipation, the decrees were regimented work codes that set norms for plantation labor. In essence, they granted a "plantation citizenship."[13]

The reason to maintain plantation agriculture was clear: France was at war in Europe and facing Spanish and British occupation forces in the colony. Without the labor of plantation workers to produce revenue-generating exports, France could not sustain the war effort in Europe or in the colony, let alone pay the salaries of their black compatriots who, as free French citizens, had joined the ranks of the French army to defend the Republic *and* general emancipation. Plantation workers were to consider themselves "soldiers-in-the-field"; their efforts, like those of their counterparts in the army, were necessary to the defense of revolutionary France who had sanctioned their freedom. The exigencies of the war economy dictated the social relations of production, land, and labor. Ironically, the war economy set the terms and conditions of freedom.

At this point, Toussaint Louverture was still allied with Spain and rebel leaders Jean-François and Biassou, while fighting for general emancipation in his own name. He remained cautious about Sonthonax's emancipation proclamation; normally only kings or other sovereigns had the power to abolish slavery. Decreed by a commissioner, emancipation might be revoked in the ever-changing course of events in France. Only after news arrived in early May 1794 of the National Convention's law of February 4 abolishing slavery did Toussaint break with his Spanish allies and join the French republican army. From then until the final evacuation of the British troops in 1798, on terms he personally negotiated as commander-in-chief of the French army in Saint-Domingue and lieutenant-governor of the colony, Toussaint rose to become the foremost figure—militarily and politically—in determining the direction and destiny of the colony. He worked to create a prosperous, self-governing territory of France, under sovereign *black* rule.

Over time, he lost confidence in the conservative post-Jacobin government of the French Directory, responsible for reorganizing the colonies into overseas departments of the Republic, "one and indivisible," and for implementing universal citizenship and equality among former slaves. The year 1797 brought a resurgence of royalist and other proslavery factions, inside and outside the government; they took control of the legislature in spring elections and were pushing toward a restoration of the slave trade and the pre-1789 colonial regime.[14] Although these elements were purged in the republican coup d'état later that year, the Directory came close to suspending application of the French constitution of 1795, which guaranteed the abolition of slavery. Finally, in early 1798, the Directory sent a military, rather than a civil agent, General Marie-Théodore-Joseph Hédouville, to represent French republican authority in Saint Domingue. For his part, Toussaint began to build the foundations for Saint-Domingue's political autonomy and, ideally, economic conditions to take an emancipated black state into the Atlantic world of the still-slaveholding great powers. But *how*? With what powers and with what consequences? What kind of a society would it be? In the absence of metropolitan guarantees, how could such an entity—on its own amid revolution and international warfare—defend emancipation? Fundamental contradictions underlay any exercise of colonial sovereignty in a plantation society without slavery.

The Road to Independence

Toussaint's state-in-the-making revolved around a number of overriding and interlocking objectives.[15] The first and most crucial was to defend general emancipation, and to do so under black rule. In the uncertain world of colonial slavery and Atlantic imperialism—not to mention the uncertainties of the French Revolution—Toussaint needed a strong army; and for this he needed the revival of exports and accumulation of foreign reserves to sustain his emerging state and the military. The path he chose toward economic recovery was built on the ruins of the pre-1789 plantation export regime, and on the post-1793 emancipationist labor regimes founded by the French civil commissioners.

To restore the colony's war-torn economy, which by 1795 left Saint Domingue's exports virtually nonexistent,[16] Toussaint reinforced, rather than reformed, the existing agrarian structure. To deter individual initiatives toward a model of production based on independent smallholding and local markets, which might undermine his regime, he placed plantation laborers under military rather than civil administration. Commercial prosperity, under slavery or freedom, came only from agricultural exports. Large-scale agriculture and plantation labor were tied to international commerce, and without commerce Toussaint could never hope to achieve his ultimate objective—a solid and sovereign black state. For Saint Domingue to reenter the commercial Atlantic as an international player, Toussaint needed free markets and open trade relations, notably with neutral countries like the United States. Inevitably this would bring him into the tangled world of international diplomacy and the vortex of Atlantic colonialism. To consolidate his own government and preserve the freedom of his people, he would need to deal directly with two major powers, Great Britain and France, and an emerging nation, the United States—each motivated by self-interest.

At the time of the British evacuation in August 1798, Toussaint sought to maximize his options and turn to advantage the terms of Britain's military troop withdrawal. He entered direct negotiations with General Maitland and, overriding France's legally constituted agent, General Hédouville, signed a mutually expedient convention by which Great Britain was guaranteed *protected and exclusive* trading relations with Saint Domingue.[17] In exchange, Great Britain would guarantee the colony's security by promising not to attack Saint Domingue for the remainder of the war with France in Europe, or to intervene in its internal affairs. For his part, Toussaint promised the same with regard to Jamaica, which meant that he would not try to export emancipation beyond Saint Domingue. The convention was a hermetic trade agreement with an enemy of France. By acting in his own name, without consulting—and without the consent of—any higher French authority, Toussaint assumed powers of head of state. He exercised a function normally reserved to sovereign states, negotiating international treaties.

Later that year, Toussaint took another step to expand Saint Domingue's commerce, this time with the United States. On November 6, 1798, he dispatched a letter to President John Adams proposing to reopen trade between the two states. Toussaint aimed to circumvent the interruption of commerce with U.S. merchants that had resulted from the diplomatic hostilities between the United States and France in their Quasi-War against each other's shipping.[18] He would legalize and expand trade that, at the time, was conducted clandestinely. For the young North American nation, the West Indies trade was crucial to commercial development; by now U.S. trade with Saint Domingue ranked second in importance only to that with Great Britain.[19] The foreign policy of the Adams administration reflected these commercial goals, even as the cautious opening to diplomatic relations with a nominally sovereign black state exposed the contradictions embedded in early U.S. attitudes toward slavery, emancipation, and race.

Renewed commerce, of course, depended on Saint Domingue's capacity to produce and export plantation crops to pay for foodstuffs, arms, and other basic goods with which to equip the army. In the first of a series of proclamations relating to land and labor resources, issued on November 15, 1798, Toussaint began to reorganize and reinforce the plantation structure by placing it under the supervision of the military. In the process, he began transforming the civil basis of the society into a military one. Toussaint specifically charged his lieutenants, the military police, and local army commanders with enforcing work discipline and the overall submission of the plantation laborers, and with forcing those who had abandoned their estates for opportunities on other plantations or in the towns, to return to those to which they belonged.[20] He also began leasing out plantations that had been sequestered by the state to leading generals and other high officers of his army. As leaseholders, they became new proprietors; for plantation laborers, they became new masters.[21]

On November 17, 1798, Toussaint issued another ordinance seeking to redress the colony's balance of trade, offset the drainage of colonial currency, and increase government revenues. He lamented: "The small volume of trade [at present] with the Americans and the Danish tends only to drain the colony of its specie. These foreign traders bring mostly luxury goods and very few staples, of which the colony is constantly deprived to meet its basic needs."[22]

The "mercantilist maneuver," as Toussaint called it, had three detrimental effects: maintaining the high cost of basic staples by reducing supplies, creating scarcity and increasing unmet demand; draining the colony of specie to pay for costly luxury goods; and, in prevailing wartime conditions, driving down prices of exports by limiting outlets for plantation production. In response, Toussaint restricted the landing of luxury goods to one-third of a ship's cargo, prohibited the export of colonial specie in any form and, to counter fraud and corruption, tightened administrative controls over customs and treasury officials.[23] As important as these measures were to improving government finances, and strengthening his government and army, without a normalization and expansion of trade with neutral powers like the United States, the reforms remained insufficient.

On February 9, 1799, Congress passed and President Adams signed into law "Toussaint's Clause," exempting Saint Domingue from the U.S. embargo on trade with France in the Quasi-War between the two countries, reopening trade with the colony. Adams appointed Edward Stevens as consul-general to Saint Domingue, a title implying official recognition of an independent Saint Domingue. For Stevens, the reopening of trade with Toussaint was good policy and an absolute necessity for the U.S. merchant houses doing business clandestinely since the initial American embargo on French ports. He urged a parallel agreement with Great Britain "in the interests of America." For Maitland on the British side, trade with Saint Domingue, if well-regulated and kept within a U.S.–Great Britain–Saint Domingue triangle, would economically benefit Britain, strike a blow at French commerce, and also isolate Saint Domingue, preventing the spread of emancipation in the Caribbean or the southern United States. A three-way alliance, known as "Heads of Regulation," was signed on

June 13, 1799. It expanded the earlier Louverture-Maitland agreement to open direct trade in Saint Domingue to both British and American shipping.[24]

Yet the arrangement had significant drawbacks for Toussaint. It prohibited Saint Domingue from building a merchant marine or navy by restricting the size of her ships to fifty tons and their navigation to five leagues from the northern coastline. While Toussaint had broadened his trading partners and widened his markets, Anglo-American commerce with Saint Domingue, including the carrying of the plantation exports Toussaint promoted, would belong exclusively to British and U.S. ships. However, the agreement did permit Toussaint to pursue another objective: eliminating his political rival, André Rigaud, military commander of the South and leader of the colony's former free-colored elite. Anticipating the impending civil war between them, Toussaint insisted that the ports of the South be excluded from the new trade agreement to prevent Rigaud from supplying his army and ensure his defeat.

The United States wanted to ensure Toussaint's victory over his rival; they saw him as the stronger of the two protagonists and one who, "were his power uncontrolled, would exercise it in protecting commerce, encouraging agriculture and establishing useful regulations for the internal government of the colony." Should he be unsuccessful, Stevens wrote, "all the arrangements we have made respecting commerce must fall to the ground. The most solemn treaty would have little weight with a man of Rigaud's capricious and tyrannical temperament."[25] Furthermore, in the view of the United States and the British, Toussaint was seeking to separate himself from French authority. As soon as Rigaud was defeated and the last French civil commissioner sent off, Stevens anticipated that Toussaint would declare the colony independent.[26] From the U.S. point of view, if *Toussaint* declared independence, the United States would bear no responsibility and could carry on trade with Saint Domingue without having to extend official diplomatic recognition, and thus contravene French sovereignty. Free trade with Toussaint was commercially beneficial, having Toussaint declare independence would be diplomatically pragmatic, and, so far as any potential threat to slavery, a safe bet. Secretary of State Timothy Pickering added that, for the time being, "and perhaps for a much longer period," Saint Domingue's foremost needs were military.[27] The population of Saint Domingue would be tied to agriculture; the Heads of Regulation ensured that Saint Domingue would never have a navy or merchant marine posing a threat to U.S. commerce.

With his final victory over Rigaud in August 1800, Toussaint could have declared independence. We may never know whether he was on the verge of doing so, but Toussaint knew he was dealing with France's enemies. He had defied French authority in the colony, while maintaining deferential relations with the metropolis; he kept British and U.S diplomats guessing about the consequences and ramifications of Saint Domingue independence. Toussaint had entered the world of nation-states and plunged into the vortex of imperialist politics; he was no dupe to the ultimate aims of British American commercial interests, and less so to those of British imperialism. Had he broken ties definitively with France in 1799 or 1800, Saint Domingue would have been little more than a protectorate of the United States and Great Britain, a pawn serving Anglo-American commerce and British imperialism. Neither the United States nor Britain encouraged Saint Domingue independence on abolitionist principles or to further black self-determination. Their only goal was to take the colony from France and further their own commerce. They accepted slave emancipation on the island of Saint Domingue alone, because there was nothing they could do about it. They hoped to contain in Saint Domingue the dangers of a black state born of slave revolt. To preserve his own and Saint Domingue's de facto independence, Toussaint remained deferential to France. As long as it maintained the abolition of slavery, he stopped just short of breaking formal ties with the metropolis.

Within the colony he reigned supreme. After defeating Rigaud in the civil war, Toussaint had arranged for his exile to France, eliminating any further challenge to his authority in Saint Domingue. To consolidate these gains, he turned to incorporating the adjacent Spanish colony of Santo Domingo (ceded to France in 1795 by the Treaty of Basel, but never formally occupied). In early January 1801, defying metropolitan prohibitions, he sent an expedition to place the Spanish territory under military occupation in the name of France. He thus extended his military and political authority over the entire island. At the same time, he placed the remaining French commissioner, Philippe Roume, under house arrest for refusing to authorize the expedition. Finally, Toussaint created a commission to draft a constitution, promulgated on July 8, 1801, conferring political sovereignty (although not formal independence) over all of Hispaniola and absolute power on himself as governor-for-life.

The constitution was not a declaration of independence. Toussaint was careful to recognize that Saint Domingue was still French and to reiterate the permanent abolition of slavery: "There cannot be any slaves on this territory; servitude here is forever abolished. All men are born, live and die here, free and French." Hence all individuals were equal before the law, which would be applied without distinction of color. Toussaint's constitution established the legal foundations for a multiracial egalitarian society. He, not France, set the terms by which Saint Domingue would be governed.

Napoleon Bonaparte had already ended the status of the colonies as overseas departments of France, previously conferred under the Directory's Constitution of 1795. Now, according to Article 91 of his new constitution of 1799, the colonies would be subject to "special laws" that addressed the specific needs of each colony. In his proclamation of December 25, 1799, to the "citizens of Saint Domingue," but directed primarily at Toussaint Louverture, at the time still engaged in the civil war against Rigaud, Bonaparte announced that the Directory's Constitution of 1795 had been replaced by a new constitutional pact "aimed at strengthening liberty," Article 91 of which concerned the colonies. Given differences in climate, customs, soil, agriculture, and types of production from those in France, the inhabitants of the colonies could not be governed by the same laws as those in the metropole. Still, it proclaimed the principles of liberty and equality for blacks to be inviolable: "Remember, brave Negroes, that only the French people recognize your freedom and the equality of your rights."[28]

Lurking in all the deflecting rhetoric, the law of February 4, 1794, which abolished slavery and extended universal citizenship to all inhabitants of the French Republic, no longer had constitutional validity. For Toussaint, the potential for a restoration of slavery became manifest. There was little doubt in his mind that Bonaparte's "special laws" would strike a terrible blow to the legal foundation of freedom and lead to a very uncertain future.

In the absence of French constitutional law, Toussaint aimed to provide clear, decisive, and sovereign black leadership for Saint Domingue, on his own terms and with his own constitution. Yet beyond the constitutional guarantees of personal security, the inviolability of domicile, the sanctity of private property, the right to be lawfully charged with an offense before arrest, the right to a trial in court, and the right of petition—"especially to the governor"—the structures Toussaint set to govern the colony and direct the economy were military.[29]

All previous laws and ordinances on agriculture and the policing of the plantation workforces were constitutionalized, as was the leasing of sequestered or abandoned estates to army generals and other high-ranking officers. Former white colonists wishing to return and take possession of their properties were encouraged. To reinforce the plantation complex and preclude the rise of a class of smallholding peasants, Toussaint passed legislation prohibiting the purchase of land under 50 *carreaux* (approximately 165 acres). Any worker or association of workers hoping to buy a few carreaux were barred. To ensure the growth of the plantation workforce and the increase of agricultural output, Toussaint's constitution gave him power to import additional laborers (presumably by purchasing them through the slave trade and then freeing them), a measure that, ironically, gave rise to rumors in the North that Toussaint intended to restore slavery. Such rumors, along with the harsh restrictions and ubiquitous presence of the military, prompted widespread popular revolt against his regime in October, only three months after the promulgation of his constitution. It was inspired by Toussaint's nephew, General Moïse; as agricultural inspector for the North he opposed the repressive measures that deprived workers of personal freedom. Following the revolt, which cost the lives of hundreds of white colonists, Toussaint ordered Moïse arrested and quickly had him tried and executed. He then enacted new measures of control requiring district military commanders to submit censuses of all farmworkers on the plantations under their jurisdiction. Anyone not a farmworker had to carry a passport proving his vocation or trade, or be arrested and sent to the fields. Any residential, occupational, or social mobility to which a farmworker might aspire was precluded; they were tied to the plantations.

Toussaint made a clear distinction between freedom as the abolition of chattel slavery (insisting that no person could be property of another), and freedom as the right of former slaves to exercise individual liberties. The latter, if allowed to plantation laborers, would, he believed, inevitably lead to widespread vagrancy and idleness, a lack of moral and civic virtues, and of parental responsibility in educating youth. Above all, it would result in the refusal to work on plantations for the profit of others, undermining the island's economic prosperity. He formalized the distinction in his constitution: there could be no slaves in Saint Domingue—all men are born, live and die free and French; but, "the colony being essentially agricultural, [it] can suffer no loss or interruption of production,"[30] lest it lead to economic ruin and leave the colony prey to slaveholding colonialist powers. Each plantation should therefore be run as a factory, with a permanent concentration of workers assembled as one family under the paternalistic authority of an owner or manager, and the absolute authority of the military. To defend slave emancipation, Toussaint effectively replaced civil society with a militarized state, making any distinction between state and society, or "the state and the nation," all but invisible, leaving the mass of the agrarian citizenry constitutionally and politically alienated.

Toussaint did achieve a limited economic recovery. Export figures for 1801–1802, at the height of his governance, are revealing. Compared with figures for 1795, when the colony exported almost nothing, those for 1801–1802 show a significant increase in coffee and cotton exports, and a lesser rise in sugar. In 1795, sugar exports, the economic lifeblood of the plantation system, were but 1.2 percent of the levels of 1789; by 1801 they had risen to 13 percent of the earlier peak, a limited growth that documented encouraging results from the opening of Anglo-American trade and the efficacy of Toussaint's labor regime, despite freed slaves resistance to the most difficult of labors. In 1795, coffee, a crop requiring far less capital investment than sugar, had dropped to 2.8 percent of the prerevolutionary peak—then rose to 57 percent by 1801. Evidently, freed slaves profited from coffee, but only when they received their entitled wages from coffee sales and only through coerced labor conditions. Cotton exports experienced a fall to only 0.7 percent of preconflict levels in 1795—by 1801 they rose to 35 percent of their 1789 levels. Certainly this was a crop the British would buy if production could increase. Only indigo, concentrated in the South, experienced a slight decline between 1795 and 1801, when British occupation and civil war disrupted production. In 1802, Saint Domingue's exports were even more favorable, with sugar reaching 38 percent, cotton 58 percent, coffee holding near 45 percent, and indigo up to 4 percent of 1789 levels.[31] The recovery enabled Toussaint to build reserve funds to strengthen the army that accounted for 60 percent of government expenditures in 1801.[32]

Toussaint had achieved a tenuous sovereignty in a world of imperial rivalry and wars, and in which there was no guarantee that slave emancipation would survive. Many events threatened to undermine the project of black self-determination. On September 30, 1800, barely two months after his victory over Rigaud, the Treaty of Mortefontaine was signed in Paris ending the Quasi-War between the United States and France, and terminating Toussaint's trade alliance with the United States. The next day, on October 1, the Treaty of San Ildelfonso confirmed the transfer of Louisiana from Spain to France; then the presidential victory of Thomas Jefferson over John Adams in early 1801 again brought into question the island's favored trade relations with the United States. The final thunderbolt came with the signing of the Amiens peace preliminaries between France and Great Britain in October 1801, allowing Bonaparte to reorganize and redeploy French troops for a military expedition to Saint Domingue, led by his brother-in-law, General Charles Victor-Emmanuel Leclerc.

With Napoleon in power and Louisiana in French hands, Saint Domingue was destined to become the cornerstone of a revived French empire extending up the Mississippi Valley. The plan, however, required a French victory over the emancipated blacks of Saint Domingue and a restoration of slavery there. For this, Bonaparte needed the support of the United States, now under

Thomas Jefferson, who had let it be known to Bonaparte that he would support a French expedition against Saint Domingue to remove Toussaint and restore the colonial regime.

However, when he realized that a French victory in Saint Domingue would lead to an expedition to occupy Louisiana, threatening the security and potential of the young republic, he withdrew support. Jefferson needed a victory by emancipated Haitians over Bonaparte's army to render Louisiana worthless to France and valuable to the United States. In a perverse irony, the Haitian victory over Bonaparte contributed to the maintenance and expansion of slavery in the United States, its total embargo of Haiti in 1806, and nonrecognition of Haiti's independence by the United States for another fifty-six years.

When Bonaparte's army landed on February 2, 1802, Toussaint's constitution became irrelevant. The terms of Haitian independence were set not by Toussaint Louverture, but by Napoleon's attempt to restore slavery. After three months of sustained resistance to Leclerc's army under the command of Toussaint's closest and most loyal generals, notably Christophe and Maurepas in the North and Dessalines in the West, and with heavy losses on both sides, Leclerc offered Toussaint a deal in early May—amnesty for the emancipator and his generals, personal asylum at a place of his choosing within the colony, and the maintenance of general emancipation.[33] At the same time, Christophe asked permission from Toussaint for a conference with Leclerc, after which he defected with over fifteen hundred colonial troops and nearly five thousand armed workers. Two days later, Toussaint accepted Leclerc's offer of asylum, leaving Dessalines militarily isolated and with little recourse but to submit in turn. In June, Leclerc summoned Toussaint to a meeting. Having laid a trap, he had him arrested, bound as a criminal, and deported to France, where he died in isolation on April 7, 1803, at Fort de Joux prison.

When news arrived that summer that slavery had been restored in Guadeloupe, the Haitian masses understood that their fate and their freedom no longer lay in the hands of the leaders now fighting in Leclerc's army. Only their own capacity to mobilize in mass insurgency, maintain individual and collective networks of resistance, to fight to the end—in short, to live free or die— could keep them free. By October, the forces of popular insurgency had reached a peak throughout the colony in a total war against slavery—despite the brutal campaigns by Dessalines and the other generals under Leclerc's orders to harass and suppress them and their chosen leaders, now mostly of African origin.

Facing an unsustainable impasse and with the mass of the population in rebellion, Dessalines and the southern mulatto general, Alexandre Pétion, deserted Leclerc to join forces and take over the direction of the independence struggle, in the process liquidating the popular revolutionary leaders who refused to submit to their authority—once again pitting the military (and ultimately the national) leadership against the masses. Yet it was the instinctive self-mobilization of the masses that rendered the defection of the generals militarily and politically feasible. As Toussaint's intrepid second in command, it was Jean-Jacques Dessalines, now commander-in-chief, who would lead the indigenous army to independence.[34]

With independence, slavery was forever abolished. The plantation economy that had made Saint Domingue the most valuable colony on the Atlantic—that drove the slave trade to new heights and flooded European markets with slave-made sugar and coffee, guaranteeing French domination of both markets— also collapsed. In less than a decade, the parallel but interlinked Spanish North American silver economy of Bajío would also collapse under pressures of popular insurgency in parallel movement toward peasant holdings and household crop production. For Haitians, however, individual acquisition of land was not the *immediate* outcome of independence; it took over two decades before the transition to an economy of household production, local markets, and, at best, of coffee cultivation for limited exports, was completed.

What Haiti's independence in 1804 did provide was the opening for other slaveholding regions, notably Cuba and Brazil, to take her place sending slave-made sugar and coffee into changing world of early nineteenth-century industrial capitalism. Confronting that world, Haiti needed to constitute and defend itself as a state, creating the institutions, revenues, and military power to sustain itself in a hostile world that would not acknowledge its legitimacy.

A Nation Divided

On January 1, 1804, Haiti defiantly proclaimed its existence to the world as a nation whose people, in conquering their liberty, had avenged the oppressed of the New World. In a more than symbolic gesture, Hayti, the original Taino name for the island, replaced the French colonial name, Saint Domingue.

Haiti's struggle to justify, define, and defend its existence, and to create a unique national identity, can be understood by examining key principles of its foundational national constitution, written and promulgated in 1805 under the regime of Dessalines. In its preamble, as Sybille Fischer demonstrates, the universalism of Haiti's existence as a free black nation is established by appealing to the Supreme Being, "before whom all mortals are equal" but whose power is revealed only through human diversity and difference among the peoples of the earth;[35] and to nature—in a disavowal of the centuries-long exclusion of Africans and those of African descent as "unworthy children." Equality, to be universal, would have to encompass racial equality, something Haiti could only achieve through the violent negation of slavery and of its perpetrators, and through a war for independence that conferred upon the new nation a historically self-determined existence. Haiti might stand as a pariah in "Western history," but it also broke the Enlightenment out of its racist Eurocentric constraints.

A close examination of some of the seminal articles of Haiti's first constitution reveals far more than lofty statements of intent. As Fischer suggests, they constitutionally historicize Haiti's identity as a black nation—the first of its kind—having overthrown a colonial past grounded in racial slavery. This explains why the 1805 Constitution stipulates that "no white man, regardless of his nationality, may set foot in this territory as a master or a landowner, nor will he ever be able to acquire any property";[36] but that white women and their children who are "naturalized as Haitian citizens," as well as the Germans and Poles (who had deserted Napoleon's army to fight alongside the blacks for Haiti's independence), would be exempt; and that "because all distinctions of color among children of the same family must necessarily cease, all Haitians will henceforth be known generically as black [noir]."[37] Although this stipulation may at first glance appear to be racial, it must be understood in light of Haiti's rejection of the colonial taxonomies that created artificial categories of color and corresponding categories of legal and social status. "Black" in the new context of Haitian independence became a political category of citizenship and national identity.[38]

Given the socioeconomic and ethnic diversity of Haiti's population, and the political, social, and cultural aspirations of each group, one may question the extent that such principles were put into practice. As with the 1812 (liberal) Constitution in Spain and in the Spanish American independence movements, as Roberto Breña points out in his essay, it is important to distinguish between lofty constitutional principles and sociopolitical practice. Contingencies of revolution and insurgency, the lack of experience of early independence leaders, the militarization of politics and selective or manipulative application of citizenship rights by those in power, or, as Jordana Dym demonstrates in her essay on Guatemala, cultural forces of regional identity that compete with national identity, all tended to short-circuit the universal application of constitutional aspirations. And Spanish liberalism had centuries of intellectual and institutional tradition to draw on in elaborating the 1812 Constitution. For Haiti, the realities of citizenship were defined on the ground by the legacies of its colonial past, particularly with respect to the peasantry. Constitutional aspirations matter; in young nations, power struggles may matter more.

In defining and defending the nation under Haiti's first postindependence regimes of Jean-Jacques Dessalines (1804–1806) and Henri Christophe (1807–1820) in the North, the universalism of the revolution's liberating aspirations and the popular nationalism of the war of independence gave way to the militarism and social inequalities that characterized the last colonial regime under Toussaint, and to power struggles among and between the new country's elites. What emerged from independence was a military state that dominated rather than governed its citizenry, the vast majority of whom were permanently excluded from participation in nation building. With independence, all lands of the former French colonists were taken into the national domain (as *biens nationaux*), making the state—a military state—the primary property owner in the country (and the biggest landowner of the entire Caribbean). The new militarized state effectively replaced the colonial master class to rule the agrarian masses and "recolonized" the labor force.[39] To restore exports and reinforce military capacities in the fledgling nation, both Dessalines and Christophe, who themselves had leased numerous plantations under Toussaint's regime, unquestioningly maintained the plantation system of land and labor. The agrarian structure of their regimes was, in many ways, a reinforced extension of that codified and constitutionalized by Toussaint, relying on the suppression of popular sovereignty, the denial of individual liberties, and the prohibition of independent peasant smallholding—the only way Haiti's agrarian laborers could organize their lives freely. In constructing an indigenous black state to defend antislavery, civil society was truncated. What emerged was not a coherent nation, but a state with a political and military elite that dominated society.

Plantation workers were not the only alienated element of the new Haitian state under Dessalines, who exacerbated the recurrent "color question" that had so often plagued Haiti's colonial past and led to civil war between Toussaint Louverture and André Rigaud in the revolutionary period. Since all properties formerly belonging to the French had been confiscated either during the revolution, by decree after 1803, or by the 1805 constitutional prohibition of white property ownership, the only potential private landowners were the former free coloreds, living primarily in the South and West. Fearing that white planters might try to entrust properties to their mulatto offspring as they fled the colony in 1803–1804, hoping to reclaim them later, Dessalines demanded verification of all transfers of land title after 1803; any land claimed by mulattoes but previously held by whites was confiscated by the state and their claims rendered null and void. Only mulattoes who could prove ownership *in their own name* and *prior* to 1803 were allowed to retain their holdings.[40]

Dessaliness land policy, as much antimulatto as antiwhite or anti-French, combined with his autocratic rule and imperial pretensions (crowning himself emperor in 1805), led to his assassination on October 17, 1806. His short-lived regime, however, was symptomatic of a deeper crisis that would exacerbate tensions and open power struggles between the country's two emergent elites over control of constitutional processes and the political and economic direction of the country. The constitutional crisis that followed the death of Dessalines led the new nation into a second civil war and a split into two political entities, the Kingdom of Haiti under Henri Christophe in the North (1807–1820) and the Republic of Haiti under Alexandre Pétion (1807–1818) in the South. As in every new American country that faced economic collapse, each Haitian leader had to confront fundamental questions of state formation: what *kind* of government, what *kind* of economy—and in the case of Haiti, what *kind* of social and labor relations should replace those that prevailed under slavery, while maintaining plantation production and commodity exports. Military defense, international relations, as well as the role of the state vis-à-vis the citizenry were all ridden with new and irreconcilable contradictions.

For the former slave majority living on the land under Christophe, there were no free choices. The land was property of the state; plantations were given in five-year leases to high-ranking army officers or members of a new "nobility"; they were worked by former slaves who preferred to be independent peasant farmers. Workers were thus tied to estates in a condition of regimented plantation labor, in perpetuity, even though they received a quarter of the profits, exempt from taxes paid by the estate holder on the crops produced. Other rights and obligations of farmworkers and estate holders were codified in Christophe's Code Henry, issued in 1811.[41] Christophe tried to convince workers cultivating cash crops for export that the harder they worked and more they produced, the greater the value of their share of the profits, and thus the greater their own well-being. Such incentives proved of little avail, as workers increasingly left plantations, either taking to the hills as "maroon" peasants or squatters, or, in the final years of his regime, migrating to live under the more tolerant regime of Pétion in the South, where government policies eventually placed land within reach of even the poorest. In the northwestern parishes of Gros Morne and Port-de-Paix, disaffected farmworkers turned to armed uprisings against Christophe's coercive plantation regime.[42]

Beside their entrenched opposition to plantation labor—painfully reminiscent of slavery—other factors also contributed to workers' rejection of the plantation model. Sugar never regained its place in Haiti's export economy, and what little sugar was produced for export could not compete with the exports of Cuba, well on its way to dominating Atlantic sugar markets by opening new lands worked by newly imported slaves. For Haiti, only coffee held its own as a major export, and it was vulnerable to price fluctuations and stiff competition from Brazil, also opening new lands with new slaves. For the Haitian workers under Christophe's regime, vulnerability to unpredictable market conditions left their quarter shares uncertain and subject to sudden decline. Such hardship reinforced the desire for a piece of land to cultivate food crops for their families and to fashion their own lives. It was a situation Christophe only addressed belatedly, in 1819, the final year of his reign; and even then his decision to parcel out portions of government estates served only the military, with soldiers and officers receiving grants according to rank: 20 carreaux (approximately 66 acres) for a colonel and 1 carreau (or 3.3 acres) for a soldier.[43]

Yet Christophe found fair success in organizing his kingdom and creating a functioning state. The economy performed fairly well despite the adverse circumstances under which he tried to reintegrate the country into Atlantic commerce. By placing the country on the gold and silver standard for trade with foreign merchants, notably those of Great Britain and neutral countries such as the United States, he ensured that exports held at sustainable levels. He raised annual averages of $3 to $3.5 million in government revenue, and on his death in 1820 left a surplus of $6 million.[44] Overall, the treasury was fiscally sound, allowing Christophe to begin financing a national education project. Most contemporary observers of Haiti confirmed the importance Christophe placed on education; as head of state (and illiterate) he understood its importance to any emerging nation. Although the primary beneficiaries were children and young adults of the upper classes and the military, Christophe's efforts remain noteworthy in a country then (and still) overwhelmingly illiterate. He understood the need for educated individuals to run the public administration and state bureaucracy, especially for the northern kingdom of Haiti with a population composed almost exclusively of ex-slaves and former free blacks, and where educated mulattoes were few. His antipathy toward the latter was notorious. Instead, he looked to Great Britain, where abolitionists supported his educational projects, and to Prussia, whose educational system was among the most progressive in Western Europe at the time.[45]

Christophe's kingdom was, to borrow an apt expression, "oddly modern"[46]—a self-proclaimed monarchy with an invented nobility. That Christophe opted to rule as a king, rather than a republican president, is understandable. In 1811, when he proclaimed his regime a monarchy, nearly all of the European powers were monarchical; as no country had recognized Haiti's independence, a monarchy might provide Christophe's government with some legitimacy and a regal aura for himself as head of state. Royal absolutism and a hereditary monarchy, as opposed to constitutional republicanism, where rights and invested powers could be contested, also short-circuited political opposition, whether from the masses below or the ranks of educated elite. It is also possible that Christophe presumed an affinity among his African-born subjects for kingship.[47] Christophe's monarchy was by no means anachronistic for the time; at least two other new Latin American countries, Mexico briefly in 1821–1822, and Brazil from 1822 to 1889, began as monarchies. For Brazil, monarchy provided conditions for long-term political consolidation and the maintenance of slavery to 1888. In Haiti, the death of Christophe in 1820 brought an end to the monarchical regime in which the state dominated the lives of plantation laborers struggling to acquire land of their own, hoping to reshape them and forge their own identity. Its end did not resolve the fundamental problems of citizenship and nationhood—which would plague so much of the Americas long into the nineteenth century.

Alternative Landholding Policies and the Peasant Economy
While Christophe's monarchy struggled to rule and maintain the plantation system in the North, in the South, the republican regime of mulatto president, Alexandre Pétion, opened the way for alternatives to large-scale plantations and coerced labor. After early and largely futile attempts to restore the plantations by adjusting tariff and tax policies on sugar and coffee, and by subsidizing them in times of declining market prices during his first two years in power, Pétion began a policy of land distribution that, by 1817, had led to the breakup and transfer of some four hundred thousand acres of land from the national domain to roughly ten thousand peasant recipients.[48] His turn to distribution reflected both an understanding of the need to address the goals of the majority and the needs of the state. First, Pétion recognized that those who had fought in the war of independence deserved to be rewarded with land in recognition of their military service to the nation (and in lieu of back wages): noncommissioned soldiers and officers received 5 carreaux (16.5 acres) each; former commissioned officers received larger grants according to rank. By 1814 he was distributing land taken from large coffee estates to active members of the military, to civil servants, hospital employees, petty administrative officials, and influential politicians.[49] By 1817 properties from the national domain were for sale at affordable prices, enabling thousands of others to become property owners.[50] Pétion believed that if peasant families owned their land they would be motivated to cultivate it and produce crops not only for their families and local markets, but

also for export. That was possible in the South, where coffee easily meshed with subsistence production, facilitating a family-based mix of production for consumption and trade. And with a stake in landholding, Pétion believed that ex-slaves become peasants would gain a stake in society: civic virtue, family values, and personal and civic responsibility would all be promoted—while government would be left to predominantly light-skinned, educated elites.

Pétion's recognition of the needs and potential of his citizens merged with other, often more pressing concerns. His government faced a serious fiscal crisis when he took office in 1807 and his early attempts at restoring the plantation economy during his first two years were dismal failures. By parceling out portions of the national domain beginning in 1810, Pétion aimed to create a mixed economy in which state revenues derived from taxes on the production of a wider and more numerous base of independent peasant landowners cultivating coffee for exports, in addition to food crops for domestic or family consumption—while remaining large estates might continue to produce for export, yet with diminishing returns.

At the southwestern extremity of the island in the region of Grand Anse, a large independent maroon community of armed peasants lived on the periphery of Pétion's emerging republic. Their leader, Jean-Baptiste Goman, had been a popular insurrectionary slave leader from the early days of the revolution and an important figure in sustaining the popular resistance forces against the French army during the war of independence. Refusing to submit to Dessalines when the indigenous army entered the South, Goman retreated into the mountains of Grand Anse, where by 1807 he led an armed peasant state numbering close to three thousand men, women, and children. Their fierce resistance to Pétion's government and crushing defeat of his troops in 1813 likely influenced the latter's agrarian policies. To undermine the attraction that the existence of Goman's armed landed community provided, and to consolidate national unity, in 1814–1815 Pétion began to implement measures to ameliorate the socioeconomic conditions of workers and accelerate the pace of land distribution.[51] Over time, Pétion's land distribution policies created a diversified peasantry, with a few rich large holders, others middle-sized, and many very small landowning peasants producing alongside tenants and sharecroppers (*de moitié* workers) on the larger estates. There remained countless landless peasants, many squatting in outlying regions, occupying land in their family name and cultivating it illegally, others working for wages as day laborers.[52]

Under Pétion and his successor Jean-Pierre Boyer (1818–1843) popular peasant demands for land were ultimately satisfied. Were the same peasants simultaneously disempowered politically at the hands of a ruling mulatto oligarchy

FIGURE 4.2. Market women in nineteenth-century Haiti.
Courtesy Archives CIDIHCA (Centre International de Documentation et
d'Information Hatienne, Caraibeenne, y Afro—Canadienne)

that progressively abandoned landholding to take control of the more lucrative
sectors of politics, commerce, and the state? Did they ensure that the peasants,
in the majority black, African-born and illiterate, would become politically ap-
athetic, inactive, and self-isolated? Scholars long maintained that the parceling
of land resulted in an "egalitarian poverty"—the root cause of Haiti's economic
stagnation during the nineteenth and twentieth centuries.[53]

Recent studies of the early nineteenth-century Haitian peasant economy
and society now challenge the prevalence of peasant apathy and political withdrawal.[54] Postindependence peasant struggles for democratization (essentially
political in nature) did exist; universal citizenship and universal male suffrage,
effective at local levels, persisted under Pétion. Peasant proprietorship and
demands for political citizenship merged; landholding peasants *and* citizens
pressed to negotiate individual citizenship rights, including those of education,
in the spaces open to them. Most politics were local, sometimes pressing de-

mands in armed rebellions. As citizens of the republic they exercised the right to petition for, and receive, land grants under the reform program instituted by Pétion. They were left to their own initiatives to make the land productive, improve their lives, and seek inclusion as citizens of the nation.

Boyer made a final attempt to restore plantation production and exports in the Rural Code of 1826—adopted in an attempt to raise revenue to pay the indemnity debt promised to France in 1825 in exchange for recognition for Haitian independence. Popular pressure demanding land and resisting plantation labor proved too strong, and by midcentury the landholding structure had been permanently transformed. The plantation system was gone and a diversified landholding peasantry dominated production. Coffee—easily grown on peasant holding of diverse size—irreversibly replaced sugar—which demanded large plantations and forced labor—as Haiti's primary export. At the same time, the state and the military institutions that sustained it operated in an enclave, disengaged from Haiti's agrarian citizenry. Left to produce and pay taxes, the landed majority was left without channels of effective political participation or protest. The structural ties between the state and civil society that might have permitted ordinary individuals to make their voices heard in meaningful ways at the state or national level did not exist. And the role of the military in the day-to-day lives of the peasantry and in relations between the peasantry and the state reinforced the cleavage between the two. Haitian peasants were neither "traditionally conservative" nor "self-isolated" politically. They were blocked by the powers concentrated in the state from exercising greater agency and active political roles.[55]

Peasant empowerment was also constrained by the rise of merchants, often former planters who had turned from landholding to seek new wealth by ruling the links between peasant producers, international markets, and a state in search of revenues. They gained virtual monopolies over peasant marketing, setting prices for household surpluses. Property holding peasants found themselves vulnerable to the price-fixing practices of speculators and merchants (themselves indebted to foreign capital) and to direct and indirect taxation by the government, whose sole source of revenue came from taxation of peasant production, especially coffee.[56] The only other source of state revenue came from customs duties and export taxes, normally paid by wholesale merchants and middlemen, but inevitably passed on to coffee peasants by uniformly lowering the price paid them for their coffee.[57] Increasingly, the independent peasantry saw small gain in producing for export markets. They carried on out of dire needs to supplement their meager incomes from household crop cultivation while they bore the burden of state financing. The same state deprived peasants of any direct means to negotiate or ameliorate the terms of their inclusion in

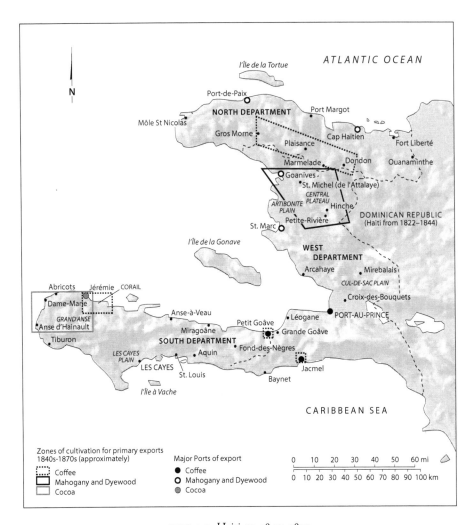

l'Île de la Tortue

Port-de-Paix

NORTH DEPARTMENT

Port Margot

Môle St Nicolas

Gros Morne

Cap Haïtien

Plaisance

Fort Liberté

Marmelade

Dondon

Ouanaminthe

Goanives

St. Michel (de l'Attalaye)

CENTRAL PLATEAU

ARTIBONITE PLAIN

Hinche

DOMINICAN REPUBLIC
(Haiti from 1822–1844)

Petite-Rivière

St. Marc

l'Île de la Gonave

WEST DEPARTMENT

Arcahaye

Mirebalais

CUL-DE-SAC PLAIN

Abricots   Jérémie   CORAIL

Croix-des-Bouquets

Dame-Marie

Anse-à-Veau

Léogane

PORT-AU-PRINCE

GRAND'ANSE

Anse d'Hainault

Petit Goâve

Miragoâne

Grande Goâve

Tiburon

SOUTH DEPARTMENT

Fond-des-Nègres

LES CAYES PLAIN

Aquin

LES CAYES

St. Louis

Jacmel

Baynet

l'Île à Vache

CARIBBEAN SEA

Zones of cultivation for primary exports
1840s-1870s (approximately)

Major Ports of export

0   10   20   30   40   50   60 mi

Coffee

● Coffee

0 10 20 30 40 50 60 70 80 90 100 km

Mahogany and Dyewood

○ Mahogany and Dyewood

Cocoa

◉ Cocoa

MAP 4.2. Haiti, ca. 1840–1870

a market economy. Their inclusion in civil society was similarly constrained. Meanwhile, former plantation owners shifted their pursuit of wealth from landholding (irrevocably in decline) to commerce, forging a working alliance for profit and power with the state.[58]

The one opportunity for a rapprochement of "state" and "nation" came in the context of the Liberal revolt of 1843 to overthrow the aging Boyer. A new generation of young Haitian elites, educated in France and eager to break the control of politics and the state held by Boyer in his twenty-five-year autocratic regime, aimed to implement basic principles of nineteenth-century liberal democracy, enabling them to play a defining role in the politics of the nation. In the face of Boyer's intransigence, the movement became a revolt that violently toppled Boyer's government. But in the elections held after they took power, and in implementing their constitutional reforms, the young liberals' professed principles of racial equality broke down. Insurrectionary peasants saw an opening to demand citizenship that would give tangible social, cultural, and economic, as well as political meaning to the rights of citizenship. They pressed a counterdiscourse of popular sovereignty and peasant democracy as experienced in their communities and peasant organizations, and practiced in daily lives. Their deception with the politics of the liberal elite was well founded; the traditional wisdom of the Kreyòl proverb "Constitusyon sé papié, bayonet sé fer" (constitutions are paper; bayonets are iron), well placed.

Jean-Jacques Accau, a former member of the rural police, led the "Army of Sufferers" in the Piquet peasant rebellion of 1844–1847. The focus was not the pursuit of individual peasant property, by then widely dispersed, but to claim the constitutional rights of social democracy. As primary spokesman, Accau argued for these with less emphasis on the distinctions of color that separated the educated light-skinned elites from the politically disempowered black peasantry and more along lines of class—of rich versus the poor. The Piquet insurrections forced open new public spaces in which rights were forcefully contested, in which political citizenship, the state, and the nation could have been redefined, and from which a new social contract might have emerged to encompass the legitimate claims of the *peuple souffrant* to integrated rights of citizenship including education, political empowerment, and social and economic justice.

By 1847, the insurrections were suppressed. An opportunity for fundamental change and national consolidation was lost as the liberal mulatto elites turned to a *politique de doublure*; a succession of black "front" presidents would be manipulated to serve the financial and commercial interests of the powerful few, maintaining the latter's indirect domination of the state. Haiti's peasantry, as Mimi Sheller plainly put it, was "ready for democracy from before the first day of emancipation, but democracy was not ready for them."[59] National consolidation never occurred as the state continued to function, when it functioned at all, as a self-contained entity which parasitically exploited the peasantry to sustain itself.

PARADOXICALLY, HAITI'S FIRST REGIMES (except Dessalines's) proved relatively durable, perhaps because the Haitian majority of ex-slaves did gain two key goals of their revolution: first and most immediately emancipation, more slowly but in time solidly access to land to consolidate lives focused on family sustenance. Simultaneously, the nation was politically isolated, and while gaining some trade and revenues from coffee, never joined the Latin American countries that in the later nineteenth century stabilized by producing commodities to sustain the industrializing countries of Europe.

Throughout, Haiti stood as a beacon of freedom to the oppressed, offering asylum and, after one year of residence, naturalization as a Haitian citizen to any person of African or Indian descent who entered Haiti, regardless of their place of birth.[60] In 1815, at a critical moment in the Spanish American wars of independence, Haitian president Alexandre Pétion provided asylum, monetary and military aid, and Haitian troops to a defeated Simón Bolívar, allowing him to continue to fight and eventually succeed in his struggle for South American liberation. He asked only that Bolívar pledge to abolish slavery in the territories he liberated.[61] A decade later, in preparatory talks for the hemispheric Panama Congress, to be held in 1826, the Federation of Gran Colombia raised the issue of Haitian independence and argued for Haiti's participation in the conference. U.S. delegates refused to recognize Haitian independence on blatantly racist grounds, guaranteeing that Haiti was excluded from the Congress and would remain on the periphery of inter-American relations long after the United States, in Civil War over slavery, recognized Haiti in 1862.

Only France recognized Haiti's full independence in 1825—at a catastrophic price. After seven years of fruitless talks with Haitian leaders, including Christophe and Pétion, about restoring French rule over the country and its people, and under the threat of French gunboats stationed on Haiti's shores, President Boyer agreed in 1825 to France's demand for an indemnity of 150 million francs (equivalent to anywhere from $12 billion to $21 billion U.S. in today's value), plus a 50 percent reduction in customs duties on all French imports. Such recognition left the Haitian government fiscally bankrupt, crippling Haiti's limited commercial economy and prejudicing political consolidation for decades to come.[62] An independence that consolidated the end of slavery and enabled the rise of a landed peasantry gained recognition from its former "mother country" only under pressure and by a deal that left the new country permeable to the power of international finance capital and economic imperialism of the great powers. In the later decades of the nineteenth century Haiti would face the economic uncertainty and political instability that earlier characterized many new Latin American republics.

THE HAITIAN REVOLUTION permanently destroyed the plantation economy of the world's foremost sugar colony, a French dependency that had fueled the international slave trade, profited home industries large and small, employing uncounted workers in a "free" France, and sending produce across Europe. The revolution was shaped by contradictions embedded in the country's colonial origins: the vast majority of the African-born had to struggle perennially to forge spaces of freedom based on independent peasant holdings—their definition of independence and the means by which to defend their freedom against slavery (and the coercions that followed), plantation production, and the state.

The leaders who rose during and after the revolution were, by the nature of the war against slavery, military men who took control of government, shaped the state in their own interests, and tried to maintain exports and revenues by perpetuating the plantation economy—which they knew required coerced labor, as former slaves who fought for independence would never willingly return to cane fields. That contradiction set off a long struggle—until by the late 1820s peasant proprietorship and household production prevailed. Former slaves living as peasants were by then better off than before—certainly more autonomous and likely better fed.

The gains—and they were real—did not bring an end to exploitation. In consolidating freedom and gaining the land, Haitian peasants faced the rise and persistence of a predatory state backed by a class of merchants trafficking the country's only viable export, coffee, in the emerging world of industrial capitalism, and sustaining themselves—state politicians and merchant predators—through a perfidious system of peasant taxation. The state became simultaneously authoritarian *and* weak and fractured within. Through the nineteenth century nationhood remained, as it remains today, a dream deferred in a new country—arguably the newest in the Americas based on its revolutionary transformation—shaped by the unresolved contradictions of revolutionary emancipation, a population adamantly grounded in autonomies on the land, and the challenges of making and sustaining a sovereign state.

Notes

1 On the "unthinkability," and recurrent denial and banalization of the Haitian Revolution, if not erasure, among contemporaries and in Western historiography generally, see Michel-Rolph Trouillot's influential essay "An Unthinkable History: The Haitian Revolution as a Non-Event," in *Silencing the Past: Power and the Production of History* (Boston: Beacon, 1995).

2 C. Fick, *The Making of Haiti: The Saint Domingue Revolution from Below* (Knoxville: University of Tennessee Press, 1990), 22–26. One of the best works on colonial Saint Domingue and the Haitian Revolution is still C. L. R. James's *The Black Jacobins* (1938), 2nd ed., rev. (New York: Vintage, 1963; reprint, London: Allison & Busby, 1980). All further references to James's work are from the 1963 edition.

3   Fick, *Making of Haiti*, 22.

4   Henri Castonnet des Fosses, *La perte d'une colonie: La révolution de Saint-Domingue* (Paris: A. Faivre, 1893), 8.

5   John Garrigus, "French Slavery," in *The Oxford Handbook of Slavery in the Americas*, ed. Robert Paquette and Mark Smith (Oxford: Oxford University Press, 2010), 173; also see Fick, *Making of Haiti*, 22, 280, nn42–44.

6   John Thornton, "'I Am the Subject of the King of Congo': African Political Ideology and the Haitian Revolution," *Journal of World History* 4:2 (Fall 1993): 185 and nn14–15. See also David Geggus, "Sugar and Coffee Cultivation in Saint Domingue and the Shaping of a Slave Labor Force," in *Cultivation and Culture: Labor and the Shaping of Slave Life in the Americas*, ed. Ira Berlin and Philip Morgan (Charlottesville: University Press of Virginia, 1993), 73–98.

7   On the composition of the slave leadership and organization of the August 22, 1791, insurrection, see Fick, *Making of Haiti*, 91–96.

8   For a larger discussion of these issues, see John Garrigus, "Colour, Class and Identity on the Eve of the Haitian Revolution: Saint Domingue's Free Coloured Elite as Colons Américains," *Slavery and Abolition* 17:1 (1996), 20–43.

9   See J. Garrigus, *Before Haiti: Race and Citizenship in French Saint Domingue* (New York: Palgrave Macmillan, 2006), 329, n 47.

10 Before long, the British would be in control of the western extremities of the northern and southern provinces, as well as significant coastal port cities of the West province.

11 Cited in Robert Stein, *Léger-Félicité Sonthonax: The Lost Sentinel of the Republic* (Rutherford, NJ: Fairleigh Dickenson University Press, 1985), 76.

12 After one year, they could, with special dispensation from a justice of the peace, contract themselves to another plantation, but whether or not this was a widespread practice under the prevailing wartime conditions in 1793–1794 is unclear. In any case, the structural features of the plantation economy and of plantation labor remained unaffected.

13 For further discussion of the duties and obligations of the workers, wage allocations, and police regulations, as well as workers' reactions and resistance to these, see C. Fick, "Emancipation in Haiti: From Plantation Labor to Peasant Proprietorship," *Slavery and Abolition* 21:2 (August 2000), 9–22. The term "plantation citizenship" is that of Vertus Saint-Louis, "Les termes de citoyen et Africain pendant la révolution de Saint-Domingue," in *L'insurrection des esclaves de Saint-Domingue (22–23 août 1791)*, ed. Laënnec Hurbon (Paris: Karthala, 2000), 75–95. See also C. Fick, "The Haitian Revolution and the Limits of Freedom: Defining Citizenship in the Revolutionary Era," *Social History* [UK] 32:4 (2007), 394–414.

14 See Bernard Gainot, "La constitutionalisation de la liberté générale sous le Directoire (1795–1800)," in *Les abolitions de l'esclavage de L. F. Sonthonax à V. Schoelcher, 1793, 1794, 1848*, ed. Marcel Dorigny (Paris: Presses Universitaires de Vincennes/Éditions UNESCO, 1995), 217–221.

15 Unless otherwise noted, parts of the following section are based on material previously published in C. Fick, "Revolutionary Saint-Domingue and the Emerging

Atlantic: Paradigms of Sovereignty," *Review: A Journal of the Fernand Braudel Center* 31:2 (2008), 121–144 and presented with permission.

16 Fick, "Emancipation in Haiti," 27.

17 These would be expanded to include the United States; see below.

18 The so-called Quasi-War, lasting roughly from 1797–1798 to 1800, resulted from a scandal, the XYZ Affair, that erupted when it became known in the United States that the three agents sent by President Adams to Paris to ease tensions between the two countries during the Quasi-War were rebuffed, insulted, and expected to pay a bribe if they wanted to begin negotiations with Minister of Foreign Affairs Charles Talleyrand. See Gordon S. Brown, *Toussaint's Clause: The Founding Fathers and the Haitian Revolution* (Jackson: University Press of Mississippi, 2005), 124–127.

19 For the extent of commercial relations between Philadelphia merchants and Saint Domingue during the 1790s, see James Alexander Dun, " 'What avenues of commerce, will you, Americans, not explore!': Commercial Philadelphia's Vantage onto the Early Haitian Revolution," *William & Mary Quarterly* 62:3 (2005), 357–364. For a penetrating interpretive analysis of early American attitudes toward (and denial of) its own *créolité* in the context of U.S.-West Indian connections, be they political, economic, or cultural, see Sean X. Goudie, *Creole America: The West Indies and the Formation of Literature and Culture in the New Republic* (Philadelphia: University of Pennsylvania Press, 2005).

20 R. P. Adolphe Cabon, *Histoire d'Haïti*, 4 vols. ([1895–1919]; reprint, Port-au-Prince: Éditions de la Petite Revue, 1940), 4:88–89; Vertus Saint-Louis, *Aux origines du drame d'Haïti: Droit et commerce maritime (1794–1806)* (Port-au-Prince: L'Imprimeur II, 2006), 131.

21 For a fuller discussion of militarized agriculture under the regime of Toussaint Louverture, see Claude Moïse, *Le projet national de Toussaint Louverture et la Constitution de 1801* (Montreal: Les Éditions du CIDIHCA, 2001), 62–65; James, *Black Jacobins*, 242; Saint-Louis, *Aux origines*, 150–155; Fick, "Emancipation in Haiti," 26–27.

22 Bibliothèque Nationale (BN) (France) MSS, 12102. Correspondance de Toussaint Louverture, vol. 2, no. 415. *Ordonnance du Citoyen Toussaint Louverture, Général en chef de l'Armée de Saint-Domingue*, le Cap, 27 brumaire An 7 (November 17, 1798).

23 BN MSS, 12102. Correspondance de Toussaint Louverture, vol. 2, no. 415. *Ordonnance*, le Cap, 27 brumaire An 7 (November 17, 1798). On Toussaint's administrative initiatives, also see Beaubrun Ardouin, *Études sur l'histoire d'Haïti*, 11 vols. ([1853–1860]; reprint, Port-au-Prince: F. Dalencourt, 1958), 4:11–12; Moïse, *Le projet national*, 56–57; V. Saint-Louis, *Aux origines*, 133–134.

24 See discussion in "The Road to Independence," above. For other specific provisions of the treaty, see Rayford Logan, *The Diplomatic Relations of the United States with Haiti, 1776–1891* (1941; reprint, New York: Kraus Reprint Co., 1969), 95; Alexander de Conde, *The Quasi-War: The Politics and Diplomacy of the Undeclared War with France, 1797–1801* (New York: Charles Scribner's Sons, 1969), 138–140; Brown, *Toussaint's Clause*, 144–161.

25   In Franklin Jameson, ed., "Letters of Toussaint Louverture and Edward Stevens, 1798–1800," *American Historical Review* 16:1 (1910), 79–80. Stevens to Pickering, Arcahaye, June 24, 1799.

26   In Jameson, "Letters," 77. Stevens to Pickering, Arcahaye, June 24, 1799 (italics in original).

27   In Logan, *Diplomatic Relations*, 83.

28   Quoted in C. Fick, "The Saint Domingue Slave Revolution and the Unfolding of Independence, 1791–1804," in *The World of the Haitian Revolution*, ed. D. Geggus and N. Fiering (Bloomington: Indiana University Press, 2009), 182–183.

29   On military control of the lives of the workers and supervision of plantation production, see C. Fick, "The Haitian Revolution and the Limits of Freedom: Defining Citizenship in the Revolutionary Era," *Social History* [UK] 32:4 (2007), 409–412.

30   Quoted in Moïse, *Le projet national*, 104, 106 (articles 3 and 14 respectively). The full text of the Constitution of 1801 is printed therein: 97–123.

31   Mats Lundahl, "Toussaint Louverture and the War Economy of Saint Domingue, 1796–1801," in *Caribbean Freedom*, ed. H. Beckles and Verene Shepherd (Princeton/London/Kingston: Markus Weiner/James Curry/Ian Randle, 1996), 4, 9.

32   Fick, "Emancipation in Haiti," 28.

33   For a detailed account of the initial resistance of the forces still loyal to Toussaint on the expedition's arrival in February 1802, and on the defection of key generals to Leclerc, see C. Fick, "La résistance populaire au corps expéditionnaire du général Leclerc et au rétablissement de l'esclavage à Saint-Domingue (1802–1804)," in *Rétablissement de l'esclavage dans les colonies françaises: Aux origines de Haïti*, ed. Y. Benot et Marcel Dorigny (Paris: Maisonneuve & Larose, 2003), 130–136; and especially James, *Black Jacobins*, 295–325.

34   For this phase of the independence struggle, in which numerous popular African leaders refused to submit to the superior command of Dessalines, and for which Dessalines and Christophe both led unrelenting campaigns to eliminate them, see Fick, "La résistance populaire," 144–148, and "The Saint Domingue Slave Revolution and the Unfolding of Independence," 190–192.

35   The concept of a "Supreme Being," as both universal and immaterial, existing outside and beyond the realm of the human condition, could also contain an embedded reference to the notion of a "Supreme Being" found in various African religious belief systems that contributed to the evolution of Haitian vodou. It is generally conceived of as a supreme, all-powerful but distant thing, or force of nature, to which all other deities (*loas*), and mortals, must ultimately submit. As a foundational document aiming to unify a country still composed in its majority of a multiplicity of African cultures and ethnicities, such reference in the preamble to the 1805 Constitution, if read in this light, might be plausible, but speculative. It is worth noting, as Sybille Fischer points out, that the early independence constitutions were written collectively, in committees, by men with formal training in France, and by ex-slaves. In *Modernity Disavowed: Haiti and the Cultures of Slavery in the Age of Revolution* (Durham, NC: Duke University Press, 2004), 228.

36   The designation of "white" to prohibit property ownership in Haiti was later changed to "foreigner" and remained in effect until 1918 under the U.S. Marine Occupation of Haiti (1915–1934).

37   Passages quoted in, and translated by Laurent Dubois and John Garrigus, *Slave Revolution in the Caribbean, 1789–1804* (Boston/New York: Bedford/St. Martin's, 2006), 192–193.

38   On this point, see Fischer, *Modernity Disavowed*, 232–236. In Haitian *Kreyòl*, the word *nègre* means simply: a person, a man, a Haitian, a human being, irrespective of color and without negative connotation.

39   See Jean Casimir, "La révolution de 1804 et l'État," in *Genèse de l'État haïtien (1804–1859)*, ed. M. Hector and L. Hurbon (Port-au-Prince: Éditions Presses Nationales d'Haïti, 2009), 93.

40   Fick, "Emancipation in Haiti," 30–31.

41   On more specific aspects of labor and property relations under the Code Henry, including allocation of small family plots, health care, working hours, duties, and mode of payment by owners to the workers, as well as taxes to the government, see Michel Hector, "Une autre voie de construction de l'État haïtien: L'expérience christophienne (1806–1820)," in *Genèse de l'État haïtien*, 255–281. Christophe's anglophilia (and bitter hatred of the French) led him to prefer the anglicized spelling of his name, Henry. See also Fick, "Emancipation in Haiti," 32.

42   Alex Dupuy, *Haiti in the World Economy: Class, Race and Underdevelopment since 1700* (Boulder, CO: Westview, 1989), 88.

43   Fick, "Emancipation in Haiti," 33. See also Paul Moral, *Le paysan haïtien: Étude sur la vie rurale en Haïti* (Paris: Maisonneuve et Larose, 1961), 33.

44   Fick, "Emancipation in Haiti," 32.

45   Hector, "Une autre voie," 267–268.

46   Fischer, *Modernity Disavowed*, 259.

47   These and other possibilities are discussed in Fischer, *Modernity Disavowed*, 245–260.

48   Fick, "Emancipation in Haiti," 34. Considering that Haiti's total land area is only slightly more than ten thousand square miles (roughly the size of the state of Delaware), and the above figure for Pétion's land transfers pertain only to his southern regime, the amount of land distributed in this manner was significant. It also set the pattern and parameters for later land acquisitions, diverse local property sales and transfers (often of portions of dilapidated or ruined plantation estates), family inheritances, and the emergence of Haiti's characteristically diverse peasantry, including those without land of their own, or land without title.

49   Fick, "Emancipation in Haiti," 34. For more detail on the sizes of the land grants according to military rank and occupation see Mimi Sheller, *Democracy after Slavery: Black Publics and Peasant Radicalism in Haiti and Jamaica* (Gainesville, FL: University Press of Florida, 2000), 93.

50   See Moral, *Le paysan haïtien*, 37.

51   M. Hector, "Les deux grandes rebellions paysannes de la première moitié du XIXè siècle haïtien," in *Rétablissement de l'esclavage*, 189–190.

52   See note 48 above. See also B. Éthéart, *La problématique foncière en Haïti* (Montréal: Les Éditions du CIDIHCA, 2014), 17–61.

53   See Sheller's discussion of these historiographical trends in *Democracy after Slavery*, 89–92.

54   Most recently in Jean-Alix René's innovative and challenging doctoral thesis, "Le culte de l'égalité: Une exploration du processus de formation de l'État et de la politique populaire en Haïti au cours de la première moitié du dix-neuvième siècle (1804–1846)" (PhD diss., Concordia University, April 2014). Also see Sheller, *Democracy after Slavery*, 89–141.

55   Sheller, *Democracy after Slavery*, 91–92.

56   Michel-Rolph Trouillot, *State against Nation* (New York: Monthly Review Press, 1990), 59–82.

57   Trouillot, *State against Nation*, 62.

58   Trouillot, *State against Nation*, 72–80.

59   Sheller, *Democracy after Slavery*, 243.

60   Article 44 of Pétion's 1806 Constitution, in Fischer, *Modernity Disavowed*, 237–241.

61   On the contingencies of Bolívar's unsuccessful attempts to gain adherence by his creole compatriots to abolition, see Carmen Bohórquez, "L'ambivalente présence d'Haïti dans l'indépendance du Vénézuela," in *Haïti: Première république noire*, ed. M. Dorigny (Saint-Denis/Paris: Société française d'histoire d'Outre-Mer/ Association pour l'Étude de la Colonisation Européenne, 2003), 227–240. See also Clément Thibaud, "La culture de guerre napoléonienne et l'Indépendance des pays bolivariens, 1810–1825," in *La France et les Amériques au temps de Jefferson et de Miranda*, ed. M. Dorigny and Marie-Jeanne Rossignol (Paris: Société des études robespierristes, 2001), 115–124.

62   The indemnity was reduced in 1838 under the July Monarchy to 90 million francs payable over the next thirty years, in addition to the initial French bank loan of 30 million (with compounded interest), i.e., the "double indemnity," to pay the first installment in 1825. For details and discussion of the entire indemnity question, see François Blancpain, *Un siècle de relations financières entre Haïti et le France (1825–1922)* (Paris: Harmattan, 2001), 43–78.

        No mention was made of the Spanish part of Hispaniola that was originally ceded to France in 1795 and then incorporated into the colonial state under Toussaint Louverture's 1801 constitution. With total disregard for Haiti's sovereignty as of 1804, France agreed to return the territory to Spain during the post-Napoleonic negotiations at the Congress of Vienna in 1815. In 1822, President Boyer led an expedition into Santo Domingo to bring it back under Haitian sovereignty. In 1844, following the liberal revolt to overthrow Boyer, the people of Santo Domingo claimed independence from Haiti and became the Dominican Republic.

5

CUBAN COUNTERPOINT

Colonialism and Continuity in the Atlantic World

DAVID SARTORIUS

On September 19, 1825, a bold call for Cuban independence cited "the instinct that all men have to search for their freedom" as the impetus to end Spanish rule on the island. For the authors of the manifesto, the tables had turned in the epic contest between civilization and barbarism: after more than a decade of war, the Americas were now the home of progress, justice, and liberty, and Spain embodied the decay and backwardness of an outdated political and economic order. According to the declaration, Cuba remained "under the dominion of a race of men who, to humanity's disgrace, cannot enter into social relations with civilized peoples"; with plenty of recent examples of the heroism of mainland patriots throughout Spanish America, Cubans could act on the "sanctity of their rights" with the full support of the new republics. In turn, Cuba's strategic location at the mouth of the Gulf of Mexico—it had long been known as the Key to the Indies—meant that its independence would guarantee the "peace, abundance, and prosperity" of all new nations in the Americas.

This appeal to free Cuba did not hail from Havana or Santiago de Cuba, or any other locale on the island. It originated in Mexico City, where conveners of a "patriotic meeting" promoting Cuban independence had directed a statement to the nascent Mexican Congress.[1] The group boasted the inclusion of some resident Cubans as well as Mexican citizens, but of the sixty men who signed the document, most were Mexican independence leaders and politicians. While Cuban luminaries José María Heredia and Father Felix Varela appear on the list, even their famous names get lost among a Who's Who of Mexican independence and statehood: Vicente Guerrero, Antonio López de Santa Ana, Nicolás Bravo, Anastasio Bustamante, Vicente Filosola, Manuel Gómez Pedraza, and many more. They all claimed to speak for the "effervescence that has produced the desire for freedom in the public spirit" of Cuba.

On the island itself, evidence of this effervescence is spotty. Ventriloquizing a desire for Cuban independence became a common gesture among leaders and citizens of newly independent republics in Spanish America. Their optimism and certainty often masked their own bumpy, uncertain transitions from colonies to nations in the Americas. Cuba's continued status as a colony until 1898 frustrated assumptions from abroad that an unstoppable desire for independence existed on the island that would inevitably topple Spanish rule. That an armed struggle against Spain did not occur until the second half of the nineteenth century disrupts a narrative that sees events in the Atlantic world between 1750 and 1850 coalescing to make the national independence of American colonies a foregone conclusion.[2] Nevertheless, highlighting Cuba's divergence from common American patterns may obscure as much as it reveals. First, even those onlookers who yearned for Cuba's liberation were themselves unclear about what political and economic practices constituted a new regional norm, especially in light of fragile postcolonial predicaments.[3] And second, to emphasize continuity in Cuba and change everywhere else is to miss new dynamics of colonial rule, exaggerate the newness of mainland Spanish American republican and liberal experiments, and prioritize the political such that the sweeping social and economic transformations that occurred on the island fade from view.

Those changes, coincidentally, have figured as the most common explanations for continuity. Explaining the persistence of colonial rule in Cuba led nineteenth-century observers, and more recent scholars too, to zero in on two factors: sugar and slavery. In the wake of the Haitian Revolution, the argument goes, the Cuban elite recognized the potential to pick up sugar production where St. Domingue left off before the Haitian Revolution, and it realized the necessity of a steady supply of African slave labor in order to do so. Rather than risk the so-cial instability that accompanied political transitions to nationhood elsewhere, wealthy Cubans—of Spanish descent in the vast majority—opted for the mili-tary safeguards, political control, and relaxed trade regulations offered by Spain.[4] To the extent that talk of freedom held appeal, concerns about its contagion among a growing slave population left white Cubans vigilant about the prospect of "another Haiti."[5] The 1825 statement to the Mexican Congress tried to assuage concerns that Cuban independence would incite revolutionary slave resistance by noting that Spanish rule in Cuba looked nothing like the weak French state and disorganized planters in late eighteenth-century St. Domingue. Few Cubans appear to have been persuaded, and the extraordinary wealth generated by sugar production throughout the nineteenth century left the Cuban creole elite, unlike their counterparts on the mainland, to accept the continuity of Spanish rule. Seen in this light, Cuba justifiably stands out as an exception to the period variously termed the Age of Revolutions, the independence period, and the beginning of the "modern period" in Latin American history.

As historians have sought to understand the period of independence as a complicated balance of continuity and change, it is useful to revisit the assump-tion of Cuban exceptionalism and opposition to the trends of the period.[6] Such polarity, with its deep roots, can prove difficult to unsettle. In 1940, Cuban anthropologist, lawyer, and activist Fernando Ortiz published *Cuban Counter-point: Tobacco and Sugar*, in which he identified the dynamic of a "multiform and persistent contrast" between modes of tobacco and sugar production and the cultures that they shaped.[7] This essay enlists that dynamic for a different pur-pose as it considers the extent to which Cuba can be contrasted to the nations in the Americas that emerged between 1750 and 1850. Did colonial rule exclude Cuba from the experiments with liberalism, representative government, and political participation that occurred elsewhere? Did the explosive economic growth of the sugar economy continue older patterns of Atlantic commerce, or did the abrupt changes on the island prevent the kind of economic stagna-tion experienced in the rest of Spanish America? Answering these questions requires critical distance from some basic assumptions about the politics and economics of the "ever-faithful isle."

Bread and Sugar: Continuity and Change in the Cuban Economy
Antonio López de Santa Anna, the Mexican general, future president, and signer of the 1825 call for Cuban independence, saw no compatibility between the island's prosperity and the continuation of Spanish rule. In 1824, only

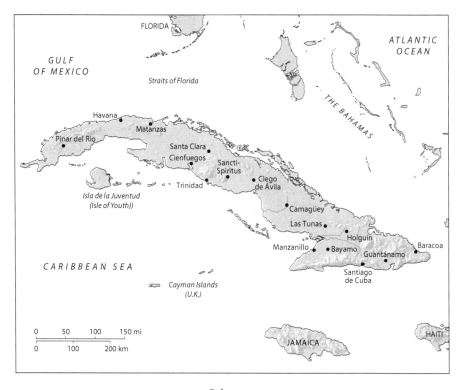

MAP 5.1. Cuba, ca. 1790–1860

months into his tenure as governor of Yucatán province, Santa Anna submitted a proposal to the central government to lead an invasion of Cuba. Spain's presence in the region, and especially around Veracruz, he argued, jeopardized Mexico's independence and made its mining economy vulnerable. But other enticing economic opportunities were at stake: a dozen Cuban exiles in Yucatán had also persuaded him of the profits to be reaped by liberating Cuba, since Mexico "would have to be compensated by a country of inexhaustible resources, given its locale, ports, fecundity, and output." And then there were Mexican exports, which could buoy the fledgling national government in Mexico City provided that they enjoyed unfettered access to Cuban markets. Santa Anna realized that the regional economy was in transition and that its spoils were up for grabs: Colombian ships were already dotting the Cuban coastline and Colombian agents had hatched the failed Soles y Rayos de Bolívar independence plot in 1823. "I repeat that this task belongs to the Mexican Nation and its magnitude merits your concern," he wrote to the war minister.[8]

In its final decades as a colony, New Spain had done its share to facilitate Cuba's economic rise: annual *situados*, or royal subventions, transferred revenues from Mexico to Cuba in an attempt to invigorate new areas of the colonial economy.[9] Whereas Santa Anna in 1825 recognized Cuba's (and perhaps Mexico's) potential to profit from Atlantic economic realignments, other observers a half century earlier were less optimistic about the region's fortunes—and about Spain's ability to stimulate them. Independence-minded creole elites in the American colonies were not unique in viewing imperial economic systems as irretrievably outmoded. In the eighteenth and early nineteenth centuries, debates gained momentum in Western Europe about the merits and viability of maintaining colonies. From Adam Smith to Montesquieu, economic and political critiques of empire accumulated, and within the Iberian world, figures such as Pedro Rodríguez Campomanes called for reforms based on a brutal assessment of Spain's policies in its colonies.[10] When Jeremy Bentham exhorted Spaniards in 1821 to "rid yourselves of the Ultramarine colonies," he was motivated less by moral injustices of colonialism than his belief that their American colonies no longer generated profits.[11] Critics of Spain's excessive focus on mainland silver mining cited the missed opportunities for sugar production in the Spanish Caribbean. As Franklin Knight proposed, "Had Cuba not been a part of the Spanish empire, it would undoubtedly have followed the earlier path of St. Domingue, Barbados, or Jamaica."[12] This economic counterfactual had occurred to many of those in Spanish America who felt the pinch of Bourbon economic policies and began to wonder whether colonialism and long-term profitability had ever been compatible and what the future might bring. Among the various charges that Denis Diderot leveled against Spain, its rigid economic policies illustrated the brutality characteristic of the Black Legend: an inability to colonize according to the "true principles of commerce" (namely mutual trade with independent countries) and greed that made "a wilderness of her own country and a grave of America."[13]

While the onset of independence movements in mainland Spanish America might only have added to doubts about Cuba's colonial status, the island's economic elite saw nothing but long overdue opportunity under Spanish rule, a new and leading role in a changing Atlantic world. One year after a massive slave rebellion began in St. Domingue, those Cubans with the means and clout to direct the island's economy formed in 1792 what became known as the Sociedad Económica de Amigos del País. The Havana group advocated for overhauling Cuba's environment, society, and infrastructure in order to accelerate the expansion of sugar, coffee, and tobacco production. Enlightenment ideas were key to this endeavor, but the writings of Smith, Montesquieu, and Bentham (often hard to acquire thanks to government censors) mattered less to most members than scientific treatises of the period, especially those that provided the botanical, chemical, and technological knowledge to improve the refinement of sugarcane. It translated studies of sugar used by French planters and technicians on St. Domingue, and for decades published its *Guía de forasteros*, an almanac for foreigners who might bring capital and commerce to the island.[14] Always on the lookout for new sources of revenue, Spanish officials listened carefully to the appeals of the society. Beginning in 1789, when Spain allowed the free trade of slaves in Cuban ports, Cubans won a number of concessions over the course of three decades that allowed them to reshape the western and central parts of the island. The structure of land ownership and land use changed drastically to clear land for sugar cultivation, and as Cuba became the world's top sugar producer, it did so in a period of an astounding increase in sugar consumption: between 1800 and 1880 the amount of sucrose production that reached the world market increased fifteenfold.[15] Little surprise, then, that planters and investors looked to agricultural expansion with wide-eyed confidence and to a political system that frequently supported them.

The engineers of this transition often thought comparatively, depicting Cuba as having mastered economic lessons that other regions had learned the hard way. Arguments for the strict surveillance and harsh control of slave workforces rested on the desire to avoid "another Haiti"—a fear of slave rebellion often willfully disconnected from aspirations to match or exceed St. Domingue's successes in sugar. By the 1810s and 1820s reformers could also warn that Spain should seek to avoid another Mexico, the loss of a prized colony due to mismanagement. One Santiago resident seeking to boost agriculture in the eastern part of the island wrote to the king in 1811 that monopoly and trade restrictions had wrecked New Spain's tobacco economy and led to an *época fatal* that Spain could forestall in Cuba.[16] But these attempts to make Cuba a counterpoint to its regional neighbors overlooked the deep connections between them that blur the borders of nominally discrete case studies. Politically and economically they often experienced linked fates both real and imagined, from the situados that Cuba enjoyed from New Spain to later Mexican designs for Cuban independence.[17] Beyond what Saint Domingue and the Haitian Revolution represented in the abstract, arrivals to Cuba of people from Saint Domingue during the height of the conflict had immediate and visible effects. In eastern Cuba, French planters established coffee farms that used slave labor, marking a change for the region but continuity for the planters and slaves themselves. As Ada Ferrer points out, the revolutionary process in Haiti briefly relocated a reactionary order to Cuba rather than destroying it outright: "People who would have remained free in Saint-Domingue/Haiti became slaves once more in Cuba.... And planters who had shipped coffee to the United States from southern Saint-Domingue now grew it and shipped it from eastern Cuba."[18] Interconnected trajectories like these complicate assessments of Cuba's exceptional status, a style of comparative thinking aided by the formation of national units that rely on assertions of distinctiveness. Explaining or justifying why Cuba took a different path than other countries can neglect the occasions on which their paths crossed, merged, and ran parallel.

A further hindrance to understanding Cuba's economic trajectory comes in considering it within the context of the Atlantic world, a frame of reference as much about time as it is about space. Given that other Caribbean slave societies that produced sugar prospered (often briefly) much earlier through Atlantic Ocean exchanges of capital, goods, and people, it is tempting to see Cuba as a latecomer to the system, an island out of step with the rest of the region.[19] Certainly, the waning of the transatlantic slave trade in the early nineteenth century complicated the expansion of slavery that accompanied the sugar revolution. When Spain loosened restrictions on the trade in 1789, the slave population more than doubled between 1792 and 1817. Yet Spain then signed a treaty with Great Britain (and received a £400,000 incentive from Britain) to end the slave trade to Cuba by 1820, and a clandestine slave trade flourished until the 1860s despite British cruisers surveilling the Cuban and African coasts and mixed Anglo-Spanish commissions attempting to enforce the ban on the island. In other words, Cuba remained an active participant in an Atlantic commercial system in decline.

But other Atlantic worlds were possible. One difficulty of the Atlantic framework for understanding nineteenth-century Cuba is that scholars have often bracketed its period of relevance between 1500 and 1800, at which point the end of certain European colonial projects in the Americas ruptured the economic and political structures that constituted the Atlantic system. Never mind that the majority of Caribbean islands remained under European rule well into the twentieth century and most of the European powers in the Atlantic continued to maintain colonies. Historians have recently attempted to extend the periodization of the Atlantic world: Emma Rothschild, for example, articulates a vision of "late Atlantic history," and José Moya defines an Atlantic world in the nineteenth century not by "early modern" standards but by the markers of what tends to count for "modernity." Suggesting an analytical path forward, they have identified new commodities, new ideas, and new migrations and connections that do not correspond neatly to the patterns characteristic of the earlier period.[20]

Seen in this light, Cuba appears not as an anachronism from a bygone era of slavery and colonialism, but as an engine of a renovated Atlantic economy. Technological advancements such as steam-driven sugar mills and rail transport between plantation regions and ports plotted Cuban sugar production squarely within the nexus of industrial capitalism. Dale Tomich has referred to a nineteenth-century "second slavery" that infused new life into the economies of Cuba, Brazil, and the United States, and complicated swift or easy plans for abolition.[21] If we shift perspective to consider questions of consumption and imports in these second slave societies, more new Atlantic connections come into view. Slavery was vital to the development of profitable export provisioning economies that used new technologies of mass production to provide sustenance for other slave societies. Brazilian coffee, for example, provided the profits that allowed Brazilian planters to buy wheat flour from places like Virginia, where slaves were active in wheat farming. Cuban demand for North American wheat spiked in the late eighteenth century, to the benefit of the fledgling economy of the United States. In fact, the Upper South's targeting of the Cuban market worried many Spanish officials, merchants, and wheat farmers. Cheap U.S. flour disadvantaged Cuba's own wheat farmers, located mainly in the central and eastern parts of the island—to the contentment of many planters and policy makers who argued that Cuba should devote itself to sugar alone.[22] Demand for subsistence goods in export-intensive agricultural areas and port cities in Cuba, Brazil, and the United States reoriented the Atlantic economy toward new regions on new terms.[23] Moreover, imports of foodstuffs in lieu of domestic production placed less pressure on planters to allow their slaves to cultivate *conucos*, or provision grounds, and at least in some regions of Cuba the rare instances when slaves could profit from their garden plots was precisely during wartime disruptions of the Atlantic food import economy.[24] Cuba remained, as Alejandro de la Fuente noted of sixteenth-century Havana, "not just a place in the Atlantic but an Atlantic place," although the Atlantic looked quite different than it had in previous centuries.[25]

That Cuba, Brazil, and the United States anchored a distinctive nineteenth-century Atlantic economy, both fueled by and fueling slavery, is a useful reminder that the persistence of slavery in the Americas and overseas commerce did not depend on a single political form such as colonial rule, national independence, or empire. Indeed, all three systems were in play, and making Cuba an exception to the transformations in the Atlantic world between 1750 and 1850 privileges one (national independence) over the others.[26] Economic historians have continued to explore the particular impact of colonialism and foreign trade in the Americas, even after the pull of dependency theory weakened in

FIGURE 5.1. Slaves making sugar in nineteenth-century Cuba:
The boiling house of the Asunción estate

the 1980s and 1990s. Research in this vein has generally demonstrated Cuba's similarity, more than disparity, with the emerging national economies of mainland Spanish America, up to a point. Contrary to the assumption that foreign trade uniformly disadvantaged the Latin American economies, other factors now better explain "how Latin America fell behind."[27] The calculations of Linda and Richard Salvucci of Cuba's terms of trade in the nineteenth century illustrate a surprising pattern. Although the end of colonial rule had severely disrupted their export economies, Mexico, Peru, Brazil, Argentina, and many other Latin American nations generally experienced a rise in their terms of trade throughout the nineteenth century. Some of their export sectors were too small to yield significant benefits, and many gains derived from commodity booms that exacted heavy economic tolls, but the fact of foreign trade itself did not necessarily produce impoverishment. One might expect Cuba, with its gargantuan export economy contributing to a decline in world sugar prices, to have suffered in contrast. Instead, improvements in productivity (likely from steam-powered mills and being one of the first countries in the world to use rail transport) prevented declining terms of trade until 1847, and they began to rise again in 1862.[28] In other words, despite presumed differences between the free trade that Spain allowed for Cuba and the free trade policies of new nations (which often included fierce protectionism), both Cuba and the nations of Latin America benefited, however indirectly and unevenly, from foreign trade. Spain eventually closed the Cuban trade system for one conspicuous commodity. Spanish officials fretted about the increasing volume of trade between Cuba and the United States, and beginning in the 1830s, Spain imposed heavy duties on wheat flour from the United States.[29] The intended beneficiaries of this protectionism were Spanish wheat farmers, not Cubans, and once the duties took effect in the 1840s and 1850s, Spanish wheat imports to Cuba nearly quadrupled.[30]

Together with the developments already mentioned, this aggressive policy suggests several conclusions about Cuba's "contrapuntal" economy in relation to those of the mainland republics. First, Spanish strategies in Cuba were neither afterthoughts nor sufficiently weak to indicate a "natural" decline in imperial might and an opening for independence. In combination with the active interventions of the Cuban elite, policy makers effected a transformation that consolidated Spanish political control. This challenges commonplace assumptions that independence and nationhood offered better alternatives to presumably restrictive colonial relationships. Second, the significance of new Atlantic realignments in the nineteenth century was not lost on Spaniards or Cubans; the island was not artificially exempt from economic relationships developing among independent states because it remained under imperial rule. Those realignments also adhere to a longer timeline that suggests similarities and connections, not simply contrasts, with other Spanish colonies and new nations. Finally, colonial officials worried not simply about the possibility of Cuban independence but about the possibility of a new power, namely the United States, acquiring commercial, if not political, control of the island. Those fears were not unfounded. By the 1830s, Cuban exports to the United States had already exceeded those to Spain, and by the 1850s almost half of Cuban exports went north.[31] Instead of viewing that influence as a late nineteenth-century development that fused U.S. political interests in Cuba to increasing U.S. investments in Cuban sugar after the Ten Years' War (1868–1878), we might see concerns about competition with new foreign rivals as a facet of the early nineteenth century that occasioned a powerful response from

Spain that resembles attempts in Mexico, Brazil, and other countries to shape the contours of British and U.S. economic interventions.

Nevertheless, the impulse to single out Cuba, and the Spanish Caribbean more broadly, as an outlier and exception has enjoyed a long history and notable adherents, including British scholar and colonial bureaucrat Herman Merivale. In 1841 he romanticized the supposedly harmonious nature of the Spanish Caribbean colonies before their economic takeoff and observed how times had changed. He wrote that "the tropical colonies of Spain were commonwealths in an epoch when those of most other nations were mere factories; they are now rapidly acquiring the degrading characteristics of factories, while ours, we may hope, are advancing toward the dignity of commonwealths."[32] Overlooking a key connective story—how Britain's sugar "factories" suffered in part from direct competition with Cuba's successful enterprise—Merivale, like others, took a dim view of Cuba's political fortunes relative to its economic prosperity while still affirming the principle that colonies could achieve from political communities for the common good.

¡Viva España! The Politics of Spanish Rule
Whether commonwealth or factory, Cuba was subject to laws and policies that were never wholly determined by economic ambitions. The idealized memory of a Spanish commonwealth based on noble, benevolent principles experienced a lengthy afterlife on the island. Shortly after Cubans drafted a progressive constitution in 1940, the historian and legal scholar Ramón Infiesta published a monumental history of constitutionalism in Cuba. He traced the origins of the island's democratic traditions not to recent efforts to challenge Gerardo Machado's dictatorship and the political influence of the United States, nor to the independence movement against Spain, but to Spanish colonialism. The 1812 Constitution, he argued, was situated at "the nexus between past Castilian freedoms and a new democratic spirit." While Infiesta admitted that the membership of the Cortes of Cádiz betrayed the inclusive ideology expressed in the constitution, he celebrated its advocacy of elections "that excluded any regard for *casta* or of privilege" and that located politics "outside the radius" of class influence.[33] These were certainly generous interpretations of "Castilian freedoms," and especially of the Cádiz Constitution; far from being race blind, it offered only a narrow window of citizenship for free men of African descent who proved their "virtue and merit." For Infiesta, any flaws in Spanish constitutional rule derived from constraints on civic life: obsessed with public order

and hunting down runaway slaves and bandits, local governments did little to foster a democratic spirit beyond the realm of institutional politics inhabited only by the privileged. Nevertheless, this early period of constitutional rule under colonialism laid the groundwork, according to Infiesta, for the democratic political culture that had culminated in a twentieth-century constitution that has long set a political standard for many Cubans.[34]

The idea that Spanish rule had championed any freedoms, or that colonial notions of sovereignty and political legitimacy might serve as models for postindependence politics, was uncommon among Spanish American elites, and has only recently has attracted the attention of historians in the case of the Cádiz Constitution.[35] More commonly, new nation-states defined themselves against the old colonial regime and professed a commitment to representative government and constitutionalism, in Jeremy Adelman's words, "building on the political achievements of defeating metropolitan monarchies."[36] In another interpretation, however, "schizophrenic" independent states struggled to reconcile republicanism with the "organicist and corporatist" ideologies left over from colonial rule.[37] To acknowledge the fuzziness of the transitions from colony to nation in mainland Spanish America, especially in the realm of political practices, is to invite curiosity about the explicit persistence of colonial politics in Cuba, albeit in the context of new visions of the Spanish nation.

Despite widespread inequalities during the colonial period along the lines of gender, race, and class, Cubans like Infiesta could look to the late nineteenth century and cite some evidence of inclusive political practices. By 1898, Cubans had come to enjoy freedoms of press and association, political parties modeled on those in Spain, and, at the end of the independence war, even a last-minute offer of full political autonomy within the Spanish empire. Aside from separatist sentiment, the presumed unimportance of popular politics in Spanish Cuba is often understood as the logical casualty of the simultaneous growth of African slavery—and, for many scholars, a reason to exclude the island from comparative considerations of nineteenth-century Spanish American political history. But innovations in Spain's nineteenth-century empire raise similar questions to those relevant to the new republics about liberalism, popular politics, civil society, and about imperial and national imaginaries not easily contained within neat periodizations that end "the colonial period" with mainland independence.[38] In this light, the relationship between institutional and popular politics in colonial Cuba becomes as ripe for analysis as it has been for the rest of Spanish America during its "modern period."[39]

One of the most apparent features of political life during Cuba's continued colonial status was the surprising degree of popular support for Spain, including that of free and enslaved people of African descent. In contrast to the stable category of royalists who emerged out of the mainland independence conflicts with patriots, loyalty to Spanish rule in Cuba was rarely a fixed or permanent political identity; allegiance to Spain was contingent and flexible. Given that all Cubans occupied some subordinate social or political position under Spanish rule, the colonial state often recognized claims to privileges from self-proclaimed loyal subjects more readily than demands for rights based on elusive national citizenship. Racial inequality, just like other built-in colonial hierarchies, contained within it the possibility of inclusion. And ultimately, symbolic acts of loyalty to the imperial project, not the promise of citizenship embodied in the 1812 Spanish Constitution, may have been what offered more secure footing to some free men of color—not despite the widespread unrest and in the Americas but precisely because of it. What many Cubans came to realize in the years of imperial crisis, as they watched other regions of Spanish America dissolve into violent conflict, was that loyalty, as opposed to exit, offered a relatively stable position from which to argue for economic reforms, improved social standing, or political recognition.[40] As for much of the colonial period, subordinate status, not equality among citizens, grounded political subjectivities, so that even humbler colonials could speak to power in the language of loyalty, so long as some means of expression was available. Just before the constitution was promulgated, for example, Pedro Galdíz, a lower officer of the pardo battalion in Havana, successfully lobbied the captain general for a portion of normal monthly pay during months of rest. In 1811, he appealed "with no pretension but obedience and hope for the return of our legitimate sovereign to his throne" for a type of recognition that could not yet have been granted by invoking the constitution. For many African-descended Cubans, the constitution seems to have stood as one, but not the primary, front on which they advanced struggles for survival, success, and mobility.[41] On most fronts, the language of loyalty figured prominently.

As in the new mainland republics, the constitution enjoyed a long afterlife in Cuba, but on the island its limitations and possibilities became especially manifest under the continuation of Spanish rule. Ferdinand VII abrogated it in 1814, it was restored in 1820–1823 following a military coup in Spain, was wrongfully reinstituted by Santiago's governor in 1836, and its protections were definitively placed out of reach from Cubans in 1837 with Spain's decision to govern the colonies by "special laws."[42] Cubans frequently looked favorably on its guarantees of free press and association, particularly during its restoration in 1820. In an initial test of those freedoms, the restoration provoked lively public commemorations that stretched the limits of what kind of public fraternizing would be tolerated. Alejandro Ramírez, and army intendant, reported on five straight days of celebration in Havana to celebrate the physical arrival of the constitution. On April 15, a Spanish ship carrying the proclamation completed its month-long voyage from La Coruña and was met by three Spanish regiments, one of them proudly headed by a colonel who had guarded Cádiz in 1812 when news of the constitution was initially proclaimed. Soldiers led music and meandering parades through the streets, and they eventually mixed with "paysanos de toda ropa," followed by "masses of blacks and mulattoes, all of them with bouquets and little paper lanterns placed on long sticks, singing, drumming, and shouting at whomever they encountered." Amid the "infernal noise," Ramírez identified groups of *negros* "who shouted 'Viva el Rey' from a distance when they heard of the Constitution's victory."[43] This, for Ramírez, was the desired outcome of loosening restrictions on public gatherings: however boisterous the Cubans of color might have been, they used public space to show support for Spanish rule—a far preferable alternative to uniting in rebellion.

As his description continued, however, the intendant snuck in some suspicion amid the praise. On the final night of the festivities, crowds proceeded down Calle Muralla—renamed Calle de la Constitución—to a plaza featuring the Arca de la Ley, a stone memorial to the constitution. There they sang patriotic hymns, toasted the new political order, and wore hats that bore the message "Viva la Constitución." Once again, soldiers mixed with civilians, "masses of people of all classes, sexes, and colors," but now many of the images and decorations that he witnessed bore "triangles, squares, and other tools of masonry, and a combination of three colors. . . . Blue-striped ribbons worn on their black coats; such dress, according to some intellectuals of the Egyptian mysteries, was analogous to the Triangular emblem." The role of Masonic lodges in many Spanish American independence movements was a fresh memory to officials like Ramírez, although Cuban lodges generally traced origins and ongoing relationships to counterparts in Spain and generally survived intense government scrutiny.[44] The concern at the end of the restoration celebrations seemed to locate the potential for subversion in Masonic iconography—an anxiety undoubtedly linked to understandings of the influences on mainland independence—much more than assumptions about the rebellious nature of Cubans of color.

Throughout the week, Ramírez expressed ambivalence that characterized the uneven development of public life in early nineteenth-century Cuba. He could not help but observe that the events "gathered all of the elements capable of generating disorder," and that the loyal sentiments of the African-descended participants were insufficient to overcome the subversive potential of general revelry. He concluded that "although the desires and intentions of the pueblo were Spanish and Patriotic, the principle that set the machine in motion was neither Patriotic nor Spanish, at the opposite extreme."[45] Could the medium have been the message? Ramírez certainly thought so, and opportunities to express support for colonial rule waxed and waned as authorities worked with qualified success to limit the forms of popular public expression that voiced political opinions, pro-Spanish or otherwise.

The second constitutional period ostensibly broadened opportunities for more Cubans, citizens or not, to engage in political discussion, but even those liberties had their limits: government censors issued 147 denunciations to various licensed newspapers in the course of the Trienio.[46] After major turning points away from expanded rights—in 1823, in 1837, with the announcement of "special laws," and after the slave revolts and La Escalera conspiracy in the 1840s—moderate reforms coming from Madrid often faced skepticism from officials on the island, such as Captain General Luis Dionisio Vives's refusal in 1823 of Spain's continuation of associational freedoms after the constitution's nullification. Such austerity left figures like Father Félix Varela, once a Cuban delegate to the Cortes, to relocate political discussion off of the island—in Varela's case to the United States, where he published *El Habanero* in Philadelphia and advocated Cuban independence. The restrictions placed on public space and association, political discussion, and publications may have intended to squelch seditious and revolutionary activities, but they also limited even expressions of support for Spanish rule.

Before 1837, the creole elite had won economic concessions in the absence of political representation, but the announcement of "special laws" for the island rightly struck them as explicitly silencing. Drawing on the ill-fitting rhetoric of human bondage, a furious José Antonio Saco, now stripped of his position in the Cortes, accused Spain of "reducing free citizens to political slavery" and wondered how it could cite fears of slave rebellion to justify its decision, given that Spain had created the system itself: Cubans owned "slaves that the Government itself brought us and forced us to buy."[47] Ramón de la Sagra, the Spanish agriculturalist who studied and taught in Cuba and often sparred with Saco, tried to give the decision a positive spin. From Paris he published an analysis of the constitution's suspension in Cuba that saw special laws as a privilege, not an insult, bestowed on white Cubans. They had the resources they needed to prosper, and lost representation in the Cortes was a small price to pay to prevent political freedoms from becoming "a seductive spectacle for an unhappy race that can neither understand nor enjoy them."[48] Things could still improve for the white population, but more importantly they were now less likely to be destroyed altogether.

All the while, talk of independence remained relatively muted. Annexation to the United States increasingly piqued the curiosity of slave-owning Cubans, reformers seeking autonomy under colonial rule floated various designs for "Spanish Cuba," and a handful of planters found a modest platform to make their interests heard in Madrid. In the 1840s and 1850s, Saco was a frequent spokesmen for Cuban planters and slave owners who met with limited success when they argued that white immigration and an end to the slave trade might create a Cuba worthy of constitutional protections. Although Cubans didn't disappear entirely from the Spanish political scene, they had to adapt their rhetoric to fit their exceptional and subordinate status. Francisco Muñoz del Monte, a wealthy Santiago liberal who became a regular presence in the court of Isabel II during the 1850s, wrote frequently for a Spanish periodical called *La América*. He still celebrated the merits of freedom, but he now paired it with order as a necessary preventive balance for unchecked liberties. He tried to fuse the interests of the Spanish and Cuban bourgeoisie with appeals to the "Iberian race" and fraternal harmony. And he watched with some exasperation after 1854 as political parties proliferated in Spain, mindful that Cubans were left out of such debates. In an article about the many "liberal parties" in Spain, he reminded readers that Spanish liberals and conservatives alike could trace their origins to the liberal ideals of the 1812 Constitution.[49]

As long as slavery and racial differences existed on the island, the Spanish government seemed disinclined to encourage hopes for the extension of constitutional rights. We should not see in this an absence of politics altogether— either as two-dimensional conjecture about Iberian absolutism or as a contrast to democratic American republics, themselves reckoning racial divisions with rights talk. Again, the promise of constitutional rights and liberal government was only one mechanism by which Cubans could achieve inclusion and justice. And as the 1812 Constitution made no attempt to curb slavery and excluded slaves from any claims to citizenship, many slaves themselves pursued political paths with older origins. Alejandro de la Fuente has discussed how the persistence of slaves in Cuban courts helped transform the centuries-old legal custom of *coartación*, or slaves' self purchase, into an institution understood as a right—though not without disagreements by planters and the colonial government.[50] One syndic in 1852 affirmed the freedom claim of a slave woman named Catalina because she had traveled with a former owner to Spain, where slavery did not exist. He reasoned that "the right of post-liminy was established to promote freedom . . . according to the wise and enduring legal code formulated by Alfonso X, 'All worldly rights always advance the interests of freedom.'"[51] Here was an invocation of freedom that did not depend on constitutional guarantees or the threat of anticolonial revolt. The fact that this anecdotal evidence does not necessarily congeal into a well-defined pattern is precisely the point: this was a system of exceptions and special cases. With the rules themselves frequently in transition, aspiring to citizenship under the Spanish constitution was rarely a stable political stance that would be uniformly recognized as allegiance to Spain.

Nevertheless, on the eve of Cuba's first war for independence, there began to appear a slight softening of the parallel rigidity among Cuban leaders to the enslaved and free descendants of Africans. Certainly, the U.S. Civil War and slave emancipation had dampened enthusiasm for annexation, and former adherents rerouted their discontent in the direction of colonial reform. Over two decades after the alleged conspiracy of La Escalera, which led to a brutal crackdown on slaves and free people of color alike, the free-colored militias had been reinstated, whitening the population became a more common goal of elites, and deceptive discussions about "free" African migrant labor at least acknowledged that slavery would not last forever. Each of these developments pointed to a need or desire for better social integration despite a wide gap between its principles and practice. Together, they ostensibly placed Cuban creoles in a stronger position to critique the political fractures and exclusions they had long suffered. Even though the Junta de Reformas de Ultramar that convened in 1865 could not align the interests of its Puerto Rican, Cuban, and metropolitan constituencies, it nevertheless offered a limited space for political deliberation. Ironically, 1865 was also the year of the founding of the Sociedad Abolicionista Española, an organization that would debate the role of former slaves and Cuba's sizable free population in preserving support for Spanish rule.

To what extent might this openness in the 1860s have been extended to the exclusions and exceptions made for Cubans of African descent? The captain general himself seemed optimistic. Domingo Dulce acknowledged the "civilizing aptitude" of the free population of color and urged the Ministerio de Ultramar to loosen up. Since he had arrived in Cuba in 1862, free people had achieved success in many professions, "even music and poetry," and Dulce recommended removing legal obstacles to their contribution to the "expansive and fusionary Spanish race." He warned that the ministry should not "draw up special laws for the *libres de color*, nor deprive them de facto and de jure of the equality before the law that they have possessed and still possess, although there are only few slight differences to repeal." The work of dismantling legal inequalities within the island might have been the necessary condition for holding at bay special laws in general, as, Dulce predicted, the "divergence of aspirations between the majority of the inhabitants and a minority of *peninsulares* will disappear."

Ultimately, though, he admitted that the "progressive amalgamation of race will be the work of time and not of legislation," and by 1868, time for musing about a racially amalgamated empire or political equality was interrupted by the outbreak of Cuba's first war for independence.[52]

While the treaty that ended that war effected an unprecedented expansion of the public sphere—far more opportunities for political deliberation, including the founding of conservative and liberal political parties—1868 begins a narrative of independence that differs from that of the other Spanish American colonies in that a national vision preceded political independence. That vision, as Ada Ferrer so persuasively articulates, was built less on the ideas of biological and cultural mixing, which fueled calls for national unity in the nineteenth-century republics, but "as the product of a revolutionary cross-racial alliance—a formulation that ostensibly acknowledged the political actions of nonwhite men and therefore carried with it powerful implications for racial and national politics in the peace and republic to follow anticolonial insurgency."[53] What happens, asks Jeremy Adelman of approaches to Spanish American independence, if we "do not suppose the existence of the nation, either as social formation or as idyll, before empires crumbled and the fires of revolution began to spread across colonial hinterlands?"[54] What happens if we examine Cuba's history as counterpoint and harmony alike: questions of political inclusion that shaped the trajectories of all American nations, but with Cuba's struggle for independence and race-transcendent nationalism a marked distinction from the creole-led movements of the early nineteenth century.

Conclusion

Another appeal for Cuban independence, made almost thirty years after the statement to the Mexican Congress, characterized anticolonial rebellion as an inevitable and foreseeable event by midcentury, prophesying that "down-trodden peoples, brutalized by ages of oppression, will rise in the rude majesty of their ungovernable might." Indeed, by now Cuban desires for political emancipation could be historically documented: the author cited an 1823 plea to Simón Bolívar for help, an 1826 plea at the Congress of American States in Panama, the 1828 conspiracy of the Aguila Negra, and the Santiago governor's 1836 attempt to reinstate the Cádiz Constitution. This time, the call came from neither a Cuban nor Mexican but a U.S. southerner. Samuel R. Walker was a New Orleans filibuster who made the case for independence in 1854 to John Perkins, a Democratic Louisiana congressman; he had in mind more than a moral crusade against "the *divine right* sacrilegiously claimed by imbecile kingcraft." A free Cuba, for Walker, was a vital issue for the southern economy. "The articles we produce are those they most need," he insisted, and England or France would never "have suffered such an incubus to have existed at the outlet of even their petty rivers, weighing down their commercial advancement." Political solidarity did not lie far from his economic ambitions, and although a full-scale invasion of Cuba might upset the delicate racial balance, Walker still asked what "the United States, the center from which these rays diverge, [would] be willing to contribute to the cause of freedom and humanity."[55] His assessment echoed the sentiments of the Mexican supporters of Cuban independence in 1825, who claimed that Cuba needed the strong "protection of a friendly nation" in order to secure its liberty.[56] As in much of the American hemisphere's history, economic and political motivations rarely separated neatly as factors in expansionary projects.

If that rhetoric portends later justifications for the 1898 U.S. intervention in Cuba's final war for independence, it should also alert us to a persistent counterpoint between the harmonious "family of nations" in the nineteenth-century Americas and the expansionary and paternalistic ambitions of some of its members, including, but not limited to, the United States. Even as European empires expanded throughout the century, and still controlled much of the Caribbean, observers from new American nations commonly proclaimed the incompatibility between colonial rule in Cuba and regional capitalist development. But the experiments with inclusionary politics and economic innovation in the last decades of Spain's presence in the Americas allow us to unfix liberalism and capitalism from their association with the nation-state. Not that Cuba alone diverged from this presumed norm. While colonialism on the island rarely approximated the liberal imperialism claimed and theorized by the British and French in their nineteenth- and twentieth-century global exploits, it was never the sole site of imperial allegiances, enduring racial hierarchies, and coerced labor in the Americas.[57] Those phenomena remained viable and prominent even in the new nations that were gradually and unevenly shaped in opposition to them. Counterpoint—between colony and nation, equality and subordination, rights and privileges—might involve different contours and rhythms, but the melodies are intrinsically interdependent.

This point was not lost on Fernando Ortiz. The oppositions that he delineated in *Cuban Counterpoint* never remained distinct; rather, the historical processes by which they informed and transformed each other laid the foundation of Ortiz's wide-ranging concept of transculturation. And this insight offers a way to understand Cuba as an integral part of the Age of Revolutions rather than a curious exception to it. Perhaps the loudest counterpoints are to be found not between individual cases but within them. Cuba, for all of its continuity, became a laboratory for experiments in economic and political reform throughout the nineteenth century. If preserving slavery was the critical explanation for maintaining colonial rule, the hierarchies that bolstered it could be mobilized not simply for economic exploitation but for membership in a public or political community that was unequal by design. The privileges and paternalism characteristic of Spanish colonial rule held the attention of many Cubans at the same time that the rights and freedoms attributed to independent nation-states were being hammered out elsewhere. Situating Cuba alongside the new nations in the Americas brings into sharper view the colonial foundations of the various "national" political cultures that emerged and the "modern" features of European empires.

Notes

1   *Representación al soberano congreso mejicano por los miembros de la reunión patriótica promotora de la libertad cubana* (Mexico City: Imprenta de la Aguila, 1825). Rare Books Division, Library of Congress. For statements of support for Cuban independence from committees formed in other Mexican cities and towns, see Archivo de la Secretaría de Relaciones Exteriores, Mexico City (hereafter ASRE), L-E-1333, números 3 and 4. On other foreign efforts to liberate Cuba, see Ramiro Guerra y Sánchez, *Manual de historia de Cuba* (Madrid: Ediciones Madras, 1985), 285–287, 298–299.

2   Arturo Sorhegui D'Mares explores the Havana elite's response to the Age of Revolutions in "La Habana y el proceso de la primera independencia en Hispanoamérica," in *Repensar la independencia de América Latina desde el Caribe*, ed. Sergio Guerra Vilaboy and Emilio Cordero Michel (Havana: Editorial de Ciencias Sociales, 2009), 268–304.

3   Concerns that new republics did not measure up to European-derived definitions of political and economic success echoed the concerns of postcolonial scholarship with troubling a shopworn image of the region's new nations as "variations on a master narrative that could be called 'the history of Europe,'" in the words of Dipesh Chakrabarty in *Provincializing Europe: Postcolonial Thought and Historical Difference* (Princeton, NJ: Princeton University Press, 2000), 27. Tulio Halperín Donghi emphasizes Argentina's divergence from the presumptive model of nationalism developed by Benedict Anderson in his influential text *Imagined Communities* (London: Verso, 1983). See Halperín Donghi, "Argentine Counterpoint: Rise of the Nation, Rise of the State," in *Beyond Imagined Communities: Reading and Writing the Nation in Nineteenth-Century Latin America*, ed. Sara Castro-Klarén and John C. Chasteen (Baltimore: Johns Hopkins University Press / Woodrow Wilson Center Press, 2003), 33–53.

4   The argument is ubiquitous, but two recent examples can be found in José A. Piqueras, "La siempre fiel isla de Cuba, o la lealtad interesada," *Historia Mexicana*

58:1 (2008), 427–486, and Dominique Goncalvès, *Le planteur et le roi: L'aristocratie havanaise et la coronne d'Espagne (1763–1838)* (Madrid: Casa de Velázquez, 2008).

5   On the circulation of information about the Haitian Revolution in Cuba, see María Dolores González-Ripoll, Consuelo Naranjo, Ada Ferrer, Gloria García, and Josef Opatrný, eds., *El rumor de Haití en Cuba: Temor, raza y rebeldía, 1789–1844* (Madrid: CSIC, 2004).

6   See, for example, Peter Guardino, *The Time of Liberty: Popular Political Culture in Oaxaca, 1750–1850* (Durham, NC: Duke University Press, 2005); Sarah C. Chambers, *From Subjects to Citizens: Honor, Gender, and Politics in Arequipa, Peru, 1780–1854* (University Park: Pennsylvania State University Press, 1999); and Karen Caplan, *Indigenous Citizens: Local Liberalism in Early National Oaxaca and Yucatán* (Stanford, CA: Stanford University Press, 2009).

7   Fernando Ortiz, *Cuban Counterpoint: Tobacco and Sugar*, trans. Harriet de Onís (Durham, NC: Duke University Press, 1995), 5.

8   Antonio López de Santa Anna to the Secretario del Ministerio de Guerra y Marina, August 18, 1824, AMRE 3–14–5155.

9   Alan J. Kuethe, "El situado mexicano, los azucareros y la fidelidad cubana: Comparaciones con Puerto Rico y Nueva Granada," in *Las Antillas en la era de las luces y la revolución*, ed. José Antonio Piqueras (Madrid: Siglo XXI, 2005), 301–318.

10   See Jeremy Adelman, *Sovereignty and Revolution in the Iberian Atlantic* (Princeton, NJ: Princeton University Press, 2006), 22–33; and Gabrielle B. Paquette, *Enlightenment, Governance, and Reform in Spain and Its Empire, 1759–1808* (New York: Palgrave Macmillan, 2008).

11   Jeremy Bentham, "Rid Yourselves of Ultramaria," in *Colonies, Commerce, and Constitutional Law: Rid Yourselves of Ultramaria and Other Writings*, ed. Philip Schofield (New York: Oxford University Press, 1995), 1–194.

12   Franklin W. Knight, *Slave Society in Cuba during the Nineteenth Century* (Madison: University of Wisconsin Press, 1970), 28.

13   Quoted in Sankar Muthu, *Enlightenment against Empire* (Princeton, NJ: Princeton University Press, 2003), 92, 106.

14   Manuel Moreno Fraginals, *El ingenio: Complejo económico social cubano del azúcar*, 3 vols. (Havana: Editorial de Ciencias Sociales, 1978), 1:105–112. Initially known as the Sociedad Patriótica, the organization had at least a dozen different names in its first century but remains best known as the Sociedad Económica de Amigos del País. On the library and publications of the Sociedad, see Izaskun Álvarez Cuartero, *Memorias de la Ilustración: Las Sociedades Económicas de Amigos del País en Cuba (1783–1832)* (Madrid: RSBAP Delegación en Corte, 2000), 107, 213–214, 222.

15   Sidney W. Mintz, *Sweetness and Power: The Place of Sugar in Modern History* (New York: Penguin Books, 1985), 197. The world's population did not even double in that same period. On sugar expansion, see Mercedes García Rodríguez, *La aventura de fundar ingenios: La refacción azucarera en la Habana del siglo XVIII* (Havana: Editorial de Ciencias Sociales, 2004), and *Entre haciendas y plantaciones: Orígenes de la manufactura azucarera en la Habana* (Havana: Editorial de Ciencias

Sociales, 2007). On land tenure, see Imilcy Balboa Navarro, *De los dominios del rey al imperio de la propiedad privada: Estructura y tenencia de la tierra en Cuba (siglos XVI–XIX)* (Madrid: Consejo Superior de Investigaciones Científicas, 2013).

16 Martin José de Palacios to Fernando VII, September 25, 1811, Archivo General de Indias, Seville, Sección Ultramar, legajo 318, cited as "Memorial de un vecino de Santiago de Cuba sobre propuesta de reformas, 1811," in *El departamento oriental en documentos, Tomo II (1800–1868)*, ed. Olga Portuondo Zúñiga (Santiago de Cuba: Editorial Oriente, 2012), 52–65.

17 On eighteenth-century connections, see Arturo Sorhegui D'Mares, "La Habana y Nueva España, el Mediterráneo americano y la administración española en el siglo XVIII," in *La Habana en el Mediterráneo americano* (Havana: Imagen Contemporánea, 2007), 221–252.

18 Ada Ferrer, *Freedom's Mirror: Cuba and Haiti in the Age of Revolution* (New York: Cambridge University Press, 2014), 182. See also Olga Portuondo Zúñiga, *Santiago de Cuba, los colonos franceses y el fomento cafetalero, 1798–1809* (Santiago: Editorial Oriente, 1992).

19 Philip D. Curtin critiqued the assumption that recognizing the ultimate successes of Saint Domingue and Cuba means that "we half expect them to have been big at the beginning" of European colonization in the Americas, although he also claims that the end of slavery was "out of phase." *The Rise and Fall of the Plantation Complex: Essays in Atlantic History* (New York: Cambridge University Press, 1990), 27, 189.

20 Emma Rothschild, "Late Atlantic History," in *The Oxford Handbook of the Atlantic World, c. 1450–c. 1850*, ed. Nicholas Canny and Philip Morgan (New York: Oxford University Press, 2011), 634–648; José C. Moya, "Modernization, Modernity, and the Trans/formation of the Atlantic World in the Nineteenth Century," in *The Atlantic in Global History, 1500–2000*, ed. Jorge Cañizares-Esguerra and Erik R. Seeman (Upper Saddle River, NJ: Pearson/Prentice Hall, 2007), 179–197. See also Christopher Schmidt-Nowara, "Continuity and Crisis: Cuban Slavery, Spanish Colonialism and the Atlantic World in the Nineteenth Century," in Cañizares-Esguerra and Seeman, *The Atlantic in Global History*, 199–217; Frederick Cooper, *Colonialism in Question: Theory, Knowledge, History* (Berkeley: University of California Press, 2005), chap. 4; Jane G. Landers, *Atlantic Creoles in the Age of Revolutions* (Cambridge, MA: Harvard University Press, 2010), and Rebecca J. Scott and Jean M. Hébrard, *Freedom Papers: An Atlantic Odyssey in the Age of Emancipation* (Cambridge, MA: Harvard University Press, 2012).

21 Dale Tomich, "The 'Second Slavery': Bonded Labor and the Transformation of the Nineteenth-Century World Economy," in *Through the Prism of Slavery: Labor, Capital, and World Economy* (Lanham, MD: Rowman and Littlefield, 2004), 56–71.

22 Linda K. Salvucci, "Supply, Demand, and the Making of a Market: Philadelphia and Havana at the Beginning of the Nineteenth Century," in *Atlantic Port Cities: Economy, Culture, and Society in the Atlantic World, 1650–1850*, ed. Franklin W. Knight and Peggy Liss (Knoxville: University of Tennessee Press, 1991), 40–57.

23 Dan Rood, "Slavery and the Amber Waves of Grain: Trade, Technology, and Middle-Class Consumption in the Richmond-Rio Circuit, 1760–1860," unpublished essay. See also Richard Graham, *Feeding the City: From Street Market to Liberal Reform in Salvador, Brazil, 1780–1860* (Austin: University of Texas Press, 2010), and Andrew Sluyter, "The Hispanic Atlantic's Tasajo Trail," *Latin American Research Review* 45:1 (2010), 98–120. For an eighteenth-century contrast, see Celia P. Torre, "La alimentación en Cuba en el siglo XVIII," *Revista de Humanidades* [Monterrey] 19 (2005), 101–116.

24 David Sartorius, "Conucos y subsistencia: El caso del ingenio Santa Rosalía," in *Espacios, silencios, y los sentidos de la libertad: Cuba entre 1878 y 1912*, ed. Fernando Martínez Heredia, Rebecca J. Scott, and Orlando F. García Martínez (Havana: Ediciones Unión, 2001), 108–127. See also Jorge Ibarra Cuesta, *Marx y los historiadores: Ante la hacienda y la plantación esclavistas* (Havana: Editorial de Ciencias Sociales, 2008), 186–187.

25 Alejandro de la Fuente (with the collaboration of César García del Pino and Bernardo Iglesias Delgado), *Havana and the Atlantic in the Sixteenth Century* (Chapel Hill: University of North Carolina Press, 2008), 223.

26 For a history of slavery and sugar that juxtaposes imperial and constitutional politics in Brazil and Cuba, see Márcia Berbel, Rafael Marquese, and Tâmis Parron, *Escravidão e política: Brasil e Cuba, c. 1790–1850* (São Paulo: Editoria Hucitec, 2010).

27 Stephen Haber, ed., *How Latin America Fell Behind: Essays on the Economic History of Brazil and Mexico* (Stanford, CA: Stanford University Press, 1997).

28 Linda K. Salvucci and Richard J. Salvucci, "Cuba and the Latin American Terms of Trade: Old Theories, New Evidence," *Journal of Interdisciplinary History* 31:2 (2000), 197–222. They note that income terms of trade rose, and the decline was limited to the net barter terms of trade and to single factoral terms of trade.

29 Antonio Santamaría García and Alejandro García Álvarez, *Economía y colonia: La economía cubana y la relación con España, 1765–1902* (Madrid: CSIC, 2004), chap. 3.

30 Salvucci and Salvucci, "Cuba and the Latin American Terms of Trade," 211. This did not deter the "natural" trade relationship between the United States and Cuba: in the second half of the nineteenth century, the flour trade increased at an average of 8.8 percent per year.

31 See Nadia Fernández de Pinedo, "Cuba y el mercado azucarero en el siglo XIX," in *Azucar y esclavitud en el final del trabajo forzado*, ed. José A. Piqueras (Mexico City: Fondo de Cultura Económica, 2002), 271–290; Linda K. Salvucci, "Atlantic Intersections: Early American Commerce and the Rise of the Spanish West Indies (Cuba)," *Business History Review* 79 (Winter 2005): 781–809; Julio le Riverend, *Historia económica de Cuba* (Havana: Editorial Pueblo y Educación, 1974), 382–394; Moreno Fraginals, *El ingenio*, 3:80.

32 Herman Merivale, *Lectures on Colonization and Colonies* (1841; reprint, New York: Kelley, 1967), 41, cited in Sidney W. Mintz, *Three Ancient Colonies: Caribbean Themes and Variations* (Cambridge, MA: Harvard University Press, 2010), 211.

33 Ramón Infiesta, *Historia constitucional de Cuba* (Havana: Editorial Selecta, 1942), 31. On questions of race and the 1940 Constitution, see Alejandra Bronfman, *Measures of Equality: Social Science, Citizenship, and Race in Cuba, 1902–1940* (Chapel Hill: University of North Carolina Press, 2004), 171–178.

34 Marifeli Pérez-Stable notes that anti-Batista opposition during the 1950s "rallied around the Constitution of 1940"; after the Cuban Revolution, the restoration of the 1940 Constitution has figured prominently on the agenda of many exiles, including José Morell Moreno, who served as a justice of the Cuban Supreme Court during the 1950s. See *The Cuban Revolution: Origins, Course, and Legacy*, 3rd ed. (New York: Oxford University Press, 2012), 82, and José Morell Moreno Papers, Cuban Heritage Collection, University of Miami Libraries.

35 See, for example, Scott Eastman and Natalia Sobrevilla, eds., *The Rise of Constitutional Government in the Iberian World: The Impact of the Cádiz Constitution of 1812* (Tuscaloosa: University of Alabama Press, 2015); François-Xavier Guerra, *Modernidad e independencias: Ensayos sobre las revoluciones hispánicas* (Madrid: Mapfre, 1992); *Cortes y Constitución de Cádiz, 200 años*, ed. José Antonio Escudero (Madrid: Espasa, 2011); and Roberto Breña, *El imperio de las circunstancias: Las independencias hispanoamericanas y la revolución liberal española* (Madrid: Marcial Pons / Colegio de México, 2012).

36 Adelman, *Sovereignty and Revolution*, 370. See also Adelman's "Introduction: The Problem of Persistence in Latin American History," in *Colonial Legacies: The Problem of Persistence in Latin American History*, ed. Jeremy Adelman (New York: Routledge, 1999), 1–13.

37 Howard J. Wiarda, *The Soul of Latin America: The Cultural and Political Tradition* (New Haven, CT: Yale University Press, 2001), 102. See also Stanley J. Stein and Barbara H. Stein, *The Colonial Heritage of Latin America: Essays on Economic Dependence in Perspective* (New York: Oxford University Press, 1970), esp. chap. 6.

38 For a sophisticated consideration of this perspective, see Josep M. Fradera, *Colonias para después de un imperio* (Barcelona: Edicions Bellaterra, 2005).

39 The literature is extensive. A few recent examples of English-language monographs include: Florencia Mallon, *Peasant and Nation: The Making of Postcolonial Mexico and Peru* (Berkeley: University of California Press, 1995); Peter Guardino, *Peasants, Politics, and the Formation of Mexico's National State: Guerrero, 1800–1857* (Stanford, CA: Stanford University Press, 1996); Hilda Sabato, *The Many and the Few: Political Participation in Republican Buenos Aires* (Stanford, CA: Stanford University Press, 2002); Brooke Larson, *Trials of Nation Making: Liberalism, Race, and Ethnicity in the Andes, 1810–1910* (Cambridge: Cambridge University Press, 2004); James E. Sanders, *Contentious Republicans: Popular Politics, Race, and Class in Nineteenth-Century Colombia* (Durham, NC: Duke University Press, 2004); Cecilia Méndez, *The Plebeian Republic: The Huanta Rebellion and the Making of the Peruvian State, 1820–1850* (Durham, NC: Duke University Press, 2005); and Pablo Piccato, *The Tyranny of Opinion: Honor in the Construction of the Mexican Public Sphere* (Durham, NC: Duke University Press, 2010). On the relationship between the constitution of popular politics and the discourse of modernity, see

James E. Sanders, "The Vanguard of the Atlantic World: Contesting Modernity in Nineteenth-Century Spanish America," *Latin American Research Review* 46:2 (2011): 104–127, and Nicola Miller and Stephen Hart, eds., *When Was Latin America Modern?* (New York: Palgrave, 2007).

40 Albert O. Hirschman, *Exit, Voice, and Loyalty: Responses to Decline in Firms, Organizations, and States* (Cambridge, MA: Harvard University Press, 1970), chap. 7.

41 Antonio de Castro to the Captain General, January 23, 1811, AGI, Cuba, Leg. 1766, Núm. 38. Ann Twinam exhaustively demonstrates how militia service laid a groundwork for claims to vassalage and citizenship by free men of color in *Purchasing Whiteness: Pardos, Mulattos, and the Quest for Social Mobility in the Spanish Indies* (Stanford, CA: Stanford University Press, 2015).

42 See Olga Portuondo Zúñiga, *Cuba: Constitución y liberalismo*, 2 vols. (Santiago de Cuba: Editorial Oriente, 2008).

43 Extracto de sucesos ocurridos en la Habana, remitido por el Intendente de Ejército al Secretario de Estado y del Despacho en Madrid, n.d., Roque Garrigó, *Historia documentada de la conspiración de los Soles y rayos de Bolívar* (Havana: Imprenta "Siglo XX," 1929), 180.

44 Eduardo Torres-Cuevas, *Historia de la masonería cubana: Seis ensayos* (Havana: Imágen Contemporánea, 2004), 48–50. Victor M. Uribe-Urán notes that mainland Latin American Masonic networks had links to France and Britain more than Spain. "The Birth of a Public Sphere in Latin America during the Age of Revolution," *Comparative Studies in Society and History*, 37:1 (2000), 425–457. See also Jossianna Arroyo, *Writing Secrecy in Caribbean Freemasonry* (New York: Palgrave Macmillan, 2013).

45 Garrigó, *Historia documentada*, 94, 97.

46 J. M. de Andueza, *Isla de Cuba pintoresca, histórica, política, literaria, mercantil é industrial* (Madrid: Boix, 1841), 112. See also Juan José Sánchez Baena, "Libertad de ideas y prensa en Cuba (1810–1823)," in *Los colores de las independencias iberoamericanas: Liberalismo, etnia, y raza*, ed. Manuel Chust and Ivana Frasquet (Madrid: Consejo Superior de Investigaciones Científicas, 2010), 55–87.

47 José Antonio Saco, *Exámen analítico del informe de la comisión especial nombrada por las Cortes . . .* (Madrid: Oficina de D. Tomas Jordan, 1837), 19.

48 Ramón de la Sagra, *Apuntes destinados a ilustrar la discusión del artículo adicional al proyecto de Constitución que dice "Las provincias de ultramar serán gobernadas por leyes especiales"* (Paris: Impr. de Maule et Renou, 1837), 32.

49 Olga Portuondo, *Un liberal cubano en la Corte de Isabel II* (Havana: Ediciones Unión, 2002), 69.

50 Alejandro de la Fuente, "Slaves and the Creation of Legal Rights in Cuba: Coartación and Papél," *Hispanic American Historical Review* 87:4 (2007), 655–692.

51 Gloria García Rodríguez, *La esclavitud desde la esclavitud: La vision de los siervos* (1996; reprint, Havana: Editorial de Ciencias Sociales, 2003), 168. The *derecho de postliminio* was a Roman legal provision that restored the rights of citizenship to returning prisoners of war. See García Rodríguez, *La esclavitud desde la esclavitud*, 203.

52 Cárlos de Sedano y Cruzat, *Cuba desde 1850 á 1875: Colección de informes, memorias, proyectos y antecedentes sobre el gobierno de la isla de Cuba, relativos al citado período que ha reunido por comisión del gobierno* (Madrid: Imprenta Nacional, 1873), 295. Dulce contrasted the "active, enterprising and dominant Anglo-Saxon" race, whose presumed unity in the United States rested on the destruction of the territory's indigenous population, to the "Latin race," which was more conservative in its actions and built its unity on the absorption of different groups.

53 Ada Ferrer, *Insurgent Cuba: Race, Nation, and Revolution, 1868–1898* (Chapel Hill: University of North Carolina Press, 1999), 4.

54 Adelman, *Sovereignty and Revolution*, 344. For a recent consideration of this question, see José M. Portillo Valdés, *Crisis atlántica: Autonomía e independencia en la crisis de la monarquía hispana* (Madrid: Fundación Carolina, Centro de Estudios Hispánicos e Iberoamericanos, 2006), and José Antonio Piqueras, *Bicentenarios de libertad: La fragua de la política en España y las Américas* (Barcelona: Ediciones Península, 2010).

55 Samuel R. Walker, *Cuba and the South* (New Orleans, May 20, 1854), Rare Book Collection, Huntington Library, San Marino, CA. On southern filibustering, see Robert E. May, *Manifest Destiny's Underworld: Filibustering in Antebellum America* (Chapel Hill: University of North Carolina Press, 2002).

56 *Representación al soberano congreso mejicano*, 4. On Mexico's interests in Cuba, see Rafael Rojas, *Cuba mexicana: Historia de una anexión imposible* (Mexico City: Secretaría de Relaciones Exteriores, 2001).

57 See, for example, Jennifer Pitts, *A Turn to Empire: The Rise of Imperial Liberalism in Britain and France* (Princeton, NJ: Princeton University Press, 2006), and Josep M. Fradera, "Reading Imperial Transitions: Spanish Contraction, British Expansion, and American Irruption," in *Colonial Crucible: Empire in the Making of the Modern American State*, ed. Alfred W. McCoy and Francisco A. Scarano (Madison: University of Wisconsin Press, 2009), 34–62.

6

ATLANTIC TRANSFORMATIONS
AND BRAZIL'S IMPERIAL INDEPENDENCE

KIRSTEN SCHULTZ

In important ways Brazil became a new country in the early nineteenth century. Following its exit from the Portuguese empire in 1822, it faced struggles over national authority and regional autonomy, including quests for provincial secession. The formation of a Brazilian nation-state—the most enduring nineteenth-century American monarchy—also entailed reckoning with transatlantic and national debates about slavery and reconsolidating an export economy in the midst of Britain's rise to industrial eminence. In all of these challenges Brazil shared conflicts and debates that shaped other new countries of the Americas. Yet, as has been noted often, Brazil faced the least conflictive path to independence. Brazilians recognized the heir to the Portuguese throne as a leader of independence; the new monarchy successfully defended its sovereignty over most of the territory of the former Portuguese colony; and in the new commercial regime of open ports and direct trade with Britain, landowners and merchants invested in the rapidly growing coffee export economy and agreed that preserving the slavery that sustained this economy was paramount.

Was Brazil, then, the least new of the new countries? Understanding how Brazilians consolidated a monarchical national state, fostered a new coffee economy, and defended slavery to hold together as the largest, most prosperous, and most politically stable South American country in the nineteenth century requires a long historical vision. The transformations that made Brazil both new and more economically prosperous and politically stable than many of its American neighbors should be traced through the whole eighteenth century and into the early decades of the nineteenth. This is not to suggest that the roots of Brazilian nationhood, or of a Brazilian nation-state, arose early in Brasil-Colônia, or that ideas and institutions of nationhood and statehood were uncontested after the 1830s. Rather, examining Brazil's transformations within the Portuguese empire's long eighteenth century illuminates the ways in which it became part of a dynamic Atlantic world in the context of a global empire—and how Brazil's place within that empire shaped how people on both sides of the Atlantic experienced the crises that ultimately led to Brazilian independence and adapted to a world increasingly defined by British industrial and military power.[1]

The eighteenth century and the first decades of the nineteenth encompassed interrelated economic, political, and administrative transformations, interpreted and addressed in various ways within the Portuguese royal court and at the local level in Brazil. They redefined the Portuguese empire, while people in both Portugal and Brazil forged a transatlantic political culture that mixed allegiance to, and critique of, monarchy and royal administration. At the start of the eighteenth century Brazil was part of an empire in transformation and a dynamic Atlantic world, linked to global markets through exports of agricultural commodities and gold, and imports of human chattel. By the middle of the century, the Crown had recognized Brazil's primacy among its territories by investing in diplomatic, administrative, and commercial policies that sought to leverage the "continental" potential of the American *ultramar* as a guarantee of the monarchy's independence within Europe. In the wake of the Napoleonic crisis and the Portuguese royal court's move to Rio de Janeiro in 1808, the legacies of these policies were manifest yet divergent. Rio-centered political elites worked to preserve the American and imperial future envisioned by eighteenth-century royal officials by liberating Brazil from colonial status within Portuguese politics and imperial commercial policy. By the 1830s these elites had forged a new independent state—a constitutional monarchy called the Empire of Brazil—and defended it against challenges from Portugal and within Brazil.

Although one royal family holding the thrones in Portugal and Brazil brought entanglements and uncertainties, Pedro I's abdication to his young Brazilian-born son, Pedro II, in 1831 affirmed the separation between Europe and America. British abolitionism notwithstanding, leaders of the new Brazilian empire also negotiated international recognition of independence and a diplomatic framework for gradual abolition that allowed for an expansion of slavery in the short term, enabling—as slave traders and slave owners insisted it would—the expanding production of wealth within a global economy that had long linked Brazil and Great Britain via Portugal. The elimination of Portugal from this network served the "interests of commerce" and opened the economic and political potential of Brazil, promoted by eighteenth-century royal officials and secured under a nineteenth-century empire linked directly if informally to industrializing Britain.

At the same time, the defense of American empire and its economic potential was inextricably linked to quests to politically transform the former colony from within. As recent historical scholarship has shown, a plurality of political projects, both old and new, shaped a complex articulation of state and nationhood in the first half of the nineteenth century. Institutional and economic continuities (slavery, monarchy, export production, British markets and merchants) provided frameworks within which people in Brazil sought to define a new nationhood in law, in political and economic practice, and in culture. In the process, visions of vassalage, monarchical authority, nationhood, and the state's sovereignty over the territory of Brazil, including its vast hinterland and disputed border zones, effaced local authorities and autonomies. As vassalage was transformed into citizenship, the ideals and practices of cultivating allegiance to the state and thereby forging a unified social and political order in the name of nationhood underwrote an entrenchment of old hierarchies and exclusions, as well as new understandings of the imperatives of territorial unity and political authority. Thus, notwithstanding the dynastic, geographic, and socioeconomic continuities so often cited as having set Brazil apart from its Spanish American neighbors, throughout the nineteenth century people living in the vast territory claimed by the new Empire of Brazil, like their counterparts across the hemisphere, contended with the contingencies and contradictions of a new sovereignty, even as the free reaped the rewards and slaves bore the burdens of Brazil's export prosperity linked to an expanding, industrial capitalism.

Global Empire and Portuguese America in the Eighteenth Century
From the fifteenth century, the Portuguese empire was a leading participant
in the creation of a complex global economy that by the late sixteenth century
linked the flow of American silver toward China and the Atlantic trades in
sugar and slaves. It was a growing economy shaped, and reshaped, by rivalry.
What Charles Boxer called "the global struggle with the Dutch," began during
the Union of the Iberian Crowns (1580–1640) and ended after the restoration
of Portuguese sovereignty under the leadership of the House of Braganza. It
led to the loss of the Moluccas (1605) and fortresses in Ceylon (1638–1658) as
well as lengthy efforts to fend off the Dutch in Africa (El Mina in 1638 and Lu-
anda from 1641 to 1648). These wars were costly and disastrous for Portuguese
Asian trade; in the 1630s, in contrast to the 1580s and 1590s when the *carreira
da India* comprised as many as fifty-nine ships, fewer than two ships arrived
at Lisbon per year with no significant increase in the following two decades.[2]

In the second half of the seventeenth century the attention of royal officials in Lisbon shifted from the Estado da Índia, the Indian Ocean network
of fortresses, merchant communities, and administrative cities, toward the Atlantic, following the generation of revenue. Yet the shift from east to west was
complex. The Dutch had set their sights on the Americas as well. In the 1620s
they attacked Salvador da Bahia and the following decade occupied the neighboring capitancy of Pernambuco—where the Portuguese under Spanish Hapsburg sovereignty had consolidated the first large-scale sugar and slave society in
the Americas. To revitalize the Brazilian enterprise, the newly restored Portuguese Crown founded the Companhia Geral do Comércio do Brasil in 1649,
providing a new venue for investment (in many cases from New Christians)
with rights to import cod, oil, and wine into Brazil, and the duty to organize
and share in the revenue from transatlantic fleets laden with slaves and sugar;
one of these fleets was instrumental in expelling the Dutch from the Brazil
in 1654. The renewed growth of Brazil's sugar economy was limited, however,
by concurrent transformations in transatlantic commerce. As the English, the
French, and the Dutch established plantations in the Caribbean, the price of
sugar declined; Portugal's revenues reached a low in the 1680s. And when Brazilian trade revived, its revenues could not compensate for what had been lost
in Asia. Nor could new links between Brazil and the Estado da Índia via the
Cape route—especially the trade in Brazilian tobacco—reverse the trend of
declining imperial revenue.[3]

A dramatic transformation and the preeminence of what some have called
an "Atlantic system"—based on the intricately linked export economies of
Brazil and Africa—took shape only at the end of the seventeenth century,

fueled initially, yet not entirely, by the discovery of gold in Portuguese America's hinterland. The adaptation of slavery to the production of gold across the uplands beyond Rio and São Paulo ensured that bound Africans would remain the base of Brazil's production. Despite the challenges of administering new settlements and extracting new resources, by the turn of the eighteenth century the empire was once again providing substantial financial resources to the Crown. Gold from Brazil had become part of a complex international political-economic conjuncture. Even as wars in Europe at the beginning of the century disrupted existing trade and commerce, they created new opportunities for Brazilian exports. In a context of war and commercial potential, the Crown of Portugal committed to a new alliance with England, signing the Methuen Treaty in 1703; it provided for low tariffs on Portuguese wines sent to England and ensured open markets in Portugal for English woolens. For Portugal, the result was a trade deficit with England, paid for with Brazilian gold. As royal officials at the time observed, it was the price of alliance with a formidable European power that would protect Portuguese territories from Franco-Spanish aggression.[4] For England, Brazilian gold sustained the momentum of its own eighteenth-century commercial enterprise. Brazil found a new place linked to Britain in a global economy that was, as Tutino explains, dynamic and polycentric.[5]

With the new Brazilian mining economy playing such a vital role in the Atlantic economy and imperial policy, the Crown remained committed to establishing control over new areas of settlement in Brazil. As thousands of settlers from Bahia, Pernambuco, São Paulo, and Portugal traveled both the official *caminhos* and newly forged and often clandestine paths to *as Minas*, the Crown first aimed to defend its sovereignty in America by limiting access to the mining region, and then turned to administrative and fiscal reforms that officials hoped would forge effective governance.[6] As officials on both sides of the Atlantic noted, governing and ensuring a steady stream of revenue from Brazilian mines carried high costs. Along with officials' salaries and the cost of freight and of building and staffing foundries, the Crown had to invest in forces of order: by the 1720s a troop of professionally trained dragoons was stationed in Minas to assist locally recruited militias in escorting gold shipments and, at times, to suppress revolts. Over time the Crown began to assume the costs of defending the Brazilian coast, once a burden borne by the residents of coastal cities. Yet if the costs of governing Minas Gerais grew, the economy that took shape around mining in the hinterland also afforded the Crown sources of revenue beyond the *quinto* (royal tax), including tolls on roads that were used to export gold and transport needed supplies to and within the region. Much of

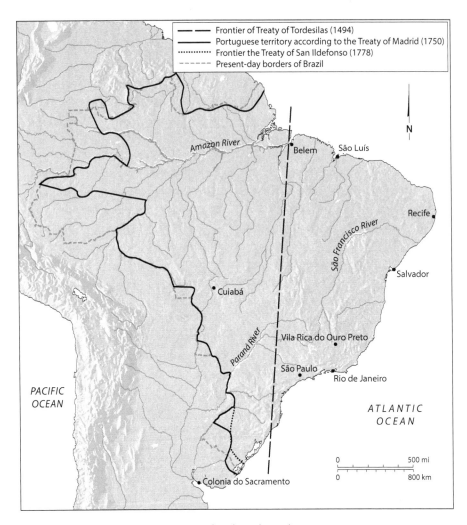

Amazon River

Belem

São Luís

N

Recife

São Francisco River

Salvador

Cuiabá

Vila Rica do Ouro Preto

Paraná River

São Paulo

Rio de Janeiro

PACIFIC
OCEAN

ATLANTIC
OCEAN

0   500 mi
0   800 km

Colonia do Sacramento

MAP 6.1. Brazil in the eighteenth century

this revenue was spent locally to sustain fiscal administration and infrastructure. Such investment "helped to reinforce government control and ultimately rendered possible the very construction of Brazil."[7]

In the second half of the eighteenth century, even as gold exports entered a period of decline, the Portuguese imperial shift from east to west endured. On the one hand, gold exports were but one source of revenue from a larger and more diverse export economy that generated revenue through customs tariffs. Indeed, as Stuart Schwartz observed, as "the gold cycle" lost dynamism around midcentury, agricultural production, including a revived sugar economy, out-paced mining. In 1760, he explains, "when Brazilian exports were valued at 4,800,000 milréis, sugar accounted for half of that figure and gold for 46%."[8] While the mix of gold and agricultural exports ensured that Brazil remained a very lucrative enterprise for the Crown, in the Estado da Índia revenues stag-nated and the Portuguese faced not only European rivals but also the ambi-tions of local rulers who sought to increase the territories under their control at the expense of the Portuguese.[9]

Facing what appeared an irreversible decline of the Asian empire and the growth of Brazil, royal officials began to articulate a new vision of an Atlantic American empire. Led by Brazilian-born Alexandre de Gusmão (1695–1753) and bolstered by increasing geographic and cartographic knowledge of the Ameri-can hinterlands, the Portuguese Crown renegotiated the borders between Spanish and Portuguese America; the new Treaty of Madrid (1750) displaced the Treaty of Tordesillas by upholding the principle of *uti possidetis* (occupa-tion) in Africa and Asia as well as the New World. The size of Portuguese claims doubled to include the vast basin of the Amazon River, while an exception was applied in Río de la Plata where the Portuguese relinquished claims to the Co-lonia do Sacramento. Although the southern borders of Portuguese America continued to generate disputes and the Treaty of Madrid was revised by the Treaty of San Ildefonso in 1777, the new western borders would endure.[10]

João V's successor, José I (r. 1750–1777), and his powerful prime minister, the future Marquês de Pombal, took up the challenge of crafting administrative and economic policy for the Amazon region and of ensuring that the whole empire remained prosperous. Pombal pursued reforms, often compared to those of the Bourbons in neighboring Spain and Spanish America, intending to strengthen Portugal's position in Europe. Without abandoning the Luso-British alliance, he sought to diminish Portugal's trade deficits with England by promoting manufacturing to reduce imports and establishing the Alto Douro Company in Portugal to curtail English control of the wine industry. Beyond what Kenneth Maxwell described as a "nationalization" of Portugal's economy through import-substitution, Pombal sought to develop colonial economies in the interest of both security and imperial trade. To exploit the Amazon basin, Pombal created the Companhia Geral do comércio do Grão Pará e Maranhão (1755), promoting the expanded use of African slave labor, the settlement of Azorean immigrants, and the diversification of the northern economy, espe-cially the cultivation of cotton and rice. To consolidate de facto royal control over the Amazon, he entrusted his brother, Francisco Xavier de Mendonça Furtado, with the task of devising a policy for the region's indigenous population;

the *Directorio que se deve observar nas Povoações dos Indios do Pará, e Maranhaõ* was published in Lisbon 1757.[11] A centerpiece in the Pombaline effort to achieve what Ângela Domingues has called the "occidentalization of Amazonian space" through greater settlement, in the wake of the expulsion of the Jesuits from the Portuguese empire in 1759 the Diretório provided the framework for governing and appropriating the labor of the indigenous populations formerly supervised by that order.[12]

As Pombal began to implement his reforms, in recognition of the growing economic and strategic importance of the Brazilian South and to further shore up Portuguese control of frontier territories there, in 1763 the Crown moved the capital of Brazil from Salvador, Bahia, to Rio de Janeiro. The Crown sent out cartographers, engineers, and natural scientists in expeditions intended to increase knowledge of the potential of its territories. To enhance its defensive and administrative capacities, the Crown raised auxiliary cavalry and infantry regiments throughout Brazil and established *juntas da fazenda* (exchequer boards) in each captaincy. The end of the requirement that ships sail within the fleet system, in turn, gave a select group of merchants more flexibility in adapting to supply and demand. In response to the British seizure of Havana in 1762, officials on both sides of the Atlantic began a series of projects aimed at fortifying the Brazilian coast. To further security and, above all, to keep commerce Portuguese and Brazilian, the Crown barred foreigners from Brazil's ports.[13]

Although Pombal fell from power following the death of Dom José in 1777, much of his reform vision weathered the criticism that found voice in the new royal court of Maria I (1777–1816). Brazilian planters and merchants, Portuguese royal officials, and what Maxwell calls "the merchant-industrial oligarchy" enriched by Pombaline protectionism continued to recognize both the overwhelming importance of Brazil within the imperial economy and that the new controls on commerce within the empire had diminished trade deficits with Britain and dismantled "the commanding role" earlier played by the British merchants in Portuguese ports. Led by Pombaline protégé Rodrigo de Sousa Coutinho, in the last decade of the eighteenth century Portuguese royal officials continued to foster the diversification of Brazil's export agriculture as well as the revival of mining. Thus, as Maxwell observes, "the South Atlantic dimension of the long Portuguese eighteenth century . . . set the chronological framework for the whole epoch."[14]

While the Portuguese defended mercantilist policies throughout the century, what contemporaries called the *antigo sistema colonial* proved "pervious." Portuguese imperial commerce linked to northern, central, and southern European shipping and finance; it included direct trade in certain commodities (i.e., cod) between northern Europe and Brazil; it extended to "intercolonial exchange" between Africa and the Indian Ocean network and, above all, to the transatlantic slave trade, much of which was controlled by Portuguese African and Brazilian traders. In Brazil, both trade with Portugal and the slave trade between Brazil and Africa fueled the development of local and regional economies, expanding commodity production, and a wealthy landed and mercantile elite.[15] Thus, in Brazil, as Tutino has noted of other American contexts, the terrain of the eighteenth-century commercial economy was not only defined by exchanges between metropoles and colonies, but also encompassed regional and subregional economic centers and ports linked in complex ways to each other and to global trade networks.[16]

The porosity of a global empire defined by what one royal official called the "interests of commerce" also shaped the ways in which royal officials perceived political-cultural challenges to Portuguese authority. If investment in the defense of the Brazilian coastline reduced the potential of foreign aggression, the problem of cultivating political allegiance and gaining administrative and fiscal control over the extraction of wealth proved to be more challenging and enduring. In the newly settled mining region, in the first three decades of the eighteenth century the Crown faced both violent challenges to political order and a general disregard for royal authority. The Crown also faced revolts against taxes in the 1710s in Salvador and São Paulo, as well as armed conflict between planters of Olinda and wealthy merchants in Recife. The Crown responded with force, as it had in Minas, to restore order and maintain control. In the first half of the eighteenth century, as officials negotiated the implementation of taxes and the recognition of local institutions, they also promoted public and collective displays of allegiance and afforded urban life and urban planning greater space in royal policy.[17] It would be in urban centers where, in the last decades of the eighteenth century, residents would receive and share news of challenges to monarchy and empire taking shape in North America, France, and Haiti, and where residents would mount their own conspiracies against royal government and rebellions against the social order that royal authority upheld. The Crown successfully confronted these challenges too—most famously the Tiradentes conspiracy of 1789 in Minas Gerais—with force and exemplary punishment.[18]

Throughout the eighteenth century the Crown also contended with an effective absence of its authority in the vast hinterlands of Portuguese America. The Pombaline Directory envisioned assimilating Indians into colonial society as laborers. In practice, the lack of resources for interior administration, local initiatives that contradicted royal policy, the corruption of directors, the encroachment on indigenous villages and lands as settlers pushed into territories under Indian control, the Indians' resistance to such settlement, and Portuguese perceptions of indigenous savagery, all mixed to stimulate local and royal efforts to militarize the hinterland and enslave, remove, and in some cases exterminate indigenous populations without effectively enhancing the governance of territories far from the historic, mostly coastal, centers of settlement. Indeed, as Hal Langfur explains, while in the hinterland of Minas the Crown sought to create a "forested no-man's land, peopled by native antagonists whose enmity . . . would prevent unauthorized access to and smuggling from the mines to the coast," even this "enforced absence" proved difficult to sustain in practice. African slavery too presented challenges to sovereignty; throughout Brazil slaves who escaped from plantations formed communities, called *mocambos* or by the eighteenth-century *quilombos*, which were economically viable and politically autonomous. In the late seventeenth century royal authorities had turned to military force to dismantle the large, populous, and long-established República dos Palmares in northeastern Brazil. Yet the use of force on the margins of Portuguese settlement, often at odds with the local imperatives of negotiation, did not mean that the sovereignty proclaimed by treaties became reality on the ground. Indeed, at the turn of the nineteenth century much of the territory claimed by the Portuguese Crown encompassed an "archipelago" of autonomous indigenous communities and quilombos. They sustained "territorialized resistance," as one historian describes it, to settlement and enslavement in places both remote from and adjacent to centers of economic and political power.[19]

Still, the fractured geography of governance and sovereignty notwithstanding, as royal officials in Portugal assessed Napoleon's undeniable ambition and the prospects of another European war, Brazil's potential loomed large. Recognized throughout the eighteenth century in diplomatic, commercial, and administrative policies that promoted settlement of American hinterland, urbanization, investment in administrative and judicial institutions, and the cultivation of political allegiance, Brazil had become the foundation of Portuguese wealth and power. Its potential grew as revolutionary ex-slaves took down the export production of sugar and coffee in Haiti, the Atlantic leader in both before 1790, opening new markets for Brazilian growers. As chief of the royal treasury Rodrigo de Sousa Coutinho surmised in 1803, "Portugal by itself is not the best and most essential part of the monarchy." If a war were to leave Portugal devastated, he concluded, "it was incumbent upon its Sovereign and its Peoples to go and create a powerful Empire in Brazil."[20]

Crisis, Independence, and Sovereignty

When in 1807 Napoleon ordered an army to march across Spain and occupy Lisbon, he brought to an end the neutrality that sustained the Portuguese commercial empire in the last quarter of the eighteenth century as well as recent debates within the Portuguese royal court about capitulation to the French or alliance with the British. In response, Prince Regent Dom João, ruling in place of his incapacitated mother Maria I, established a regency, counseled his vassals against armed resistance, assured them they would endure his absence only "until the General Peace" was attained, and, with thousands of courtiers and a British naval escort, crossed the Atlantic.[21] While Brazil officially became a short-term haven from war and occupation, key royal counselors saw the move to Brazil as a continuation of eighteenth-century visions of Western ascendance and recent conjecture about American potential. Sousa Coutinho, now minister of foreign affairs and war, dramatically restated his optimistic appraisal of the reorganization of imperial space. Rather than embarking on an exile, the prince regent, he posited in the "Declaration of War against the French," was headed for "a new empire, which he will create."[22]

In the years that followed, royal officials insisted that the "new empire" stood against revolution and in defense of political tradition and hierarchy, while recognizing that it would also bring significant change. In Bahia in 1808, before arriving at Rio, the prince regent issued a charter that opened Brazil's ports to allow commerce and the collection of revenue to continue during the war and the occupation of Portugal. Officially defined as "interim and provisional," merchants and officials across the empire recognized that the measure marked the end of the "old colonial system" of mercantilist monopoly and the beginning of "free trade" for Brazil. In a time of war and British naval and commercial dominance in the Atlantic, trade links to Britain became direct, while markets for Brazilian export commodities grew steadily in the 1810s.[23]

As the Peninsular War ended in 1814, demonstrations of political allegiance and transatlantic solidarity began to fracture. Vassals of the Portuguese monarchy questioned the empire's new configuration, with its capital in Rio. In 1817 in Pernambuco, as sugar prices fluctuated and the fiscal demands of the Rio government appeared to jeopardize prosperity, provincial elites staged an insurrection demanding more autonomy. The same year, discontent in Portugal with postwar conditions led a group of officers to plot against the interim government of British marshal Beresford in favor of "independence" and a constitutional monarchy. Although the Crown moved swiftly and successfully to repress both movements, it faced growing criticism of the political and economic ramifications of the alliance with Great Britain, expressed in an ex-patriot press in London, in public squares in Portugal and Brazil, and at the royal court itself.

The key concern among Portuguese merchants was a new commercial regime, created by the Treaties of Commerce and Navigation of 1810, upheld in subsequent agreements, and characterized by Alan Manchester as "British preeminence" in Brazil. Desired by imperial and commercial interests in London before the transfer of the court, temporarily undercut by the 1808 charter that opened Brazil's ports to all nations, the 1810 treaties gave British traders and goods a preferential status in Brazilian ports: import duties of 15 percent on British goods were lower than those applied to Portuguese merchandise and other international goods. And while Portugal gained "most favored nation" status within the British empire, Brazilian sugar and coffee, "articles similar to the products of the British colonies," were denied direct entrance to British markets. Within Brazil the British also gained the unreciprocated privilege of selling retail. Although the 1810 treaties were at first accepted in Portugal as essential in wartime, when it became clear that the postwar regime would not bring changes that favored merchants in Portugal, acceptance gave way to disenchantment.[24]

In Brazil, if merchants and local economies did not suffer as dramatically from the opening of Brazil's ports, many residents viewed the British as having gained the upper hand in trade and, as some protested, in local economies as well. Complaints about the British presence in local markets and frictions generated by growing British communities in Brazilian port cities resonated with perceptions of the larger threat of Great Britain's imperial ambition in South America. Brazilian elites especially opposed British demands that the Portuguese Crown curtail the slave trade. While the presence of royalty in Rio de Janeiro had raised questions about both the moral and cultural effects of slavery, and the Haitian Revolution had raised doubts about security, the majority of Luso-Brazilian elites saw slavery as integral to imperial prosperity.[25]

At the end of the decade the perception of besieged economic and political sovereignties and a more general dissatisfaction with the local politics of the new political economy of empire, the "internal conflicts" of the Luso-Brazilian empire came to a head and laid bare the political limits of the wartime imperial reconfiguration. The center of the crisis formed not in the royal court of Rio de Janeiro, but in Portugal where the Crown failed to convince its vassals of the promise of a new American future. Instead both the British postwar occupation and the opening of Brazil's ports were read as signs of the former metropolis's new "colonial" status. In Portugal growing criticism of the trend toward "national decadence" focused on the nature of sovereignty itself. In August 1820 a group of property owners, merchants, low-ranking military officers, magistrates and clergy, and some members of the nobility in Porto, called on Dom João to return to Portugal. There the monarch could usher in a "regeneration" of the Portuguese nation by convoking the Cortes, a formerly consultative institution that represented the kingdom in the reunion of three estates. Inspired by the experience of Cádiz in 1812, they called on representatives to write a constitution for Portugal and its empire.

While the movement professed loyal to the monarchy, its loyalty was based on Dom João's allegiance to the Cortes and a new constitution that would circumscribe royal power and restrict it to the role of executive. The nation, not the Crown, would be sovereign. The news of the rebellion reached Rio in October 1820. A steady stream of rumor and reports followed, including news that confirmed the spread of the rebellion to Lisbon where the Cortes Gerais, Extraordinárias e Constituintes da Nação Portuguesa, would convene. As royal counselors debated how to respond, political actions in Brazil redefined emerging challenges. Beginning in January 1821 local expressions of support for the Cortes from officials and Portuguese troops in the Northeast and in Rio began to include demands that the Spanish Constitution of Cádiz, drafted in 1812 during the French occupation of Spain and recently reimplemented at the insistence of Spanish military men, serve as a provisional charter of the global Portuguese nation. In response, Dom João pledged support for the deliberations of the Lisbon Cortes.[26]

When, in recognition of the Cortes's demands, Dom João set sail for Portugal in 1821, he left behind his son Dom Pedro as regent of Brazil and uncertainty about whether the new constitutional order would endure and, if it did, what it would mean for the empire. One draft of a new Portuguese constitution defined the Portuguese nation as the "union of all Portuguese of both hemispheres," including "free men born and living in Portuguese territory" and "the slaves born in the ultramarine possessions that obtain manumission."[27] Thus, the ideal of national representation would itself serve as the basis for future imperial integrity and prosperity. In practice, imperial integrity would be guaranteed by the presence in the Lisbon Cortes of deputies from Brazil, elected to provide representation for each province and, with other representatives of the Portuguese "nation," to deliberate on the "new order of things." Yet constitutionalist politics and political culture produced manifold visions and debates. Within the now uncensored press, pamphleteers raised the question of whether the nation, monarchy, and empire were coterminous.

Were they products of history and tradition, language and law, and a will to live together in a political community, or illusions that would succumb to perceptions of cultural, geographic, and racial differences?[28]

Indeed, although Dom Pedro accepted his father's pledge to defend the future constitution and respect the authority of the Lisbon Cortes, by the middle of 1822, the ideal of a constitutionally sanctioned representation that promised to preserve the unity of the empire became the basis of rupture. As "citizens" on both sides of the Atlantic debated the empire's future, many in Brazil began to claim publicly that the promised representation and "equality of rights" would not necessarily serve what they defined as Brazilian "interests" and "causes." At the same time, by August 1821, with Brazilian delegates a minority, and before many of them had arrived in Lisbon, the Cortes began to pass measures interpreted in Brazil as efforts to "reduce Brazil to the old status of colony": commercial regulations that had inhibited the interests of peninsular merchants were repealed; Rio was stripped of its status as a political capital with the creation of provincial governments directly subordinate to Lisbon; additional troops were sent to Brazil; the high courts established in Rio following the transfer of the court were abolished; and, perhaps most threatening, Prince Regent Dom Pedro, heir to the throne, was ordered, as his father João VI had been in 1821, to return to Portugal.[29] Thus, as was the case in the Cádiz deliberations, as the promoters of the Lisbon Cortes offered constitutionalism as a way to integrate the empire through representation, Portuguese representatives worked to affirm Lisbon's rule within the empire. As in Spain's domains, first in Cádiz and then with the 1820 reinstitution of the constitution, the attempt to use constitutional liberalism to integrate an empire came with limits and impositions that led American representatives and those they represented to consider separation.

Local and provincial governments in the Brazilian Northeast, with strong commercial ties to Portugal and the first to embrace constitutionalism, remained loyal to the Cortes that, in turn, acknowledged their authority, seeking to drive a wedge between them and Dom Pedro's regency. In Bahia, armed conflict between Portuguese expeditionary forces and local Brazilian regiments left Portuguese merchants and the military governor in Salvador to face mounting opposition to the Cortes in nearby towns and the countryside. Some refugees from the city, including militiamen of color, together with slaves and other laborers, saw an end to Portuguese sovereignty as an opportunity for social change; at the same time plantation and sugar mill owners surmised that a government led by Dom Pedro would preserve slavery and the social hierarchies that underwrote their wealth.[30]

FIGURE 6.1. An emperor for a New World empire: Acclaiming Dom Pedro, 1822

Contrasting visions of uncertain changes could lead to a common pursuit of separation. In Rio and surrounding provinces the Cortes's decrees also inspired people with diverse political and social aspirations to mobilize in support of the prince regent's remaining in Brazil. Dom Pedro responded favorably, pledging in January 1822 to defy the Cortes and stay.[31] The following May, with increasing organized support for his leadership, Dom Pedro complied with a request from Rio's city council to call a representative body that would evaluate the conditions for union between Portugal and Brazil, and whether and how the constitution drafted by the Lisbon Cortes would apply to Brazil.[32]

Dom Pedro hoped that the new assembly in Rio and the Cortes in Lisbon would work together to maintain the integrity of the Portuguese monarchy and empire, a vision similar to the 1821 Plan de Iguala that aimed to hold Mexico and Spain together under Bourbon sovereignty. But in Rio in 1822 public support for "independence" as a guarantee of Brazil's post-1808 status began to take shape.[33] Meanwhile, in the Lisbon Cortes, as representatives from Brazil defended autonomy, the majority of delegates expressed skepticism about the maintenance of a government in Brazil led by the prince regent. On September 7, informed of the Cortes's decision to defend its undivided sovereignty over American territory with force, Dom Pedro pledged to secure Brazil's complete separation from his native Portugal. In October, Dom Pedro was acclaimed emperor of the new Empire of Brazil. Originally called as a "Luso-Brazilian Assembly," the representatives gathered in Rio de Janeiro were charged to write the new empire's constitution.[34]

To consolidate the Empire of Brazil, Dom Pedro and his allies faced the challenges of establishing the empire's sovereignty in all the territory of the former colony and of defining political practice. While Brazil's independence is often seen as a relatively peaceful counterpoint to the violent struggles that unfolded across Spanish America, Dom Pedro's rupture with the Cortes was challenged. The confrontations between those defending the new empire and those defending Portuguese sovereignty, provincial autonomy, or both, were often bloody. To gain control over the North and the South Dom Pedro and his allies purchased arms and recruited foreign military officers; naval forces led by Thomas Cochrane aided local insurgents' ultimately successful blockade of Salvador, together forcing the departure of Portuguese forces in July 1823. Following two years of fighting that included the use of brutal and at times indiscriminate force the empire's armies prevailed.

The effort to define constitutional practice in Brazil, if less bloody, was no less contested. As the new Constituent Assembly debated the scope of the emperor's and its own authority, a nativist press inflamed tensions between Brazilian- and Portuguese-born residents of Rio de Janeiro, leading Dom Pedro to denounce the assembly as a source of disorder. He sent troops to disband it. The Constitution of 1824, written by a council of men subsequently appointed by Dom Pedro and promulgated by him in March of that year, recognized both a general assembly and the emperor as representatives of the "Brazilian Nation." It also established central administrative authority over local sovereignties and provincial autonomies.[35]

Although Brazil's fight for independence stood in contrast to that of Spanish America, where a once vast empire fragmented into ten different and debated nations, the new empire continued to face local and regional challenges. Indeed, beyond Rio de Janeiro the new constitutional order was rejected. As was the case in 1817 and 1822, the northeastern provinces rebelled against monarchical authority and proclaimed their own understandings of liberal governance. Allegiance to a new "Confederation of Ecuador" took shape in Pernambuco and in the northern provinces of Alagoas, Paraíba, Río Grande do Norte, and Ceará. In response, lacking Portuguese recognition of Brazil's independence and anticipating the arrival of Portuguese forces, Dom Pedro's government had

MAP 6.2. Brazil in the nineteenth century

to calculate whether a deployment of forces to assert authority in the North would jeopardize the defense of Rio de Janeiro. Mobilizing British mercenaries and local allies, imperial forces defeated the Confederation; its leaders were arrested and incarcerated or executed.[36] In the South, the empire had less success. In the mid-1820s rebels in the Banda Oriental challenged Dom Pedro's authority and Brazilian sovereignty and aligned themselves with the United Provinces of Río de la Plata. By 1827, after decisive defeat on the battlefield and with Great Britain mediating the dispute, Brazil had to recognize the loss of the territory that three years later became Uruguay.

Following these initial decades of conflict, the empire went on to preside over a political stability and prosperity that stood in sharp contrast to much of the Americas for decades. The question of why has elicited numerous debates. Historians have examined the complex social and political arrangements of the early nineteenth century in which Brazilians negotiated transformations and continuities. The development of an economy of export diversity during the long eighteenth century, promoted by Portugal while always linked to Britain, also underwrote early national stability. During the wars that shook the Atlantic world from 1790, Brazil gained new export opportunities opened by the slave revolution in Haiti, became the center of a global empire in 1808, and found prosperity in expanding export growth increasingly linked directly to Britain during the years after 1810. When the conflicts that led to the experiment in liberalism and then Brazilian imperial separation came to a head in the early 1820s, Brazilian export prosperity linked to British commercial ascendancy held strong. As it rose to global industrial and military hegemony, Great Britain facilitated the independence and unity of Brazil. Britain mediated border disputes, negotiated international recognition of the empire's independence, and financed the 2 million pounds sterling the empire agreed to pay Portugal as an indemnity. All that opened the way for formal guarantees of British traders' rights to operate in Brazilian ports, facilitating their dominant place in Brazil's commercial and export economy during a period of great growth as the cultivation and export of coffee expanded in the region around Rio de Janeiro.[37] The Empire of Brazil, in this sense, inherited Portugal's historic commercial and political alliance with Great Britain, as the latter soared to new power and prosperity.

The new Brazilian empire also inherited ongoing negotiations over the future of the slave trade as British foreign policy embraced the use of political and economic power and recognition of South American independence as leverage for demanding the immediate end of the trade between Africa and the new states. In Brazil, some powerful political elites, including José Bonifácio de Andrada e Silva, expressed support for the end of the slave trade and of the institution of slavery in the future. They also insisted, pointing to recent events in Haiti, that only a very gradual and nonviolent abolition would avert disaster for Brazil's export economy. After two centuries of plantation production grounded in slavery and a second century in which the bondage of Africans became the base of gold mining, slavery was deeply entrenched in Brazilian society; slaves supplied the labor on both plantations and more modest holdings, in mines and cities. As the Brazilian political elite staunchly upheld both the trade and slavery itself, even as most new Spanish American republics agreed to abolish the trade in the 1820s, within British official circles Brazil became "the slave trade personified."[38]

Between 1821 and 1826 in both London and Rio de Janeiro, in negotiations over recognition of independence and commercial arrangements between Great Britain and Brazil, British and Brazilian representatives took up the question of a time frame for ending the slave trade as well as of how to characterize the Empire of Brazil's commitment to earlier conventions between Portugal and Great Britain, which limited the trade to below the equator. Some in the British cabinet expected an agreement that would make the end of the slave trade a condition for recognition of independence. British officials, however, also saw a need to balance the moral project of abolition with the commercial interests of their own empire. Accepting Brazil's refusal of immediate abolition, the British government recognized Brazilian independence in 1825 prior to a settlement over the question of the trade. The British maintained their commitment to abolition by stipulating that the Empire of Brazil could not unite with former Portuguese colonies in Africa, a union that would have created a national, rather than international, transatlantic slave trade. After a new round of negotiations the following year, the governments of Great Britain and Brazil ratified an antitrade treaty in 1827. Brazil agreed to observe the obligations of earlier treaties that limited the trade to south of the equator; beyond the line, it had three years to continue the trade before the British would begin to regard it as piracy.[39]

Although the treaty found support among Dom Pedro's closest allies, many among the political elite regarded the outcome as the unfortunate result of the emperor's excessive power and British imperial ambitions.[40] As the negotiations over the treaty had unfolded, another political crisis contributed to an erosion of both elite and popular confidence in the emperor. Following Dom João's death in Portugal in 1826, Dom Pedro's interest in Portuguese politics, specifically his daughter's claims to the throne, called into question his political allegiances and priorities, especially among Brazilian-born elites who feared a reunion with Portugal. Feelings of uncertainty over the political future of Brazil mounted in the context of fiscal crisis (the Bank of Brazil, founded on the arrival of the royal court to Rio, closed in 1829), while the loss of territory that became Uruguay on the Río de la Plata left military commanders disenchanted with the imperial government. In 1831, as demonstrations both for and against his authority engulfed the city of Rio de Janeiro, Dom Pedro abdicated to his five-year-old son and namesake.[41]

The end of Pedro I's reign marked the end of the decades of conflicts and transition that made Brazil a new country—a constitutional monarchy of vast territorial claims that found a rising prosperity for a powerful few by sustaining export production grounded on growing numbers of enslaved laborers. In Portugal's American empire responses to the crises shaped by the Haitian Revolution, the fall of the European empires, and the rise of British industrial hegemony were conditioned by the ways eighteenth-century Brazil had become a dominant export economy, first within the Portuguese empire and then linked to Britain during the key decade of conflict and transition after 1810. Initially, revolution in the United States, France, and Saint Domingue provided opportunity, as Brazilian exports took the place of Caribbean competition undermined by local violence. With the arrival of the Portuguese court in Rio, the colony continued to prosper while guaranteeing the survival of the monarchy. The crisis of authority in Brazil and Portugal that followed the Napoleonic wars led to an embrace of a monarchy "emancipated" from absolutism by "national sovereignty." In the 1820s in political discourse and practice, the residents of Brazil's historic urban centers, together with statesmen on both sides of the Atlantic, came to recognize Brazil as an "autonomous political body."[42]

The economic basis for the empire's prosperity—export commodities made by slave labor—was ensured in a constitution that both recognized the legacies of slavery for citizenship (freed slaves born in Brazil were citizens) and allowed slavery to expand.[43] Notwithstanding British abolitionism and its appeal among members of the British government, the Empire of Brazil secured recognition of its independence from Portugal only three years after Dom Pedro had pledged to defend it with his life. Brazilian diplomacy—and the promise of profitable export trades—produced a framework for ending the transatlantic trade that was sufficiently porous to allow rising imports of enslaved Africans. As slaveholders and political elites responded to slave rebellions with repression, policing, and efforts to effectively "administer" slaves as laborers, the fear generated among slave owners by news from Haiti and by local rebellions in Brazil did not displace violence or greed. Although the legislature later strengthened the legal framework for the abolition of the trade, the Brazilian government for decades showed neither the interest nor a capacity to enforce the ban. No surprise to a British government which sought to protect its own interests in the Brazilian export economy, neither the slave trade treaty's ratification nor the end of the years of "tolerance" led to a decline in the number of Africans brought to Brazil. Indeed, some Brazilian elites began to forge a proslavery discourse in the legislative assembly and in the press, countering arguments in favor of even a gradual abolition in a distant future. It is difficult to exaggerate the tragic dimensions of the consequences: between 1831 and 1850, Brazil, together with the Spanish colony of Cuba, received 10 percent of the

FIGURE 6.2. Slaves carrying coffee in nineteenth-century Brazil

total number of Africans brought to the New World in the entire 350 years of the transatlantic trade. In the expanding coffee regions around São Paulo, Minas Gerais, and Rio de Janeiro planters imported three times the number of slaves in 1836–1840 as their predecessors had in the centuries before 1835. Meanwhile, in sugar-producing Pernambuco the annual number of imported slaves tripled between 1837 and 1840.[44] The export economy grew, serving British and North Atlantic markets, financed by British banks. British merchants and Brazilian planters reaped the rewards.[45] The Brazilian expansion of slavery thus converged with other American experiences examined in this volume; with Cuba, where slave imports increased, and with the United States, where southern planters drew a growing local population of slaves westward toward Louisiana and Texas. Across the hemisphere, links to British industry yielded American prosperity, profits, and enduring human costs.

Territory and the Predicaments of Sovereignty in the New State
Viewed from the capital in Rio, provincial port cities, and the coffee and sugar plantations that sustained their wealth by sending slave-made exports to Britain as it forged a new industrial world, mid-nineteenth-century Brazil appeared a consolidated new country. The economic dynamism and diplomatic negotiations that enabled the political elite's commitments to both constitutional monarchy and slavery did not, however, end the fractured nature of de facto sovereignty in Brazil. Although the continuities that marked independence grounded elite prosperity in key coastal zones and nearby interior enclaves of the vast territory claimed by the new empire, the continuities included persistent historic tensions as well. As noted above, imperial authority (now based in Rio) was often at odds with provincial elite and popular demands for autonomy. The empire also encompassed conflicts between elites and a range of peoples and communities seeking to escape slavery or preserve indigenous independence. Thus, even as slave-based export prosperity stood in sharp contrast to Spanish South America, the challenges of internal integration and local sovereignty were shared across the continent. Indeed, in Brazil the politically turbulent decade of the Regency that followed Pedro I's abdication laid bare the weak consensus among elites and the popular classes about the institutional frameworks for governance at the national and regional level, and about the scope of imperial authority and provincial autonomy. Only in the middle of the nineteenth century, after two decades of provincial rebellion, a decentralization and then recentralization of power in the executive branch, reform of the judiciary, reforms of the military and the creation of a National Guard, and the end of the Regency and Dom Pedro II's assumption of the throne in 1840 did the imperial state consolidate its authority in provincial urban centers and their hinterlands.

The forging of ideas and practices of nationhood and administrative sovereignty across the empire's larger territory was an even more protracted process.[46] The resistance and persistence of quilombos on the outskirts of coastal cities and plantation zones forced political leaders and planters to recognize their incapacity to eradicate communities of freedom whose residents often worked nearby on plantations and in cities for wages. As Yuko Miki has explained, living as free people within societies and spaces in which the law defined them as slaves, *quilombolas* (maroons) forged an "insurgent geography" of citizenship that allowed them to control their own labor and maintain family ties.[47]

For the indigenous, in turn, even as nineteenth-century novelists imagined their unions with settlers leading to the birth of an amalgamating nation, independence from Portugal did not bring significant shifts in their relations with frontier settlers and political elites. Legislators recognized Indians and their capacity for "civilization" in debates in the constituent assembly of 1823, as had eighteenth-century royal legislation, but the status of the indigenous was not addressed in the Constitution of 1824. As before independence, nineteenth-century policies privileged assimilation and acculturation while marginalizing Indians from social and political agency as legal dependents. The Pombaline Directory, dismantled at the end of the eighteenth century, was not replaced with a new administrative structure for indigenous communities (the mid-nineteenth-century office of Director-General of Indians was not put into practice). As Hal Langfur explains, although the declaration of war against "savages" and cannibals in 1808 centralized the violence that was already a feature of Indian-Portuguese relations at the local level, by the 1830s the Crown had given up on the Botocudo war as a means to force territorial incorporation in the vast hinterland beyond Rio and São Paulo; it did not have the resources necessary to sustain it. This suggests the emergence of spaces for indigenous independence in the Brazilian backlands parallel to those Erick Langer details for the frontiers of Spanish South America. Yet in many parts of Brazil, indigenous prosperity and autonomy were challenged by elite efforts to gain control over the hinterland. Land legislation abetted the shift, already under way in the eighteenth century, away from efforts to appropriate Indians' labor to dispossessing them of their land. Indeed, in the "just war" against the Botocudo, the Crown, while insisting it intended to "civilize" Indians, took the opportunity to redefine and reinforce its control over frontier lands by taking them as *terrenos devolutos* to be demarcated, settled, and despoiled.[48] As in the United States east of the Mississippi, a flourishing slave-based export economy drove the search for lands westward in Brazil, limiting the chances for indigenous independence that proved better on the margins of nations with economies in crisis.

Thus, the new Empire of Brazil inherited from the Portuguese Crown a "continental" geography defended in the Treaty of Madrid, a fractured sovereignty over that huge territory, as well as economic, cultural, political, and legal frameworks for conquest and settlement that would, over the course of the nineteenth century, diminish but not entirely eradicate indigenous autonomy. The gap between ideal and real sovereignty sustained the new state's relationship to what James Holston describes as the "distinctly porous enclosure" of an "inclusively inegalitarian" national society that shaped the empire and endured long after its fall.[49] Amid these contradictions, the independent empire sustained slave-based export economies—the older sugar plantations and mills in the Northeast and the new and expanding coffee cultivation in the South—as British capital and commerce (British abolitionism notwithstanding) facilitated profitable ties to the Atlantic economy. If the empire presided over the end of slavery in 1888, it bequeathed the export economy and its own less decisive presence in an interior, where diverse peoples continued to negotiate the possibilities and uncertainties of their relative autonomy, to its successor, the "Republic of the United States of Brazil," a year later.

Notes

For their many illuminating comments and suggestions, I would like to thank the participants in the "New Nations in a New World, 1750–1850" conference, Georgetown University, 2011, and the subsequent panels at the Latin American Studies Association Meeting, 2012, especially John Tutino, who read carefully and critically many drafts.

1 Among the most seminal accounts of Brazil's transition from colony to empire are Caio Prado Júnior, *Evolução Política do Brasil, Colônia e Império* (1933), 18th ed. (São Paulo: Brasiliense, n.d.) and *Formação do Brasil Contemporâneo* (1942), 20th ed. (São Paulo: Brasiliense, 1987), and Fernando A. Novais, *Portugal e Brasil na Crise do Antigo Sistema Colonial (1777–1808)* (São Paulo: Hucitec, 1979). More recent scholarship both builds on this work and reconsiders the contingencies of imperial, continental, national, and international economies and politics to challenge the assumption that the end of the Portuguese empire in America was tantamount to the creation of the state and the nation, as well as the more recent claim that it was the state that forged the nation in the nineteenth century. See especially the collaborative research project "A fundação do Estado e da Nação brasileiros, c. 1750/1850" led by Wilma Peres Costa, Cecilia Helena de Salles Oliveira, and the late István Jancsó, the results of which are being disseminated in various forms and venues including monographs, collections of essays, and the journal *Almanack Brasiliense*, published online from 2005 to 2010 by the Instituto de Estudos Brasileiros, Universidade de São Paulo at http://www.almanack.usp.br/, and most recently at the Universidade Federal de São Paulo as *Almanack* at http://www.almanack.unifesp.br. For an overview of the conceptual foundations of the project see Costa and Salles de Oliveira, preface, in Márcia Berbel, Rafael Marquese, and Tâmis Parron, *Escravidão*

e Política, Brasil e Cuba, 1790–1850 (São Paulo: Fapesp/Hucitec, 2010). For extended essays on the historiography of Brazilian independence see István Jancsó, ed., *Independência: Historia e Historiografia* (São Paulo: Hucitec, 2005), and Maria Odila Silva Dias, "A interiorização da metrópole" (1972), in *A interiorização da metrópole e outros estudos*, ed. Silva Dias (São Paulo: Alameda, 2005). For a discussion of notions of nation, patria, and the people, see István Jancsó and João Paulo G. Pimenta, "Peças de um mosaico (ou apontamentos para o estudo da emergência da identidade nacional brasileira)," in *Viagem Incompleta: A experiencia brasileira (1500–2000)*, in *Formação: Histórias*, ed. Carlos Guilherme Mota, 2nd ed. (São Paulo: SENAC, 2000).

2   C. R. Boxer, *The Portuguese Seaborne Empire, 1415–1825* (1969) (Manchester: Carcanet, 1991); Sanjay Subrahmanyam, *The Portuguese Empire in Asia 1500–1700, a Political and Economic History* (London: Longman, 1993); Jorge M. Pedreira, "Costs and Financial Trends in the Portuguese Empire, 1415–1822," in *Portuguese Oceanic Expansion, 1400–1800*, ed. Francisco Bethencourt and Diogo Ramada Curto (New York: Cambridge University Press, 2007), 62.

3   Pedreira, "Costs and Financial Trends," 64–66.

4   Pedreira, "Costs and Financial Trends"; José Luís Cardoso, "Leitura e interpretação do Tratado de Methuen: Balanço histórico e historiográfico," in *O Tratado de Methuen (1703): Diplomacia, guerra, política e economia*, ed. José Luís Cardoso (Lisbon: Livros Horizonte, 2003).

5   John Tutino, chapter 1 in this volume.

6   On Minas Gerais see J. R. Russell-Wood, "The Gold Cycle, c. 1690–1750," in *Colonial Brazil*, ed. Leslie Bethell (New York: Cambridge University Press, 1987); Júnia Ferreira Furtado, *Homens de negócio: A interiorização da metrópole e do comércio das Minas setecentistas* (São Paulo: Huctitec, 1999), 149–150; Laura de Mello e Souza, *Desclassificados do Ouro: A pobreza mineira no século XVIII* (Rio de Janeiro: Edições Graal, 1982); Adriana Romeiro, *Paulistas e emboabas no coração das Minas: Idéias, práticas e imaginário político no século XVIII* (Belo Horizonte: Editora UFMG, 2008); Robert Allan White, "Fiscal Policy and Royal Sovereignty in Minas Gerais: The Capitation Tax of 1735," *The Americas* 34:2 (October 1977), 207–229; Boxer, *The Golden Age of Brazil: Growing Pains of a Colonial Society, 1695–1750* (Berkeley: University of California Press, 1962), 188–203.

7   Pedreira, "Costs and Financial Trends," 68.

8   Stuart B. Schwartz, "The Economy of the Portuguese Empire," in Bethencourt and Curto, *Portuguese Oceanic Expansion*, 38.

9   Maria de Jesus dos Martires Lopes, *Tradition and Modernity in Eighteenth-Century Goa (1750–1800)* (Lisbon: CHAM/Manohar, 2006); Schwartz, "Economy of the Portuguese Empire," 34.

10   Luís Ferrand de Almeida, *Alexandre de Gusmão, o Brasil e o Tratado de Madrid (1735–1750)* (Coimbra: Universidade de Coimbra, 1990); Íris Kantor, "Usos diplomáticos da Ilha-Brasil: Polêmicas cartograficas e historiográficas," *Varia Historia (Belo Horizonte)* 23:37 (January/June 2007), 70–80; Júnia Ferreira Furtado, *Oráculos da Geografia Iluminista: Dom Luís da Cunha e Jean-Baptiste Bourguignon*

D'Anville na construção da cartografia do Brasil (Belo Horizonte: Editora UGMG, 2012).

11 *Directorio que se deve observar nas Povoações dos Indios do Pará, e Maranhaõ em quanto Sua Majestade naõ mandar o contrario* (Lisbon: Na Officina de Miguel Rodrigues, 1757).

12 Ângela Domingues, *Quando os índios eram vassalos: Colonização e relações de poder no Norte do Brasil na segunda metade do século XVIII* (Lisbon: CNCDP, 2000); Rita Heloísa de Almeida, *O Diretório dos índios: Um projeto de "civilização" no Brasil no século XVIII* (Brasília: EditoraUnB, 1997); Hal Langfur, *The Forbidden Lands: Colonial Identity, Frontier Violence, and the Persistence of Brazil's Eastern Indians, 1750–1830* (Stanford, CA: Stanford University Press, 2006), 60–62. Pombal, convinced that the Jesuits, who had defined European relations with the indigenous in the Amazon, were obstacles to effective royal government there, led the campaign to expel the order from the empire. See Kenneth Maxwell, "The Spark: The Amazon and the Suppression of the Jesuits," in *Naked Tropics: Essays on Empire and Other Rogues* (New York: Routledge, 2003).

13 Kenneth Maxwell, *Pombal: Paradox of the Enlightenment* (New York: Cambridge University Press, 1995), 88–89, 114, 118–130.

14 Maxwell, *Pombal*, 149–153; 162; Pedreira, "From Growth to Collapse: Portugal, Brazil, and the Breakdown of the Old Colonial System (1760–1830)," *Hispanic American Historical Review* 80:4 (2000), 841. See also Novais, *Portugal e Brasil*, 289–294, and Francisco José Calazans Falcon, *A Época Pombalina (Política Econômica e Monarquia Ilustrada)* (São Paulo: Ática, 1982).

15 Pedreira, "From Growth to Collapse," 861–863; João Luís Ribeiro Fragoso, *Homens de grossa aventura: Acumulação e hierarquia na praça mercantile do Rio de Janeiro (1790–1830)* (Rio de Janeiro: Arquito Nacional, 1992).

16 See Tutino, "Introduction," in this volume.

17 Rodrigo Bentes Monteiro, *O rei no espelho: A monarquia portuguesa e a colonização da América, 1640–1720* (São Paulo: Hucitec, 2002); Nestor Goulart Reis, *Evolução urbana do Brasil, 1500/1720*, 2nd ed. (São Paulo: Pini, 2000); Paulo César Garcez Marins, *Através da rótula: Sociedade e arquitectura urbana no Brasil, séculos XVII a XX* (São Paulo: Humanitas/FFLCH/USP, 2001), 71–72; Boxer, *Golden Age*, 127–130, 135–136, 147–148, 158–161.

18 Rebellion and revolution in other Atlantic empires resonated in the *Inconfidência mineira* (Minas Gerais, 1789) and the *Revolta dos alfaiates* or *Conjuração bahiana* (Salvador, 1798), as well as dissident gatherings in Rio in the 1790s.

19 Genaro Vilanova Miranda de Oliveira, "Independent from Independence: Indigenous Nations and Maroon Societies during the Emergence of the Brazilian National State," *Journal of Iberian and Latin American Research* 17:2 (December 2011), 166–168; Langfur, *The Forbidden Lands*, 37, 49; chaps. 1 and 2; B. J. Barickman, "'Tame Indians,' 'Wild Heathens,' and Settlers in Southern Bahia in the Late Eighteenth and Early Nineteenth Centuries," *The Americas* 51:3 (January 1995), 325–368; "Quilombo" and "República dos Palmares," in Clóvis Moura, *Dicionário da escravidão negra no Brasil* (São Paulo: EDUSP, 2004), 335–339, 347–352.

20 Rodrigo de Sousa Coutinho, "Quadro da Situação Política da Europa...," (August 16, 1803), in Ângelo Pereira, *D. João VI, príncipe e rei*, vol. 1 (Lisbon: Emprensa de Publicidade, 1953), 127–136.

21 Alan Manchester, "The Transfer of the Portuguese Court to Brazil," in *Conflict and Continuity in Brazilian Society*, ed. Henry Keith and S. F. Edwards (Columbia: University of South Carolina Press, 1969), 156–159.

22 "Manifesto de Declaração de Guerra aos Francezes," May 1, 1808 ([Rio de Janeiro]: Impressão Régia, [1808]).

23 "Carta Régia," January 28, 1808; Alan Manchester, *British Preëminence in Brazil, Its Rise and Decline: A Study in European Expansion* (1933) (New York: Octagon, 1964), 70–74; Valentim Alexandre, *Os sentidos do império: Questão nacional e questão colonial na crise do antigo regime português* (Porto: Edições Afrontamento, 1993), 212; José Luís Cardoso, "A transferência da Corte e a Abertura dos Portos: Portugal e Brasil entre a ilustração e o liberalismo economico," in *A Abertura dos Portos*, ed. Luís Valente de Oliveira and Rubens Ricupero (São Paulo: SENAC, 2007), 166–195.

24 Manchester, *British Preëminence*, 78; Valentim Alexandre, "O nacionalismo vintista e a questão brasileira: Esboço de análise política," in *O liberalismo na península ibérica na primeira metade do século XIX*, vol. 1, ed. Miriam Halpern Pereira (Lisbon: Livaria Sá da Costa, 1982), 290–291.

25 Kirsten Schultz, *Tropical Versailles: Empire, Monarchy, and the Portuguese Royal Court in Rio de Janeiro, 1808–1821* (New York: Routledge, 2001).

26 See "Decreto," dated February 18, 1821, published February 22, 1821, in *Código Brasiliense* ([Rio de Janeiro: Impressão Régia, 1817–1822]); "Processo da revolta na praça do commércio," *Documentos para a história da independencia*, vol. 1 (Rio de Janeiro: Biblioteca Nacional, 1923) (hereafter *DHI*), 277–325; *Constituição política da monarquia portuguesa feita pelas Cortes...* (Lisbon: Impressão Nacional, 1821). On constitutionalism see Lúcia Maria Bastos Pereira das Neves, *Corcundas e Constitucionais: A cultura política da independência (1820–1822)* (Rio de Janeiro: Revan/Faperj, 2003); Iara Lis Carvalho Souza, *Pátria coroada: O Brasil como corpo político autônomo, 1780–1831* (São Paulo: Editora UNESP, 1999), chap. 4; Schultz, *Tropical Versailles*, 235–276; Andréa Slemian, *Vida Política em Tempo de Crise: Rio de Janeiro (1808–1824)* (São Paulo: HUCITEC, 2004); Raymundo Faoro, "Folhetos da independência," in *O debate político no processo da independência*, ed. Raymundo Faoro (Rio de Janeiro: Conselho Federal de Cultura, 1973).

27 *Constituição política da monarquia portuguesa feita pelas Cortes.*

28 António D'Oliva de Souza Sequeira, *Projeto para o establecimento politico do Reino Unido de Portugal, Brasil e Algarves...* (reprint) (Rio de Janeiro: n.p., 1821), 3; Faoro, *Debate político*; Schultz, *Tropical Versailles*, 247–265.

29 On the Portuguese Cortes and Brazilian representation there see M. E. Gomes de Carvalho, *Os Deputados Brasileiros nas Cortes de Lisboa* (Brasília: Senado Federal/ Editora da Universidade de Brasília, 1979); and Márcia Regina Berbel, *A nação como artefato: Deputados Brasileiros nas Cortes Portugueses (1821–1822)* (São Paulo: Editor Hucitec/Fapesp, 1999).

30 Richard Graham, *Feeding the City: From Street Market to Liberal Reform in Salvador, Brazil, 1780–1860* (Austin: University of Texas Press, 2010), 140–155.

31 Neill Macaulay, *Dom Pedro: The Struggle for Liberty in Brazil and Portugal, 1798–1834* (Durham, NC: Duke University Press, 1986), 120–121; Isabel Lustosa, *D. Pedro I: Um herói sem nenhum caráter* (São Paulo: Companhia das Letras, 2006), 138–141.

32 "Representação do Senado da Camara do Rio de Janeiro, pedindo a convocação de uma Assembléa Geral das Provincias do Brasil," in *DHI*, 378–383; José Honório Rodrigues, *A Assembléia Constituinte de 1823* (Petrópolis: Vozes, 1974), 291–299.

33 As Isabel Lustosa shows, the concern with the Cortes's quest to "recolonize" Brazil cannot be separated from a transformation in print culture in Brazilian cities in 1821 and 1822. See Lustosa, *Insultos Impressos: A guerra dos jornalistas na independência, 1821–1823* (São Paulo: Companhia das Letras, 2000).

34 Rodrigues, *Assembléia Constituinte*, 29, 30–34; Macaulay, *Dom Pedro*, 145–147; Roderick Barman, *Brazil: The Forging of a Nation, 1798–1852* (Stanford, CA: Stanford University Press, 1988), 65–96; Andréa Slemian and João Paulo G. Pimenta, *O "nascimento político" do Brasil: As origens do estado e da nação (1808–1825)* (Rio de Janeiro: DP and A Editora, 2003).

35 Graham, *Feeding the City*, 151–155; Barman, *Brazil*, 97–129; Macaulay, *Dom Pedro*, 146, 154–158; Francisco C. Falcon and Ilmar Rohloff de Mattos, "O processo de independência no Rio de Janeiro," in *1822: Dimensões*, ed. Carlos Guilherme Mota (São Paulo: Editora Perspectiva, 1972), 328; Rodrigues, *Assembléia Constituinte*, 44, 64, 66–67, 198–248, 305; Lustosa, *Insultos*, 395–407; Gladys Sabina Ribeiro, *A liberdade em construção: Identidade nacional e conflitos antilusitanos no primeiro reinado* (Rio de Janeiro: Relume Dumará / FAPERJ, 2002), 80–87.

36 Evaldo Cabral de Mello, *A outra independência: O federalismo pernambucano de 1817 a 1824* (São Paulo: Editora 34, 2004).

37 Robin Blackburn, *The Overthrow of Colonial Slavery, 1776–1848* (London: Verso, 1988), 406.

38 José Bonifácio de Andrada e Silva, "Representação a Assembléia Geral e Constituinte e Legislativa do Império do Brasil sobre a escravatura," in *José Bonifácio de Andrada e Silva*, ed. Jorge Caldeira (São Paulo: Editora 24, 2002), 200–217; Ana Rosa Cloclet da Silva, *Construção da nação e escravidão no pensamento de José Bonifácio, 1783–1823* (Campinas, SP: Editora da UNICAMP, 1999); Stuart B. Schwartz, *Sugar Plantations in the Formation of Brazilian Society, 1550–1835* (New York: Cambridge University Press, 1985); Wilberforce cited in Leslie Bethell, *The Abolition of the Brazilian Slave Trade: Britain, Brazil and the Slave Trade Question, 1807–1869* (New York: Cambridge University Press, 1970), 31. See also Jaime Rodrigues, *O infame comércio: Propostas e experiências no final do tráfico de Africanos para o Brasil (1800–1850)* (Campinas, SP: Editora da UNICAMP/CECULT, 2000), 82–92.

39 Bethell, *Abolition*, 49, 60–61.

40 Bethell, *Abolition*, 62–63; Rodrigues, *O infame comércio*, 101–107; Berbel, Marquese, and Parron, *Escravidão e política*, 185–200.

41   Macaulay, *Dom Pedro*, chap. 7; Lustosa, *D. Pedro I*, 278–281, 293–301; Ribeiro's *Liberdade em construção* provides an examination of the political culture of Dom Pedro's reign with a focus on the question of national identity and anti-Portuguese discourses. On the Bank of Brazil see José Luís Cardoso, "Novos elementos para a história do Banco do Brasil (1808–1829): Crónica de um fracasso anunciado," *Revista Brasileira de Historia* (São Paulo) 30:59 (2010), 167–192.

42   Carvalho Souza, *Pátria coroada*, 17.

43   Hebe Maria Mattos, *Escravidão e cidadania no Brasil monárquico* (Rio de Janeiro: Jorge Zahar Editor, 2000).

44   Bethell, *Abolition*, chaps. 3 and 4; Berbel, Marquese, and Parron, *Escravidão e política*, 220, 232–233, 348–349.

45   Berbel, Marquese, and Parron, *Escravidão e política*, 91–93; Rafael de Bivar Marquese, *Administração e escravidão: Ideáis sobre a gestão da agricultura escravista brasileira*, preface by Antonio Penalves Rocha (São Paulo: Editora Hucitec/Fapesp, 1999).

46   The bibliography on politics and political culture in the nineteenth-century empire after 1830 is vast. Among the most seminal works is Ilmar Rohloff de Mattos, *O tempo saquarema* (São Paulo: Hucitec, 1987). Along with Barman, *Brazil*, more recent work on the local and imperial politics of state formation includes Judy Bieber, *Power, Patronage, and Political Violence: State Building on a Brazilian Frontier, 1822–1889* (Lincoln: University of Nebraska Press, 1999); Matthias Röhrig Assunção, "Elite Politics and Popular Rebellion in the Construction of Post-colonial Order: The Case of Maranhão, Brazil (1820–41)," *Journal of Latin American Studies* 31:1 (February 1999), 1–38; Maria de Fátima Silva Gouvêa, *O império das provincias: Rio de Janeiro, 1822–1889* (Rio de Janeiro: Civilização Brasileira, 2008), and Jeffrey Needell, *The Party of Order: The Conservatives, the State, and Slavery in the Brazilian Monarchy, 1831–1871* (Stanford, CA: Stanford University Press, 2006); Francivaldo Alves Nunes, "A Amazônia e a formação do Estado Imperial no Brasil: Unidade do território e expansão de domínio," *Almanack* (UNIFESP), no. 3 (2012), 54–55. A recent examination of the interplay and tensions between local, regional, national, and Atlantic politics and economies is Graham, *Feeding the City*.

47   Yuko Miki, "Fleeing into Slavery: The Insurgent Geographies of Brazilian Quilombolas (Maroons), 1880–1881," *The Americas* 68:4 (April 2012), 495–528; Marcus J. M. de Carvalho, "O outro lado da Independência: Quilombolas, negros e pardos em Pernambuco (Brazil), 1817–23," *Luso-Brazilian Review* 43:1 (2006), 1–30.

48   Kirsten Schultz, "La independencia de Brasil, la ciudadanía y el problema de la esclavitud: *A Assembléia Constituente de 1823*," in *Revolución, independencia y lasnuevasnaciones de América*, ed. Jaime E. Rodríguez O. (Madrid: Mapfre/Tavera, 2005), 442–443; "Constituição de 1824," *Political Database for the Americas*, Center for Latin American Studies, Georgetown University: http://pdba.georgetown .edu/Constitutions/Brazil/brazil1824.html; accessed May 14, 2015; Hal Langfur, "Cannibalism and the Body Politic: Independent Indians in the Era of Brazilian Independence" (manuscript); Manuela Carneiro da Cunha, "Política indigenista

no século XIX," in *História dos Índios no Brasil*, ed. Manuela Carneiro da Cunha (São Paulo: Companhia das Letras/Fapesp/Secretaria Municipal de Cultura, 1992); Fernanda Sposito, "Liberdade para os índios no Império do Brasil: A revogação das guerras justas em 1831," *Almanack* (UNIFESP), no. 1 (2011): 52–65; James Holston, *Insurgent Citizenship: Disjunctions of Democracy and Modernity in Brazil* (Princeton, NJ: Princeton University Press, 2008), 73. For nineteenth-century law pertaining to the indigenous see Manuela Carneiro da Cunha, ed., *Legislação indigenista no século XIX: Uma compilação (1808–1889)* (São Paulo: Edusp, 1992).

49 Holston, *Insurgent Citizenship*, 64, 80; Jens Andermann, *The Optic of the State: Visuality and Power in Argentina and Brazil* (Pittsburgh: University of Pittsburgh Press, 2007), especially chap. 4. On the protracted history of defining Indians as social and political dependents see Holston, *Insurgent Citizenship*, 70–76; Alcida Rita Ramos, "The Special (or Specious?) Status of Brazilian Indians," *Citizenship Studies* 7:4 (2003), 401–420. On Indians and the Brazilian state in the twentieth century see Seth Garfield, *Indigenous Struggle at the Heart of Brazil: State Policy, Frontier Expansion, and the Xavante Indians, 1937–1988* (Durham, NC: Duke University Press, 2001).

PART III

SPANISH AMERICAN INVERSIONS

7

BECOMING MEXICO

The Conflictive Search for a North American Nation

ALFREDO ÁVILA AND JOHN TUTINO

During the eighteenth century, New Spain was the most economically dynamic region of the Americas. Its silver drove global commerce. The Spanish monarchy, however uncertain at home, ruled New Spain with skill—promoting silver production and expanding trades, keeping the peace through limited participations and judicial mediations, negotiating to contain the few political and popular challenges that came before 1800. Then, beginning in 1808, the breakdown of sovereignty in the Spanish empire led to constitutional debates, political wars, and popular insurgencies that culminated in Mexican independence in 1821. A vibrant political culture shaped contested national and provincial politics; a brief flirtation with monarchy in 1821 gave way to a decentralizing federal republic by the Constitution of 1824, followed by a turn to greater central power in 1835—a trajectory not unlike that of the United States, which began in confederation and then turned to stronger central powers in the Constitution of 1787.

Yet just as the nation began, it faced the fall of silver and a rapidly changing world economy. Constitutional creativity could not generate profit or state revenues or calm political conflict. The search for a new economy proved slow and uncertain. Instability continued into the 1840s, when the United States turned to war to take the northern half of Mexico's territory. Both North American nations faced deep political and social conflicts into the 1860s. When they ended, the United States emerged a continental power set to compete for global hegemony; Mexico still searched for political stability, economic possibilities, shared prosperity—and a national culture that might integrate historic diversities.[1]

New Spain: Silver Economies and Social Stability to 1810

Visiting New Spain as the nineteenth century began, Alexander von Humboldt wrote his four-volume *Political Essay*, detailing economic dynamism and the importance of silver to global and Atlantic trades—and lamenting the deep inequities that sustained them.[2] By the time the work became widely available, Mexico was becoming a nation. Later analysts have suspected that Humboldt was wrong about "Mexico's legendary wealth." He was not. New Spain was as rich and as important to the world as he portrayed it—when he visited, before 1810.

New Spain began in the early sixteenth century with the conquest of the Mexica (Aztecs) and the rapid subordination of the other states of Mesoamerica. A devastating depopulation driven by smallpox and other Old World diseases enabled the conquest and continued long after, reaching 90 percent by the 1620s. In the middle of the sixteenth century, however, destructions began to mix with opportunities—mostly for Euro-Americans—stimulated by a newly integrating world economy. Silver production had begun at Taxco in the 1530s and at Pachuca in the 1550s, both near Mexico City in the heart of Mesoamerica. Zacatecas and Guanajuato rose as mining centers to the north, in the lands of the mobile and warring Chichimecas. Their resistance delayed development. Later their defeat in the 1590s opened the way for the deeply commercial society of Spanish North America.

Responding to Chinese demand, New Spain developed two silver societies— one grounded in landed indigenous republics in Spanish Mesoamerica, the other founded in the Bajío and driving north with commercial dynamism to create Spanish North America. Together, the silver economies of New Spain stimulated global trades for centuries.[3]

MAP 7.1. New Spain in North America, ca. 1790

There were coercions and exploitations in the reconstruction of Mesoamerica, but the opportunity of silver, the scarcity of the native population, and the rights to land and self-rule granted to new native republics led to negotiations of inequities that kept the silver economy strong and indigenous communities essential. The republics sustained local families and markets and became sites of vibrant indigenous adaptations of Catholicism focused on Christ, the Virgin, and diverse saints.[4] By the early 1600s, silver boomed, the native population hit bottom, republics consolidated, and colonial courts mediated conflicts, stabilizing inequities across Spanish Mesoamerica.[5] In regions reaching south across

Oaxaca, Yucatán, and Chiapas, and into Guatemala, few mines developed and the stimulus of silver was weak. There, the consolidation of indigenous republics kept communities strong and limited Spanish exploitations.[6] The defining characteristic of Spanish Mesoamerica was the grafting of a commercial economy on a foundation of landed communities reconstituted as native republics.

The richest silver mines and most dynamic commercial economy in New Spain developed north of the states and cultivating communities of Mesoamerica. About two hundred kilometers northwest of Mexico City, the fertile Bajío basin was a frontier contested by Mesoamerican states and mobile Chichimecas around 1500. Soon after the conquest, Otomí communities drove north from Mesoamerica to settle Querétaro. But the great push came after the discovery of silver at Zacatecas in the 1540s and Guanajuato in the 1550s. Europeans, African slaves, and diverse Mesoamericans flooded north. Spaniards and Mesoamericans fought as allies against state-free Chichimecas—who also faced the destructions of Old World plagues. The opening of the north to silver mining, stock grazing, and irrigated cultivation in vast regions with few landed republics forged a distinctly commercial colonial society around 1600.[7]

In many ways, the eighteenth century was the century of New Spain. Population tripled, silver production quadrupled, trade with Europe and Asia soared, and settlement drove north into California. New Spain's treasury funded Spain's regime across the northern Americas—including Cuba and Louisiana. From 1700 to the 1750s, strong demand and high prices in China stimulated silver in New Spain; the Bourbon regime solidified in Spain and pressed little reform in the Americas. Silver production in New Spain rose from 4 million pesos yearly around 1700 to nearly 13 million pesos in the 1750s.[8] A drop below 12 million pesos annually from 1760 to 1765, linked to falling Chinese demand, coincided with Spain's role in the Seven Years' War (1756–1763). The peace brought demand for new revenues and military recruitment—assertions similar to the demands for revenues and new powers that set off the conflicts that led to the U.S. independence a decade later. In New Spain, tax hikes and recruitment provoked risings by irate mine workers and others in and near silver centers at Guanajuato, Real del Monte, Guanajuato, and San Luis Potosí in 1766 and 1767. Yet an alliance of officials and local entrepreneurs mobilized to end resistance, resume mining, and turn the regime to promoting silver production.

After 1770, Spain's rulers stimulated silver with tax breaks and cheap mercury. All of Europe's Atlantic powers aimed to gain as much silver as they could—in trade if possible, by war if necessary. New Spain's production rose from about 12 million pesos yearly in the late 1760s to hold near 23 million pesos from 1791 to 1810. Production held strong amid wars, trade disruptions, and revolutions. A key to that strength was a regime that stimulated production while keeping social order—at little cost relative to the revenues it gained in New Spain. Indigenous republics funded local rule and religious life with community lands; Spanish city councilmen purchased seats and gained little pay; local landlord-commanders funded militias; new city patrols were small and paid little. There were almost no professional military forces in the colony before the 1750s; when armed forces expanded later, militias funded by local elites still prevailed.[9]

Generating soaring silver for trade and state coffers, Bourbon New Spain maintained an inexpensive regime, weak in coercive force, dependent on judicial mediations. The dearth of coercive power left officials to negotiate rule and legitimacy with their subjects, usually in court. The revenues of silver, *alcabalas* on trade, the tribute paid by natives and mulattos, and the Tobacco Monopoly built in the 1760s, funded administration in New Spain, missions and presidios on the frontier, and subsidies for Cuba and Louisiana—with ample surpluses for Madrid.[10]

Mexico City, the largest city in the Americas around 1800, grew to over 130,000 people as the center of government and trade, religion and education for both Spanish Mesoamerica and Spanish North America. Near the capital, the mines at Taxco flourished into the 1750s; Real de Monte boomed in the 1760s and 1770s—all surrounded and sustained by landed republics and commercial estates. As population grew, the people of the republics faced land shortages; to compensate they sent expanding gangs of men and boys to gain wages at nearby estates—which supplied mines and city markets. Estate operators profited; villagers survived—and the courts continued to mediate.[11] During the crisis of the 1760s, there was little violent conflict in the central highlands. Only at Real del Monte, where mine workers faced wage cuts, did they rise in a revolt that was quickly suppressed—and mediated to resume silver flows.[12] Local disputes and riots proliferated during the decades after 1770—but most were still resolved in the courts. The economy grew and social stability held around Mexico City to 1810.

In southern Mesoamerica, the stimulus of silver remained weak in the eighteenth century. Growing populations created limited pressures on still ample community lands; small cities and limited demand kept estates small. Conflict rose—perhaps heightened by the lack of commercial opportunity, leaving frustrated entrepreneurs to press on entrenched communities. Again, the courts mediated. In Oaxaca's mountains, Mixtec villagers raised cochineal—a brilliant red dye made by drying and crushing insects that grew on local cactus—for international markets. As Europe increased cloth production, demand for cochineal rose. Made by women in Mixtec households, it was marketed by district magistrates who doubled as merchants. Tensions between growers and traders rose as profits favored magistrate-merchants. Conflicts increased but were still resolved in the courts. Social stability held through the eighteenth century.[13]

Spanish North America was different.[14] Silver production soared at Zacatecas and in far northern Chihuahua before 1750, at Guanajuato, San Luis Potosí, and Catorce after 1770. As population and production grew, commercial cultivation expanded across the Bajío. Cloth production boomed at Querétaro and San Miguel el Grande. Grazing shifted northward, as did the search for new mines. Conflict and trade with independent natives, now often Apaches, drove northward, too, along with missions to draw them to lives of laboring Christian dependence. Population, commercial ways, and trade rose everywhere. North of the Bajío, that combination brought opportunity for entrepreneurs and chances for diverse settlers—who held together in the face of conflicts with independent natives.

In contrast, in the Bajío the mix of demographic and economic growth became socially polarizing after 1770. Mining soared to new heights at Guanajuato, the leading producer of silver in New Spain and the world from 1770 to 1810.[15] After containing the risings of 1767, mine owners continued to press down on workers' earnings, aiming to end the ore shares that had made them partners in production and profit. The regime offered tax breaks and subsidized mercury to mine operators and expanded city patrols and militias to solidify social controls. State power backed by coercion was a new focus—a turn away from judicial mediation. Meanwhile, reformers in Madrid favored Spanish cloth exports, aiming to draw silver to Europe, threatening Bajío textile shops. The result was not decline in the Bajío, but a shift from large shops to family weaving ruled by merchant financiers who pressed falling earnings on struggling households.

Across the rural Bajío, estates continued to expand irrigation and commercial cropping. When a mix of early frost and severe drought brought unprecedented dearth, famine, and death in 1785 and 1786, estates profited from famine prices, took fields back from tenants, and forced worker salaries down. The years from 1790 to 1810 brought deepening pressures on the lives of Bajío mine workers, cloth makers, and rural producers.[16] Social exploitation was compounded by escalating cultural conflicts as promoters of a new "enlightened" religion maligned popular practices as superstitions. Still, production boomed and stability held—until Napoleon broke the Spanish empire in 1808, followed by two years of political debates as drought again ravaged the Bajío.

Politics in New Spain

The history of New Spain often appears without politics, which seems to be a creation of independence in Mexico. If politics requires competitions to select leaders for large jurisdictions, there was no politics in New Spain before 1808. But if politics involves participation in shaping and influencing the institutions of governance and justice that orient everyday life, then politics flourished throughout New Spain. Across Spanish Mesoamerica, politics was pivotal to the powerful in key cities and towns—and to the native majority in thousands of indigenous republics. In Spanish North America, city and town politics was a regular concern of the powerful—but with few indigenous republics, the majority found few avenues of participation before 1810.

There were three overlapping levels of politics in New Spain: the politics of indigenous republics; the politics of Spanish city councils; and the politics of imperial administration. They were integrated by a judicial structure that focused on the mediation of disputes at every level. A mix of segmented politics and judicial mediation was pivotal to the stabilization of New Spain during the decades of economic dynamism and social polarization that peaked around 1800. They must be understood to analyze the diverse regional and social participations in the political conflicts and popular risings that led to independence. And they must be understood to analyze the political conflicts and social instabilities that persisted long after 1821—when national and regional politics flourished, while judicial mediations waned.[17]

The politics of the indigenous republics of New Spain are often studied, but rarely as politics. Established in the second half of the sixteenth century, they integrated head towns and outlying villages, all ruled by governors and councilmen elected annually by (and among) minorities of notables designated *principales*. The republics held land to fund local government and religious festivals, to provide modest commercial holdings to notables, and give subsistence plots to the majority. Republics oversaw local religious life and local justice—and regularly petitioned the General Indigenous Court in Mexico City when problems within or between republics, or with Spanish officials, merchants, or estates, could not be resolved locally.[18]

With such important roles, there was a lively and often contested political life in the native republics. Factions contested power, building coalitions within the republics and allies without; one group might court the local priest, another turn to a trader or the manager of a nearby estate. The indigenous republics of Spanish Mesoamerica—county-sized jurisdictions—lived active political lives in the eighteenth century. Officeholding favored leading families; participation in elections included only principales. Still, contested politics often led to coalitions that mobilized much of the local populace around key local questions. Such local political actions, by contrast, were scarce in Spanish North America, where there were few republics. The rural majority lived as commercial dependents of landed estates and faced rising pressures in the eighteenth century—without republican politics and with limited access to the judicial mediations those politics facilitated.[19]

A less participatory politics focused on the Spanish councils that ruled the cities that centered the commercial economies of New Spain. Men of old wealth held most seats permanently; from the 1770s many included rotating "honorary" councilmen elected by established members—bringing in men of new wealth often claimed in mining and trade and invested in commercial estates. Councilmen also elected annually the local magistrates who oversaw urban justice. Such councils oversaw public affairs in Mexico City; at Querétaro, Guanajuato, Zacatecas, and other centers in the North; in Puebla, Oaxaca, Mérida, and other towns in Mesoamerican regions stretching east and south. They organized city markets and public works; they oversaw education and religious celebrations; they mobilized relief in times of dearth and disease; they orchestrated the militias and urban patrols that expanded after 1765. Spanish city councils sent agents to represent them before officials in Mexico City, Seville, and Madrid, petitioning in judicial processes to negotiate local needs. Formal council politics were internal, limiting political participations. Still, councils had to maintain political bases; they could be challenged in court by disgruntled citizens—and by republics that organized native populations in Mexico City and Querétaro. Across New Spain, Spanish cities and towns lived vibrant politics that were less participatory that those of the indigenous republics.[20]

The highest level of politics in New Spain focused on imperial power and the silver economy—the viceroy, the High Court, treasury officials, intendants, and others. While formal power concentrated in Madrid, imperial prosperity depended on the Americas—especially New Spain's silver. The regime understood that balance of power. It recognized merchant chambers and mining boards that provided a voice and a measure of self-governance to the entrepreneurs who kept the silver flowing. Recent analysts call it a stakeholder regime, in which key entrepreneurs played sanctioned roles in planning and governance—to the mutual benefit of entrepreneurs and the regime.[21] New studies also show vibrant conflicts and emerging political networks in the late eighteenth century, forming a new public opinion in New Spain.[22]

The politics of imperial power in New Spain extended beyond sanctioned institutions and stakeholder participation. Leading financiers and mining magnates, merchants and landlords forged ties with key regime leaders. In some cases, they were linked by business affairs. In addition, top colonial officials, including many sent by the Bourbons to assert Spanish power over colonial subjects, found marriage ties and rich inheritances in the families of New Spain's leading entrepreneurs. Treasury officials, High Court judges, and viceroys built such links. In New Spain and in Spain they became advocates for the powerful few who ruled the silver economy of New Spain.[23]

From 1790 to 1808, while the silver economy boomed and war brought rising demands for regime revenues, mining soared, the regime claimed rising revenues, and entrepreneurs in mining and global trades profited. Middling entrepreneurs and the Church lenders that funded them faced financial stress. Textile producers lived hard times when imports flowed freely, then boom times when war blocked trade and local production soared. Indigenous republics in Mesoamerica used established rights and access to courts to blunt impositions and retain autonomies. In the far north, the same years brought uncertain opportunities to those ready to risk trade and war with independent natives.

The Bajío, pivotal to economic growth after 1770, mixed mining boom, textile uncertainties, tobacco growth, and expanding cultivation in times of polarization. While entrepreneurs negotiated policies that promoted commercial profits and regime revenues, the people lacked institutions of political participation and social negotiation. The rich profited, or at least adapted, in times of opportunity and challenge; the populace faced deepening difficulties. Mine workers saw ore shares cut while wages fell—driven down in part by the refineries' recruitment of women to sort ores for low pay. Large textile workshops closed and family producers faced falling earnings between 1770 and 1793; then wartime blockades mixed with respites of peace to bring alternating years of boom and bust. The rural majority faced rising rents, evictions, and falling wages.[24]

The producing majority in the Bajío lacked the political rights and judicial access to negotiate rising impositions and deteriorating lives. A few tried, going to court to claim lands, councils, and religious rights as indigenous republics. They understood the value of such rights in fending off entrepreneurial demands and regime claims. Most failed. When the Bourbon regime fell to Napoleon in 1808, setting off a war for independence in Spain and debates about sovereignty across the Americas, in New Spain nearly every group—Spanish city councils and indigenous republics, merchant chambers, royal officials, and High Court judges—negotiated unimagined challenges through established political channels. The populace of the Bajío faced deepening difficulties without indigenous republics and with limited access to the courts. When a provincial priest backed by a few militia officers called them to arms in 1810, they rose in the tens of thousands to challenge a regime and economy that had prejudiced their lives for decades.

From Imperial Crisis to Provincial Insurgency, 1808–1811

The conflicts that led to Mexican independence in 1821 did not begin in New Spain. During the eighteenth century, Great Britain and France, Spain and Portugal engaged in wars that aimed to increase trade and revenues in American possessions. After the global war of 1757 to 1763, all expected colonial subjects to pay the costs of imperial contests. All enacted reforms to increase revenues and make collection more efficient. In the face of urban resistance among mine workers and others in Guanajuato and nearby, New Spain's entrepreneurs and Bourbon rulers came together to crush the resistance and reenergize the silver economy—leading to the boom of 1770–1810.

New Spain sustained soaring silver production, booming trade, rising agricultural production, and growing regime revenues past 1800. But drawn into escalating wars in the 1790s, Spain saw its naval power collapse after 1800. Spanish traders struggled to maintain commercial ties with American domains while war between Britain and Napoleonic France pressed the Spanish monarchy, which faced military and financial exhaustion even as New Spain's economy carried on despite fiscal demands.

Carlos IV, through his "favorite" minister, Manuel Godoy, entered a difficult alliance with Napoleon. Dependent on French military power, the Spanish Crown submitted to every demand. In 1803, Madrid signed a Treaty of Subsidy with France, agreeing to pay 6 million livres (or about 1.5 million pesos) monthly; the imagined total of 18 million pesos yearly would deliver to Napoleon the equivalent of 75 percent of all New Spain's silver. Godoy committed American revenues directly to foreign creditors. Rising demands led to discontent in Spain and New Spain, resentments heightened by knowledge that revenues were flowing to bankers sustaining imperial rivals. Leading aristocrats and politicians began to see in Fernando, prince of Asturias, an alternative to the dangerous dependence on Napoleon built by Carlos and Godoy. The idea that Godoy aimed to sell the kingdom to France found widening acceptance.[25]

In 1804, the king decreed the Consolidation of Royal Bonds, demanding that pious foundations across Spain's Americas sell income properties, call in loans, and deliver the proceeds in royal coffers. Many feared that the program would damage colonial production. Convents, cathedral chapters, and other

Church institutions had long served as sources of credit. They had to call in loans and, if the creditor could not pay, auction property. Those who challenged the decree—Querétaro corregidor Miguel Domínguez, Michoacán canon Manuel Abad y Queipo, and Mexico City councilman Francisco Primo de Verdad—faced the ire of Viceroy José de Iturrigaray. In a negotiated implementation, rich entrepreneurs paid little, convent-banks in Mexico City and elsewhere lost most, and capital became scarce for middling landowners who depended on ecclesiastical mortgages to develop estates.[26] The greatest impact of the Consolidation was the discontent it provoked. Collectors, including Viceroy Iturrigaray, gained fees and were easily seen as profiteering from war and the Consolidation.[27]

In 1807, Spain signed a treaty allowing French armies to cross Spanish territory to occupy Portugal. France took Lisbon, but the monarchy escaped with British help to Brazil, making Rio de Janeiro the capital of the Portuguese empire and a British dependency. Napoleon turned his armies on Spain in the spring of 1808. Having lost the wealth of Saint Domingue to the Haitian Revolution, Napoleon aimed to take Portugal and Brazil; when that failed, he turned on his Spanish ally in pursuit of American silver.

As French armies entered Spain, the discovery of a plot against Godoy linking powerful aristocrats and Fernando offered clear evidence of Napoleon's involvement in Spain's affairs. When Godoy tried to follow the Portuguese example and take Carlos and the monarchy to America, riots at Aranjuez blocked the plan. Carlos IV was forced to abdicate, his son proclaimed king as Fernando VII. Soon, however, Napoleon drew both Carlos and Fernando to Bayonne; father and son abdicated to their "beloved friend and ally" Napoleon, who delivered the Spanish throne to his brother, José Bonaparte.

The Napoleonic intervention—armed and dynastic—set off an unprecedented crisis. The collaboration of high authorities with the French led others across Spain to form juntas to organize resistance and preserve Bourbon rights. The Bayonne renunciations created a constitutional crisis. Many rejected the abdication, presuming that Carlos IV was forced—and that he had no legal right to abdicate. Many more recognized Fernando, whose name—even in captivity—symbolized opposition to Napoleon. In Spain and the Americas, many refused to recognize either Carlos IV or José I.

Across a suddenly beheaded empire, juntas claimed control of the monarchy's powers, arguing that they were conserving Fernando's domains until he reclaimed the throne. As the Mexico City Council stated, the monarchy held the kingdom in trust; no king could legally alienate his domains. Nor could the kingdom ever be without a king; there was always a successor, based on the laws

GUERRERO, HÉROE DE LA INDEPENDENCIA

FIGURE 7.1. Vicente Guerrero

of succession. As a result, as Francisco Primo de Verdad insisted, the viceroy could obey neither José Bonaparte nor any junta claiming to govern in Spain. The latter could rule only their home territories. Across New Spain city councils and indigenous republics promised to fight any delivery of the kingdom to the French.[28]

The absence of a legitimate king in Spain left enormous potential power in the hands of the viceroy in Mexico City. To ensure that Iturrigaray did not rule arbitrarily, key leaders—including High Court Judge Jacobo de Villaurrutia and most Mexico City councilmen—proposed a junta parallel to those in Spain. It would represent the interests of New Spain in times of crisis. Nearly all other High Court judges, Church leaders, and top regime officials argued otherwise: the viceroy should rule only in concert with the established High Court, ensuring the power of Spain in New Spain. The two factions faced off in meetings in Mexico City in August and September 1808. After they failed to reach a resolution, a group of merchants, high officials, and military mobilized the merchants' militia to arrest the promoters of a junta and the viceroy. In the wake of the first coup in Mexican history, the conspirators named a weak viceroy; recognized the Seville Junta, which claimed to rule in Spain; and promised support for the war against Napoleon.

In Spain, as Roberto Breña shows in chapter 2, the crisis of 1808 triggered a political revolution that led to the proclamation of a liberal constitution in 1812. The Cortes de Cádiz declared the sovereignty of a nation that included all imperial dominions. In New Spain, elections came in the summer of 1810. Deputies from New Spain took important roles in the Cortes' debates. Miguel Ramos Arizpe, from Coahuila, led the Cortes to establish Provincial Deputations, regional boards charged with promoting the common welfare. José Miguel Guridi y Alcocer, born in Tlaxcala, argued that Spanish America should have representation equal to Spain. But Spain's deputies held a strong majority and blocked that key American demand. A leading Spanish liberal, Agustín Arguelles, stated directly that because Americans outnumbered Iberians, they could not have proportional representation.

After two years of unprecedented political uncertainties and debates, in September 1810 Francisco Xavier Venegas arrived in New Spain as viceroy, sent by the Regency that called the Cortes to write a constitution for a transatlantic Spanish nation. Simultaneously, militia officers Ignacio Allende and Mariano Abasolo, the priest Miguel Hidalgo, and Josefa Ortiz, wife of Querétaro's Corregidor Domínguez, were denounced for joining other Bajío notables in meetings to promote provincial rights and limit subordination to France or Spain. Learning of the denunciations, Hidalgo called to his parishioners on the morning of

September 16, in an event tradition re-created as "El Grito de Dolores." Hidalgo's call to defend the kingdom from French imposition and "be done with oppression" raised thousands of men. In weeks, the Bajío, the pivot of the silver economy, was in flames—literally and politically. Wherever the few troops and vast populace following Hidalgo and Allende marched, European Spaniards, reviled as *gachupines*, lost power and faced imprisonment and sometimes death. American Spaniards took over. In a few months, rebel governments ruled Guanajuato, San Luis Potosí, Zacatecas, Guadalajara, and Valladolid (now Morelia) and other key towns. The rising found its strength in the Bajío. From San Luis Potosí, Félix Calleja—soon to lead the counterinsurgency—reported that the offer of self-government attracted many American Spaniards, and some from Spain too.[29]

In Valladolid, Hidalgo set up a government of American Spaniards, ordering reforms including the end of tributes to improve the lives of indigenous communities, people of African descent, and other subject groups. Later in Guadalajara, Hidalgo reaffirmed and extended his reforms. He sought support among the populace and found backing among elites whose enlightened views recognized the need for reform. But political violence against immigrant Spaniards (mostly officials and merchants) and mass assaults on urban stores and estate granaries, created apprehension. The occupation and the sacking of the mining city of Guanajuato provoked fear. Manuel Abad y Queipo, once Hidalgo's close friend, condemned and excommunicated the insurgent priest. Many city dwellers welcomed the strong measures taken by Viceroy Venegas against rebels—who found most support among rural people who had lived decades of declining earnings, evictions, deepening insecurities, and two years of drought and famine just ending.

In January 1811 outside Guadalajara, Hidalgo, Allende, and insurgent forces faced defeat by provincial militias, mostly Americans. Insurgent leaders fled north, where most were soon arrested. Hidalgo, Allende, and others were executed. Calleja began a campaign of repression. In Aguascalientes, he called for locally recruited and financed defense forces in every town and city. He limited the viceregal army to defending the mining center of Guanajuato and pursuing leading political rebels. In the long run, local forces helped cities and towns defend their own interests—which might change over time. Outside the Bajío, where the rising began and many rebels returned home to carry on guerrilla resistance, 1811 saw quick pacification even as Ignacio Rayón formed a Junta Americana in isolated uplands around Zitácuaro and José María Morelos turned to armed political resistance in Pacific coastal lowlands.[30]

The Cortes carried on in Cádiz, aiming to hold Spain and its Americas together and to give communities new opportunities to promote and defend
their interests—within legal institutions. In 1812 it promulgated a constitution
promising liberal rights.[31] Its first articles stated that sovereignty belonged to
the Spanish nation, including all inhabitants of Spain, Spanish America, the
Philippines in Asia, and a few possessions in North Africa. The nation was defined
as a totality of people subject to the same laws and with the same rights. Government included three branches: the Cortes, the king, and a Supreme Judicial
Tribunal. All descendants of Spaniards and indigenous Americans were citizens; people of African descent were excluded—and discounted in determining representation (a concession to Spanish Cubans committed to slavery). The
constitution called for one deputy for every seventy thousand people (excluding
castas of African origin).

The creation of Provincial Deputations and Constitutional City Councils
elected by citizens satisfied demands for self-rule in many cities and towns.
Freedom of the press allowed the emergence of a new journalism in New
Spain, notably *El pensador mexicano* (*The Mexican Thinker*), published by José
Joaquín Fernández de Lizardi, and *El Juguetillo* (*The Little Jester*), published
by Carlos María de Bustamente. They and others promoted participation and
the exercise of rights, especially voting. Late 1812 and early 1813 brought the
first popular elections in New Spain. All adult men, excluding castas of African
origins and a few others (criminals, friars, etc.), were called to elect councilmen.
Voting was in levels, first in parishes, which sent electors to join city or town
elections. It is impossible to know how many voted, yet the turnout surprised
the authorities. Many of African ancestry voted; after centuries of mixing, lines
were hard to see. In Mexico City, the results worried authorities. The majority of men elected were Americans favoring self-rule. Some sympathized with,
even assisted, insurgents in the provinces. Viceregal officials suspended the
elections and freedom of the press.[32]

A focus on counterinsurgency conditioned the implementation of the constitution. The liberal insistence that all citizens contribute to the treasury, thus
to the costs of counterinsurgency, pleased the viceroy and his commanders. The
High Court, pivotal to maintaining the link between Spain and New Spain in
the coup of 1808, continued as a council of government—despite its prohibition in the constitution. The founding of a Provincial Deputation in Mexico
City was delayed to avoid limiting the viceroy's political and military powers.

While the Cádiz Constitution was written in Spain and implemented in New Spain, insurgencies, political and popular, proliferated across New Spain. During 1811, the pacification led by Calleja claimed major victories. Loyal authorities reclaimed most mining centers, cities, and towns. But the popular resistance that had fueled the first mass insurgency carried on to threaten power and production. It persisted south of Guadalajara, where Hidalgo had made his last political stand. It continued north of Mexico City in the Mezquital, a dry basin where Otomí villagers threatened commercial estates and the mines at Real de Monte. And most damaging to the silver economy, the original rebels from the Bajío, tens of thousands strong, returned home in January 1811 to take control of the fertile basin that sustained Guanajuato and its mines.

Calleja took his troops to occupy Guanajuato—knowing the importance of reviving mining there. For a year, he tried to coordinate a campaign to pacify the Bajío—and failed. Insurgent families ruled the countryside, claiming estate lands and livestock, producing for sustenance, and supplying local markets as they found useful. Most Bajío towns were islands of loyalists surrounded by an insurgent countryside. Mining held below 50 percent of the level of 1810. While popular insurgents ruled the Bajío countryside and Calleja remained surrounded in Guanajuato, political rebels organized the Junta Nacional Americana at Zitácuaro—in rugged uplands between Mexico City and the Bajío, protected by the insurgency there. When Calleja realized at the end of 1811 that he could not alter the stalemate in the Bajío, he moved to dislodge the junta. It was too late: popular insurgents ruled the Bajío, and the silver economy remained besieged.[33] From 1812 on, most Bajío cities held in loyalist control; Guanajuato struggled to resume silver production. But cities surrounded by rebel communities faced unprecedented threats and costs: sustenance came from insurgent cultivators; shipping silver to Mexico City required costly convoys—and payment to insurgent patrols. A limited resumption of mining paid for both insurgency and counterinsurgency, yet neither mining nor the commercial economy approached their previous dynamism in the Bajío after 1810.

The regime had to implement constitutional innovations that aimed to strengthen loyalty to Spain by granting new participations in New Spain—while fighting popular insurgencies that undermined the commercial economy in the Bajío and elsewhere, and while resisting political rebels who found new strength. The well-known political insurgents such as José María Morelos neither mobilized nor led the popular movements. They developed in distinct regions, Morelos based in the Pacific lowlands, popular insurgency grounded in the Bajío. Still, they were mutually reinforcing, making the regime fight two very different foes simultaneously. Political insurgents like Morelos fought for political autonomies that led toward national independence; popular insurgents in the Bajío, the Mezquital, and elsewhere sought autonomies of production and culture that would limit the power of any state.[34]

Some political rebels like Francisco Osorno, who ruled the Apan plains and the Puebla sierra into 1816, built alliances with insurgent communities. He imposed taxes on local merchants and estates, creating authorities that operated as insurgent states.[35] More typical, the Villagrán family led political insurgency in the uplands of Huichapan, dealing irregularly with the Otomí communities that persisted in insurgency across the Mezquital from 1811 to 1815—threatening the mines at Real del Monte. They might ally briefly in skirmishes with common foes; most of the time they took mutual advantage of loyalist forces' difficulties facing both simultaneously.[36] Meanwhile, Guadalupe Victoria built power in the highlands of Veracruz, near the Gulf Coast, surrounded by resistant Totonac villages in the northern Huasteca and rebellious Africans and mulattos, slave and free, to the south.[37] Victoria, too, depended on popular insurgents more than he led them.

In Pacific lowlands from southern Michoacán, past Acapulco, and into Oaxaca José María Morelos coordinated resistance that recruited key landlords seeking local rule, indigenous communities seeking greater autonomy, and diverse mulattos (including muleteer Vicente Guerrero, Mexico's second president, in 1828). Morelos led a mobile guerrilla army that at times held the mines at Taxco, the sugar basin around Cuernavaca south of Mexico City, and the city of Oaxaca—but never threatened Mexico City.[38]

Through 1812 and into 1813, diverse and disconnected insurgent groups, political and popular, held a line that began in the mountains of Veracruz and passed through the Puebla sierra, across the Apan plains and the Mexquital into the Huichapan uplands. The line of resistance broke at Querétaro—a key to regime survival—but held the core of the Bajío and the nearby uplands, surrounding the Guanajuato mines and extending toward Guadalajara. Meanwhile, Morelos and his allies held strong in Pacific hills and lowlands. Officials and loyalists ruled Mexico City and most cities, working to implement the Cádiz Constitution there and in indigenous republics across Mesoamerica. Insurgent power in the Bajío and other zones cut transports links with the North and threatened routes to Atlantic and Pacific ports. The future of New Spain was uncertain at best.

Loyalism and liberalism engaged each other and political and popular insurgents in complex conflicts and negotiations. Early in 1812, Calleja besieged Morelos and his army at Cuautla, southeast of Mexico City. Calleja's victory ensured that no insurgency would again approach Mexico City; Morelos's escape with most of his forces south to Oaxaca guaranteed that insurgency would survive to challenge regional rulers and economic integration.[39] In Oaxaca, Morelos began the insurgents' most ambitious political project. Carlos María de Bustamente, a lawyer and journalist who had organized elections in Mexico City in November 1812, only to see victories overturned and face persecution by loyalist officials, energized the work. He concluded that monarchical rule was by nature authoritarian and would never respect liberal laws. His leadership gave Morelos's political project its salient characteristic: it would be constitutional but, unlike Cádiz, would reject the monarchy.

During 1813, while Morelos besieged Acapulco (cutting trade ties with Asia), his movement held elections where it could. Amid war, only Oaxaca and Tecpan (southern zones of the Intendancy of Mexico) elected deputies. Other delegates were substitutes serving regions under loyalist rule. On September 13 a Congress opened in Chilpancingo. Morelos offered key principles in his celebrated *Sentimientos de la nación*: American independence; the abolition of slavery and racial distinctions; self-government; and protection of Catholic religion. The Congress published a Declaration of Independence.[40]

Morelos's political advance, however, came with military collapse. Troops arriving from Spain reinforced viceregal armies. Calleja was named viceroy and began new campaigns against the rebels. In 1814 the Treaty of Valençay returned the Spanish throne to Fernando VII, who abolished of the Cádiz Constitution and dissolved the Cortes—turning against those who fought hardest for his return. In New Spain, Calleja dissolved liberal institutions. Provincial Deputations and constitutional city and town councils disappeared, yet previous ways did not fully return. War brought profound changes—not easily reversed. Calleja kept some Cádiz innovations—notably the constitution's tax provisions. Absolutism returned to focus the fight against insurgency.

The political insurgents around Morelos offered an alternative to absolutism. At Apatzingán in October 1814, a Congress promulgated a Constitutional Decree for the Liberation of Mexican America (América mexicana). It prescribed a separation of powers in three branches, recognized the rights of citizens, and protected Catholic worship. The decree offered the people of New Spain a constitutional alternative to the return of Fernando and the abolition of the Cádiz Constitution—in part the inspiration of the new Mexican charter. But mounting defeats left the Apatzingán Constitution to have force but briefly in towns of the *tierra caliente*—the south of the Intendancies of Michoacán and Mexico. The capture and execution of Morelos late in 1815 all but ended insurgent constitutional government.

Popular insurgencies persisted, notably in the Bajío. This was a common sequence: the Villagrans faced defeat in the summer of 1813; Otomí insurgents held the Mezquital into 1815. With the defeat of Morelos in 1815, political insurgency survived only in isolated retreats, notably with Vicente Guerrero in the south and Guadalupe Victoria in Gulf uplands. Yet loyalists only pacified popular insurgents in the Bajío between 1818 and 1820. From 1811 to 1815, the dilemma of loyalist forces, first liberal and then absolutist, was how to contain the popular insurgencies in the Bajío and elsewhere that prejudiced production and regime revenues while also fighting the political threat of Morelos and his allies in southern strongholds. Both insurgencies, political and popular, endured longer thanks to the presence of the other. Almost everywhere, popular insurgencies proved stronger—or at least lasted longer.[41]

The persistence of popular insurgency across the Bajío for five years after the defeat of political insurgency meant that while authorities might try to restore pre-1808 ways, they could not return the silver economy to pre-1810 dynamism. Mining carried on at Guanajuato, but capital proved scarce and supplies expensive. Operators dug ore without investing in infrastructure and drainage. They took limited silver and lesser profits, paying taxes that funded counterinsurgency and exactions that sustained insurgents. Disaster came in 1820, just as the surrounding countryside seemed pacified: the Valenciana mines flooded. The Guanajuato council reported that the city, New Spain, and the world would be forever changed.[42]

With the collapse of mining, rural pacification could not return the Bajío to its long-profitable ways. Peace came between 1818 and 1820, as commanders saw that the only way to reestablish property rights was to allow families that had taken lands as insurgents to retain their ranchos, enabling them to continue family production on the promise of small rents (paid irregularly). The summer of 1820 brought the end of popular insurgency, the collapse of silver mining, and a turn to family production across the Bajío. The regime's triumph was also a victory for popular communities. Ten years of popular insurgency made revival of the Bajío silver economy impossible.

Six years' experience with the debates and experiments of Cádiz liberalism made the return of Bourbon absolutism problematic. Ten years of war brought other irreversible changes. The number of men at arms increased radically; compared to late colonial times there was a sudden militarization of society. Even with Bourbon efforts to build military power, standing troops were few in 1810. Most forces remained militias, funded and led by provincial elites. Some had joined in insurgency, led by Allende in 1810; many more mobilized in counterinsurgency, called out by Calleja to defend the regime. Ten years of war created armed forces everywhere. Troops began to arrive from Spain in 1812. Militias were at arms so long they became standing forces. Estates fearing popular insurgents paid local defense troops. Native republics, on losing municipal rights in the return of absolutism in 1814, kept local militias for "patriotic defense."[43]

From 1815 to 1820, as pacification progressed slowly, New Spain did not become less military. Troops pressed remaining insurgents to take amnesties, which often included the right to keep arms as patriotic militias. Militias and amnestied insurgents often linked—to rebel again, then claim another amnesty. Guerrillas, insurgents, and bandits mixed to keep New Spain a violent place. When Viceroy Juan de Apodaca reported to the authorities in Spain that peace reigned in 1820, he was lying. Conflicts continued and regional commanders took advantage to amass more troops and more power. José de la Cruz, captain general at Guadalajara, led forces that challenged the viceroy. Joaquín Arredondo ruled the Northeast with autonomy, like many commanders in the North, where years of conflict in the Bajío had cut ties with Mexico City.

Revived Spanish Liberalism and the Experiment in Mexican Monarchy, 1820–1823

Most insurgency, political and popular, ended by 1820; deep economic, social, and political challenges remained when news arrived from Spain of a return to liberal rule. Spanish military forces refused to sail to face Bolívar in the Andes unless Fernando reinstated the Cádiz Charter. Fernando, knowing his rule rested on military power, acquiesced and called a new Cortes. Reactions differed in New Spain. Many military leaders feared that new constitutional authorities would prosecute excesses committed during the wars. Meanwhile, constitutional councils revived in many cities and towns; Puebla and Valladolid demanded Provincial Deputations. Renewed press freedom allowed expressions of support for the constitution—while others argued that true rights required a break with Spain.

In 1821, a group of American deputies presented the Cortes a proposal to create three kingdoms in America, all recognizing Fernando, each with its own Cortes—thus its own laws. Inevitably, the Iberian majority rejected the plan. Before leaving for Spain, many of New Spain's representatives knew that political and military leaders were planning to call the king or a member of his family to become emperor of Mexico. Agustín de Iturbide, a former loyalist commander in the Bajío, led the effort; he recruited high churchmen and leading entrepreneurs in the capital and gained adherence by Vicente Guerrero, still in the field and committed to independence in his southern stronghold.

In February 1821, the Plan of Iguala declared Mexico independent, offering the throne to Fernando VII, promising a constitution appropriate to Mexico, and offering citizenship to all men, including those of African origin—addressing a key demand pressed by Guerrero, whose African roots left him no rights under the 1812 charter. Iturbide's Plan also defended Catholic institutions and religion. The anticlerical turn of Spanish liberalism in 1820, absent in 1812, drew many in New Spain to independence.

Through spring and into the summer of 1821, Iturbide and Guerrero led an alliance of former loyalists and insurgents seeking support for a reformed monarchical-constitutional Mexico. Victory came with the adherence of key commanders and city councils in the Bajío and nearby: Guanajuato, Guadalajara, San Luis Potosí—and, pivotally, Querétaro in early July. The city that had anchored counterinsurgency for a decade joined the Iguala movement, uniting the entire Bajío—or at least its urban elites—in support of independence for the first time.[44] The rural majority, entrenched on family ranchos and exhausted by a decade of conflict, stood aside. Iturbide and the Iguala movement took power by linking military commanders and urban councils. There were few real battles; cities and armies joined in a new route to power.[45]

Facing rising opposition, Viceroy Apodaca ended freedom of the press in Mexico City. On July 5, as Querétaro joined the opposition, the Mexico City garrison deposed the viceroy. Spanish commanders found his defense of the regime timid. They offered a replacement, but neither the Mexico City council nor the Provincial Deputation recognized him. As in 1808, leaders of fragile legality fell, replaced by others without legitimacy. Juan O'Donojú, sent from Spain to pacify New Spain, chose to deal with Iturbide. In August, O'Donojú accepted the Plan de Iguala and Mexican independence.[46]

Soon after, the Army of the Three Guarantees—religion, independence, and union—entered Mexico City. Iturbide named a provisional junta, which named a Regency and Iturbide its president. On September 28, 1821, the junta proclaimed an Act of Independence of the Mexican empire. It would rule from Panama to California. Soon news arrived that Fernando has refused the Mexican throne and the Spanish Cortes did not recognize Mexican independence, declaring it a rebellious province. Iturbide took power, a less than fully legitimate emperor.

Thirteen years of unprecedented conflict—political, military, ideological, social, and cultural—made the kingdom of New Spain independent. Nothing else was resolved in 1821. The economy faced collapse. Iturbide proposed a constitutional monarchy, and for a time ruled as emperor. Others sought a republic—and still others pursued provincial autonomies. Spain resisted the loss of the kingdom that had sustained its power in the world. How would a young United States and an industrializing Britain react? Mexico's challenges had only begun. Conflicts of nation making persisted through the 1860s. In part they resulted from the nature of independence: insurgents suddenly allied with counterinsurgents to break with Spain; in 1821 they agreed on that and little else. In part too, long political debates resulted from the creative political experiences of 1808 to 1821: monarchists faced republicans; defenders of imperial traditions engaged liberal innovations, all complicated by tensions between central powers grounded in the historic capital of Mexico City, provincial interests focused on intendancies becoming states, and cities and towns with councils committed to traditions of urban sovereignty.[47]

All those potential fault lines were hardened by the new universalism of the age of nations. The imperial monarchies of the early modern era recognized diverse subjects with diverse laws, rights, and privileges—and multiple ways of justice to resolve disputes. New nations sought a new universalism, at least within their borders. Rights grounded in popular sovereignty must apply to all people. Such visions grounded Spanish liberalism; its legacies shaped Mexican state making in powerful ways. To liberals, the corporate rights to land, self-rule, and separate justice that defined indigenous republics were "privileges" that had to end. Yet in many communities, liberal promises of universal rights seemed assaults on the right to be an indigenous republic.[48]

The new militarization of state and society added further challenges. Under the monarchy before 1808, coercive powers were limited; disputes were settled at the highest levels by stakeholder negotiations, across the wider society by judicial mediation. Wars for and against independence created militaries. After 1821 troops were everywhere and political disputes often led to mobilizations of force. Military power gave a new edge to the debates of nation making. And military power was expensive. Governments at every level—national, provincial, and local—faced new costs. Armed men who forged and then contested new state powers were difficult to deny when they demanded pay. The costs of government were much higher in the new nation.

Yet the means to pay those costs were limited—and also contested. The tributes long collected from the indigenous and mulatto majority were abolished amid political wars and popular risings before 1815. The collapse of silver mining radically cut regime revenues and the stimulus to commercial life. Internal collections shrank, as did international trade and revenues. Fundamental political, ideological, and cultural divisions mixed in a context of militarization, economic collapse, and sparse revenues. Mexican nation making must be seen in that context.

As emperor, Iturbide faced rising difficulties. Powerful economic actors and churchmen backed him; popular neighborhoods in Mexico City hailed his coronation.[49] But asserting independence and taking a throne proved easier than building a regime. Debates over how to elect a Congress and relations between Congress and the executive led to grave conflicts. No judicial power was built, no fiscal system created, no constitution written. Eleven years of war and revolution had fragmented society. Many refused to pay taxes. Others paid, but revenues never reached Mexico City as provincial authorities kept funds. Iturbide could not meet the demands of both the military and provincial powers. In October 1822, facing stalemate, he dissolved Congress. In December, Antonio López de Santa Anna, commander at the key port of Veracruz, rebelled with a group of republican conspirators.[50]

At first the rising found little support. But the imperial army lacked the arms and ammunition to retake Veracruz. When Antonio Echavarrí, the general sent to defeat Santa Anna, saw he was about to lose command, he pronounced in favor of a new Congress and peace with the rebels on February 1, 1823, at Casa Mata, near Veracruz. Iturbide's rivals in the army joined the movement; José Morán, commander at Puebla, proclaimed himself head of a liberating army. In March, Iturbide reinstated Congress and fled the country, leaving the monarchy in disarray.[51] Politics, for centuries focused on seeking influence within established monarchical institutions, was now an unbridled competition over who should govern and how.

In the summer of 1823, life in the lands drawn into the Mexican empire was difficult, the future uncertain. Mining struggled to revive; entrepreneurs lacked funds to invest. During years of conflict, immigrant merchants returned to Spain, taking what capital they had. Without the stimulus of silver, international trade languished; without capital to revive mines, struggling operators looked for foreign investors. Commercial agriculture also struggled, leaving urban food supplies uncertain. Bajío tenants with lands taken in insurgency and Mesoamerican villagers who pushed back liberal attempts to privatize their lands continued to cultivate. They fed families and communities first, marketing only limited surpluses. Estates remained, but few were profitable; rural social relations shifted to favor-producing families.[52]

The dimensions of the Mexican republic remained uncertain. Population concentrated in the center and south. Mexico City held perhaps 150,000 people. About half of the nation's 6 million people lived in communities with Mesoamerican roots and long ago made into indigenous republics in regions from the heartland around Mexico City south to Yucatán. Coastal lowlands were little populated, mixing people of Spanish, indigenous, and African ancestry. The Bajío remained densely settled with mixed peoples; commercial dynamism had given way to family production. Population held sparse to the north. The largest city there, Zacatecas, had 30,000 residents. Durango, Chihuahua, Saltillo, and Monterrey were small towns. On the Pacific, San Blas and Mazatlán were ports with few residents; on the Gulf, Tampico and Matamoros were small but growing, as Veracruz no longer monopolized Atlantic trade.

With the fall of silver, economic dynamism waned in northern regions. The frontiers became isolated: El Paso and Santa Fe lost trades with regions south—and looked toward the United States via the Santa Fe trail. The residents of San Antonio, Texas, began to see newcomers from the U.S. South who came to grow cotton with slave laborers. In California, missions congregated small numbers of natives while rancheros grazed growing herds. Most important, independent Comanche used long adaptations to Spanish power and trade to build armed forces and assert power between New Mexico, Texas, and the Mississippi. There were many contenders and uncertainties in new struggles to shape North America.

Founding a Federal Republic, Searching for a New Economy, 1823–1830

Most of the provinces aimed to maintain a Mexican union. They had all come out of New Spain, remembered its economic dynamism, shared important customs and institutions—old and new—and feared reconquest by Spain. They also worked to keep autonomies gained in years of civil war and shaped by liberal institutions. With Iturbide gone, few recognized the Imperial Congress or the executive power it named. In that context, negotiations led by Lucas Alamán proved pivotal. The educated son of a Guanajuato mining entrepreneur, Alamán convinced the provinces to recognize the government in Mexico City. As secretary of internal and international relations, he brokered deals with leading politicians in provincial capitals and other cities; he sent troops to Puebla and Jalisco when negotiations failed. He kept Chiapas within Mexico when Guatemala led Central America into a separate federation.[53]

Alamán was also central to writing the Founding Act of the Mexican Federation. A new national Congress met in November 1823 and approved the act early in 1824. In key debates, some deputies proposed a loose federation parallel to the early United States under the Articles of Confederation. Others sought a unified national state, looking to French and Spanish traditions. The final project came from Miguel Ramos Arizpe: a federation akin to the United States as remade in the Constitution of 1787—but with articles on religion, municipal rights, voting, and more derived from the Cádiz Charter of 1812.[54]

The constitution founding Mexico as a Federal Republic was signed in 1824. It declared that sovereignty derived from the people, but first settled in the states being created in provinces extending from Yucatán, through the core of New Spain, to northern regions. Asserting that sovereignty belonged to the people, and to the states they created, paralleled developments in the United States. That assertion, however, was neither an imposition nor an imitation in Mexico.[55] The provinces created by Bourbon Intendancies and the Cádiz Constitution's Provincial Deputations prepared the way for state sovereignty. The 1824 Constitution made a considered choice to lodge sovereignty in the people and to constitute it first in regional states. The federal government would serve— and hopefully balance—popular and provincial sovereignties.

The founders of the republic rejected the alternative of lodging sovereignty in a unitary abstraction called the nation—a legacy of the French revolution adopted by Spanish liberals in 1812. They also rejected the Hispanic tradition of the sovereignty of the pueblos—towns and cities with councils. The 1824 Constitution chose popular sovereignty and provincial priority over municipal rights and national sovereignty, the latter a route to more centralized national power. Yet both traditions remained vibrant in Mexico. When central rule returned in the 1830s, it built on urban bases. Throughout Mexico's national history the pueblos have never been passive. Hispanic towns and indigenous villages have pressed their interests and negotiated demands with political parties, government officials, military powers, and other political actors.[56]

In the Federal Republic, national legislative powers divided into two chambers: one of deputies representing the people, another of senators representing the states. The president was elected by the state congresses—in turn chosen by the people of the states. Each state wrote a constitution, defining citizens and their rights, including who could vote and hold office—always limited to men. Property qualifications were few; tiered elections derived from the Cádiz Constitution allowed all adult men to vote locally for electors; the latter repeatedly chose propertied, educated, and politically experienced men for office. The Federal Republic remained Catholic, endorsing a culture shared by all.

In October 1824, the state congresses voted Guadalupe Victoria Mexico's first president. Nicolás Bravo, a landed insurgent who had joined Morelos, backed Guerrero, and then Iturbide, came in second to become vice president. Both had strong insurgent credentials, though Bravo was suspected of centralist leanings. Victoria named a cabinet of diverse tendencies, leaving no group satisfied. The new regime faced many challenges.

External threats seemed everywhere. Spain refused to accept the loss of its richest colony and threatened to send troops. The United States and the other new nations of the Americas had recognized Mexican independence under the Iturbide's empire. More important powers remained aloof. Neither Pope Leo XII nor his successors accepted Mexican sovereignty before Fernando VII died in 1833. That was not only a cultural challenge to a deeply Catholic country; it blocked the naming of bishops and other Church officials, limiting the Church in a most Catholic nation. France and other monarchical allies of Spain also refused recognition.[57]

That left Great Britain pivotal. Britain had known the importance of New Spain's silver since the eighteenth century. As allies of Spain's liberals in the fight against Napoleon, British merchants and ships took direct roles in that trade in 1808. Britain emerged from the Napoleonic wars militarily triumphant, dominant in Atlantic trade, and with a rising industrial economy driving toward global hegemony. In 1824, Mexico needed British recognition, capital, and trade.

Meanwhile, the new republic faced economic collapse. The treasury seemed always empty, while bureaucrats and troops demanded pay. The constitution left direct taxes to the states; revenues from silver and commerce (should they revive) belonged to the states, as would any property or head taxes (which might replace colonial tributes). Only tariffs on international trade and revenues from the Federal District, including Mexico City, funded the national regime. The states negotiated annual contributions to the national treasury, but while the economy struggled, contributions were low and inconsistently paid. Making matters worse, powerful interests that had loaned vast sums to the colonial treasury before 1821 forced national officials to recognize their claims as the price of accepting the new regime.[58]

Into that vortex came the British government, bankers, and investors. Victoria's national government needed cash and recognition. British officials sought open access and low tariffs for British textiles. But low tariffs would limit the only revenue that funded national power—and a flood of cheap textiles threatened Mexican cloth makers, mostly artisans. The British solution: recognition, low tariffs, and loans from British banks to fund national power. Britain would get open markets and control of Mexican national purse strings. Victoria accepted. British loans made him the only president to complete a term during Mexico's early decades; the debts that resulted plagued national leaders for half a century. Mexican cloth makers faced losses that fueled discontent.

Economic struggles continued. However distributed, revenues depended on trade, internal and international, all historically stimulated by silver. The decade of insurgency had undermined the silver economy in the Bajío and limited it elsewhere. The dearth of silver and the commerce it stimulated cut the sources of capital that had financed New Spain's economy. Again, the solution appeared to come from Britain. Coal mines there had perfected steam pumps that might rapidly drain flooded mines. But bringing new technology to the Mexican highlands increased capital costs—and Mexicans had no capital. Led by Lucas Alamán, mine operators like the Condes de Regla at Real del Monte, the Condes de Valenciana at Guanajuato, and others at Zacatecas and elsewhere negotiated joint ventures with British capitalists. British funds, technology, and workers came to Mexico—and for the first time, returns on capital flowed out of Mexico to London and elsewhere. Nothing announced the transformation of the mining economy between 1808 and 1824 more clearly than the turn to foreign financing.

Still, the mines were slow to revive—revealing the enormity of the task and the difficulty of importing capital and technology. Zacatecas, least pummeled by insurgency and civil war, revived in the late 1820s; Guanajuato most devastated by insurgency, did not flourish until the 1840s; Real del Monte's revival was even slower. When mines did revive, their revenues filled state treasuries: first at Zacatecas, later in Guanajuato. The national regime never found revenues to sustain its costs, including those of the military, nor to pay its debts to British and other bondholders. For decades after 1824, bankers made short-term loans at exorbitant rates; famous *agiotistas* both funded and plagued the national regime.[59]

While the national government and the silver economy struggled, some states found prosperity. Along the Gulf Veracruz gained from commerce; its rich lands raised food, cotton, and tobacco. Yucatán profited from trade with Havana as Cuba's sugar and slave economy filled markets opened by Haitian revolutionaries. Puebla saw steady cultivation, but cloth makers suffered from British competition. The State of Mexico, surrounding Mexico City and reaching far north and south, might be the richest of all—with mines at Real del Monte and Taxco, rich fields in the Valleys of Mexico and Toluca, sugar around Cuernavaca, and coastal lowlands around Acapulco. But mines struggled to revive, and estate operators saw profits plummet; they blamed villagers who controlled too much land and asked too much to harvest crops.[60] Michoacán and Jalisco prospered—but not as much as Zacatecas with its recuperating silver mines. Guanajuato and Querétaro were slow to regain prosperity. Local leaders lamented that tenants prospered more than landowners—and that women showed too much independence.[61]

Some states found political stability; others lived years of turbulence. Without political parties, groups seeking power organized in diverse ways. The army became a political force—defending its right to separate justice while claiming power to resolve others' disputes. In the 1820s, many political actors organized in Masonic lodges. Leading members of government in 1823 and 1824 joined Scottish Rite lodges founded by republicans who had opposed the empire. Iturbide's partisans met in other lodges, such as the Black Eagle later headed by President Guadalupe Victoria. It affiliated with the York Rite, backed by Joel Poinsett, first U.S. minister in Mexico. The Yorkinos promoted popular mobilizations and gained influence in local elections. They accused their foes of centralism and inflamed a campaign against remaining Spanish immigrants. In 1826, Yorkinos won congressional elections; several gained ministries in Victoria's cabinet, notably Manuel Gómez Pedraza as secretary of war. They found power in many state governments. Their triumphs led to radical demands, including the expulsion of Spanish immigrants (all legally Mexicans). By 1827, Yorkinos were dominant and divided. As the 1828 elections approached, one faction, the Impartials, pressed the rights and interests of the states (including Coahuila's Miguel Ramos Arispe and Zacatecas's Francisco García) and backed Manuel Gómez Pedraza for president. Radical Yorkinos led by State of Mexico governor Lorenzo de Zavala backed popular ex-insurgent Vicente Guerrero.[62]

In 1828, popular elections for a new national Congress favored radical Yorkinos, but the vote for president came from existing state congresses. As a result, Gómez Pedraza came first, Guerrero second, and General Anastasio Bustamente third—backed by a few enemies of Zavala. The split radical vote denied Guerrero, the popular choice, the presidency. Before final results were known, Santa Anna rose in arms against a Veracruz state Congress that voted for Gómez Pedraza, arguing that the people favored Guerrero. In Mexico City, Zavala promoted a protest that turned into a riot that destroyed the Parián market—where the rich bought Asian and European wares in front of the National Palace. President Victoria could not resist the pressure: he named Guerrero secretary of war. Gómez Pedraza renounced his claim to office and fled to Jalisco. The new Congress named Guerrero president and Bustamente vice president.[63]

Near the end of 1828, several states that backed Gómez Pedraza built a coalition against Guerrero, insisting he had been imposed from the center. Guanajuato and others called militias to arms—but lower officers and troops sympathized with Guerrero and refused to move against him. The strength of the new regime lay in its popular bases and it addressed their concerns. It expelled immigrant Spaniards, often merchants and easy scapegoats for economic dislocations and urban poverty. Guerrero prohibited imports of cloth and other goods to preserve markets for national producers, mostly artisans. The cut in trade hit already paltry national revenues, worsening underlying regime difficulties.

Guerrero faced challenges governing. His secretary of the treasury, Lorenzo de Zavala, tried to collect direct taxes, but they were resisted by provinces as unconstitutional. Without funds, Guerrero turned to the agiotistas, gaining small revenues for large obligations. Meanwhile, the nation faced a Spanish invasion. An expedition landed at Tampico on the northern Gulf Coast. Santa Anna mobilized forces in Veracruz, as did Manuel de Mier y Terán in Tamaulipas; they defeated the invaders on September 11, 1829. Mexicans lived a brief but intense moment of patriotic fervor; independence seemed assured.

The situation soon deteriorated. In December, an army camped in Xalapa to guard against Spanish incursions demanded a return to constitutional rule. Vice president Bustamente led a coalition opposing Guerrero for having claimed extraordinary powers to suspend freedom of expression, collect direct taxes, and impose forced contributions on sovereign states. The ex-insurgent and arguably Mexico's most popular early president fled home to the rugged south of Mexico State. Bustamente assumed the presidency in early 1830 and named Lucas Alamán secretary of internal and international relations.[64] Again Congress exceeded its faculties: it declared Bustamente's Plan of Jalapa just, recognized his rule—and made Guerrero ineligible.

New Beginnings, Escalating Conflicts, and Texas Sucession in the 1830s

In the 1820s, political Mexicans debated central power versus provincial rights in a context of economic collapse. In the 1830s, they forged new coalitions and visions that came to be labeled conservative and liberal, aiming in different ways to find economic revival and political consolidation. The decade shaped Mexico's future: conservative and liberal visions contended for national primacy past midcentury while the secession of Texas led to a war in the 1840s that saw an expansive United States take Mexico's vast northern territories.

Though Bustamente sat as president, Lucas Alamán ruled from 1830 to 1832. He promised social order and a full national treasury, yet pursued divisive political policies. He sent the military against Guerrero; after months on the run the popular strongman who fought for independence and became president was captured, charged, summarily tried, and executed. Alamán also persecuted Yorkino partisans, especially those who won the 1828 state congressional elections. Many saw their state sovereignty attacked. Even state governments that backed Bustamente strengthened militaries to resist centralization. Bustamente's secretary of war tried to strengthen the army, reducing the power of the civic militias that served state governors. The attempt provoked more discontent.

In economic affairs, Alamán reversed Guerrero's policies. The new minister opened ports to cloth and other imports, charging tariffs to fund the government and a bank to finance imports of machinery for Mexican factories. The Banco de Avío, the world's first national development bank, aimed to back entrepreneurs committed to industrial production.[65] It revealed Alamán's vision of a new Mexican economy. In the 1820s he promoted British investment to revive silver mining. In the 1830s he used tariffs to facilitate industrial development in Mexico—to limit British imports. Alamán hoped to balance revived silver mines and new industries. By the mid-1830s factories operated in Puebla, around Mexico City, and at Querétaro. They made industrial cottons, competed with imports, and employed growing numbers of workers—threatening the household cloth makers that Guerrero had aimed to protect. Nothing proved easy or unifying—but Alamán had a vision of a new Mexico.

Alamán's policies alienated merchants, including many importers at Veracruz. Their ire reinforced opposition among those committed to state autonomy and resisted impositions from the center. In 1832, Santa Anna led a coalition of merchants and popular groups at Veracruz in another rising to topple a national government he accused of taking power illegally, promoting centralism, and ruling outside the constitution.

At first, Santa Anna's movement gained little response. Other states were working to return to the legal ways broken in 1828. New presidential elections were due in 1832, and Manuel de Mier y Terán seemed an ideal candidate to leaders of important states like Zacatecas, San Luis Potosí, and Jalisco. But Mier y Terán committed suicide, leaving federalists without a leader. Fearful that Alamán would become president, frustrated states joined Santa Anna in rebellion—on condition that that Gómez Pedraza return to complete the term he won in 1828. It was an ingenious plan to reclaim a broken legal order. Bustamente saw the force arrayed against him and resigned.

In April 1833, elections in the state congresses chose Santa Anna as president and Valentín Gómez Farías as vice president, both strong federalists. For the first time in Mexico, radical liberals led by Gómez Farías took aim at the economic power and cultural role of the Church.[66] Since independence in 1821, state governments had sought the *patronato*, the right granted by the papacy to Spanish kings to name bishops and other high clerics. The Vatican insisted that such rights did not extend to the nation or the states. Denied power over the Church, states desperate for revenue eyed ecclesiastical wealth. The states of Mexico, Michoacán, Jalisco, and Veracruz began to sell Church properties. Some radicals, inspired by eighteenth-century Spanish reformers, argued that Church lands should be distributed among small farmers to promote production and popular welfare. Often proposed, redistributions rarely happened. Conflict between liberals seeking revenues and churchmen defending clerical rights and properties escalated. Most liberals were Catholics; most churchmen accepted the nation and civil authorities—but resisted state intervention in Church affairs.[67]

The dispute was not entirely about wealth and power. Church institutions monopolized education in New Spain. José María Luis Mora, a liberal cleric from Guanajuato, offered a plan for higher education focused on citizenship, not religion. Governments would set programs of study based on the needs of the republic. Oaxaca, Zacatecas, and the State of Mexico founded Institutes of Arts and Sciences to educate new generations of liberals. Churchmen saw wealth, power, and control of education attacked; they mobilized in opposition, insisting that liberals were attacking religion.[68]

Santa Anna left governing to his vice president; to implement reforms, Gómez Farías was backed by a liberal national Congress elected in 1833 and by powerful federalist interests. Still, reform provoked opposition. The vice president dissolved the Mexico City Council, replacing it with one favorable to his plans; he prohibited publications critical of his program; he passed laws removing political enemies. Many faced punishment without trials, fair or otherwise. Opposition intensified.

When Gómez Farías and his congressional backers ended mandatory tithes and state enforcement of clerical vows, the Church protested but acquiesced. When the government gave states the right to name priests to vacant parishes, the Church would not obey, and Gómez Farías suspended the law. Then in 1834 Congress decreed that bishops who did not accept state powers faced exile. As divisions escalated, Generals Gabriel Durán and Mariano Arista led part of the army in rebellion; Santa Anna defeated them—yet proved ambivalent toward the policies of a government he led as president. He backed liberal measures, but insisted that solving revenue difficulties came first. He balked when Congress began to reform the military.[69]

Meanwhile, challenges mounted on Mexico's northeastern frontier. Settlement in Texas focused on San Antonio and grazing estates all around. Missions extended farther out, aiming to subordinate native peoples. Independence and the collapse of the silver economy ended the markets for Texas livestock and other economic ties with regions south. A Comanche empire asserted power north and west. Meanwhile, the United States emerged from the War of 1812 with independence confirmed and control of the Mississippi basin. The 1820 Missouri Compromise settled the question of the expansion of slavery. The United States was poised for growth: industry flourished in the Northeast; cotton and slavery drove west across the South; expansion across the Mississippi basin raised crops that fed eastern cities, southern plantations, and expanding trade.[70]

Texas became the vortex where struggles to shape a Mexico facing economic collapse met rising Comanche power, and the expanding United States. Waves of settlers from the United States and Europe entered Texas, most committed to expanding cotton and slavery on rich coastal plains. The politics of Texas settlement began in 1819 when Spanish authorities announced that people from Florida and Louisiana, Spanish domains before they joined the United States, were welcome in Texas. Iturbide's empire confirmed the rights of the settlers and promoted the arrival of more. The Constitution of 1824 made colonization a question for the states. Texas merged with Coahuila in one extensive frontier state—a concession to the power of Miguel Ramos Arizpe. *Coahuiltejano* governors ratified immigrant rights and granted new concessions to entrepreneurs who sought land in Texas to settle colonists. Soon, newcomers outnumbered *tejanos* in Texas.

The question of slavery brought rising challenges. The Constitution of Coahuila and Texas declared all persons born in the state free—allowing new settlers to keep the slaves they brought with them, but face a generational transition to free labor. In 1829, Mexican national authorities abolished slavery, but permitted its persistence in Texas while prohibiting imports. The end of slave labor would accelerate. In 1830, Alamán decreed national power over immigration and colonization, and prohibited foreign settlement near the borders of their country of origin. The rights of U.S. migrants to settle and maintain slavery in Texas were challenged again. They began to discuss secession and annexation to the United States.

Texans met in assemblies calling for the separation of Texas from Coahuila. English-speaking settlers, the powerful among them committed to cotton and slavery, would be a majority in the new state. In 1833, leading Texas entrepreneur and colonizer Stephen Austin trekked to Mexico City seeking separation from Coahuila, the repeal of the immigration law of 1830, and tax exemptions. Congress repealed the law, a centralist act unpopular with many federalists, and extended Texas tax exemptions for three years. But without Mexican authorization, Austin wrote to Texas calling for a state government. Gómez Farías learned of the letter and arrested Austin, who was held in Mexico City until 1835. The situation was tense as 1833 became 1834.[71] Samuel Houston and other Texas leaders built armies to fight for Texas independence, aiming to later join the United States. The threat alarmed Mexicans. Many saw a need for a more centralized regime to prevent the fracture of the nation.

In 1834, Santa Anna reclaimed power from Gómez Farías and appointed a cabinet of moderate federalists. Elections for Congress brought deputies who opposed their predecessors' radical measures. The new government began to search for a political center. While Santa Anna, his cabinet, and the new Congress agreed on the need to reform the constitution to prevent secessions from breaking the nation, by 1835, several states seemed ready to defend their autonomies with arms. Many feared that the nation was on the verge of disintegration—not unimaginable given ongoing fragmentations in Central America and the Río de la Plata. In Campeche on the Yucatán Peninsula and at Cuernavaca just south of the capital, armed movements offered to defend national unity against separatist threats. Santa Anna, long a staunch defender of federalism as it favored Veracruz, began to see that states' rights might lead to disunion. He decided to fortify national power by reducing state militias. Resistance came quickly, notably in silver-rich Zacatecas. Santa Anna sent the national army against the Zacatecas militia—and faced acquiescence rather than resistance. Mining wealth might fund provincial power; it also reduced incentives to disruptive violence.

Authorities in Coahuila and Texas opposed the limits on state militias, while local conflict set the governor against the state commander. Texas colonists saw opportunity and refused to recognize either the state or the national regime—though Austin convinced them not to declare independence. He knew a declaration would end Mexican federalists' support for Texas. But when Santa Anna organized an expedition to end the rebellion, Texans saw no reason for restraint. In March 1836 they met in convention to declare the Republic of Texas. David Burnet was its first president; Lorenzo de Zavala—the Mexican federalist pivotal to Guerrero's rule in the late 1820s—was vice president. Santa Anna claimed an (in)famous victory at the Alamo in San Antonio, but Houston's troops, mostly recruits from the United States, defeated him at San Jacinto. Captured, Santa Anna recognized Texas.[72]

Defeat in Texas—though Mexican authorities did not recognize its secession—intersected with rising discontent across Mexico. The press became alarmed. In 1833, cholera had ravaged cities and rural regions from Veracruz, through Puebla, and Mexico City and the surrounding State of Mexico—the national heartland. The epidemic brought death to thousands and rising food prices to the living; cholera blocked communications, closed mills, paralyzed trade, and cut tax revenues.[73] Meanwhile, cloth imports and new industries spread discontent among artisans. Dispersed powers had no cure. Attacks on the Church and the loss of Texas convinced many that liberal federalism had failed.

Congress began work on a new constitution. In 1836 it promulgated Siete Leyes Constitucionales—Seven Constitutional Laws—ending the Federal Republic and creating central rule. Sovereignty no longer focused on states or belonged to the people. Rather, it derived from the nation, to be exercised by central authorities. The shift fused Spanish tradition and Cádiz liberalism. The name Siete Leyes evoked the medieval Siete Partidas; politics became a relationship between central powers and city councils. The center and the cities displaced the states and the people.[74] National authorities named provincial administrators to replace elected governors. The Leyes raised the population required to keep municipal councils, denying self-rule to many towns and most former indigenous republics. To vote, citizens faced income requirements for the first time. Departments that replaced the states did elect juntas (reminiscent of Provincial Deputations)—but power came from the capital. The founders of the new polity feared congresses, national and provincial. They aimed to strengthen national power, yet divided it between the president and a new Supremo Poder Conservador—creating fractures at the top.[75]

Constitutional change could not alter entrenched ways; national officials struggled to rule distant provinces and outlying communities. Cities and towns kept autonomies. It proved difficult to limit political participation. The Siete Leyes set income limits on voting and higher levels to old office; implementation was uneven. Departments, like the states they replaced, resisted national claims on revenues. Unable to end financial shortfalls, Anastasio Bustamente, now president under centralism, raised import taxes and turned once more to the agiotistas, again trading short-term funds for mounting debts.[76]

The War for North America and the Struggle for Mexico

Mexico faced serious problems in the 1840s. Political life seemed a disaster. In 1840 a revolt led by General José Urrea and Valentín Gómez Farías called for a return to federalism, but forces backing Bustamente prevailed. Fears of persistent instability and escalating violence led to new coalitions and old propositions. Some concluded that Mexicans could not govern themselves with republican institutions because colonial customs and traditions prevailed. In August 1840 José María Gutiérrez Estrada proposed a return to constitutional monarchy.

Military leaders argued that only military rule could save the nation, yet the military failed to impose order—and often provoked disorder. When Nicolás Bravo followed Bustamente as president under the new centralizing charter, congressional voting favored the Federalists.[77] Under changing constitutions, elections documented deepening fragmentation of political visions and interests. There was never enough revenue to fund governments, national or provincial—or to pay militaries that were always discontented and ready to back the next political project. Ironically, in the same years the economy finally began to strengthen.[78] Mining had revived at Zacatecas in the 1830s; it came back at Guanajuato in the 1840s. Meanwhile, a national textile industry took hold. Mechanized factories concentrated growing numbers of workers at Puebla and around Mexico City; the Hercules mill flourished in the canyon east of Querétaro.

Reviving silver mines began to generate employment, profit, and revenue, and stimulated trade that created more. Yet textile industrialization, British or Mexican, threatened artisan families—and the income of women who spun thread in struggling households. Villagers, tenants, and rancheros still ruled most rural production, limiting profits among landlords who longed for colonial agrarian capitalism. Still, as the 1840s began, economic revival was under way and calls for political balance were rising.[79]

Texas remained a headache. Politicians and military commanders saw a rebel province; none had the power or resources to force reincorporation. A greater problem was that Texas leaders claimed the Río Grande as its southern and western boundary; they dreamed of sovereignty including northern Tamaulipas and half of New Mexico, even as the Comanche ruled west of Austin. No Mexican president could accept such claims. The land between the Río Grande and the Nueces, the historic border between Tamaulipas and Texas, became the focus of discord and excuse for war.[80]

From the moment of secession in 1836, Texans sought union with the United States. They failed because they would be a slave state, disrupting the Missouri Compromise. In 1845, views in Washington were changing. James Polk won the presidency with southern and expansionist backing, while the Texas Republic faced fiscal crisis and rising debts. The U.S. Congress approved annexation knowing that Mexico would see it as an act of war. The press in both nations excited war fever. Mexican president José Joaquín de Herrera knew he could not win a war against the United States—yet he could not state that publicly. He might have accepted an independent Texas defined by historic boundaries, but not with the new claims. Polk sent John Slidell to Mexico to buy San Francisco and northern California. The acquisition would bring gold, rich lands, Pacific ports, and a way to rebalance slave and free states in an expanded Union. Herrera refused to meet Slidell. The Mexican press inflamed tensions, accusing Herrera of preparing to cave to U.S. pressure.[81]

In December, General Mariano Paredes y Arrillaga, charged to lead an army to defend the North, instead toppled the government. Lucas Alamán backed him, as did other conservatives, arguing that monarchy was the only way to keep Mexico from falling to the United States. Alamán also knew that Mexico could not win a war against the United States—and that no government could survive without promising to reclaim Texas.[82] Polk was ready take Texas—and more. He sent General Zachary Taylor to the banks of the Río Grande. The United States had invaded Mexico.

Hostilities began. Mexico, a quarter century past independence, had neither a strong national regime nor a viable economy; it lacked a military ready for international war; it had no navy; and it had neither the unity nor the resources to mobilize for war. By contrast, the United States, seventy-five years a nation, had forged a regime grounded in a burgeoning economy combining southern cotton, northern industry, and westward expansion; it had professional armed forces trained at West Point and Annapolis; its resources for war were beyond any Mexico could muster. Mexican leaders knew all this, as did men in Washington—who saw the chance to take a continent before Mexico might reach a consolidation that allowed resistance.

As war began, Mexican divisions persisted. State leaders often looked to local interests, promising to defend their states while providing few troops or funds to defend the border, ports, or the capital. As the U.S. navy blocked Mexican ports, Yucatán declared neutrality to prevent an invasion; merchants in Culiacán, Sinaloa, took advantage of U.S. occupation to profit. There was realism in such decisions, but little national patriotism.[83] Some indigenous groups, rarely committed to a national project that threatened their lands and autonomies as often as it offered rights and inclusion, took the war as a time to rise for local and regional independence—among Zapotecs at the Isthmus of Tehuantepec; among the diverse people of the Sierra Gorda (north of Querétaro); and famously among the Maya of Yucatán, who rose in what Mexicans called a Caste War. Movements for indigenous independence caused fear among Mexican elites.[84]

Taylor's army crossed the Río Grande to take Mexico's northern cities. Small U.S. forces took New Mexico and California. Winfield Scott landed at Veracruz and quickly left disease-ridden lowlands to march to the capital. Facing multiple invading forces that were well armed and well provisioned, Mexican politicians and generals concluded that only Santa Anna could raise a defense. He did what he could in impossible circumstances, slowing the drive of Taylor's forces from the north. But in August 1847, Scott's army was poised outside Mexico City. National Guard forces, cadets of the Colegio Militar, some regular troops, and common citizens joined resistance at Churubusco, Molino del Rey, and Chapultepec. Nothing stopped U.S. troops. National leaders left the capital to keep government alive in Querétaro. For two days in September the working people of Mexico City rose to hurl stones at U.S. soldiers, defending their city even if their leaders and army could not defend the nation and its capital.[85]

In Querétaro, a new president, Manuel de la Peña, assembled a cabinet and Congress. Radical federalists argued to continue the war—an irony as the states whose interests they defended contributed so few men and resources. The government entered peace negotiations early in 1848. It recognized Texas as a state of the United States. It accepted the loss of New Mexico (including Arizona) and California in exchange for an indemnity of 15 million pesos. The treaty signed at Guadalupe led to long challenges. Many Mexicans remained north of the border. By treaty, the United States committed to defend their rights as citizens and landholders, rights repeatedly abrogated in practice. By treaty, too, the United States accepted the duty to protect the border, a commitment also rarely kept.

After the War That Decided Everything

The war of 1846 to 1848 set the future course of Mexico, the United States, and North America. Important issues took decades and many lives to resolve: the roles of central powers, liberal policies, and indigenous communities in Mexico; the questions of slavery, its expansion, and national unity in the United States. Still, by 1850 it was clear that Mexico would be a nation without a North to settle and develop, and that the United States would be a continental power driving across a new West. In the new world of industrial capitalism, the United States took hemispheric hegemony as Mexico faced limited development. We can only ask what Mexico might have become with the lands from Texas through California, and what the United States would be without them.

Both nations needed two decades after the war to set national politics and find ways forward. In the United States, new territories reopened the question of slavery's expansion, driving divisions that led to Civil War—the deadliest of all conflicts of nation making in the Americas. The 1865 Union victory ended slavery, setting the expanded nation on course to industrialization and expansion, sustained by mines and lands once Mexican.[86]

MAP 7.2. Mexico in North America, ca. 1855

Mexico struggled through postwar years of national doubt. A moderate regime gave way to centralist conservatism uniting Alamán and Santa Anna and hinting of monarchism. A revived liberal movement took power in 1855 and began a radical transformation. Reformers ended the separate jurisdictions of the Church and the military—and privatized the lands of Church institutions and indigenous communities. A Church-backed reaction (most communities stood aside) brought the Reform War of 1858 to 1860. Liberal victory came with soaring debts, facilitating conservatives' recruitment of a European intervention, French occupation, and the imposed monarchy of Maximilian in 1864—a short-lived regime that proved more liberal than many Mexican liberals. The

1867 restoration of the republic under the long-resistant Benito Juárez brought a welcome to U.S. capital, a turn to privatizing community lands, a new round of regional revolts, and in time the consolidation of a politically authoritarian, economically liberal regime under Porfirio Díaz—who had fought French occupation but welcomed a new Mexico rebuilt as an economic dependency of the United States.[87]

Notes

1 John Tutino, "Capitalist Foundations: Spanish North America, Mexico, and the United States," in *Mexico and Mexicans in the Making of the United States*, ed. Tutino (Austin: University of Texas Press, 2012).

2 Alexander von Humboldt, *Ensayo político sobre el reino de Nueva España* (Mexico City: Porrúa, 1966).

3 Dennis Flynn and Arturo Giráldez, "Cycles of Silver: Global Economic Unity through the Mid-Eighteenth Century," *Journal of World History* 13:2 (2002), 391–427.

4 John Tutino, "Haciendas y comunidades en el Valle de México: El crecimiento commercial y la persistencia de los pueblos a la sombra del capital colonial, 1500–1800," in *Historia general del Estado de México*, ed. María Teresa Jarquín Ortega (Zinacatepec: El Colegio Mexiquense, 2011).

5 See Brian Owensby, *Empire of Law and Indian Justice in Colonial Mexico* (Stanford, CA: Stanford University Press, 2008).

6 On the South, the place to begin is Karen Caplan, *Indigenous Citizens: Local Liberalism in Early National Oaxaca and Yucatán* (Stanford, CA: Stanford University Press, 2009).

7 Tutino, *Making a New World: Founding Capitalism in the Bajío and Spanish North America* (Durham, NC: Duke University Press, 2011), part 1.

8 This section's discussion of the eighteenth-century silver economy synthesizes Tutino, *Making a New World*, part 2.

9 On local militias, see Virginia Guedea, "La organización militar," in *El gobierno provincial en la Nueva España 1570–1787*, ed. Woodrow Borah (Mexico City: UNAM, 1985), 125–148; for the army, Christon I. Archer, *The Army in Bourbon Mexico, 1760–1810* (Albuquerque: University of New Mexico Press, 1977).

10 See Carlos Marichal, *La bancarrota del virreinato: Nueva España y las finanzas del imperio español, 1780–1810* (Mexico City: Fondo de Cultura Económica, 1999).

11 Tutino, "Haciendas y comunidades."

12 Doris Ladd, *The Making of a Strike: Mexican Silver Workers Struggles in Real del Monte, 1766–1775* (Lincoln: University of Nebraska Press, 1988).

13 See Rodolfo Pastor, *Campesinos y reformas: La mixteca, 1700–1856* (Mexico City: El Colegio de México, 1987); Brian R. Hamnett, *Politics and Trade in Southern Mexico 1750–1821* (Cambridge: Cambridge University Press, 1871); and Jeremy Baskes, *Indians, Merchants, and Markets: A Reinterpretation of the Repartimiento*

and Spanish-Indian Economic Relations in Colonial Oaxaca, 1750–1821 (Stanford, CA: Stanford University Press, 2000).

14　Again, this section's discussion of the North and the Bajío synthesizes Tutino, *Making a New World*.

15　Felipe Castro Gutiérrez, *Nueva ley y nuevo rey: Reformas borbónicas y rebeliones populares en Nueva España* (Zamora: El Colegio de Michoacán, 1996) and Tutino, *Making a New World*, chap. 4.

16　Real wages fell across New Spain in the late eighteenth century. See Amílcar Chaullú and Aurora Gómez Galvariato, "Mexico's Real Wages in the Age of Divergence, 1780–1930," *Revista de historia económica* 33:1 (2015), 83–122.

17　José Miranda, *Las ideas y las instituciones políticas mexicanas: Primera parte 1521–1820* (Mexico City: UNAM, 1978).

18　For the regions near Mexico City, see Charles Gibson, *The Aztecs under Spanish Rule* (Stanford, CA: Stanford University Press, 1964), and James Lockhart, *The Nahuas after the Conquest* (Stanford, CA: Stanford University Press, 1994). For regions south, see Pastor, *Campesinos y reformas*, and Caplan, *Indigenous Citizens*. On judicial mediations, see Owensby, *Empire of Law*, on the early period and William Taylor's classic *Drinking, Homicide, and Rebellion in Colonial Mexican Villages* (Stanford, CA: Stanford University Press, 1979) on the eighteenth century.

19　See John Tutino, "Provincial Spaniards, Haciendas, and Indian Towns," in *Provinces of Early Mexico*, ed. Ida Altman and James Lockhart (Los Angeles: UCLA Latin American Center, 1976), 177–194, and Claudia Guarisco, *Los indios del valle de México y la construcción de una nueva sociabilidad política, 1777–1835* (Zinacatepec: El Colegio Mexiquense, 2003).

20　This reflects Tutino, *Making a New World*. On Spanish council politics, see Beatriz Rojas, *Las instituciones de gobierno y la élite local: Aguascalientes del siglo XVII hasta la independencia* (Zamora: El Colegio de Michoacán, 1998); Gabriel Torres Puga, "La ciudad novohispana: Ensayo sobre su vida política, 1521–1800," in *Historia política de la Ciudad de México desde su fundación hasta el año 2000*, ed. Ariel Rodríguez Kuri (Mexico City: El Colegio de México, 2012), 143–158; and Esteban Sánchez de Tagle, *Del gobierno y su tutela: La reforma a las haciendas locales del siglo XVIII y el cabildo de México* (Mexico City: INAH, 2014).

21　Alejandra Irigoin and Regina Grafe, "Bargaining for Absolutism: A Spanish Path to Nation-State and Empire Building," *Hispanic American Historical Review* 88:2 (2008), 173–209; Iván Escamilla González, *Los intereses mal entendidos: El Consulado de Comerciantes de México y la monarquía española, 1700–1739* (Mexico City: UNAM, 2011).

22　Gabriel Torres Puga, *Opinión pública y censura en Nueva España: Indicios de un silencio imposible, 1767–1794* (Mexico City: El Colegio de México, 2010).

23　See Tutino, *Making a New World*, chap. 5.

24　Again, this discussion of social pressures in the Bajío synthesizes Tutino, *Making a New World*, part 2.

25　Emilio La Parra, *Manuel Godoy: La aventura del poder* (Madrid: Taurus, 2002).

26 See Gisela von Wobeser, *Dominación colonial: La consolidación de vales reales, 1804–1812* (Mexico City: UNAM, 2003).

27 Tomás Antonio Rodríguez Campomanes to Duque de Medinaceli Santisteban, San Juan Bautista Xiquipulco, Mexico, January 2, 1808, and T. A. Rodriguez Campomanes to Fernando, Prince of Asturias, January 2, 1808, in Archivo Histórico Nacional, Spain, *Estado*, vol. 57, documents 46–47. See also Guillermina del Valle Pavón, *Finanzas piadosas y redes de negocios: Los mercaderes de la ciiudad de México ante de la Crisis de Nueva España, 1804–1808* (Mexico City: Instituto Mora, 2012).

28 A. Ávila, "Nueva España, 1808–1809," in *En el umbral de las revoluciones hispánicas: El bienio 1808–1810*, ed. Roberto Breña (Mexico City: El Colegio de México, 2010), 129–148.

29 The rise and fall of Hidalgo's insurgency is outlined in John Tutino, *From Insurrection to Revolution in Mexico: Social Bases of Agrarian Violence, 1750–1940* (Princeton, NJ: Princeton University Press, 1986); on Querétaro loyalty, see John Tutino, "Querétaro y los orígenes de la nación mexicana: Las políticas étnicas de soberanía, contrainsurgencia, y independencia," in *México a la luz de sus revoluciones*, ed. Laura Rojas and Susan Deeds (Mexico City: El Colegio de México, 2014), 17–64. On Hidalgo, see Carlos Herrejón Peredo, *Hidalgo, maestro, párroco, insurgente* (Mexico City: Clío, 2011).

30 A. Ávila, J. A. Serrano, and Juan Ortiz Escamilla, *Actores y escenarios de la Independencia. Guerra, pensamiento e instituciones 1808–1825*, ed. Enrique Florescano (Mexico City: FCE, 2010), 115–203.

31 On the Cádiz project, see Roberto Breña, *El primer liberalismo español y los procesos de emancipación de América, 1808–1824* (Mexico City: El Colegio de México, 2008).

32 The politics of the era are synthesized in A. Ávila, *En nombre de la nación* (Mexico City: Taurus, 2002). See also Jaime Rodriguez, *We Are Now the True Spaniards: Sovereignty, Independence, and the Emergence of the Federal Republic of Mexico, 1808–1824* (Stanford, CA: Stanford University Press, 2012).

33 John Tutino, "De Hidalgo a Apatzingán: Insurgencia popular y proyectos politicos en la Neuva España revolucionaria 1811–1814," in *La insurgencia Mexicana y la Constitución de Apatzingán, 1808–1824*, ed. Ana Carolina Ibarra (Mexico City: UNAM, 2014), 49–78; and John Tutino, "The Revolution in Mexican Independence: Insurgency and the Renegotiation of Property, Production, and Patriarchy in the Bajío, 1800–1855," *Hispanic American Historical Review* 78:3 (1998), 367–418.

34 John Tutino, "Soberanía quebrada, insurgencias populares y la independencia de México: La guerra de independencias, 1808–1821," *Historia Mexicana* 59:1 (2009), 11–75.

35 See Virginia Guedea, *La insurgencia en el Departamento del Norte: Los Llanos de Apan y la Sierra de Puebla, 1810–1816* (Mexico City: UNAM, 1996).

36 On the Villagráns and other regional rebels, the key work is Eric Van Young, *The Other Rebellion: Popular Violence, Ideology, and the Struggle for Mexican Independence, 1810–1821* (Stanford, CA: Stanford University Press, 2001); on Otomí insurgency, see John Tutino, "Buscando independencias populares: Conflicto social

y insurgencia agrariań en el Mexquital mexicano, 1800–1815," in *Las guerras de independencia en la América española*, ed. Marta Terán and José Antonio Serrano Ortega (Zamora: El Colegio de Michoacán, 2002), 295–321.

37 On the Huasteca, see Michael Ducey, *A Nation of Villages: Riot and Rebellion in the Mexican Huasteca, 1750–1850* (Tucson: University of Arizona Press, 2004); on Veracruz, see Juan Ortiz Escamilla, *El teatro de la guerra: Veracruz, 1750–1825* (Valencia: Universitat Jaume I, 2008).

38 The classic work is Ernesto Lemoine, *Morelos y la revolución de 1810* (Mexico City: UNAM, 1979); see also Peter Guardino, *Peasants, Politics, and the Formation of Mexico's National State: Guerrero, 1800–1857* (Stanford, CA: Stanford University Press, 1996), and *In the Time of Liberty: Popular Political Culture in Oaxaca, 1750–1850* (Durham, NC: Duke University Press, 2005).

39 Brian Hamnett, *Roots of Insurgency: Mexican Regions, 1750–1824* (Cambridge: Cambridge University Press, 2002), 150–177.

40 Ávila, *En nombre de la nación*, chapter 4.

41 See Tutino, "The Revolution in Mexican Independence."

42 See María Eugenia Romero Sotelo, *Minería guerra: La economía de Nueva España, 1810–1821* (Mexico City: El Colegio de México, 1887).

43 On the military, the key study is Juan Ortiz Escamilla, *Guerra y gobierno: Los pueblos y la independencia de México,* 2nd ed. (Mexico City: El Colegio de México, 2014); on communities and patriotic militias, see Guarisco, *Los indios del valle de México.*

44 This is detailed in Tutino, "Querétaro y los orígenes de la nación."

45 The Iguala movement is synthesized in Ávila, *En nombre de la nación*, and Tutino, "Soberanía quebrada."

46 The best analysis of 1820–1821, the military, and independence is Rodrigo Moreno Gutiérrez, "Las fuerzas armadas en el proceso de consumación de independencia: Nueva España, 1820–1821" (PhD diss., UNAM, Mexico City, 2014).

47 Timothy Anna, *Forging Mexico 1821–1835* (Lincoln: University of Nebraska Press, 1998).

48 John Tutino, "National State, Liberal Utopia, and Indigenous Communities," paper presented at the Colegio de México, October 2009.

49 On Iturbide's popular base, see Torcuato S. Di Tella, *National Popular Politics in Early Independent Mexico, 1820–1847* (Albuquerque: University of New Mexico Press, 1996), 105–132, and Richard Warren, *Vagrants and Citizens: Politics and the Masses in Mexico City from Colony to Republic* (Wilmington, DE: Scholarly Resources, 2001).

50 A. Ávila, *Para la libertad: Los republicanos en tiempos del imperio 1821–1823* (Mexico City: UNAM, 2004).

51 Lucas Alamán, in his *Historia de Méjico*, 709–713, assumes that the Acta de Casa Mata originated in the Masonic lodges; our view derives from Ávila, *Para la libertad*, 257.

52 See John Tutino, "Hacienda Social Relations in Mexico: The Chalco Region in the Era of Independence," *Hispanic American Historical Review* 55:3 (1975), 496–528;

From Insurrection to Revolution in Mexico; and "The Revolution in Mexican Independence."

53 Alamán is usually seen as conservative, centralist and monarchist; as a federalist, see A. Ávila, "La Constitución de la República Federal," in *México: Un siglo de historia constitucional (1808–1917): Estudios y perspectivas*, ed. Cecilia Noriega and Alicia Salmerón (Mexico City: Poder Judicial de la Federación/Instituto Mora, 2009), 43–61. On Chiapas annexation, see Mario Vázquez Olivera, "Chiapas, entre Centroamérica y México, 1821–1826," in *El establecimiento del federalismo en México*, ed. Josefina Zoraida Vázquez (Mexico City: El Colegio de México, 2003), 582–608.

54 Ávila, *En nombre de la nación*, 262–280.

55 See Nettie Lee Benson, *The Provincial Deputation in Mexico: Harbinger of Provincial Autonomy, Independence, and Federalism* (Austin: University of Texas Press, 1992).

56 A. Ávila, "Liberalismos decimonónicos: De la historia de las ideas a la historia cultural e intellectual," in *Ensayos sobre la nueva historia política de América Latina, siglo XIX*, ed. Guillermo Palacios (Mexico City: El Colegio de México, n.d.). On popular liberalism, see Jesús Hernández Jaimes, "Actores indios y Estado nacional: Las rebeliones indígenas en el sur de México 1842–1846," *Estudios de Historia Moderna y Contemporánea de México* 26 (July–December 2003), 5–44.

57 Josefina Z. Vázquez, "El reconocimiento y tratados comerciales: Cartas de identidad de un nuevo estado," in *Tratados de México: Soberanía y territorio 1821–1910*, ed. J. Z. Vázquez and M. del R. González (Mexico City: Secretaría de Relaciones Exteriores, 2000), 19–107.

58 Jesús Hernández Jaimes, *La formación de la Hacienda pública mexicana y las tensiones centro-periferia, 1821–1835* (Mexico City: El Colegio de México, 2013).

59 Barbara Tenenbaum, *México en la época do los agiotistas, 1821–1857* (Mexico City: Fondo de Cultura Económica, 1990).

60 Tutino, "Hacienda Social Relations." For studies of the states, see J. Z. Vázquez, *El establecimiento del federalismo en México* (Mexico City: El Colegio de México, 2003).

61 Tutino, "The Revolution in Mexican Independence."

62 M. E. Vázquez Semadeni, *La formación de una cultura política republicana: El debate público sobre la masonería, México, 1821–1830* (Mexico City: UNAM/El Colegio de Michoacán, 2010); Di Tella, *National Popular Politics.*

63 See Ávila, "La presidencia de Vicente Guerrero," in *Gobernantes mexicanos*, ed. Will Fowler (Mexico City: Fondo de Cultura Económica, 2008), 75–96.

64 Catherine Andrews, *Entre la espada y la constitución. El general Anastasio Bustamante, 1780–1853* (Ciudad Victoria: Universidad Autónoma de Tamaulipas, 2008).

65 Robert Potash, *El Banco de Avío en México: El fomento de la industria, 1821–1857* (Mexico City: Fondo de Cultura Económica, 1959), and Walter Berneker, *De agiotistas a empresarios: En torno a la temprana industrialización mexicana, siglo XIX* (Mexico City: Universidad Iberoamericana, 1992).

66 Josefina Z. Vázquez, "La primera presidencia de Antonio López de Santa Anna,"

in Fowler, *Gobernantes mexicanos*, 97–117; Will Fowler, *Santa Anna of Mexico* (Lincoln: University of Nebraska Press, 2007).

67 Brian Connaughton, *Entre la voz de Dios y el llamado de la patria: Religión, identidad y ciudadanía en México, siglo XIX* (Mexico City: Fondo de Cultura Económica, 2010).

68 Mora, "Revista política," in *Obras sueltas* (Paris: Librería de Rosa, 1837), 1, clxxxii–ccxxxv. On reforms, see Charles Hale, *Mexican Liberalism in the Age of Mora 1821–1853* (New Haven, CT: Yale University Press, 1968).

69 Vázquez, "La primera presidencia."

70 See Andreas Reichstein, *Rise of Lone Star: The Making of Texas* (College Station: Texas A&M University Press, 1989).

71 Vázquez, "La primera presidencia," and J. Z. Vázquez, *Décadas de inestabilidad y amenazas México, 1821–1848* (Mexico City: El Colegio de México, 2010).

72 See Randolph Campbell, *An Empire for Slavery* (Baton Rouge: LSU Press, 1989), and Paul Lack, *The Texas Revolutionary Experience* (College Station: Texas A&M University Press, 1992).

73 Hernández Jaimes, *La formación de la Hacienda pública.*

74 Reynaldo Sordo Cedeño, *El congreso en la primera república centralista* (Mexico City: El Colegio de México, 1993).

75 David Pantoja Morán, *El Supremo poder conservador: El diseño institucional en las primeras constituciones mexicanas* (Mexico City: El Colegio de México, 2005).

76 See Michael Costeloe, *The Central Republic in Mexico: Hombres de bien in the Age of Santa Anna* (Cambridge: Cambridge University Press, 1993).

77 Cecilia Noriega Elío, *El Constituyente de 1842* (Mexico City: UNAM, 1986).

78 See Araceli Ibarra Bellón, *El comercio y el poder en México, 1821–1864* (Mexico City: Fondo de Cultura Económica, 1998).

79 See Mariano Otero, *Ensayo sobre el verdadero estado de la cuestión social y política que se agita en la Republica mexicana* (Mexico City: Ignacio Cumplido, 1842).

80 On navigation of the Río Grande: David Montejano, *Anglos and Mexicans in the Making of Texas, 1836–1986* (Austin: University of Texas Press, 1986).

81 David Pletcher, *The Diplomacy of Annexation: Texas, Oregon and the Mexican War* (Bloomington: Indiana University Press, 1973).

82 Miguel Soto, *La conspiración monárquica en México, 1845–1846* (Mexico City: EOSA, 1988).

83 On provincial politics in times of war, see Laura Herrera Serna, ed., *México en guerra (1846–1848)* (Mexico City: Conaculta, 1997), and J. Z. Vázquez, ed., *México al tiempo de su guerra con Estados Unidos, 1846–1848* (Mexico City: FCE, 1997); on indigenous insurgencies, Tutino, *From Insurrection to Revolution in Mexico.*

84 On indigenous independence, see chapter 10 by Erick Langer.

85 Luis Fernando Granados, *Sueñan las piedras: Alzamiento ocurrido en la ciudad de México, 14, 15, 16 de Septiembre de 1847* (Mexico City: Era, 2003).

86 That the U.S. Civil War came out of the war with Mexico has been recognized at least since John Ashworth, *Slavery, Capitalism, and Politics in the Antebellum Republic*, vol. 1, *Commerce and Compromise, 1820–1850* (Cambridge: Cambridge

University Press, 1995); Adam Rothman's chapter 3 in this volume reflects the scholarly consensus.

87 The 1850s turn to liberalism in Mexico begs for a new synthesis. The best work in English is Richard Sinkin, *The Mexican Reform, 1855–1876* (Austin: University of Texas Press, 1976). Erika Pani, *Para mexicanizar el Segundo imperio* (Mexico City: Colegio de México, 2001), provides an essential rethinking of Maximilian's empire. For contrasting studies of the later consolidation, see François-Xavier Guerra, *Del antiguo regimen a la revolución*, 2 vols. (Mexico City: Fondo de Cultura Económica, 1988), and John Hart, *Empire and Revolution* (Berkeley: University of California Press, 2002).

8

THE REPUBLIC OF GUATEMALA

Stitching Together a New Country

JORDANA DYM

In October 1825, London's *New Monthly Magazine* commented that Guatemala, like America's other newly independent countries, "fixed the attention of
the sixteenth century, [and] deserves no less to occupy the undivided consideration of the nineteenth" with "a distinct place in the geography of modern
America, and [to] claim forcibly the attention of the commercial world."[1] But
the article described not today's country, but all of Central America, a newly
declared republic that claimed the territory stretching from Chiapas to Costa
Rica, which had been part of the Spanish Kingdom of Guatemala. Thus the
magazine fixed its attention on colonial "Guatemala," not the single federal
state that bore the name in 1825. The confusion had many causes, not least a
tradition of conflating the history of Guatemala City with that of the kingdom,
familiar to English audiences from the 1823 translation of Domingo Juarros's

history (1808–1821), but dating back at least to the seventeenth-century *Recordación Florida* of Francisco Antonio Fuentes y Guzmán.[2]

While the state of Guatemala struggled to teach foreigners to associate its name with its territory, internally the challenge was to stitch many and diverse local identities and ambitions into a single "Guatemalan" framework. The principle of *uti possedetis* allowed independent Spanish American states to establish countries based on colonial territories,[3] but didn't guide new governments' internal redistricting. Between separatist movements in the western highlands and rebellions in the eastern lowlands from the 1820s into the 1840s, getting the seven departments of the new state to identify as "Guatemalan" was as large a challenge to the new country as getting foreign powers to distinguish Guatemala from the other states of the Central American federation.

Encouraging foreigners to scale down their understanding and citizens to scale up their identity to include the newly assembled state meant teaching both groups to put aside political, economic, and demographic understandings inherited from the eighteenth-century Bourbon monarchy's reformist policies and the early nineteenth-century constitutional monarchy's revolutionary innovations, neither of which had created a polity that looked like independent Guatemala. Considering Guatemala as an innovation or invention of independence goes against the grain of much Guatemalan historiography; otherwise nuanced scholarship anachronistically takes "Guatemala" as an entity back into the colonial period or as an unquestioned result of independence and pessimistically follows the union's failure, not the state's complex endurance.[4] The distinctive shape of the twentieth-century country frequently accompanies studies of the nineteenth century, although contemporary maps show a more amorphous and less determined territory more closely related to its contingent and emergent reality.[5]

Yet the story of the birth and consolidation of this country is not unique. As Alfredo Ávila, John Tutino, and Roberto Breña argue in this volume, Guatemala's divided origins, built partly on Mesoamerican and partly on Spanish structures, compare with that of New Spain (Mexico). The crisis of the Spanish monarch (1808–1814) offered opportunity as well as disruption. Chambers's study of how postindependence Peru and Bolivia "traced and retraced" former Inca territories offers another parallel. The dissolution of Gran Columbia into Venezuela, Ecuador, and Colombia produced states that also acquired full sovereignty after emerging from a larger polity.

In essence, fledgling Guatemala experienced similar challenges to Spanish American countries that remained united: cycles of reform and resistance;

dissension among elites divided by region, family, and ideas about the rhythm and depth of innovation needed; the actions and interests of popular classes inclined to resist changes perceived as economically destructive or politically alien and unwelcome; the implanting of republican and constitutional systems of government interspersed with periods of less representative rule; and the influence of European and North American commercial interests. Considering the origins, birth, and eventual stabilization of Guatemala as a polity, this essay describes two processes: first, how districts without central ties and individuals with initial loyalties to only a locality, class, or ethnic community learned to accept a place within a Guatemalan republic; second, the emergence by 1851 of a viable country that still faced tensions between government and society. The story of Guatemala is thus a story of the emergence of an independent country out of a larger federation that merits comparison with similar "survivor" states from the former Gran Colombia and across Spanish America.

Isthmian Origins (1542–1821)

The territories and peoples that formed the state of Guatemala in 1825 owed much to pre-European Maya civilizations, the initial organization of the Spanish empire, and the reorganization of the state-society relationship during the eighteenth-century Bourbon monarchy. Spanish Central America, known as the Kingdom, Audiencia (territorial court), or Captaincy General of Guatemala, was established by the Hapsburg monarchy in 1542, administratively uniting communities and territories conquered by half a dozen Spanish *adelantados* and their diverse native allies between today's Chiapas (Mexico) and Costa Rica.[6] Hernán Cortés's deputy Pedro de Alvarado defeated the Quiché and Kaqchiquel kingdoms of highland Guatemala as well as the Pipil regions of what is now El Salvador; the Montejo family similarly conquered the peoples of today's Honduras and Yucatán Peninsula, while Pedrarias Dávila's forces took much of today's Nicaragua and Costa Rica. So the broad strokes of Guatemala's core territory and Central America's regional organization and capitals, including approximate ethnic and political divides, date to the early sixteenth century. So, too, does the emergence of Alvarado's capital, the multiply relocated Guatemala City—in its present location since 1773—as the political, commercial, religious, fiscal, educational, and judicial capital.

Independent Guatemala's demography also owes much to the colonial period. What would later be "Guatemalan" highland districts were originally settled by Mayan peoples who retained their culture and languages while granted lands and limited self-rule as indigenous republics during centuries of Spanish rule. On the cusp of independence, Juarros catalogued languages including Kiche, Kakchiquel, Mam, Pocomam, Nahuatl, and Zutuhil, still spoken today.[7] Late eighteenth-century censuses suggested the provinces in today's Guatemala were about half Maya, 10 percent European, and 40 percent "mixed race" (ladino, mulatto, mestizo) with European, American, and/or African ancestry. Geographically, the Maya lived predominantly in the western highlands, in mountains, the most densely populated part of the isthmus. What would become the coffee piedmont, the southern (Pacific) coast, and the Oriente highlands were both more "ladino" and less densely populated.[8] In addition to the estimated half a million people living under Spanish rule, independent indigenous communities like the Lacandones or Itzá lived in the Petén area bordering New Spain (Mexico). [9]

Guatemala's colonial communities did not form a single political entity but half a dozen territorial jurisdictions that operated as three distinct economic regions. The central valley and highlands (*altiplano*) combined agriculture and artisan textile and other productions, supplying urban centers.[10] In 1819, Antigua and Amatitlán in the central valley received Crown authorization to produce *grana*, a red dye extracted from crushing an insect that fed on the nopal cactus; it became the country's principal export in the 1840s.[11] Significant highland produce went north to trade in southern Mexico. The more sparsely settled Oriente (its principal populations: Santa Rosa, Quaquiniquilapa, and Mataquesquintla), was connected by the Royal Road that led to Salvadoran indigo zones and Honduran and Nicaraguan cattle ranches. Along the road, the mostly mulatto people of the Oriente provided pasturage for cattle heading to Guatemala City and worked as mule-drivers.[12] The eighteenth-century military district of Petén, now frequented by tourists visiting Mayan ruins, was a sparsely inhabited zone where the first archaeological finds—"perfectly spherical" stones—were just coming to government attention.[13]

Economically, each district was tied to Guatemala City, the principal commercial center and the region's link to Europe through Atlantic ports, via legal trade with Spain and illicit trade with Great Britain. But producers and consumers also bypassed the capital for regional trade in Central America's largely self-sufficient internal market that cushioned residents from the worst blows of the declining world market for indigo. Internal trade fueled efforts made to retain Central American political as well as economic unity.[14] Guatemala City businessmen developed financial investments (and often family ties) to San Salvador, which produced indigo, the region's principal export crop;[15] to Chiapas, Honduras, and Costa Rica (which raised tobacco); to Tegucigalpa and Chiquimula (where limited silver was mined); and to Comayagua and

Nicaragua (where cattle grazed and mules were raised). Internal trade and business ties, though important, did not prove strong enough to draw distinct economies into a single state system after independence.

In the eighteenth century, a wave of Spanish immigration (especially Basques, including the Aycinena family) and Enlightenment-oriented royal officials did not appreciably change the area's overall demography; it did help revitalize elite commercial ties to the metropolis and revive intellectual inquiry and the foundation of important institutions, including a merchants' chamber and a lawyers' guild.[16] Along with university professors and alumni (Guatemala's San Carlos graduated over thirteen hundred from 1775 to 1821), they were deeply involved with Bourbon officials in creating a short-lived Sociedad Económica de Amantes del País devoted to improving the kingdom's political economy, and the *Gazeta de Guatemala* (1797–1816), a newspaper that was based in Guatemala City but imagined a Central American public that it would inform and instruct. Indigenous peoples—one of whose great ancient centers at Palenque (Chiapas) was just being explored—were encouraged to join modern society by adopting Spanish clothes and language; all "learned" men were invited to be useful, regardless of "birth or class."[17]

Guatemala City retained its centrality as an intellectual hub. However, Carlos III's (r. 1759–1788) reforms encouraging increased accountability to Spain diluted the capital's authority within the kingdom and future state. Fiscal reforms (1760s) established royal coffers in the provinces and increased sales taxes,[18] while territorial reforms (1784 and 1786) consolidated over a dozen districts into four intendancies—Comayagua (Honduras), León (Nicaragua), Ciudad Real (Chiapas), and San Salvador (El Salvador).[19] Notably, the area that became the state of Guatemala remained fragmented as a patchwork of small districts reporting directly to the kingdom's capital rather than a consolidated administration.[20] In efforts to reduce the extension, both literal and indirect, of Guatemala City and its cabildo over "its" valley, the Crown essentially halved the original jurisdiction when relocating the capital to the Valle de la Ermita in 1773 after a devastating earthquake.[21] Thus, on the cusp of imperial crisis, priest and chronicler Domingo Juarros's 1808 history identified ten "provinces" in the future state of Guatemala, grouped into southern (Pacific), "central" (landbound), and northern (Atlantic) regions.[22] The formal political consolidation experienced in the rest of the isthmus did not occur in "Guatemala."

Ironically, fragmentation deepened even as government authority strengthened. Bourbon policy promoted reviving or establishing city councils to improve imperial communication and control, creating political representation and institutions that supported creole, indigenous, and ladino communities

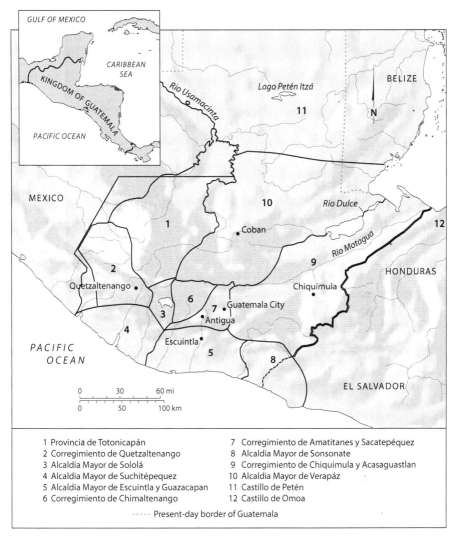

MAP 8.1. Districts of the Kingdom of Guatemala that became
part of the state of Guatemala

in distinct locales. Creole—American Spanish—"provincianos" in the western highlands organized politically around two different towns that became a counterweight to Guatemala City: Antigua (Sacatepéquez), the earthquake-destroyed capital that reestablished its municipal government and political voice in 1799,[23] and Quezaltenango, an important center of agricultural products where creole and peninsular migrants established their own cabildo and power center in addition to the existing native cabildo in 1805. These two cabildos immediately protected the interests of powerful families from the influence of those based in Guatemala City, helping royal agents to govern the region.[24] Others, too, had a say in the new system. The new jurisdictions created to reduce Guatemala City's reach incorporated Petapa, Amatitan, and Escuinta as villas "with a separate government" for their Spanish and mulatto residents. Indigenous communities, too, felt the heavier hand of government through new settlements including Chamiquín (Verapaz).[25]

Arguably, the Bourbon emphasis on expanded municipal government did the most to create a region and identity in the Oriente. There, primarily ladino or mestizo communities lacked a *cabildo de españoles* or *pueblo de indios* until Bourbon royal officials set up municipal governments to increase tax revenue and promote militia recruitment while bringing "political and social (civil) life for their inhabitants to live in peace and justice" in Christian society and rule. New urban centers were established in Iztapa, a Pacific Coast port, and Santa Rosa, in the Oriente's Valle de Jumay in the military district of Verapaz.[26] The new communities, which in the short term increased secular authority, often played important roles in postindependence revolts and negotiations with state capitals as, not coincidentally, the town institutions founded to serve imperial interests often rallied residents for their own purposes.

On the Cusp of Independence

Despite its intellectual vibrancy, by the turn of the nineteenth century the core area of Guatemala struggled economically, in large part due to external constraints. The aggressive Bourbon drive to raise revenue eventually prevailed: declines in Indian tribute were offset by increased sales tax and state monopoly revenues, but those, in turn, were offset by the costs of defending Spanish interests.[27] Between the tax policy, the *consolidación* of Church debt in 1804 and later *donativos* sent to support Spain's war against Bonaparte, Central America expatriated much of its specie and reached independence running a government deficit that was regularly filled by subsidies from New Spain's booming silver economy.[28] Britain's blockades in the late eighteenth century kept indigo waiting in ports, prompting trading families to make connections with Anglo-Americans. Some even engaged in the illicit trade in silks and velvets that they hypocritically decried as harmful to government and their own interests, sponsoring trading trips to Philadelphia, Belize, Kingston, and Havana. Postindependence claims of Guatemala's being "unknown" in the Atlantic world were implausible.[29]

Nor did the period described as the "Cádiz experiment" (1810–1814; 1820–1823) set the stage for a future Guatemalan state. Although they were economically promiscuous, politically Guatemala City's elite strongly supported Spain's war against Bonaparte and the Cádiz constitutional monarchy, preferring autonomy in the empire over full independence. Guatemala City alcalde Antonio Juarros organized an elaborate series of public events in late 1808 to support Fernando VII, legitimizing the government through claims of Kiche and Kaqchiquel monarchies as predecessors to the Hapsburg and Spanish monarchies.[30] Yet, like earlier "Guatemala City" histories, the report of the ceremony emphasized city and isthmus, not city and valley. This wider identity was matched in the cabildo's actions: Juarros and other city councilors helped Captain General José de Bustamante negotiate a peaceful end to a radical movement in El Salvador in 1811 and offered only moral support to rebels from Granada (Nicaragua) who reached the capital in chains after Bustamante squelched their movement for autonomy later that year.

Peninsular decisions that sought to foster loyalty by providing a role for overseas provinces in imperial interim governments also discouraged Central American and future Guatemalan unity by authorizing election of representatives to many kinds of "province" between 1809 and 1821. These ranged from one delegate to an early Junta Central to fifteen deputies to a later Cortes.[31] Yet the moment also hinted at connections that would underpin the later state consolidation: Guatemala City and Quetzaltenango consulted together in 1809 and 1810 to select representatives to interim Spanish government posts.[32] Both cities accepted the possibility of a "Guatemalan" territorial unit larger than each jurisdiction alone, although without recognition of a proto-Guatemalan state they operated as members of a community of cities within a Spanish imperial framework.[33] Quetzaltenango's subsequent instructions to its deputy in 1814 showed the limits of alliance, proposing a separate bishopric and intendancy as well as seeking to lower royal monopolies (*estancos*) and increase judicial autonomy.[34]

The Cortes's adoption and promulgation of the Constitución de la Monarquía Española in 1812, implemented in the Kingdom of Guatemala, introduced modern representative government to residents. Through indirect elections

FIGURE 8.1. Pledging loyalty to Fernando VII: The Kingdom of Guatemala, 1809. José Casildo España, "Las provincias del reino de Guatemala ofreciendo SLlS corazones al holocaust." In [Domingo Juarros], *Guatemala por Fernando VII* (Guatemala, *1809*). Private collection. This engraving, one of several illustrations in a pamphlet celebrating the Kingdom of Guatemala's loyalty to Spain during the imperial crisis unleashed by Napoleon's invasion of Spain in 1808, represents the territories many provinces, each with a distinct identity, professing loyalty to Spain.

—

of members of the constitutionally mandated *ayuntamientos constitucionales*, two *diputaciones provinciales* (Provincial Deputations), and Cortes deputies, Central America's residents learned the mechanisms of democratic governance; they began to experience the rights and duties of citizenship that would continue after independence.[35] Still, political innovation did not consolidate a "Guatemalan" territory or identity within the captaincy general. The Cortes created two deputations for the kingdom, one each for Guatemala and Nicaragua, in an effort to mitigate regional tensions.[36] The Cortes's Guatemalan diputación included seven districts in what are now Chiapas (Mexico), Honduras, and El Salvador as well as Guatemala.

Where the shape or outline of future Guatemala did become evident was in the districts sending the kingdom's deputies to ordinary Cortes sessions after

1812. The constitutional system introduced proportional representation by population. As a result, five of the kingdom's twelve deputies (one per seventy thousand inhabitants) represented districts that later joined the state of Guatemala.[37] Perhaps not surprisingly, the preponderance of "Guatemalan" deputies did not contribute to greater internal connections. Rather, elections fostered localist creole and ladino "dreams" for more autonomy within the system; the instructions issued to parish priest José Cleto Montiel, the *diputado* of Totonicapán and Quetzaltenango, repeated in 1821 recommendations for the separate institutions that the Quezaltenango ayuntamiento had proposed in 1814.[38] In short, we can see a strong "Guatemalan" representation at the same time as a notable regionalism that would later influence independence from Spain, both mixed with "liberal" demands for better education and "conservative" interest in a stronger ecclesiastic presence.

One constitutional change with important postindependence ramifications for Guatemala and the other federal states had to do with incorporating new communities as partners and citizens in the body politic. The constitutional period offered the indigenous pueblos and castas the opportunity to participate in the government and to elect representatives with the full support of local and imperial officials—although some, like Quezaltenango's Spanish city council, argued that since the indigenous were equal under the law, they should also be gently stimulated to be more productive.[39] José Mariano Méndez in 1821 was only repeating points made by Central American delegates since 1810 when he defended the region's mulattos' right to vote, arguing that it was difficult to verify whether they were in fact African in origin.[40] Beyond taking an active role in the region's indirect elections, the K'iche communities of Totonicapán rose up in 1820 to insist on implementation of constitutional provisions, successfully getting decrees abolishing tribute payments enforced.[41]

Since the new system also abolished protective institutions like separate cabildos for Spaniards and indigenous residents, the changes also revealed fissures. The corregidor at Quetzaltenango unsuccessfully sought to reserve a third of the seats in a now combined city council for indigenous residents—a majority of the jurisdiction's people. Was the refusal a lack compassion or flexibility among local Creoles or an attempt to facilitate indigenous exclusion in the representative system?[42] In 1820, the Quezaltenango cabildo sent the ladino militia to help put down an indigenous uprising at Totonicapán, outside its official jurisdiction.[43] This example puts the spotlight on the highland capital's ambition to be a provincial and not just district capital, and on the militarization of disputes between ladino Quetzaltenango leadership and indigenous Totonicapán, a tendency that would resonate and amplify after independence from Spain, when Totonicapán sometimes sought support from Guatemala City against its neighbor.

Essentially, in the decade leading to independence, ideas of political community and popular sovereignty offered optimism of a new contract between government and society, one based on participation and negotiation rather than imperial rule. Guatemala's leaders adapted the inclusionary and individual political and individual citizenship of Cádiz and extended it in practice to all residents of European, indigenous, and African ancestry—ending separate rights for indigenous republics, rights liberals often saw as privileges. The period saw expanded municipal governments and provincial organization, which increased an institutional base for local and regional agendas. However, the Cádiz experiment, which aimed to bind the Americas to Spain, did not forge provincial structures that could help mold identities at a Guatermalan "state" level.

In the jurisdictions closest to Guatemala City, the highlands and Oriente drifted further apart, both in demography and economic interest, with no political structure in place to bind them to each other or to Guatemala City. Los Altos continued to look north to Mexican trade; the Oriente looked south to the cattle business with Honduras and Nicaragua, while shuttling indigo to Atlantic ports. Guatemala City's role as arbiter and central tax authority was insufficient to build community or consensus in a system that had a limited economic integration and no institutional base. So in August–December 1821, that is, at the moment of independence, there was no unitary "Guatemalan" polity, ethnic, economic, or geographic. Any new state would be formed out of many and diverse districts, a composite organization with much to accomplish.

The Fissures of Independence

The formation of a single Guatemalan state incorporating the three distinct regions did not happen in the period of Central America's initial independence from 1821 to 1823. As they chose separation from Spain in the fall of 1821, Central America's territories opted (not without difficulties) to unite first with the nascent and short-lived Mexican empire of Agustín Iturbide, a process called "conditional" independence by historian Mario Rodríguez.[44] Guatemala City leaders tried and failed to control a process that began with the decision of the town of Comitán, in the intendancy of Chiapas, to join Mexico. Despite an act of provisional independence issued in Guatemala City on September 15, 1821, offering full citizenship to those of African origin and inviting a meeting of district representatives elected under Cádiz rules to a Central American Congress to determine the isthmus' political future, constitutional city councils and provincial deputations issued their own acts, and many sought separate integration with Mexico.

Among the districts choosing independence from Spain and also Guatemala City, Quetzaltenango stood out, since it would later joined the Guatemalan state. In late 1821, the town's cabildo, aided by other officials in Los Altos, as historian Arturo Taracena writes, "succeeded little by little in centralizing discontent of Sololá, Suchitepéquez, and Huehuetenango toward the city of Guatemala."[45] A similar divisive dynamic emerged in the territories that would soon form Honduras and Nicaragua. Sparring cities sought either to control or split provinces. Totonicapán again opposed Quetzaltenango's ambition "to make itself capital and elevate itself to the Rank of intendancy,"[46] skeptical that Quetzaltenango's creoles and ladinos would respect Totonicapán's K'iche majority.[47] Thus, two cities, Quezaltenango and Guatemala, offered themselves to Iturbide as separate provincial or regional powers in the area that is now Guatemala. In the end, the Mexican government supported neither and, in 1822, divided the districts of the former captaincy general into three military commands with capitals in Chiapas, Guatemala, and León (Nicaragua). Keeping Guatemala City as a regional capital, Iturbide essentially repeated the north/south divide established in Cádiz while carving off Chiapas, the only Central American province that republican Mexico kept when Iturbide's empire dissolved in 1823.

Concerned with advancing political fragmentation, Central America's provinces (minus Chiapas) separated from Mexico in 1823, elected representatives to a National Constituent Assembly (ANC) and put animosity aside to form the federal Republic of Central America. Although the federation's fifteen-year life was plagued by conflict, decisions taken at the ANC had long-term effects not only on the forms of government in the isthmus, but on the shape and size of the states that emerged as republics by the 1840s.

Not surprisingly, one contentious topic addressed by the ANC's almost three dozen representatives was how many and which states would or should comprise the new union.[48] Guatemala City leaders wanted to continue as capital city of a powerful and large Guatemalan state including nearby valleys as well as cacao-producing Soconusco, the sugar and indigo region of Sonsonate, and intensively cultivated and textile-producing Quezaltenango. By contrast, deputies from several districts expressed reservations about the consequences of forming a strong Guatemalan state that included around a third of the isthmian population. Guatemalans won out when several delegates from the highlands (Altenses) with strong ties to the capital city supported their goal, rather than formation of a separate Los Altos with its capital in Quezaltenango.[49] In April 1824, the ANC refused Quezaltenango deputy Cirilo Flores's request to postpone Guatemala's election of a state assembly pending a constitutional committee meeting, putting Altense dreams on hold.[50] On May 11, 1824, the ANC decreed state congresses for Guatemala, San Salvador, Honduras, Nicaragua, and Costa Rica, its hand forced by assemblies already convened in El Salvador and Costa Rica, paving the way for a federation composed of these five states.

Guatemala became the federation's largest state, incorporating Quezaltenango, the Central Valley, the Oriente, the Petén, and Verapaz, with a population of about six hundred thousand, around 60 percent of Central America's overall population. This configuration assured the young state's access to both Atlantic and Pacific Oceans and markets.[51] Why did federal delegates agree to a Guatemalan state with more than half the isthmian population? The indigenous majority of the highlands likely influenced the decision. If Central American deputies did not agree with the *New Monthly Magazine*'s correspondent that the "Indians in the vicinity of Guatemala are as yet in a wild state; they speak the indigenous language, and clothe themselves like savages," they were perhaps aware that Los Altos might be less appealing to the international community as a viable state when other Central American states' Indians largely spoke Spanish and dressed "after the European fashion" and thus seemed "more civilized."[52] The ANC's federal state making thus bundled three regions into a single state, leaving the Creole powers concentrated in Guatemala City and the ladinos of the Oriente to engage the Maya majority of the highlands. They would spend the next quarter century seeking a new political order and negotiating to make that union work.

Forming the State from Within

Forging enduring Guatemalan unity out of multiple colonial districts became the work of several generations. In its first year, however, the state of Guatemala seemed to get off to a relatively strong political and economic start. In October 1825, the Guatemalan constituent assembly adopted a state constitution. It enacted decrees identifying territorial divisions and raising the status of several towns throughout the territory. Taken together, the founding documents showed aspirations to create a modern state and build trust among the districts that combined to form it.

Politically, the constitution established a "republican, popular, and representative" government. Guatemala retained Catholicism as the official religion, but permitted private worship for other sects. A system of indirect elections (with popular, district, and departmental *juntas electorales*) adapted from the

Cádiz constitution offered a familiar system and increased representation to one congressman for every 30,000 (rather than 70,000) inhabitants. It provided town governments for settlements with as few as 200 residents (rather than Cádiz's 1,000).[53] This emphasis on population as a basis for political representation gave the highland districts with over 200,000 mostly indigenous people considerable weight; the more ladino Oriente had 130,000.[54] The magna carta explicitly maintained the possibility of creating a new state from part of Guatemala's territory, perhaps to ensure that Los Altos's aspirations would not delay adoption. It also welcomed Sonsonate, should the federal government determine that the district should join Guatemala instead of El Salvador.[55] In seeking unity, the founding texts of the new Guatemala left much unresolved.

Internally, consolidation also proved a challenge. The 1825 state constitution identified sixteen districts, which it combined into seven departments.[56] Over the next fifty years, that consolidation would be undone in pursuits of local rights: by 1877 Guatemala had twenty-two separate departments. The initial instinct to create departments equal in size, population, and economic importance reflected the three major geographic regions: the Oriente included Verapaz and Chiquimula, bordering Mexico, Honduras, and El Salvador; the Central Valleys provided the districts of Guatemala/Escuintla and Sacatepéquez/Chimaltenango; the populous, indigenous western highlands gained Quetzaltenango/Soconusco, Totonicapán/Huehuetenango, and Suchitepéquez/Sololá.

The division sought economic coherence. Sacatepéquez and Chimaltenango were the breadbaskets of Guatemala City. By uniting Guatemala and Escuintla, Guatemala City achieved control of indigo-producing coastal regions as that colonial economic motor entered its last days.[57] It also sought political peace, or at least balance: Totonicapán and Quezaltenango both became capitals, recognized in promotions to villa and city status, respectively.[58] Verapaz took in Petén—a region subsequent governments considered largely underdeveloped, underpopulated, and ripe for colonization. Relocation of the new state's capital from Antigua, midway between Quezaltenago and Guatemala City, to the latter in July 1825, however, worried highlands leaders.[59] The highland elite's ambitions remained alive. In 1838 and again in 1848, the chiefs of this area would lead separatist movements seeking their own state.

The founding documents aimed to create a unitary population in a society of distinct pueblos. On paper, independent Guatemala was optimistic, almost utopian. The egalitarian propositions of Cádiz and the act of independence were embedded in both federal and state constitutions, by which, as the *New Monthly Magazine* observed, "the Indians have acquired the right of citizenship, and are placed completely on an equality with the descendants of the Span-iards." Where later historians saw hypocrisy or error, many contemporaries shared Guatemala's enthusiasm for the social experiment, reporting that "they [the Indians] cannot, therefore, be otherwise than attached to the new system, and many of their entire towns are open partizans of the republican govern-ment."[60] The author believed that Guatemala could create a modern country by including rather than by separating and subjugating its indigenous inhabitants. He observed that, "in the first Constituent Assembly of Guatemala, in 1823, three Indian deputies took their seats, of whom two were ecclesiastics. Besides which, an Indian was elected Senator, and sat in the assembly of the republic; . . . nor is it improbable that in the first sittings of the Congress, several Indians will appear as deputies." Further, while acknowledging that the Indians "lead a life of great hardship," he noted that "in the province of Guatemala and those of Quetzaltenango, there are many who possess sheep in abundance. These persons avail themselves of the wool to weave stuffs of various kinds. . . . The Indians also manufacture cotton cloth higher in price than the stuffs we have just mentioned, and of which the Indian women make use for dress, as well as the poor classes of people in the cities."[61] The happy incorporation failed to materialize.

The combination of three distinct economies and geographic regions into a single state opened diverse economic possibilities. In its first year, Guatemala appeared poised to establish its importance to the international dye trade; in 1824 the optimistic official newspaper reported an extension of commerce and the spread of production of grana (cochineal) in Sacatepéquez, Sololá, and Verapaz.[62] In 1825, traveler Dr. Lavagnino reported on both indigo and cochi-neal as "most known to commerce and most esteemed" in the *New Monthly Magazine* and also referred to "many mines of silver in the provinces," princi-pally the Chiquimula area in Guatemala as well as Tegucigalpa in Honduras.[63] Pursuit of export economies, however, sowed the seeds of later conflict. The agrarian reform promulgated in Decree 27 (1825) promoted the expropriation of underutilized private property, giving the government power not only to sell to individual owners, but also to reserve one-third of both coasts and some of the interior for colonization. Discontent rose among small landowners, many of whom were mulatto or ladino.[64]

A composite Guatemala, with its capital in Guatemala City but with po-litical and geographic units recognizing existing divisions, seemed poised for growth. An expanding economy that might draw Creole, foreign, and indig-enous elites to work with the new government might lead the way. At least tem-porarily, the *altense* leadership was committed to participating in the composite state; Cirilo Flores of Quezaltenango served as vice president to President Juan

Barrundia Zepeda, both committed to a "liberal" program of economic development and political republicanism. Had this state been a fully independent country, perhaps this initial collaboration would have had time to mature. The challenge of being the largest and most diverse state in a federation kept old conflicts alive—and created new ones.

The Challenges of Federation and Foreigners

Guatemala's first years as a single entity were complicated by antagonistic relations between the state and the federal governments. Federal president Manuel José Arce was politically more moderate (and centralist) than the first Guatemalan elected chief of state, the federalist Juan Barrundia.[65] With both governments based in Guatemala City, political disputes escalated into military conflict between 1826 and 1830. In 1826, Arce deposed Barrundia, and Guatemala's vice chief, medical doctor Cirilo Flores, tried to govern from Quetzaltenango. His radical liberal legislation—which abolished the merchants' chamber, reduced the Church tithe by 50 percent, and permitted the children of clergymen to inherit Church property—was not welcomed in highland communities. Although Flores was a local son and had represented the region in the Mexican Congress of 1822–1823, his political career and life ended simultaneously in October 1826 when a crowd referred to variously as a "mob of fanatical Indians," rabble, and the *populacho*, and led by women, followed him into the sanctuary of a church, dragged him from the pulpit, and killed him.[66] Without executive authority, Guatemala's first government collapsed.

A dynamic that would repeat itself until the end of federation ensued. Stability would be established when federal and state governments were in sympathy, but fall apart either due to federal interference, as in 1825, or because of internal divisions—either between Guatemala City and the regions, or within the ranks of Guatemala City's leadership. From 1826 to 1829, Guatemala's instability came from within. Federal president Arce convened a new Guatemalan Congress, and the more conservative Mariano Aycinena was elected as chief of state.[67] His government is largely described as dictatorial and inflexible, although this son of Guatemala's Basque "aristocracy" succeeded in strengthening the state against federal pressures.[68] Still, a civil war in which liberal governments in Honduras and El Salvador fought Guatemala's leaders and federation forces continued from 1827 to early 1829, when the liberals, led by future federal president Francisco Morazán, achieved victory, sending Aycinena into exile in the United States—leaving a divided elite to face economic ruin.[69]

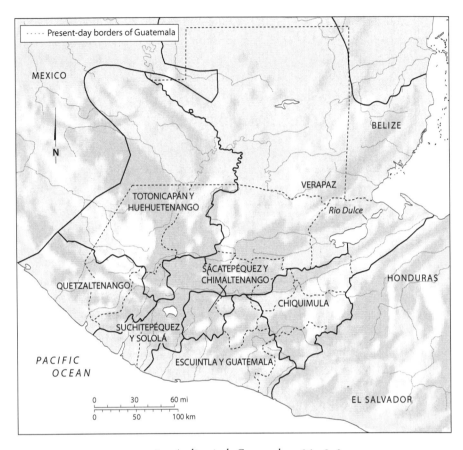

Legend: ····· Present-day borders of Guatemala

MEXICO

BELIZE

N

VERAPAZ

TOTONICAPÁN Y
HUEHUETENANGO

Rio Dulce

SACATEPÉQUEZ Y
CHIMALTENANGO

QUETZALTENANGO

HONDURAS

CHIQUIMULA

SUCHITEPÉQUEZ
Y SOLOLÁ

PACIFIC
OCEAN

ESCUINTLA Y GUATEMALA

0   30   60 mi

0   50   100 km

EL SALVADOR

MAP 8.2. Audiencia de Guatemala, 1786–1808

In 1829, a "liberal" government took office in Guatemala after returning the capital to Antigua. It was led by vice chief of state José Gregorio Márquez, who had represented the central district of Chimaltenango in the 1825 constituent assembly.[70] War had reduced the economic bases of the new state, particularly in the Oriente whose towns and pastures were on a road now transited more by soldiers than by cattle.[71] José Cecilio del Valle, in a pessimistic article for the Sociedad Económica in 1830, reported abundant natural resources and potential, but failure in "artisanal" development; the country lacked exports due to the abandonment of grana and indigo; it had failed to follow Havana's lead and invest in coffee; and it lacked industry and roads for either interior or exterior commerce. Aware of competition from textile production from Europe and

Asia, he did note that independence brought free trade policies that increased the number of ships trading in local ports.[72]

Despite (or perhaps because of) these difficulties, Guatemala's principal families disdained compromise. Conservatives refused an invitation to participate in a triumvirate executive that might have offered some balance to the government. Without them, a more radical legislative assembly abolished all the decrees of 1826–1829 and exiled many Spanish-born residents, including the archbishop and members of the former government; it assigned "forced loans" to those they called traitors, abolished religious orders and confiscated their properties.[73] A few years of self-government achieved what independence could not: a hard break between Spaniard and Creole; several Spanish families were sent into exile.

Six years after its constitution and foundational legislation, the state of Guatemala received a respite from internal and external pressures. With the election of Mariano Gálvez as president, a new liberal government pursued Guatemala's economic and political promise through transforming legislation. Under Gálvez the Guatemalan and federation governments cohabitated in Guatemala City, until the latter moved to San Salvador in 1834; for a time they collaborated, and experienced the necessary peace to experiment with state building. A sign that the new Guatemalan state was getting ready to claim the world's attention was Gálvez's commission of the country's first history and map, influenced by José Cecilio del Valle's recommendations. A former imperial bureaucrat and a long-term thinker, del Valle understood a point later historians would underline: maps and the knowledge they represented were tools for the government to use internally to exert control and externally to make political and economic connections abroad.[74]

Guatemala's first atlas, published in 1832 by Miguel Rivera Maestre, with one map of the whole country and a map of each department, [75] complemented a history of the contemporary period commissioned by Alejandro Marure. The legislature, for its part, commissioned a compilation of state laws in 1836.[76] Gálvez also sent Juan Galindo, Marure, and others to inspect and document pre-Hispanic ruins to help claim and recover Guatemala's ancient past.[77] Map, history, and legal record—all three texts spoke to a consolidating Guatemala with a land, a past, and a legal code focused on its current territory, not the entire isthmus. When Marure's second edition of *Bosquejo histórico de las revoluciones de Centroamérica* was published in 1877, historian Lorenzo Montúfar emphasized that Gálvez had commissioned it so "his patria could be known in both worlds."[78] At the level of state government, Guatemala was taking shape. Still, the frontiers with Mexico and Belize remain vague.

FIGURE 8.2. Mapping a new country: Guatemala, 1832.
Courtesy of the Latin American Library, Tulane University

———

Part of becoming known was applying what many considered foreign principles in the new state. The Gálvez government embraced the idea of legislating
progress and building a new nation as well as a new state. In his 1836 message
to the Guatemalan Congress, Gálvez emphasized "innovation." He insisted on
making "everything new, everything republican: nothing of the colonial, monarchical system" because, otherwise, "for Independence, we would have done
nothing more than change the name of things."[79] To deliver this program, his
government undertook to change legal and social culture, and to impose a new
liberal political system that emphasized equality under the law as the way to
end distinctions among persons of different race or class, and to provide equal
opportunities. Many laws passed between 1832 and 1836 sought to reduce
Church influence in society: in 1833 the formerly Jesuit University of San Carlos was converted into a secular Academy of Studies; in 1837, the legislature
enacted civil matrimony, allowing not only nullification but divorce; it abolished payment of Church tithes, ended religious holidays, declared freedom
of conscience (religion), and more.[80] To broaden political participation, the

296—Jordana Dym

Gálvez government extended more autonomy to the municipalities, enabling the "pueblos [to} administer their business" and use that independence to join in "the practical applications of the representative and federal system."[81]

The most innovative effort was to "modernize" the judicial system by translating and adapting the Livingston Codes. Gálvez considered a system that mixed old Spanish laws and orders with Cádiz-era and federation documents a disorded mess that contributed to criminal behavior. A committee adapted the Livingston system (created and then rejected by the Louisiana legislature) to the Guatemalan context. The assembly approved five codes and a definitional law between 1834 and 1836 and published "lessons" in the *Seminario Guatemalteco* and other newspapers in 1837.[82] The new jury system proposed a turn away from long-standing traditions of separate justice for different social and ethnic groups—and differening bodies such as the Church and the military. The goal was to create a liberal and modern nation-state by ending the role of single salaried judges and having people on juries take on judicial responsibilities.[83] Implementation proved difficult and in practice the results were negligible. With the exception of habeas corpus provisions, in March 1838 the new codes were suspended due to "the sad results of this premature intent and great discontent in the pueblos."[84] Did the latter prefer traditional ways of separate justice?

Gálvez's interest in innovation was sometimes offset by practical considerations. When a national law did not exist, legislation indicated that the government should rely on Spanish precedent.[85] The executive branch relied on *jefes de departamento* who played almost the same role as the governors and *jefes políticos* of the ancient regime and Cádiz experiment. Nor did Gálvez try to change the role of municipalities, created under Cádiz, which collected the new taxes, built and maintained prisons, administered primary schools, and recruited for the military. The Church did not stop registering births, marriage, and death, even if the law had removed this responsibility. Further, traditional alcaldes (magistrates) continued to serve as local judges, either under the new legal system or, after elected judges (*jueces de primera instancia*) were established, de facto when there were not enough legally trained individuals to hold these offices; a jury system, again adopted, was rejected by many citizens as well.[86]

At the socioeconomic level, Gálvez promoted cochineal and indigo production; imported the first coffee seeds from Havana; planned roads, ports, and other public works; designed a new public education system; and dreamed of prosperity for the new country, which he achieved to a limited extent.[87] With amicable relations between state and federation, there were economic advances. In his address to Congress in 1837, the chief of state boasted that commerce had doubled from 1834 to 1836. In this economic climate, it is perhaps not surprising that there was a measure of reconciliation between those who lost the civil war of 1826–1829 and the liberal government. Notably, in 1834 "the aristocracy" attended the Independence Day celebration (September 15), followed by Gálvez's reelection in 1835, symbolically sealing the rapprochement.[88]

Unfortunately, elite consensus in the capital prompted conflict with large segments of society in both the Oriente and the highlands. The Gálvez administration's promotion of commercial development, in the form of individual and private company acquisition of what the government defined as public land, frequently infringed on lands owned by Maya communities and ladino peasants in central and eastern Guatemala—despite a stated respect for communal lands. Such policies provoked increasing challenges, not only by the poor but also by men like mulatto landowner Teodoro Mexía of Santa Rosa.[89] While an April 17, 1835, legislative order established a commission to hear and respond to land disputes, little changed before rebellions broke out throughout the Southeast in 1837.[90]

In addition, despite aspirations to create more equitable socioeconomic relations based on equality before the law, the state government sometimes abandoned theory for repressive practice. In 1835, President Gálvez responded to news of insecurity and an assault on the road to El Salvador by abolishing municipal governments in the Oriente, "substituting in their place local justices."[91] In the pueblos of Santa Rosa Department, including Jalpatagua and Moyuta, a general discontent centered on what seemed an arbitrary state interest in reducing local governmental autonomy to "organize the social, religious, cultural and economic life of the communities."[92]

In the Oriente, or Montaña, discontent grew in response to policies that promoted foreign investment and "colonization" (or expropriation of land for foreigners) in about half the state's territory—through contracts Gálvez signed with Belgian and British companies with support from the federal government.[93] While cochineal production assured Guatemala a "dominant position among the Central American states in its trade with England," former Bonapartist officers from France, unscrupulous bankers from England, Protestant missionaries and educators from the United States, and Belgian colonists who found their way into Guatemalan society created tensions within the new country. Although they were only a handful, and some established joint companies with local merchants, foreign residents resisted paying war taxes. Their tendency to support their own, rather than local, interests and call on their consuls to bring in warships to defend them made them flashpoints for local dissatisfaction.[94]

A cholera morbus epidemic in Verapáz and Chiquimula compounded the challenges. Recent Protestant settlers were imagined responsible; doctors and officials trying to contain the outbreak were accused on being "poisoners," sparking a revolt in June 1837 that transformed into the "war of the Mountain."[95] An uprising begun by rural residents shouting "Long live religion and death to foreigners!" spread with the support of those whose power had diminished under liberal influence—namely, merchants and powerful families in Guatemala City, some members of the Church hierarchy, as well as landed people in the Montaña increasingly beleaguered by state policies. Gálvez, who had repeatedly resisted accepting election to a second term, was forced from office in February 1838.[96] As Ralph Lee Woodward concluded, the force necessary to implement the liberal programs seemed to contradict the rhetoric of liberty.[97]

As the state was embattled in the Oriente, Quetzaltenango's ambitions to form its own country resurfaced. On February 2, 1838, deputies met in Quetzaltenango and declared the state of Los Altos. The federal Congress, meeting in El Salvador, authorized the secession, despite its own waning authority. Guatemala's Congress accepted the decision.[98] Guatemala City's interest in the highlands proved insufficient to give leaders an appetite for civil war, or a war that might pit it against even a weakened federation government.

Quetzaltenango's ambitions were also, as Arturo Taracena argues, an indigenous nightmare. If Los Altos's ladinos protested liberal reforms, the indigenous in some communities preferred the central Guatemalan government. The Los Altos leadership enticed three towns of Suchitepéquez to join their sixth state in 1838 by offering department status to their unified districts.[99] Other Indian villages met and opposed the Altense project to create a sixth Central American state. Throughout February and March, Zutuhil municipalities— San Pedro, San Juan La Laguna, San Marcos la Laguna, and Santiago Atitlán— wrote to the Guatemalan government opposing a state they claimed would harm established commerce between the lake zone and Guatemala City and lead to double taxation. Kuiché municipality Joyabaj also mistrusted Quetzaltenango's reassurances. When Quetzaltenango sought to collect taxes in Santa Catarina Ixtahuacán (Sololá) and San Sebastián (Retahuleu), the villages held *cabildos abiertos* and refused. In short, some highland communities turned to Guatemala's government for support against Quetzaltanango's ladinos, only to find that that the state quickly warned Los Altos of complaints from "subjects of an independent state." The indigenous municipalities first sought to resolve their conflict directly with Los Altos authorities, and then with Guatemala's aid. Only when both state governments appeared deaf to their complaints did they join Rafael Carrera and the Oriente's forces to compel change at the top.[100] Once both the highlands and Oriente opposed the central government, the Gálvez administration fell.

From State to Republic

By late 1838 Guatemala's survival, whether as a federal state or independent country, was in doubt. In 1839, president Mariano Rivera Paz called on the patriotism of Guatemala's constituent assembly to help restore a country whose "society seemed dissolved," led to the brink of "misery and disorganization" by inexperience, "revolutionary furor," and a fetish for "all that is new and the desire to destroy all that existed."[101] Yet conservative policies proved equally divisive. Guatemala required a decade to transition from weak federal state to viable republic, twice forcibly putting down revolt in the Oriente and reincorporating Los Altos (1839). It declared provisional separation from the federation (1839), defeated federal president Francisco Morazán and his largely Honduran and Salvadoran forces (1840), and suppressed a new rebellion in the Oriente (1847).[102] Still, Guatemala's general outlines became clear soon after Gálvez's government collapsed. Under a government established by an Oriente rebel, the mestizo or ladino Rafael Carrera, a veneer of normalcy returned, albeit with more emphasis on economic than on universal rights. Guatemalan legislators repealed many "innovations" of the first period—abandoning the experiment in universal and individual rights, as well as Gálvez's anticlerical policy—in search of formulas that contributed to stability. Carrera was an implacable enemy of the federation after its army had tried to vanquish him. The leadership of Mariano Rivera Paz (1839–1844), and Carrera (1844–1848; 1851–1865) led to Guatemala's emergence as an independent republic in 1847 and prevented Central America's other states from reestablishing the union.

Carrera's humble origins as an illiterate pig-herder from the Oriente and his mixed-race ancestry led many nineteenth-century critics to label him a "celebrated Indian despot" (1857)[103] and "dark colored and ill-looking mestizo."[104] His support, according to many contemporaries, came from the priesthood and "his subordinate instruments, generally Indian or half breeds" [105] or merely from the Indians, while all other "classes . . . have never ceased to hate and fear him, and watch for an opportunity to overturn his power."[106] Ralph Lee Woodward Jr., René Reeves, Douglass Sullivan-González, and others have championed a more nuanced approach to his career, which put the first acknowledged non-European in control of the country and, for some, initiated the rise of the ladino state.[107] Sullivan-González in particular shows that the Church, under

DON RAFAEL CARRERA,
CAPITAN GENERAL Y
PRESIDENTE DE LA REPUBLICA DE GUATEMALA.

FIGURE 8.3. Leading a new country: Rafael Carrera

Antonio Larrazábal and later Antonio García Peláez, was a tentative ally, willing to call for patriotism and unity although not always to put its wealth or
clergy into rebellious communities.[108] During what many call the conservative regime (1839–1871), Guatemala's
leaders failed to pass a new constitution. They governed with "Constitutive
Laws" approved in 1839 by a Constituent Assembly: one each for executive (Decree 65) and judicial (Decree 75) power, and (Decree 76): Declaration of the
Rights of the State and its Inhabitants.[109] Decree 65 heralded an increasingly
powerful executive, adopting the title of "president" for the supreme executive

authority.[110] Decree 76 declared the state "sovereign, free and Independent," while still insisting on the sovereignty of the internal pueblos; it reestablished Catholicism as the official religion and created a separate status for the indigenous, who supposedly lacked "the *ilustración* (understanding/education) sufficient to know and defend their own rights." The code protected the property of any "population, corporation or person" and insisted on individual rights, including those of making wills and expressing opinions, while it prohibited torture and illegal detention.[111]

Other legislation overtly recalled the colonial system. In 1838, the assembly reestablished the mint and the merchant's chamber with their separate rights, or *fueros*. It then replaced *jefes departamentales* with corregidores, reestablished ecclesiastic supervision of education and adopted a system of residencies (end of term reviews) for state officials; it reestablished the Church's *fuero*.[112] Voting for city councilors was restricted to sitting members, who were required to choose among former councilors.[113] The legislative assembly also revoked the exile of Archbishop Ramón Casáus y Torres, appointed by King Ferdinand VII, reopened monastic orders, and resumed collecting Church tithes. Courts, too, returned to using the Recopilación de Indias in cases that seemed appropriate.[114]

For those who saw the liberal-republican system as a menace to local autonomy and the culture of indigenous republics, this policy represented not a retreat from modernity, but an attempt to overcome the government's clear weakness and inability to control the country.[115] The reversion to political processes grounded in ways that had ruled for centuries before 1808 resolved problems inherent in a country with a large rural, illiterate population—long adapted to earlier Spanish ways. A deputy in Guatemala's 1839 legislature reported that the town of Comalapa (Chimaltenango) lived "major disorder" in all aspects of governance from the administration of justice to tax collection, maintenance of town buildings, including the jail, which "is a lake inside." According to one Indian alcalde, the disasters stemmed in part from the move from perpetual to elected alcaldes, who were replaced before they began to undertake projects.[116] In other towns, lack of literate residents to serve municipal posts undermined new ways of government. The governor of Verapáz reported to Congress that only one ladino in the Indian villages of Cahabón and Lanquín could read and speak Spanish. Over the ladino's protests, the governor named him alcalde and ordered him to communicate government decrees and orders. The unwilling official reported back that the towns' *municipales* (councilors) were inebriated and spent locally the funds collected for the national war tax.[117] Such reports suggest that many indigenous communities preferred to live by their own cultures—and keep revenues at home. No wonder earlier administrations' attempts to press structural changes had proved both ineffective and unpopular. Gálvez's anticlerical policies had led to reductions in the number of clergy in rural parishes; with the return of stronger Church-state relations, priests resumed their function as official and unofficial state agents in communities long accustomed to their presence, helping to inculcate a Guatemalan identity as well as religious values in their sermons.[118]

While socially conservative steps aimed to stabilize the Guatemalan state, much new law passed between 1838 and 1848 promoted exports and commercial life, as in the foundation of a national bank.[119] The new government continued to welcome European immigrants, with a little more caution than Gálvez had shown. Under Carrera and his supporters, German colonists established farms on what would emerge as the Costa Cuca coffee regions in the western highlands.[120] Under conservative government, legal compilations—the first by Alejandro Marure, covering to 1841, and the second by Andrés Fuentes Franco, reaching to 1856—were published.[121] Also, if Guatemala under Carrera reestablished religious education and the colonial Universidad de San Carlos, the latter retained "liberal" professors like Friar José Mariano Herrarte (theology and law) to promote what historian Blake Pattridge calls "catholic liberalism"—the parts of liberalism that remained in effect until the Reforma of 1871 reestablished a government that called itself liberal. Pattridge found a dynamic curriculum, with students embarking on professional studies in French and English languages, surveyors' training, and programs in medicine and law. The conservative government attempted to balance a still precarious political situation with programs promoting commercial development.

A Conservative Republic

At the end of the period considered here, as Guatemala finally called the world's attention to itself as a fully independent republic, a liberal "revolution" in 1848 came followed by the establishment in 1851 of a conservative republic that institutionalized presidential government and militarized the state. Both remained axes of national authority into the twentieth century. It took a personalist dictatorship that recognized regional and local differences rather than a democracy that attempted to legislate homogenizing laws and common rights to link three regions and distinct interest groups—economic, ethnic, political—together in a single country.

On March 21, 1847, Rafael Carrera declared Guatemala a republic. He rejected the right of the western highlands, Los Altos, to form a separate state. For the first time, he declared Guatemala "indivisible."[122] In addition, he signaled his hope that Central America's other federal states would follow his example. According to Carrera, the states "despite the reduction suffered in their wealth and population . . . comprise sufficient elements to constitute themselves into independent Republics, and in the full capacity of political bodies. Thus they have existed, in fact, since the Federation dissolved, or better said, since they shook off the yoke of Spain."[123] Carrera astutely and accurately presented his decision as consonant with liberal policy, citing a law approved by two legislatures in 1833 that permitted the state of Guatemala "if the federal pact were to falter" to consider itself as "organized prior to that pact" to form a new social compact or "constitute itself for itself alone."[124] At the request of José Francisco Barrundia, a former radical, the Guatemalan constituent assembly ratified Carrera's decision for independence and absolute sovereignty. On the same date, Carrera called on Guatemalans to watch over "the Republic that I leave founded . . . with great elements of power."[125]

If Guatemala's entry into the world as an independent republic began auspiciously, over the next four years the country suffered regional conflicts similar to those that divided it after the hasty marriage of Los Altos, Oriente, and Guatemala City in 1825. Ralph Lee Woodward describes 1848 as a decisive year and a failed revolution. More comprehensively, Douglass Sullivan-González sees 1847–1851 as marked by a civil war brought on by Carrera's inability to address the needs of struggling sharecroppers in the Oriente—while dealing with overtures to British colonization projects, liberal opportunism, and western highland indigenous communities' resistance to land challenges pressed by ladinos.[126] A generation into statehood, Guatemala still lacked a unitary trajectory. Both conservative constitutional rule and liberal governance had proved ineffective at creating political unity—and no new economy had risen to integrate the imagined nation within or to forge strong ties to an emerging industrial world.

In early 1847, a new rebellion broke out in the Montaña on Carrera's Palencia estate. The president dedicated the next year to pacifying the Oriente's peoples. He cited laws Gálvez passed against his own revolt to justify application of military justice to the rebels.[127] He agreed to call elections for a new legislative assembly, a demand by liberals who then won, installed their legislative assembly, and established a government in August 1848, surprising many.[128] Carrera withdrew to Mexico for the next year. Instead of bringing peace, the new liberal government exacerbated problems.

Its forces proved as incapable as Carrera's in pacifying the Oriente. In the western highlands Quetzaltenango leveraged the crisis to again demand separation and an independent state. Neither rebellion's leaders accepted amnesty and invitations to become departmental governors, despite an offer to establish new *ejidos* for Oriente communities that had lost their lands. On August 26, 1848, the Quetzaltenango city council pronounced its separation from Guatemala. It saw the June 15, 1838, federal decree and reintegration in 1840 as the "effect of force and terror," thus Los Altos's reincorporation into Guatemala was illegal. With Carrera's temporary fall in 1848, they insisted on having been "placed anew in the exercise of their Sovereignty and Independence."[129] With support from leaders from the Montaña, Quetzaltenango formed a governing junta representing four of six Los Altos districts (Sololá and Suchitepéquez sent no delegates); an interim government pronounced in favor of the Los Altos constitution. El Salvador recognized the new state. In Guatemala, a committee of the legislative assembly studying the case vacillated; it would make no decision until every Altense municipality expressed its opinion.[130] Guatemala's interim president, Juan Antonio Martínez, then declared war against the Los Altos junta, capturing Quetzaltenango on October 25. The separatist movement withered, and the region was permanently integrated into the Guatemalan republic.

By late 1848, with the Oriente rebellion led by brothers Serapio and Vicente Cruz still strong and after two changes of executive power, Guatemala's liberal assembly named Colonel Mariano Paredes interim president. An apolitical military man, Paredes reestablished order, working with moderates while increasing military influence. His ascendancy signaled the end of liberal government in Guatemala for a quarter century. Carrera returned from exile in Mexico and little by little reinserted himself into public life, helping put down Altense and Oriente rebellions, and recovering the presidency in 1851. Although Decree 76 continued "in force as fundamental law" until 1871, Carrera's return brought important modifications. An October 19 constitutive act created a presidentialist state run by a president who was both "first magistrate" and "governing authority of the nation."[131] Elected not by the people, but by a "general assembly" composed of members of the legislative chamber, the archbishop, supreme court, and members of the Council of State, the president was eligible for four-year renewable terms in office. The fifty-five representatives were not considered "legislators" because they shared the work of legislating with the president.[132] This charter was revised on January 29, 1855, to name Rafael Carrera president for life (*presidente vitalicio*), a position he retained until his death in 1865.[133] The experiment of a national state built on popular sovereignty was suspended.

Country of Continuities and Ruptures

The history of Guatemala from 1759 to 1851 is one of rupture and reconciliation. Under Bourbon reforms and Cádiz government, the districts around Guatemala City participated in the modernization of the relationship between government and society, accepting greater government authority and experimenting with direct and indirect elections and equality before the law. They did not, however, form a single polity or society. The challenge of independence was to join territories with distinct populations, economies, and leaderships into a whole. Nation formation did not build on enduring political relationships, but re-created them in thirty years of trial and error from 1821 to 1851. The Republic of Guatemala was very much a new country.

From the establishment of the Guatemalan state in 1825, with its constitution and representative government, until the fall of Mariano Gálvez's government in 1838, the Hispanic revolution that was part of the Atlantic revolutions was implemented first to break with ancien régime practices and then to continue the "Cádiz revolution" in an independent country. With the revolution or rebellion "of the Montaña" in 1838, the pendulum swung back and conservatives found in caudillo Rafael Carrera the possibility to break with Gálvez-era "innovation." A third revolution in 1848 briefly returned more moderate "innovators" to promote their system of liberties, individual rights, and representative institutions until Carrera initiated autocratic government (under constitutional laws) until 1871. If they began with different ideas about how to build a state, Guatemalan leaders came to accept the need to establish enduring institutions that covered the three major geographic regions brought together together in 1825.

They participated under Barrundia, Gálvez, and Carrera's leadership by seeking to develop agricultural products for export, to improve state infrastructure, and to offer national and international investors a population that would work hard and respect the rules. Gálvez and the liberals tried (at least on paper) to create a nation of equals before the law—a national pueblo. By midcentury, Carrera and his allies and successors paused that experiment to focus on binding together regional, ethnic, and economic interests that remained disperate, despite liberal efforts to legislate unity.

By 1851, Guatemala was a sovereign republic. Although its international limits required formal recognition by its neighbors, the country's territory and existence were largely accepted at home and abroad. Los Altos and Oriente accepted Guatemala's authority. The government deployed military, ecclesiastic, and civil authorities to promote the state agenda in the countryside. The population remained largely rural, but cities started to attract new residents. The first coffee producers were finding an export market. Privatization of indigenous lands had started, pushed in part by the arrival of entrepreneurial European immigrants, even though grandiose projects for foreign colonization fizzled. Some indigenous "became" ladinos, a process of cultural assimilation common in Central America, but substantial Mayan populations retained their languages, customs, and tendency to cooperate with or defy the state to suit local interests. The rise of "ladino" power was not yet fully part of the political, economic, or cultural landscape.

By 1841, national laws were codified—without a constitutional implantation of national sovereignty and legistlative rights to serve as bulwark against executive power. The mid-nineteenth-century Guatemalan state was personalist, the price of a fragile unity. Future governments would seek to solve problems by legistlating for "Guatemalan" conditions that remained marked by deep internal disparities, often forgetting their origins in the three separate political, economic, and cultural entities stiched together to make a nation.

Notes

1   "Guatemala," *New Monthly Magazine and Literary Journal* 10 (1825), 578.
2   Francisco Antonio Fuentes y Guzmán, *Recordación Florida* (Madrid: L. Navarro, 1882), and Domingo Juarros, *Compendio de la historia de la ciudad de Guatemala* (Guatemala: Ignacio Beteta, 1808–1818). English-language readers learned the lesson in the English translation: Domingo Juarros, *A Statistical and Commercial History of the Kingdom of Guatemala, in Spanish America*, trans. John Baily (London: Printed for J. Hearne by J. F. Dove, 1823).
3   See Steven R. Ratner, "Drawing a Better Line: *Uti possidetis* and the Borders of New States," *American Journal of International Law* 90:4 (1996), 590–624.
4   National histories emerge in the late nineteenth century, e.g., Rafael Aguirre Cinta, *Lecciones de historia general de Guatemala desde los tiempos primitivos hasta nuestros días* (Guatemala: Tipografía Nacional, 1899); the most complete is Jorge Luján Muñoz, ed., *Historia General de Guatemala*, 6 vols., vol. 4: *Desde la República federal hasta 1898*, ed. Alberto Herrarte (Guatemala: Asociación de Amigos del País, 1993–1999). For an overview of twentieth-century scholarship, see Jordana Dym, "La república de Guatemala: La emergencia de un país, 1808–1851," in *De las independencias iberoamericanas a los estados nacionales (1810–1850): 200 años de historia*, ed. Ivana Frasquet and Andréa Slemian (Madrid: AHILA, Iberoamericana-Vervuet, 2009), 218–220.
5   See for example David McCreery, "Development and the State in Reforma Guatemala, 1871–1885," *Ohio University Center Latin American Studies, Latin America Series* 10 (1983), 9.
6   See the excellent essays in Michel R. Oudjik and Laura Matthew, eds., *Indian Conquistadors: Indigenous Allies in the Conquest of Mesoamerica* (Norman: University of Oklahoma Press, 2007).

7   The rest of Central America had lower percentages of indigenous languages. See Jordana Dym and Christophe Belaubre, introduction to *Politics, Economy and Society in Bourbon Central America, 1759–1821*, ed. Dym and Belaubre (Boulder: University Press of Colorado, 2007), and Juarros, *Compendio*.

8   The African origin of some of Guatemala's ladino or mulatto population, largely free and Hispanicized by the eighteenth century, is a recently recovered history. See Paul Lokken, "From the 'Kingdoms of Angola' to Santiago de Guatemala: The Portuguese Asientos and Spanish Central America, 1595–1640," *Hispanic American Historical Review* 93:2 (2013), 171–203; and essays by Lokken, "Angolans in Amatitlán: Sugar, African Migrants, and Gente Ladina in Colonial Guatemala," and Catherine Komisaruk, "Becoming Free, Becoming Ladino: Slave Emancipation and Mestizaje in Colonial Guatemala," in *Blacks and Blackness in Central America between Race and Place*, ed. Lowell Gudmundson and Justin Wolfe (Durham, NC: Duke University Press, 2010).

9   See Ralph Lee Woodward Jr., *Central America: A Nation Divided* (New York: Oxford University Press, 1985), 79; Richmond Brown, *Juan Fermín de Aycinena Central American Colonial Entrepreneur, 1729–1796* (Norman: University of Oklahoma Press, 1997), 16–17. See also W. George Lovell and Christopher H. Lutz, *Demography and Empire: A Guide to the Population History of Spanish Central America, 1500–1821* (Boulder: University Press of Colorado, 1995).

10 For a seventeenth-century list of products, see Fuentes y Guzmán, *Recordación florida*.

11 LaVerne M. Dutton, "Cochineal: A Bright Red Animal Dye" (MS in Environmental Archaeology, Baylor University, 1992), available at http://www.cochineal.info /; Jeremy Baskes, *Indians, Merchants, and Markets: A Reinterpretation of the Repartimiento and Spanish-Indian Economic Relations in Colonial Oaxaca, 1750–1821* (Stanford, CA: Stanford University Press, 2007), 185.

12 Juan Carlos Sarazúa Pérez, "Centralización política y centralización territorial en Guatemala," *Diálogos Revista Electrónica de Historia* 8:2 (2007–2008), 18–20. See also Sylvia Sellers-García, *Distance and Documents at the Spanish Empire's Periphery* (Stanford, CA: Stanford University Press, 2013), for a study of the colonial mails that connected the kingdom.

13 Juarros, *Compendio*, 25.

14 For the kingdom's products ca. 1800, see the list attributed to Spanish merchant Juan de Zavala (1753–1800) published in Carlos Meléndez, ed., *Textos Fundamentales de la Independencia Centroamericana* (San José, Costa Rica: Editorial Universitaria Centroamericana, 1971), 66–67.

15 See José Fernández, *Pintando el mundo de azul: El auge añilero y el mercado centroamericano, 1750–1810* (San Salvador: Dirección de Publicaciones e Impresos, Consejo Nacional para la Cultura y el Arte, 2003).

16 Richmond F. Brown, *Juan Fermín de Aycinena: Central American Colonial Entrepreneur, 1729–1796* (Norman: University of Oklahoma Press, 1997); Gustavo Palma Murga, "Núcleos de poder local y relaciones familiares en la ciudad de Guatemala a finales del siglo XVIII," *Mesoamérica* 12 (1986): 241–308.

17 Jordana Dym, "'Conceiving Central America: Public, Patria and Nation in the Gazeta de Guatemala (1797–1807)," in *Enlightened Reform in Southern Europe and Its Atlantic Colonies, c. 1750–1830*, ed. Gabriel Paquette (Aldershot, UK: Ashgate, 2009), 99–118, 105, 107–108, 111; John Tate Lanning, *The Eighteenth-Century Enlightenment in the University of San Carlos de Guatemala* (Ithaca, NY: Cornell University Press, 1956).

18 See Miles Wortman, *Government and Society in Central America, 1680–1840* (New York: Columbia University Press, 1982), 140–145; Miles Wortman, "Bourbon Reforms in Central America, 1750–1786," *The Americas* 32:2 (1975), 228–230; Jorge H. González, "State Reform, Popular Resistance, and the Negotiation of Rule in Late Bourbon Guatemala: The Quetzaltenango Aguardiente Monopoly, 1785–1807," in Dym and Belaubre, *Politics, Economy and Society in Bourbon Central America*, 131–157.

19 See John Lynch, *Bourbon Spain, 1700–1808* (Oxford: Basil Blackwell, 1989).

20 For more detail, see Jordana Dym, *From Sovereign Villages to National States: City, State and Federation in Central America, 1759–1839* (Albuquerque: University of New Mexico Press, 2006), chap. 2; and Hector H. Samayoa Guevara, *Implantación del Régimen de Intendencias en el Reino de Guatemala* (Guatemala: Editorial del Ministerio de Educación Pública, 1960).

21 Dym, *From Sovereign Villages*, 42–46.

22 Domingo Juarros, *Compendio de la historia del Reino de Guatemala (1500–1800)* (1808–1818; reprint, Guatemala: Editorial Piedra Santa, 1981), 56.

23 Julio César Pinto Soria, *Ladinos e indígenas en la nación criolla guatemalteca; de la colonia al régimen conservador* (Guatemala: USAC, CEUR, 1998).

24 Arturo Taracena Arriola, *Invención criolla, sueño ladino, pesadilla indígena: Los Altos de Guatemala: De región a Estado, 1740–1850* (Antigua, Guatemala: CIRMA, 1999), 78–79; and Sarazúa Pérez, "Centralización política," passim; there is need for an equally detailed study of the area around Antigua, Guatemala.

25 Dym, *From Sovereign Villages*, 42–46.

26 Archivo General de Indias (AGI), Seville, Guatemala 446, Pieza 4, Erección de Cabildo en el pueblo de ladinos de Jumay (1764), Guatemala; Archivo Histórico Nacional, Madrid, Consejos 20953, Pieza 74, Reducción a población de los mulatos de Ystapa (1764), ff. 5, 12.

27 Lynch, *Bourbon Spain*, 344–345; David A. Brading, "Bourbon Spain and Its American Empire," in *Colonial Spanish America*, ed. Leslie Bethell (Cambridge: Cambridge University Press, 1987), 130; Bernabé Fernández Hernández, *El Reino de Guatemala durante el Gobierno de Antonio González Saravia, 1801–1811* (Guatemala: Comisión Interuniversitaria Guatemalteca de Conmemoración del Quinto Centenario del Descubrimiento de América, 1993), 227, 280–283.

28 Wortman, *Government and Society*, cited in González, "State Reform," 151.

29 See Gustavo Palma Murga, "Between Fidelity and Pragmatism: Guatemala's Commercial Elite Responds to Bourbon Reforms on Trade and Contraband," in Dym and Belaubre, *Politics, Economy and Society in Bourbon Central America*, 103–129, esp. 112, 120. See also Brown, "Profits, Prestige, and Persistence"; Palma

Murga, "Núcleos de poder local"; and Miles Wortman, "Government Revenue and Economic Trends in Central America, 1787–1819," *Hispanic American Historical Review* 55 (1975), 251–286.

30 Dym, "'Enseñanza en los jeroglíficos y emblemas': Igualdad y lealtad en Guatemala por Fernando VII (1810)," *Secuencia, Numero Conmemorativo* (Mexico) (2008), 75–99.

31 *Gazeta de Guatemala* 13:131 (March 7, 1810), 273–285. See also Xiomara Avendaño Rojas, "Procesos Electorales y Clase Política en la Federación de Centroamérica, 1810–1840" (PhD diss., Colegio de México, 1995), 39–42.

32 See Mario Rodríguez, *The Cádiz Experiment in Central America, 1808–1826* (Berkeley: University of California Press, 1978), and Dym, *From Sovereign Villages,* and Archivo General de Centroamérica (AGCA) B 496–8454, Ayuntamiento de Quezaltenango al Ayto. de Guatemala, October 8, 1811.

33 José María Peynado, *Instrucciones para la constitución fundamental de la Monarquía Española y su Gobierno, . . . dadas por el M. I. Ayuntamiento de la M. N. . y L. Ciudad de Guatemala a su diputado el Sr. Dr. D. Antonio de Larrazábal . . .* (Guatemala: Editorial del Ministerio de Educación Pública, 1953), articles 68–71; AGCA A Legajo 12189, Expediente 15737, July 15, 1811, José María Peynado al cabildo; AGCA B Legajo 496, Expediente 8454, Ayuntamiento de Quezaltenango al Ayto. de Guatemala, October 8, 1811.

34 AGI Guatemala 629, Instrucción del ayuntamiento de Quezaltenango, July 9, 1813; José Cleto Montiel letter, July 1, 1814; Taracena Arriola, *Invención criolla,* 78–81. The instructions also asked to improve the education of indigenous and ladino residents, and to ensure a clergyman in each village.

35 See Jordana Dym, "'Our Pueblos, Fractions with No Central Unity': Municipal Sovereignty in Central America, 1808–1821," *Hispanic American Historical Review* 86:3 (2006), 431–466.

36 *Diario de las discusiones y actas de las Cortes,* January 13, 1812 (Cádiz: Imprenta Real, 1813), 260. The 1821 Cortes authorized a diputación for each intendancy.

37 Rodríguez, *Cádiz Experiment,* 108; Newberry Library, Ayer Ms 1131, Tabla para facilitar la elección de los diputados de Cortes suplentes y de la provincia de Guatemala [1812].

38 AGI Guatemala 629, Instrucción del ayuntamiento de Quezaltenango, July 9, 1813; carta de José Cleto Montiel, July 1, 1814; Taracena Arriola, *Invención criolla,* 78–81.

39 AGI, Guatemala 629, Instrucción, July 9, 1813.

40 AGI Indiferente General 1569, 146–1-16, José Mariano Méndez to Secretario del despacho de la Governación de Ultramar, Madrid, July 4, 1821.

41 See Aaron Pollack, *Levantamiento k'iche' en Totonicapán, 1820: Los lugares de las políticas subalternas* (Guatemala City: Instituto AVANCSO, 2008), and J. Daniel Contreras R., *Una rebelión indígena en el partido de Totonicapán en 1820: El indio y la independencia* (Guatemala: Universidad de San Carlos de Guatemala, 1968).

42 Dym, *From Sovereign Villages,* 132–135.

43 Taracena Arriola, *Invención criolla,* 83.

44 See Rodríguez, *Cádiz Experiment,* chap. 6, and Jordana Dym, "Actas de independencia: De la Capitanía General de Guatemala a la República Federal de Cen-

troamérica," in *Independencias Latinoamericanas: Interpretación 200 años después*, ed. Marco Palacios (Bogotá: Grupo Editorial Norma, 2009), 339–366.

45 Taracena Arriola, *Invención criolla*, 87.

46 Ayuntamiento of Totonicapán to Iturbide, cited in Taracena Arriola, *Invención criolla*, 93.

47 Aaron Pollack, "Crear una región: Luchas sociales en los altos de Guatemala en la primera parte del siglo XIX," *Scripta Nova revista electrónica de geografía y ciencias sociales* 10:218 (2006), http://www.ub.edu/geocrit/sn/sn-218-36.htm.

48 Taracena Arriola, *Invención criolla*, 90–91.

49 Taracena Arriola, *Invención criolla*, 108–112.

50 AGCA B Legajo 91, Expediente 2462, Cirilo Flores, Proposal, April 1, 1824, ff. 1, 27.

51 Arturo Taracena Arriola, Juan Pablo Pira, and Celia Marcos, *Los departamentos y la construcción del territorio nacional en Guatemala, 1825–2002* (Guatemala: ASIES, Fundación Soros Guatemala, 2002), 4; see also Gustavo Palma Murga, ed., *La administración político-territorial en Guatemala: Una aproximación histórica* (Guatemala: Escuela de Historia, USAC, 1993).

52 "Guatemala," *New Monthly Magazine and Literary Journal* 10 (1825), 590.

53 Guatemala (State), Constitución de Guatemala, 1825, Articles 39, 45, 50–75, 161–162; Decreto 60, October 12, 1825.

54 See José Cecilio del Valle's statistics in the 1830 *Mensual de la Sociedad Económica*, 29–52 (see note 71) for the region and department breakdowns. The seventeen representatives in state and federal congresses from Guatemala reflected regional populations: seven (41.2 percent), Western Highlands; four (23.5 percent), Oriente; and six (35 percent), Center.

55 Constitución de Guatemala, 1825, Articles 36, 76.

56 Guatemala's sister federal states also used the language of pueblos in early constitutions. For an early analysis, see "Republic of Central America," *North American Review* (January 1828), 136–142; see also Constitution of Guatemala (1825), Preamble, Articles 2, 162–163.

57 Arturo Taracena, Arriola Juan Pablo Pira, and Celia Marcos, "La construcción nacional del territorio de Guatemala, 1825–1934," *Revista Historia* (Costa Rica), 45 (January–June 2002), 9–33.

58 Asamblea Constituyente del Estado de Guatemala, Decreto 63, October 29, 1825, Archivo Histórico del Arquidiocesis de Guatemala, C, T1/105. Escuintla was also promoted.

59 Asamblea Constituyente del Estado de Guatemala, Decreto 49, July 22, 1825.

60 "Guatemala," 591.

61 "Guatemala," 592.

62 *Gaceta del Gobierno Supremo de Guatemala* 9, May 7, 1824, 66.

63 "Guatemala," 580.

64 Michael F. Fry, "Política agraria y reacción campesina en Guatemala: Región de La Montaña, 1821–1838," *Mesoamérica* 9:15 (1988), 37; Ann Jefferson, "The Rebellion of Mita, Eastern Guatemala in 1837" (PhD diss., University of Massachusetts at Amherst, 2000).

65   Hubert Howe Bancroft, *History of Central America*, vol. 3 (1801–1887) (San Francisco: History Company, 1887), 113. Barrundia had a policy that "did him honor," shaming Great Britain to give up claims to Roatán.

66   See Bancroft, *History of Central America*, 3:88n38.

67   For more on the Aycinena clan, see Brown, *"Juan Fermín de Aycinena"* and "Dilemmas of a Creole Loyalist: José de Aycinena and the Crisis of Central American Independence, 1808–1824," *Colonial Latin American Historical Review* 12:3 (2003), 249–273.

68   Ralph Lee Woodward, *Rafael Carrera and the Emergence of the Republic of Guatemala, 1821–1871* (Athens: University of Georgia Press, 1993), 30–31.

69   Fry, "Política agraria y reacción campesina, 37–38.

70   Lorenzo Montúfar, *Reseña histórica de Centro-américa* (Guatemala: Tip. "El Progreso," 1878), V.1, 274.

71   Sarazúa Pérez, "Centralización política."

72   José Cecilio del Valle, "Descripción Geográfica," *Mensual de la Sociedad Económica de Amigos del Estado de Guatemala* 1 (April 1830), 9–24, presents the country; "Continua la Descripción Geográfica del Estado de Guatemala," *Mensual* 2 (May 1830), 27–52, offers departmental information.

73   Woodward, *Rafael Carrera*, 37–39.

74   José Cecilio del Valle, "Carta Geográfica," *Mensual de la Sociedad Económica de Amigos del Estado de Guatemala* 3 (June 1830), 59.

75   Miguel Rivera Maestre, *Atlas Guatemalteco en ocho cartas formadas y grabadas en Guatemala* (Guatemala: Ministerio de Relaciones Exteriores, 1832). This is the first national map of Guatemala, if we discount the map in British diplomat George Thompson's 1828 travel account, which had del Valle's input. See Jordana Dym, "Initial Boundaries," in *Mapping Latin America: A Cartographic Reader*, ed. Jordana Dym and Karl Offen (Chicago: University of Chicago Press, 2011), 144–147.

76   Alejandro Marure's *Catálogo*, published in 1841 after Gálvez fell, was the first of its kind in the state and region.

77   Taracena Arriola, *Invención criolla*, 223–224; Oswaldo Chinchilla Mazariegos, "Archaeology and Nationalism in Guatemala at the Time of Independence," *Antiquity* 72 (1988), 376–386; William J. Griffith, "Juan Galindo, Central American Chauvinist," *Hispanic American Historical Review* 40:1 (1960), 25–52.

78   Alejandro Marure, *Bosquejo histórica de las revoluciones de Centroamérica desde 1811 hasta 1834* (Guatemala: El Progreso, 1877), with prologue by Lorenzo Montúfar, n.p.; Woodward, *Rafael Carrera*, 44.

79   Cited in Julio César Pinto Soria, *Reformismo liberal, régimen municipal, ciudadanía y conflicto étnico en Guatemala (1821–1840)* (Guatemala City: CEUR, 1997), 19n44.

80   Woodward, *Rafael Carrera*, 52; Jorge Luján Muñoz, *Breve historia contemporánea de Guatemala* (México: Fondo de Cultura Económica, 1998), 97; see also Miriam Williford, "Las Luces y la Civilización: The Social Reforms of Mariano Gálvez," in *Applied Enlightenment: 19th Century Liberalism, 1830–1839* (New Orleans: Middle America Research Institute, 1969). For university reforms, see Blake Pattridge,

Institution Building and State Formation in Nineteenth-Century Latin America: The University of San Carlos, Guatemala (New York: P. Lang, 2004).

81 Manuel Pineda de Mont, *Recopilación de las leyes de Guatemala*, 1:492–494, Decreto de la Asamblea Legislativa, September 28, 1836, municipal regulations, preamble, arts. 1 and 2 (Guatemala: Imprenta de la Paz, 1869–1872). See also Dym, *From Sovereign Villages*, and Sonia Alda Mejías, *La participación indígena en la construcción de la República de Guatemala, S. XIX* (Madrid: UAM Ediciones, 2000).

82 Luján Muñoz, *Breve historia*, 91. See also Mario Rodríguez, "The Livingston Codes in the Guatemalan Crisis of 1837–1838," in *Applied Enlightenment: 19th Century Liberalism, 1830–1839* (New Orleans: Middle America Research Institute, 1955).

83 Luján Muñoz, *Breve historia*, 92.

84 Alejandro Marure, *Efemérides: Hechos notables acaecidos en la República de Centroamérica desde el año de 1821 hasta el de 1842 . . .* (1844, rpt. Guatemala City: Ministerio de Educación Pública. 1956), 91–92.

85 Luján Muñoz, *Breve historia*, 97.

86 Dym, *From Sovereign Villages*, chap. 7. For the impact of indigenous villages, see Alda Mejías, *La participación indígena*.

87 Woodward, *Rafael Carrera*, 44, 382. See René Reeves, *Ladinos with Ladinos, Indians with Indians: Land, Labor and Regional Conflict in the Making of Guatemala* (Stanford, CA: Stanford University Press, 2006), 4–5, for a table showing the rise of coffee exports starting in the 1850s.

88 Woodward, *Rafael Carrera*, 47–48.

89 Jefferson, "The Rebellion of Mita," 1–3.

90 Woodward, *Rafael Carrera*, 51; Fry, "Política agraria y reacción campesina," 40–42.

91 Pinto Soria, *Reformismo liberal*, 14n29.

92 Pinto Soria, *Reformismo liberal*, 15.

93 William J. Griffith, *Empires in the Wilderness; Foreign Colonization and Development in Guatemala, 1834–1844* (Chapel Hill: University of North Carolina Press, 1965).

94 Robert A. Naylor, *Influencia británica en el comercio centroamericano durante las primeras décadas de la Independencia (1821–1851)* (Woodstock, VT: Antigua, Guatemala: Plumsock Mesoamerican Studies/CIRMA, 1988), citation from 93–95.

95 Woodward, *Rafael Carrera*, 52–53; Pinto Soria, *Reformismo liberal*, 18.

96 Douglass Sullivan-González, *Piety, Power, and Politics: Religion and Nation Formation in Guatemala, 1821–1871* (Pittsburgh: University of Pittsburgh Press, 1998), 8, 86.

97 AGCA B Legajo 214, Expediente 4941, Decreto 43, División Territorial del Estado; Woodward, *Rafael Carrera*, 53–54.

98 Taracena Arriola et al., "La construction nacional," 16–17.

99 Taracena Arriola, *Invención criolla*, 166–167.

100 Taracena Arriola, *Invención criolla*, 313–314. Taracena Arriola found indigenous pueblos' letters in Montúfar, *Reseña histórica de Centro-américa*, 3:150–154.

101 Mariano Rivera Paz, *Memoria que presente a la Asamblea constituyente en su primera sessión, el Consejro Gefe del Estado de Guatemala* . . . (Guatemala: Imprenta del Gobierno del Estado . . . , 1839), 1.

102 After reincorporation, the Guatemalan government split Los Altos's territories into six departments (Quetzaltenango, Totonicapán, Sololá, Suchitepéquez, Huehuetenango, and San Marcos).

103 "Revolutions in Central America," *United States Democratic Review* 40:4 (1857), 326.

104 Dunlop cited in "Revolutions in Central America," 326.

105 "Revolutions in Central America," 326.

106 William V. Wells, *Explorations and Adventures in Honduras* (New York: Harper & Co., 1857), cited in "Revolutions in Central America," 326.

107 Woodward, *Rafael Carrera*; Reeves, *Ladinos with Ladinos, Indians with Indians*; Sullivan-González, *Piety, Power, and Politics*.

108 See Sullivan-González, *Piety, Power, and Politics*.

109 For original texts, see Jorge Mario García Laguardia, *Constituciones Iberoamericanas: Guatemala* (México: Instituto de Investigaciones Jurídicas, UNAM, 2006; Decreto 76 (1839), sec. 1, arts. 2, 3, 6.

110 AGCA B Legajo 214, Expediente 4941, f. 588, for the ms. copy of Decreto 65 (1839).

111 Decreto 76 (1839), sec. 2, arts. 3, 11, 12, 14, 19. See also Pinto Soria, *Reformismo liberal*, 19–22.

112 Ralph Lee Woodward Jr., "Changes in the Nineteenth-Century Guatemalan State and Its Indian Policies," in *Guatemalan Indians and the State*, ed. Carol A. Smith (Austin: University of Texas Press, 1990), 65.

113 Manuel Pineda Mont, *Recopilación de las leyes de Guatemala* (Guatemala City: Imprenta de la Paz, 1869–1872), 510–511, Decreto, October 2, 1839, arts. 56–62; and Decreto, September 21, 1845, 572–574.

114 Luján Muñoz, *Breve historia*, 96–97.

115 Pinto Soria, *Reformismo liberal*, 16–18.

116 AGCA C1 Leg. 56, Exp. 1569, Organización territorial del estado, August–September 1839, ff. 30–31.

117 AGCA C1 Leg. 38, Exp. 942, JP Arriaga (Verapáz) to Guatemalan Congress, April 24, 1839, ff. 5–12.

118 Sullivan-González, *Piety, Power, and Politics*.

119 Woodward, "Changes," 65; Pattridge, *Institution Building*, esp. chap. 5.

120 See Griffith, *Empires in the Wilderness*.

121 Jorge Luján Muñoz, "Del derecho colonial al derecho nacional: El caso de Guatemala," *Jahrbuch für Geshhichte Lateinamerikas* 38 (2001), http://www-gewi.uni-graz.at/jbla/jahr01.html; Alejandro Marure, *Catálogo de las leyes promulgadas en el estado de Guatemala, entre 1824 y 1841* (Guatemala: Imprenta La Paz, 1841). Andrés Fuentes Franco updated this collection with laws from 1842 to 1856 with a *Catálogo razonado* in 1856.

122 Taracena Arriola, *Invención criolla*, 331.

123 *Manifiesto y Decreto N. 15 del Exmo. Señor Presidente del Estado de Guatemala, del 21 de Marzo de 1847, erigiendo dicho Estado en República independiente* [facsímile] (Guatemala: Universidad del Valle, 1997), 8.

124 Guatemala, *Decreto N. 15* (1847), 8–11, passim.

125 Guatemala, Decree, March 21, 1847, in Pineda Mont, *Recopilación* T, 1, 73–75.

126 Sullivan-González, *Piety, Power, and Politics*, 99–100.

127 Woodward, *Rafael Carrera*, 196.

128 Taracena Arriola, *Invención criolla*, 332.

129 Cited in Taracena Arriola, *Invención criolla*, 336.

130 Taracena Arriola, *Invención criolla*, 337–339.

131 Guatemala, Acta Constitutiva, October 19, 1851, arts. 3, 4, and 6.

132 Guatemala, Acta Constitutiva, 1851, arts. 5 and 11.

133 Woodward, *Rafael Carrera*, chap. 11.

9

___

FROM ONE PATRIA, TWO NATIONS

IN THE ANDEAN HEARTLAND

SARAH C. CHAMBERS

I have taken only those measures that have been necessary for the support, protection, tranquility, and conservation of the Spanish criollos, of the mestizos, zambos and Indians. For all of them [are] countrymen and compatriots born in our land. —JOSÉ GABRIEL TÚPAC AMARU, 1780

Bolivia and southern Peru are homogeneous. . . . My goal is to do well and raise these two portions of territory, if I am able, to the height of civilization and common welfare. —ANDRÉS DE SANTA CRUZ, 1837

At first glance, Andean history illustrates well the theme of divergence in the era of New World independence. In 1500, the Inkas exerted influence over the most expansive American empire from Cusco; before the end of that century the new Spanish metropolis of Potosí became a nerve center of the global economy. But silver production declined after 1650, and in the early nineteenth century the region broke into multiple countries governed by weak states and lacking cohesive national identities.[1] That outcome was not inevitable. This chapter explores the forces of convergence and divergence within the Andean heartland—core highlands ranging from the regions around the once Inka capital at Cusco to the later mining metropolis at Potosí and its hinterlands—to understand how peoples with a long history of interactions came to separate into two nations: Peru and Bolivia.[2]

Inka roads, armies, and exchanges integrated the heartland in the fifteenth century. Spanish rule linked the region to the global silver economy in the sixteenth century, but preserved strong indigenous leadership, ways of production, and cultural customs at the local level. Although the heartland was split between two viceroyalties in 1776, economic, social, and cultural integrations persisted as evidenced by the uprisings of the 1780s, famously led by Túpac Amaru. Although political rivalries during the wars of independence led to the establishment of separate nations, the foundation of Peru and Bolivia as new countries was contingent—a historical process in need of explanation.

The heartland was the core of what had been a larger Andean zone of resource exchange and empire building. Beginning almost four thousand years ago, Andean peoples began to develop settled agricultural communities and systems of exchange that distributed products such as corn, tubers, wool, and coca among highly diversified ecological zones from the coast to the high altitude plains. From the shores of Lake Titicaca, Tiwanaku expanded its influence over much of the southern Andes between 550 and 950, while the Wari held sway over the central zone (much of contemporary Peru). Over the course of the fifteenth century the Inka built an empire—Tawantinsuyu or the Land of Four Quarters—that expanded even beyond the former Tiwanaku and Wari territories. Some of those recently conquered Andean peoples helped Spanish invaders defeat the Inka in the sixteenth century, and under this new empire the silver extracted by indigenous laborers from the rich mountain of Potosí flowed across both the Atlantic and Pacific, much of it to meet high demand in China.[3] Wealthy Spanish miners, in turn, could import luxurious silks and wines to make life in the harsh environment more tolerable. Silver also stimulated commerce throughout the Andes to meet the needs of workers and provide supplies for mining: woolens arrived from far-off Quito, while mules raised to the south near Tucumán met demand for power and transportation.[4]

Spanish colonialism dramatically affected Andean society by pulling native peoples into a commercial economy and siphoning labor power from agricultural communities to the mines. Nonetheless, unlike the case of mining centers in Spanish North America, as analyzed by Alfredo Ávila and John Tutino, these forces did not make "a new world."[5] Rather, native Andeans in the heartland resiliently adapted their cultural traditions and social relations to changing conditions and demands. Although Potosí itself was a new metropolis—with a population in 1600 of about one hundred thousand at an elevation of thirteen thousand feet—it grew within a long-settled region. Despite dramatic demographic decline, the indigenous population of the Andean heartland provided labor for the mines, about half of it from a forced draft (the mitá). In addition to taxes on silver and trade, a separate tax on the indigenous population was critical to colonial (and later national) revenue. Traditional authorities (kurakas in Quechua, caciques in Spanish) and many commoners viewed this tribute as guaranteeing a degree of self-rule, access to communal landholdings, and an exemption from sales taxes when they sold their products in markets. Native Andeans without land or herds, on the other hand, often resisted payment.[6] From 1630 to 1730, silver production in Potosí declined, but agriculturalists and herders in the heartland—many of them members of indigenous communities—continued to exchange goods through regional trade networks. When silver began a modest recovery in the eighteenth century, the south-central highlands along with their connected tropical valleys (*yungas*) were able to meet the demand for supplies: sugar, cocoa, wine and brandy, woolen textiles and hides, meat, grains and tubers. While much reduced from the Inka realm of Tawantinsuyu, this region included much of its former core (Cusco and the heartlands of the southeastern quarter named Kollasuyu).

The integration created by cultural ties, trade networks, and labor migration, however, was repeatedly ignored when political authorities drew and redrew borders in the eighteenth and nineteenth centuries. In 1776, the Spanish Bourbons removed the provinces of Upper Peru, including Puno, from the authority of Lima and joined them to the newly created Viceroyalty of Río de la Plata, with its capital in the Atlantic port of Buenos Aires. The break, however, was anything but clean. Although silver from Potosí was henceforth exported through Buenos Aires, communities on both sides of the new administrative border continued to provide labor and supplies. With the establishment of a Cusco Audiencia (High Court) in 1788, three provinces of Puno were put under its jurisdiction, while the rest continued to report to the Audiencia of Charcas in Chuquisaca until the entire Intendancy of Puno was returned to Peru in 1796. An 1801 proposal to create a new viceroyalty encompassing heartland provinces of Cusco, Puno, and Charcas made sense, but did not come to fruition.[7] In 1825, Simón Bolívar sanctioned the creation of a nation, named in his honor, independent of either Peru or the United Provinces of the Río de la

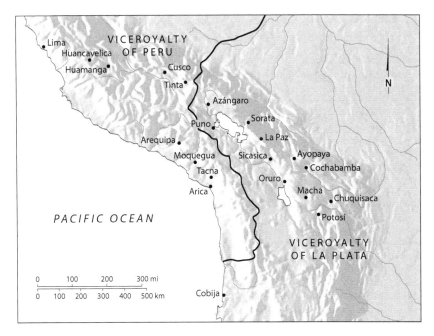

MAP 9.1. The Andean heartland, ca. 1776

Plata (which included the future Paraguay and Uruguay as well as Argentina). He still hoped to build a grand Andean federation that never materialized. Finally, in the wake of the War of the Pacific (1879–1883), Bolivia lost its Pacific port and Peru its rich nitrate fields to the expanding nation of Chile.

Despite cultural diversity and economic differentiation within the Andean heartland, one does not need to resort to counterfactuals to find political attempts to reintegrate the region. The great Andean rebellions of 1780 to 1782 encompassed this entire zone, and when the capture of Fernando VII created an imperial crisis in 1808, Viceroy José Fernando de Abascal reclaimed Upper Peru in a bid to weaken the rebels of Buenos Aires. The last Spanish viceroy of Peru, José de la Serna, retreated to the highlands, making Cusco the effective capital and allowing members of its cabildo and Audiencia to imagine a Hispanic reincarnation of the Inka empire. Independence-era leaders did not view the division of the region into separate nations a foregone conclusion. Even after a congress in "Upper Peru" declared its independence as Bolivia in 1825, various schemes imagined reuniting the two "Perus." Andrés de Santa Cruz led the most promising attempt; he saw himself as a citizen of both nations and joined them in confederation from 1836 to 1839.

Although the attempts at independence-era political integration of the Andean heartland failed, owing to internal rivalries as well as external opposition, they challenge us to consider alternatives to the separate nations of Peru and Bolivia. As in Central America, drawing national boundaries after independence was a complicated and contingent process. There, as Jordana Dym traces, Guatemala emerged from processes of both fragmentation (separation from the larger federation) and integration (strengthening the economic and political ties among three distinct regions).[8] In the Andes, inhabitants of a territory that had been cohesive for centuries were unable to overcome administrative divisions introduced by the Bourbons and reaffirmed out of political expediency after the defeat of the royal army.

Given the contingency of their separation, we should not lose sight of the commonalities between northern Bolivia and southern Peru. This region shared a resilient indigenous peasantry who was neither passive nor isolated and at least some elites and intellectuals who envisioned polities that would incorporate, rather than exclude and dispossess, such communities. Both before and after independence from Spain, the term "patria" was invoked to convey common membership in a polity, allowing Spanish concepts of *vecinos* as rights-bearing residents of a corporate community to overlap and interpenetrate both indigenous understandings of communal membership and evolving notions of citizenship in broader republics. Belonging to a patria asserted a degree of shared identity without negating internal diversity. Finally, the borders of a homeland represented by the patria were flexible, rooted in but reaching beyond the local community.[9] This chapter draws on the rich historiography of both Peru and Bolivia, as well as sources from the early nineteenth century, to reassemble those elements into an alternative view of a patria, if not a fully realized nation, integrated through culture and trade routes as well as political imaginings. Along the way, this counternarrative will cross several periods whose chronological boundaries are as imprecise as those geographic borders.

Economic Resilience and Movements for Home Rule (ca. 1750–1805)

The history of Peru is often told as a story of decline. Before the arrival of the Spaniards, native Andeans had developed technologies of agriculture, storage, and transport that supported dense populations, laying the foundations for the expansive Inka empire. In the first century of colonialism, Spaniards harnessed these human and material resources to an expanding global market. Peruvian silver funded the rise of Spain as a world power and stimulated trade from Europe to China. So famous in Europe was the remote Andean metropolis that the term "Potosí" became synonymous with striking it rich. Then silver production entered a long decline and the territory named Peru gradually shrank from encompassing all Spanish claims in South America to a medium-sized nation of uncertain prosperity by the end of the nineteenth century.

If we reconsider the Andean heartland during the eighteenth century from the vantage point of the altiplano rather than Lima, alternative narratives emerge to challenge expectations of dependency theory that extractive enterprises oriented toward the global market would create enclaves of dynamism within larger zones of underdevelopment.[10] The forced labor draft (mitá) did constitute a double exploitation of indigenous communities, by siphoning off local resources (wool, foodstuffs, llamas) along with their labor power. Nonetheless, native Andeans (women as well as men) responded to these pressures with resilience, continuing traditional exchanges of products among ecological zones and even selling surpluses in the new markets. As silver production declined and the population of Potosí shrank in the later seventeenth century, the peasant economy did not collapse. Some of the reduction in officially registered silver, moreover, reflected both tax evasion by large refiners and informal production by groups of skilled indigenous wage laborers.[11] Finally, after 1730, both the indigenous population and the production of silver began to recover from their long decline.[12]

Although Peru's value to the Spanish empire could not rival New Spain's in the eighteenth century, the Bourbon monarchs did not ignore its potential as they promoted economic revival and increased revenue collection throughout the eighteenth century. To stimulate mining, Madrid reduced the tax on silver, made mercury for processing more readily available, and provided technical help for upgrading excavations and water pumping. Equally important for the profits of silver entrepreneurs in Potosí, Spanish officials continued to enforce the mitá despite growing calls for its abolition and looked the other way as increasing quotas lengthened the shifts of forced laborers. Throughout the century, Andean silver production increased at an average annual rate of 1.2 percent, although it regained its earlier peak only briefly in the 1780s.[13] In the midst of the recovery, Bourbon reformers opened more ports to trade and reorganized colonial administration to increase oversight and tax collection. Travel from the altiplano to either coast was difficult, but shipping silver from Buenos Aires eliminated the overland Panama route, avoided Caribbean attacks by imperial rivals, and reduced silver exported directly across the Pacific. Moreover, authorities in Buenos Aires could increase vigilance against the contraband silver that had flowed through Brazil since the seventeenth century. Despite the shifts in export patterns, however, Andean products continued to move freely across the new boundary between the viceroyalties of Peru and Río de la Plata.

Demand from the reviving mining centers and expanding cities no longer drew trade from as widespread an area, in large part because producers in the Andean heartland met regional needs. Native Andeans were exempt from the sales tax (*alcabala*), an exception some nonindigenous traders and colonial officials viewed as an unfair competitive edge; thus it is difficult to measure and track commodities produced by indigenous peasants. Sources from 1793, when that exemption was briefly abolished, suggest that native provisioning accounted for a significant proportion of goods consumed in mining areas.[14] Although the vast majority of *European* goods entering Potosí that year (80 percent) were imported through Buenos Aires, almost three-quarters of commodities (as measured by value) were produced in the Andean heartland, including brandy from Tacna and Arequipa, cloth from Cusco, and coca from La Paz. Notably, much of the coca was produced and transported by native Andeans. Although large coca haciendas also expanded in response to demand from mining centers, indigenous communities often found markets for their cheaper coca during periods of silver contraction.[15] Indigenous peasants and other small farmers in the regions north of Potosí and in Cochabamba similarly provisioned both the mining areas and the city of La Paz with wheat and corn, and native Andeans flocked to major trade centers in the region of Oruro.[16] Although brandy and cloth were produced on larger enterprises and traded by Hispanic merchants, the abundance of these commodities in the markets and shops of Potosí demonstrate that the transfer of Upper Peru to the jurisdiction of Río de la Plata did not discourage trade across the new border.[17]

While Potosí remained the single most productive mining center in the Andean heartland, silver production rose throughout Upper and Lower Peru. Moreover, growing populations in cities like Arequipa also created demand for foodstuffs and other locally produced goods in addition to European imports.[18] Cusco, where producers specialized in sugar, textiles, coca, and hot peppers (*ají*), experienced greater economic stagnation than Arequipa; on the other hand, the obstacles to making quick profits limited encroachment by non-Indians onto communal lands around Cusco. The major trade routes passed through the altiplano region around Lake Titicaca, where as much as two-thirds of the livestock was in indigenous hands and many worked transporting goods on packs of camelids and mules throughout the south-central Andes. Residents of the high plains sent the products of herding (wool, hides, meat) as well as crafts (leather goods and pottery) in both directions: to Arequipa and Cusco as well as to Oruro and Potosí.[19] Although indigenous labor and commodities both received low compensation, the flexibility of peasant household production allowed for subsistence survival in hard times and modest surpluses when markets improved.[20] In contrast to Mexico and Haiti, where popular rebellions destroyed export economies to establish familial subsistence production, external and internal trade and commercial and family production continued to converge in the Andean heartland.

Although regional trade offered opportunities to some, demographic and administrative changes in the eighteenth century also resulted in economic hardship. The recovery of the indigenous population, after the last great epidemic of the 1720s, placed pressure on the land base of communities. Moreover, Bourbon measures to increase colonial revenues resulted in more efficient collection of "tribute," the indigenous head tax, in part by ending exemptions for *forasteros* ("migrants" who may have been residents of a given community for generations).[21] In 1751, Madrid also legalized the customary practice undertaken by governors (corregidores) to require communities to buy goods, often at inflated prices. Cusco elites forged economic and marital alliances with authorities in Upper Peru, for example, that allowed them to market their textiles through such *repartos*.[22] Finally, in the 1770s, colonial authorities raised the sales tax from 2 to 4 and then 6 percent, and increased the range of commodities subject to taxation. Although indigenous traders selling products from community plots or herds were exempt from taxation, they were liable for tax on "Castilian" goods that they marketed. Given this loophole, many indigenous traders feared that more of their cargos would be taxed than had been customary, especially when the sales tax was extended to coca and grains in 1779 and 1780.[23]

Colonial subjects in the Andean heartland responded in various ways to these increasing economic and fiscal pressures. As they had since the conquest, indigenous communities filed petitions and lawsuits aimed at staking claims to land, lessening the burden of their tax and labor obligations, and protesting abuses by both colonial authorities and some kurakas.[24] When Bourbon officials proved less open to negotiation than their predecessors, however, many peasants and traders turned to open revolt.[25] Crowds attacked customhouses newly established across this economic zone to collect the expanded sales tax, first in Cochabamba (1774), then La Paz (1777 and 1780) and Arequipa (1780), and finally there were plans to protest a proposed *aduana* in Cusco (1780). Evidence suggests that participation was widespread across classes and ethnic groups, and the opposition to an expanded alcabala reflected the potential links between economic circuits and potential polities.[26] Although uprisings might respond to a trigger event, they drew from historical memory of alternative forms of rule and envisioned new arrangements of power. And trade networks,

FIGURE 9.1. Traders with llamas in nineteenth-century Bolivia.
Courtesy the Archivo y Biblioteca Nacionales de Bolivia

especially the circuits plied by muleteers and *trajinantes* (who used llamas as
pack animals), were an important means of coordinating actions throughout
a wider region. [27]

As such a trader, José Gabriel Condorcanqui (1738–1781) had built up a network of contacts that cut across various ethnic and socioeconomic categories.[28]
He was educated in the Jesuit college in Cusco established for the children of
the indigenous nobility, and later in Lima met intellectuals associated with the
University of San Marcos, where professors evaded censorship to discuss enlightenment texts. He was on good terms with many of the regional elite, and
his network widened with marriage to mestiza Micaela Bastidas, who played a
key role in their joint economic and political endeavors.[29] Despite his education
and commercial success, he too ran up against colonial, specifically Bourbon,
forms of exploitation. His uncle Marcos Thupa Amaro, kuraka of Surimana, was
"bankrupted by the seizure of a train of mules and a hundred pesos' worth of
goods because his mitá quota was one man short."[30] Condorcanqui, in turn, had
to pay increased taxes on his trade goods in 1777 and disputed the reparto with
several corregidores, one of whom jailed him for debts.[31] Like other indigenous
elites, he repeatedly went to court to establish his claim as hereditary kuraka
of Tinta in the region of Cusco and his royal descent from Inka ruler Túpac
Amaru, executed in 1572 by Viceroy Francisco de Toledo. It sent a powerful

message when the kuraka, taking the name of Túpac Amaru, launched his movement by executing Corregidor Antonio de Arriaga in 1780.

Historians have long debated the causes and goals of the great Andean rebellion.[32] Túpac Amaru claimed to be acting with orders from the Spanish monarch, but the language and content of his proclamations and letters were clearly anticolonial. Issuing orders authoritatively as an Inka, he called for the reduction of tribute and sales tax rates and the abolition of the mitá.[33] He participated in and drew from an eighteenth-century revival of Inka history that included the circulation of Garcilaso de la Vega's *Royal Commentaries of the Incas*, the composition and legal use of Inka genealogies, and portraiture of kurakas and their wives in Inka dress.[34] But Túpac Amaru was also reinventing what it meant to be an Inka; he declared his Christian faith, prohibiting harm to priests or desecration of churches, and in his efforts to recruit allies, he implied that the Andean patria over which he claimed authority could be embedded within the larger empire of the Catholic sovereigns of Castile. Túpac Amaru appealed to all fellow countrymen born in "Peru" (referring to the full Andean region rather than the recently reduced viceroyalty)—American Spaniards, mestizos, and zambos (mulattos) as well as Indians—to unite as compatriots in opposition to the corrupt and exploitative officials who came from Spain.[35] Even before securing Cusco, he led his troops toward Lake Titicaca; rebels in that region continued fighting until 1783.[36] In the heartland of Tawantinsuyu, where stories of a returning or regenerated Inka (Inkarri) had and would continue to circulate, some non-Indians as well as native Andeans could imagine their place within a polity governed by an Inka.

Certainly, these coalitions were fragile. Some hereditary nobles chose not to recognize Túpac Amaru's overarching authority, but they did not necessarily reject the larger vision of a reinvigorated authority for their class.[37] Similarly, indigenous peasants had their own interpretations of who were and were not their fellow countrymen, often ignoring orders not to kill locals of Spanish or mixed descent, thus scaring off some of the allies Túpac Amaru sought.[38] Although Charles Walker rejects Peruvian nationalist narratives that claim Túpac Amaru as a precursor to the independence movements of 1810 to 1825, he does argue that the movement and its ideology constituted a militant "protonationalism." Although the rebellion did not succeed in establishing a new polity, its leaders spoke in the name of a patria, indicating "the existence of a unique body of people and the attempt to attain political gains for this body or nation."[39]

Even before Túpac Amaru's execution of Arriaga, another anticolonial movement was taking shape from the bottom up among the Aymara-speaking communities around La Paz and Potosí. In this region, the legitimacy of hereditary ethnic leaders had eroded to a greater degree than around Cusco, and local community authorities (often elected to the colonial office of village alcaldes) took the initiative in protesting the abusive practices of corregidores in forced sales and collection of tribute.[40] Such local efforts were not new, but an illiterate peasant from the community of Macha came to spearhead a wider collective strategy. Interestingly, Tomás Katari and his allies initially sought the support of new Bourbon officials against the entrenched local elite. Katari promised that in return for being allowed to determine among themselves how to apportion tribute payments, communal authorities could in fact increase revenue by cutting out corrupt middlemen. When Corregidor Joaquín Alós refused to recognize his authority, Katari traveled over two thousand miles to Buenos Aires, where he obtained a viceregal order to the Audiencia of Charcas to investigate the community claims and enact a just settlement. Instead the Audiencia ordered Katari's arrest, and its troops subsequently killed the captive. This act triggered open revolt by Katari's followers. Although Katari's leadership was distinct from that of Túpac Amaru, his movement also expressed a vision of indigenous authority at the local level that grew out of "a long-term process of cultural and political empowerment of the Andean peoples."[41]

The Amaru (Quechua) movement formed a tenuous alliance with the community-led (Aymara) revolt under a new leader from the Sicasica province near La Paz. Julián Apasa earned his living selling coca and woolens within the south-central Andean trade circuit, an occupation that allowed him to spread anticolonial plans and forge a political network. Taking the name Tupaj Katari ("Resplendent Serpent") and embodying physical and spiritual characteristics associated with Aymara warriors, Apasa effectively mobilized his peasant troops, twice setting siege to La Paz for 109 and 75 days, respectively.[42] Although Tupaj Katari was in communication with Diego Cristóbal Túpac Amaru, who was trying to maintain a multiethnic alliance from Cuzco, the Aymara soldiers often took retribution on all who gained in colonial exploitation, rather than distinguishing those born in America from those who arrived from Europe.[43] Tupaj Katari rose to prominence at the height of anticolonial protest, but had emerged out of longer-term strategies aimed at reinforcing local authority. Smaller revolts in the region of La Paz during the preceding decades had demonstrated an emerging "democracy" in action in which leaders consulted communal assemblies and Aymara peasants experimented with incorporating Spaniards and mestizos on indigenous terms into visions of a new polity.[44]

Visions of the polity that might result from Andean rebellion in the 1780s ranged from Túpac Amaru's multiethnic patria under Inka rule to Tupaj Katari's bottom-up federation of mostly Aymara communities. Revolts in which

Quechua and Aymara leaders alike experimented with practices and rituals that might incorporate non-Indians (albeit in ways those American Spaniards and mestizos might not welcome) suggest that native Andeans did not necessarily reject all outsiders from their idea of patria. As later in Haiti, where all citizens were declared "black," as Carolyn Fick shows, all members of an Andean patria might be imagined as indigenous.[45] Andrés Túpac Amaru, for example, ordered non-Indians in the town of Sorata "to dress in Indian garb, chew coca, go barefoot, and call themselves Qollas" (a reference to the Inka territory of Kollasuyu); in the mining center of Oruro Hispanic rebels voluntarily donned Inka tunics.[46] Such initiatives provide evidence to support Sinclair Thomson's claim that "race war," rather than inevitable, "was a result of political and military processes from among an array of different possibilities."[47] Although none of these revolts prevailed, nor easily conform to Western notions of nationhood, such movements can be seen as alternative projects to establish home rule of the patria, some more inclusive but authoritarian, others more exclusive but potentially more democratic.

Several decades would pass after the suppression of the rebellions of the early 1780s before major political and military movements again shook the Andes. From their role as critical intermediaries who controlled access to Andean labor and resources for Spanish conquerors, kurakas had seen the gradual erosion of their influence in the face of regime pressures. The defeat of Túpac Amaru brought an intensification of that trend. In addition to executing or deposing kurakas who had supported Túpac Amaru, colonial officials prohibited displays of Inka heritage; they even took from many loyal kurakas the authority to collect tribute.[48] Viceroy of Peru Teodoro de Croix (1784–1790) also led reforms to create a more centralized and disciplined military force that could respond to uprisings more effectively than the local militias who had performed poorly in 1780.[49]

It would be a mistake, however, to see a period after 1782 as one of complete quiescence. Provincial elites (Hispanic by reputation but often of mixed ancestry) pursued strategies of negotiation and evasion to limit the negative impacts of the Bourbon reforms, and indigenous communities returned primarily to the courts in the ongoing effort to protect their resources and limit outside exploitation.[50] One sign of the ongoing appeal of an alternative polity—for diverse inhabitants of the region—was a conspiracy in 1805. Despite memories of indigenous violence in 1780, two Hispanic provincials searched for a descendant of the Inkas to legitimate a plan to topple Spanish rule. Juan Manuel Ubalde was born in Arequipa, studied in Cusco, practiced law in Lima, and was appointed as a substitute member of the recently established Audiencia of Cusco in 1805.

His coconspirator, mineralogist Gabriel Aguilar, was born farther north in Huánuco, but had traveled widely through the trading circuits of the south-central Andes.[51] Their peregrinations traced possible boundaries of an Andean patria. Although their plans were discovered before they could be carried out, less than a decade later creoles and kurakas from Cusco jointly launched a rebellion, seizing territory from Arequipa to La Paz.

Imperial and Separatist Visions of an Andean Patria (ca. 1809–1825)
Because histories of Spanish American independence focus their studies on the nations that emerged and work their way back in time, many artificially separate Bolivian and Peruvian separatist movements. In most accounts, Peruvians are identified as the "reluctant rebels"; in these interpretations, elites remembered Túpac Amaru and feared provoking another race war, while native Andeans took no interest in the disputes between Spaniards, whether American or European.[52] Although Lima elites did remain largely royalist, many in the highlands led or joined revolts. "Bolivians" (the term did not yet exist) have a somewhat more rebellious reputation, but are noted for their formation of small *republiquetas* rather than a united front.[53] In both cases, of course, Spanish forces were defeated only with the assistance of troops arriving from the more autonomist regions of Greater Colombia and Río de la Plata. Although some Andeans (like their counterparts across Spanish America) initially remained loyal to the Spanish Crown and others opted earlier for independence, most shared a vision of a patria that encompassed territory on both shores of Lake Titicaca. And leaders in diverse political factions saw the importance of incorporating the majority indigenous population into their plans.

Urban elites throughout the Spanish empire responded to Napoleon's capture of Fernando VII by forming assemblies (juntas) to govern locally in his name, but their goals varied: some regarded their actions as a temporary measure until monarchism could be restored, others hoped to create a space for greater home rule within a reformed imperial structure, and a few envisioned a movement toward full autonomy. Lima, where both officials and merchants dreamed of reconstituting its former glory as the viceregal capital and exclusive port for Spanish South America, was notably absent from this trend. Cities in the Andean heartland, however, were among the first to establish juntas: gatherings in Chuquisaca and La Paz in 1809 preceded the formation the following year of the more famous assemblies in Caracas and Buenos Aires, and Cochabamba, Oruro, and Tacna quickly followed in 1810 and 1811.

Although members of the Hispanic elite initiated the junta in La Paz, they invited indigenous communities to send representatives. Supporters from below, moreover, pressured for measures such as the abolition of the mitá, the temporary suspension of tribute and sales taxes, and the election of local leaders. Strikingly reminiscent of earlier attempts to identify all members of an Andean patria as indigenous, rebels occasionally used the term *indio* to refer to all those born locally, grouping together "white, almost white (or having white skin), and real Indians."[54] In addition to attempting to forge an inclusive alliance within the region around La Paz, leaders planned to extend their movement throughout the Andean heartland. Their initial declaration was addressed to the "courageous inhabitants of La Paz and of the entire empire of Peru." They quickly gained adherents as far south as Potosí and Chuquisaca and sent troops toward Lower Peru and the port of Arica.[55] Although they could not hold the city of La Paz, many continued to fight for their "patria" as guerrillas in the Republiqueta of Ayopaya, a territory that included landless Aymara, indigenous communities, and mestizo and Hispanic smallholders.[56] Notably, rebel authorities adopted many of the tactics used decades earlier in the area by the Kataristas, and financed their operations in part by marketing coca.[57]

The revolts in Upper Peru envisioned an Andean patria that straddled the boundary between Peru and Río de la Plata, while authorities in Lima and Buenos Aires also vied for control over altiplano territory. Juan José Castelli, who led the first expedition to extend the power of the *porteño* junta, proclaimed that the movement aimed to liberate the indigenous population along with everyone else. As far away as Huánuco, where American Spaniards were trying to recruit support among the surrounding villages for a revolt, rumors circulated that the "Inka King Castelli" would arrive to liberate the communities and that members should prepare to greet him with traditional dances.[58] From the other direction, Viceroy José de Abascal in Lima seized upon the crisis as an opportunity to reunite Lower and Upper Peru, sending troops that scored victories over both local juntas and porteño forces. Abascal had intensified military reform, increasing the size and effectiveness of the Peruvian royal army.[59] In an effort to reinforce loyalty to the Crown, he recruited a diverse leadership to command the largely indigenous and mestizo troops. Among royal officers were loyal kurakas from Puno and Cusco, notably Mateo García Pumacahua, earlier decorated for his role in defeating Túpac Amaru. In 1812 Pumacahua was promoted to brigadier and interim president of the Cusco Audiencia, but then passed over by the permanent appointment of peninsular Manuel Pardo. American Spaniards from Arequipa, including Pío Tristan and José Manuel de

Goyeneche, returned from military service in Spain to take command of the army of Upper Peru. Mestizos such as Agustín Gamarra (Cusco) and Andrés de Santa Cruz (La Paz) also rose through the ranks.[60]

Just as Abascal was rewarding loyalty through military commissions, the convocation of the Cortes in Cádiz further altered political possibilities in the empire. In a reversal of earlier rebel attempts to Andeanize Spaniards and mestizos, the 1812 Constitution extended "Spanish" nationality to indigenous inhabitants, declaring them citizens eligible to vote and abolishing the tribute they had been assessed since conquest. The exclusion of people of African descent from citizenship would affect many along both the Pacific and Atlantic Coasts, but few in the Andean highlands. Many from various classes enthusiastically embraced the constitution during the brief periods it was in force (1812–1814 and 1820–1823).[61] Presumably they shared its vision of a new national polity in which Spaniards included all "free men who were born and reside anywhere in Spanish dominions, as well as their children" (article 5, section 1).[62] The nation, thus defined, was far vaster than the Andean heartland, much less the later nations of Peru and Bolivia. But the constitution did grant significant authority to locally elected bodies. A pyramid of municipalities and provinces within a constitutional monarchy was not so different from what Tristan Platt suggests was the indigenous vision of "cantons and provinces, departments and nations as simply the ascending levels of a segmentary system whose smallest units were to be found within the kinship and residential group."[63]

Defense of the constitution was one trigger of a major autonomist movement that began in Cusco. As in the aborted conspiracy of 1805, this rebellion was initiated by American Spaniards who sought indigenous allies; unlike the messianic dreams of Aguilar and Ubalde, its vision grew out of a new political context and its plans were more realizable. In late 1812, a lawyer circulated a letter signed by thirty-seven local notables protesting the delay in calling elections for the town council (cabildo). The Audiencia tried to restore calm by arresting some more vocal agitators, but these measures had the opposite effect of mobilizing a protest under José Angulo. When Abascal ordered a hard line against the protestors, Pumacahua, perhaps smarting from not being confirmed in his Audiencia post, joined the rebellion. Although he was cautious about his use of Inka symbolism, his descent from Huayna Capac likely bolstered his legitimacy among some, indigenous and nonindigenous alike.[64] In 1814, autonomist forces fanned out, north to Huamanga and Huancavelica and south to Arequipa, Puno, and La Paz, where they were more successful. Many soldiers and officers, like Pumacahua, had just served in the suppression of the revolts in Upper Peru, but were now mobilized for a new cause. Although the rebels were defeated by royal troops in 1815—after the restored King Fernando's abrogation of the constitution—it revealed again the potential for political alliances that crossed class and ethnic categories, and the border that had divided the two Perus in 1776.[65] As rebels in the province of Aymaraes expressed it in 1818, "We are now all of the same body, *españoles* and tribute-paying Indians."[66]

By 1820—when the Cádiz Constitution was reinstated and peninsular troops prepared to sail to South America—the royal army still controlled much Andean territory. The leaders of the increasingly successful moves toward independence elsewhere in South America recognized that they must end Spanish rule in the Andes to consolidate their own autonomy. José de San Martín landed near Lima in 1820 with soldiers from Chile and the Río de la Plata; Simón Bolívar came with Colombian troops (from regions now Venezuela, Colombia, and Ecuador) and took over patriot command in 1822. The new viceroy of Peru, José de la Serna, moved his administration from Lima to Cusco, which he called "the ancient capital of Peru," opening a last opportunity between 1821 and 1824 to construct an Andean patria within the framework of the Spanish Constitution. A local newspaper published a poem that envisioned an empire stretching across the Andes from the Pacific to the Atlantic, led by La Serna from Cusco.[67]

Despite the last stand by La Serna, local guerrillas who favored independence slowly extended their control of territory across the altiplano, while forces commanded by Bolívar and Antonio José de Sucre advanced from the north. As the balance of power tipped, American-born officers in the royal army one by one shifted allegiance to the cause of independence. The biographies of two reveal common roots in the provincial elite of the Andean heartland and the ongoing ties between Lower and Upper Peru. Agustín Gamarra was born in 1785 in Cusco, where he learned Quechua before studying Latin. He joined the king's army in 1809 to fight insurgency in Upper Peru and later the followers of Pumacahua, and by 1818 he was promoted to colonel. Then he switched sides in early 1821, volunteering to serve under San Martín.[68] Gamarra's enemies insinuated that his mother was an Indian; the mixed heritage of his future rival Andrés de Santa Cruz is undisputed. The father of Santa Cruz, originally from Huamanga, was a career military officer and midlevel royal bureaucrat, serving the viceroyalties of Peru and Río de la Plata. In the 1780s he was in La Paz to suppress the Katarista rebellion, and he later married a woman of the indigenous elite whose family remained loyal to Spain. Andrés was born in La Paz but educated in Cusco, where he courted the daughter of an Audiencia judge whom he later married in Arequipa. He pursued a career similar to Gamarra, joining the royal army in 1809 and rising to the rank of lieutenant colonel in

1817, when he was taken prisoner of war. Escaping to rejoining the royal army in Peru, he fell captive once again—and changed sides.

In addition to adapting to the fortunes of war, American-born officers saw that their chances of promotion in the Spanish army were limited. In the independence forces, by contrast, Santa Cruz rose quickly to become Bolívar's chief of staff for the Peruvian division. The gambits of Santa Cruz and Gamarra paid off in 1824 with the definitive patriot victories at Junín (where Santa Cruz fought) and Ayacucho (where Gamarra participated). Although Bolívar favored a union of the two Perus, he followed Sucre's advice to convene a congress in 1825 that founded a separate Bolivia.

An Andean Nation Briefly Realized: Trade Circuits and Confederation (ca. 1825–1839)

Before picking up the story of the intertwined political trajectories of Gamarra and Santa Cruz and their roles in promoting an Andean patria from bases in Peru and Bolivia respectively, let us revisit the regional economy during the first half of the nineteenth century. The prolonged fighting between separatist and royalist forces between 1809 and 1825 took a serious toll on production across region. Peasants and workers were pressed into service, armies requisitioned supplies from communities, and mining came almost to a halt. Nonetheless, the production of silver and other minerals resumed more quickly than often assumed, albeit with regional variations. Moderate levels of silver extraction continued in Potosí, much of it by indigenous and mestizo small-scale producers, as the mitá draft was abolished at independence. Puno also remained an important mining center integrated into both regional trade circuits and the global market.[69] Exports from and imports to Bolivia went through both the new country's only port at Cobija on the Pacific, as well as the established trading center of Arica, which remained part of Peru until 1883. With production below pre-1810 levels, however, much Bolivian silver was minted and used to buy supplies from the regions of Cusco and Arequipa rather than reaching any port.[70]

Jurist José María Dalence, a native of Oruro educated in Chuquisaca, published an overview on the geography, demography, and economy of Bolivia in 1851 that reveals continuities from late colonial times. La Paz remained the most populous department, and the most indigenous; along with parts of Potosí and Oruro, it still produced large quantities of coca and herds of camelids. Dalence noted that while most of the nation's borders were secure, the boundary between La Paz and Puno down to Arica remained porous. In addition to Bolivia's large

FIGURE 9.2. Coinage of a realm that briefly was: The Peru-Bolivia Confederation, 1838

imbalance in global trade, the nation imported more wine, liquor, and sugar from Cusco, Puno, and Arequipa, than the value of its exports to Peru.[71] Strikingly, much of this transborder trade was transacted with small-denomination coins (known as the *peso feble*) minted in Bolivia with lower silver content than either the colonial peso or the postindependence Peruvian currency. For the most part, European merchants refused to accept this new currency, as did the Chilean government, which was trying to gain control of new import trades through its port of Valparaíso. Authorities in Lima periodically protested the devalued coins, but they continued to circulate within southern Peru. Informally, the Andean heartland had its own currency that crossed national boundaries.[72]

Although the regional economy experienced much continuity, new export products also emerged in response to demands of an industrializing Europe. Southern Peru became an important source of wool for British textile mills. Trading houses in Arequipa sent mestizo middlemen up into the altiplano to buy both sheep and alpaca wool, which was shipped out through the port of Islay; until at least the middle of the nineteenth century, producers also directly marketed wool at regional fairs in the highlands.[73] Although both old and new exports were important to the postindependence economy of the south-central Andes, volumes were small compared to the colonial period or the later nineteenth century. With low revenue from customs duties, the new governments of Peru and Bolivia continued to collect head taxes (renamed from "tribute" to "contribution") from the substantial indigenous populations of the highland regions. This taxation policy had contradictory effects. On the one hand, it distinguished Indians from other Peruvians and Bolivians, setting them up for second-class citizenship. On the other hand, paying tribute protected communities from privatization and dispossession of their land base.[74] As Erick Langer details, the decades after independence allowed indigenous people in the Andes and elsewhere to gain greater control over their livelihoods.[75]

Native Andeans constituted a majority in this region, and there were liberals on both sides of the new border who were relatively optimistic about the possibilities of integrating them into their vision for a new patria. José Domingo Choquehuanca, a subprefect and elected representative from Azángaro (near Lake Titicaca), provides an interesting example. Through his father, a priest, he was descended from Inka Huayna Capac, but his grandfather, cacique Diego Chukiwanka, had opposed Túpac Amaru, provoking local rebels to sack his properties in revenge.[76] Choquehuanca, by contrast, joined with other students at the university in Chuquisaca to support independence, and he tied their struggle to earlier indigenous rebellions. He praised the brave fight of indigenous rebels for independence since 1780, emphasizing that Azángaro warriors had rallied to rebellion in 1814, joined in expeditions to both Arequipa and La Paz, and continued to fight even after the rebellion's leaders saw their cause as lost.[77]

As he compiled a report on the province's population and economy covering the five years after independence, Choquehuanca envisioned indigenous citizens as key participants. According to his figures, the citizens on the civic registries varied from 20 to 40 percent of the adult male population of each district, proportions including native Andeans.[78] He estimated that as many as two-thirds of indigenous property owners along with some mestizos belonged to the middle class (what he called the *acomodados*).[79] District by district, he provided estimates of agricultural and textile production, tracking export of textiles and animal products to Arequipa, Cusco, and La Paz and imports of coca, liquor, and grains from these regions. According to his estimates, about 64 percent of the province's wool-producing sheep and 71 percent of cattle were in indigenous hands. Choquehuanca criticized landowners and officials who called Indians lazy and mistreated them, pointing out that the indigenous population had learned from colonialism that any outward sign of economic success was an invitation to expropriation and coerced labor. "Pay them according to the law," he asserted, "and there would be more than enough workers for all manner of labor."[80] Although he acknowledged the difficulties of educating a population who were not raised to speak Spanish, he claimed that the middling indigenous population already sent their children to Arequipa to learn Spanish in order to expand their trading networks.[81] Choquehuanca supported the political reunification of the Andean heartland, and was later accused by his political opponents of not being a true citizen of Peru due to his 1789 birth in Chuquisaca.[82] In spirit, he was a citizen of an Andean patria still held together by a regional economy in which mineral production stimulated agriculture and small-scale manufacturing.

While trade circuits continued to integrate southern Peru and Bolivia, despite the new national border, economic development in central and northern Peru followed a distinct path. The greatest mining revival in Peru occurred to the northeast of Lima at Cerro de Pasco, where copper would eventually replace silver as the primary export. Demand for manufactures and foodstuffs was largely met in its immediate hinterland. Sugar and cotton plantations expanded along the northern coast, but only later would be integrated into the world market. During the 1820s and 1830s, protectionist, politically conservative elites in Lima and the North faced off against free traders and liberals in the South, especially Arequipa.[83] After 1840, world demand for fertilizers triggered the infamous guano boom, which for several decades provided the central government in Lima with critical revenues and enriched the capital's merchant elite—but did little to transform the country's interior highlands, especially in the South.[84]

Given economic interests distinct from Lima and northern Peru, elites in southern Peru and Bolivia, including Gamarra and Santa Cruz, kept alive political plans to reunite the Andean heartland after its partition at independence. The choices before the congress that convened in La Paz in 1825 were to join Peru, to join the United Provinces (the former viceroyalty of Río de la Plata) or to declare autonomy. Either of the first two options could have thrown off the delicate balance of power among emerging republics; local elites were wary of submitting to authorities in either Lima or Buenos Aires. The congress voted to establish an entirely new country, named Bolivia in honor of the "Liberator."[85] (In 1839 the capital's name was changed from Chuquisaca to Sucre, honoring the country's first president.) Santa Cruz, who agreed to be a representative despite his concern that it would harm his political future in Peru, wrote to a friend that an important minority, notably delegates from La Paz (who were underrepresented relative to the department's population), favored union with Peru. Although the independence of Bolivia was an expedient political compromise in 1825, the constitution proposed by Bolívar and approved the following year left open the possibility of federation with Peru and even Colombia.[86]

Despite the creation of two nations, the constitutions of both Peru and Bolivia granted citizenship to all who had fought in the patriot army. Therefore, Santa Cruz was able to serve as interim chief executive of Peru in 1827 and as elected president of Bolivia the next year. Gamarra began by establishing his power base as prefect of Cusco, from where he crossed the border into Bolivia in 1828 to overthrow the "foreigner" Sucre before launching his own presidency of Peru in 1829. The two caudillos became rivals, each eyeing the territory governed by the other. As conservative Gamarra fought Peruvian liberals over trade policies and constitutions, Santa Cruz seized an opportunity to ally with southern liberals to reunite Bolivia and Peru. From 1836 to 1839 he forged a Peru-Bolivian confederation of three states: Northern Peru, Southern Peru, and Bolivia.

Several models influenced the polity Santa Cruz aimed to construct. He shared Bolívar's belief that a strong military guaranteed political stability while providing upward mobility for capable soldiers (uniformed in fine cloth from Cusco). His promulgation of new civil and criminal codes drew heavily from Napoleonic laws, adapted to an Andean society that was corporatist and hierarchical rather than composed of theoretically equal individuals. Santa Cruz's continuation of paternalist policies that protected separate jurisdictions for indigenous communities allowed local Aymara and Quechua authorities to exercise a degree of sovereignty at the local level. It was no coincidence that he chose Puno as the site to issue a lengthy decree detailing rights and protections for indigenous citizens, including exemption from all taxes other than the "direct contribution" (i.e., tribute).[87] In May and June 1836, Santa Cruz visited Arequipa, Cusco, and Puno, dispensing orders and promoting state institutions that would appeal to his supporters in Southern Peru: schools and law faculties (reserving places for descendants of the Inkas in Cusco) and compensation for property losses at the hands of the confederation's enemies in the "heroic" city of Arequipa. Most important, he abolished trade barriers. The continuous movement of Santa Cruz, in his role as "protector" of the confederation, throughout southern Peru and Bolivia prevented one city in the heartland from claiming preeminence over the others—but did nothing to allay fears in Lima and northern Peru that their state had a subordinate status.

We will never know what forms of governance might eventually have emerged within the Andean federation. The union of Peru and Bolivia was seen as a threat by neighboring Chile, whose leaders allied with Gamarra to defeat Santa Cruz's army in 1839. The confederation also faced internal tensions. Although support for union was strong in La Paz, elites in Chuquisaca feared that Peruvians would dominate. In Peru, southern free traders were enthusiastic about the abolition of internal borders, but northerners had little to gain from those markets. The Lima aristocracy feared losing power to competitors in indigenous highlands, and Felipe Pardo y Aliaga relentlessly lampooned the confederation

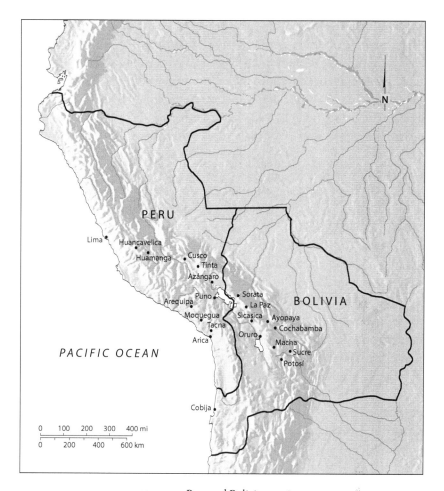

MAP 9.2. Peru and Bolivia, ca. 1840

and Santa Cruz in satiric verses that ridiculed the notion of indigenous citizen-ship and leadership.[88] Hispanic elites in Lima would neither relinquish their claim to southern Peru nor accept a broader union where the political center of gravity could shift from the coast to the Andean heartland.

Conclusions

The economic and political integration of an Andean patria centered on Lake Titicaca reached its apogee under the Peru-Bolivian Confederation, but it did not collapse in 1839. While subsequent governments in Peru and Bolivia continually renegotiated commercial treaties, merchants in La Paz and southern Peru continued to advocate reunification into the 1840s.[89] After midcentury, however, divergence predominated. Distinct export booms of silver in Bolivia and wool in southern Peru pulled trade circuits toward these nodes within the global market and away from trans-Andean commerce. As revenue from exports increased, moreover, national states relied less on the taxes paid by indigenous populations and the regional currency, the *peso feble*, depreciated. Later, with the construction of railroads to get newly valuable commodities to ports, opportunities declined for indigenous traders with mule or llama trains.[90] These economic shifts were accompanied by policies to privatize communal land, laying the groundwork for the expansion of commercial haciendas in the second half of the century.[91]

Some provincial elites and intellectuals continued to imagine regional integration, but their visions were increasingly disconnected from the economic activities and movements of the heartland's majority. As late as 1868, Bolivian artist Melchor María Mercado, who was born in Chuquisaca and traveled throughout Bolivia and southern Peru, painted a series of landscapes linking the mountains around La Paz down to the coastal cities of Tacna and Arica.[92] And as the War of the Pacific heated up in 1880, Peruvian commander-in-chief Nicolás de Piérola proposed a federation with Bolivia similar to that tried under Santa Cruz, which his father had supported. Invoking a shared history of struggle against Spain from 1780 to 1825, Piérola declared that when citizens of the renewed federation were asked about their nationality, they would respond, "I am Inca." Inka, but presumably not indigenous, as the speeches and draft treaties mentioned "Indians" merely six times.[93] Native Andeans for their part continued to resist threats to their livelihoods; but increasingly their movements and alliances were contained within the national borders of Peru and Bolivia and targeted officials in their respective capitals.[94]

Advocates of an Andean patria centered in the altiplano did not succeed in building an enduring nation-state, but not because such plans lacked support or a material basis between the middle of the eighteenth and the middle of the nineteenth centuries. Boundaries and polities throughout the Americas were in flux in this period, as detailed by the essays in this volume. Although we tend to associate nations with republics, we have American examples of successful constitutional monarchies in Cuba and Brazil—and several experiments in Mexico from 1821 to 1867. The early Andean heartland movements that looked to an Inka sovereign or a Spanish monarch, were not radically distinct from the Peru-Bolivia Confederation, with its powerful military caudillo. All these imagined communities, moreover, were rooted in corporatist politics that recognized a degree of local authority in communities—Hispanic cabildos or in-digenous councils.[95] The imagined and contested patrias linked communities in spaces continuously being constructed rather than rigidly bounded.

As drivers of mules and llamas plied their trade along highland routes throughout the Andean heartland, they carried with them more than wool, coca, and wheat. News of tax policy, of war and rebellion, of the rise of new Inkas, and of grievances against Spaniards traversed these same routes. Such reports were not received and interpreted in identical ways in different provinces or by distinct social groups. Nevertheless, broad coalitions repeatedly converged to challenge not just orders from Madrid, but from Lima and Buenos Aires. Ethnic conflict was always possible, but at key times Spanish liberals declared Indians to be "Spanish," and rebels called Spanish Americans "indios." They failed, it is true, to establish alternative polities for more than a few years at a time, facing overwhelming military force from outside, whether Lima or San-tiago, as well as ongoing internal tensions. But the nations that were established struggled with their own challenges: to develop strong economic foundations and promote a common identity, and to resist foreign invasions that further reduced their borders by the end of the nineteenth century. To observers in Cusco in 1780, La Paz in 1809, or Arequipa in 1836, such boundaries—on maps as well as in political belonging—were by no means foreordained.

Notes

Conversations with the contributors to this volume helped to shape my thinking. I would particularly like to thank John Tutino, Erick Langer, and Sinclair Thomson for their constructive feedback on written drafts. The first epigraph is from Ward Stavig and Ella Schmidt, eds. and trans., *The Tupac Amaru and Catarista Rebellions: An Anthology of Sources* (Indianapolis and Cambridge: Hackett, 2008), 73; the sec-ond is Santa Cruz as quoted from Juan Gualberto Valdivia in Alfonso Crespo, *Santa Cruz: El cóndor indio* (Mexico City: Fondo de Cultura Económica, 1944), 206.

1 Brooke Larson, *Trials of Nation Making: Liberalism, Race, and Ethnicity in the Andes, 1810–1910* (Cambridge: Cambridge University Press, 2004).

2 It is difficult (and indeed contrary to the spirit of this essay) to draw precise bound-aries for this region. It could include part of modern-day Ayacucho in Peru, but likely excludes the eastern and far southern regions of Bolivia (i.e., Santa Cruz and Tarija). Much of the literature refers to this region as the southern Andes (*sur andino*), but to clearly distinguish it from either southern Peru or areas even farther south, I will use the term Andean heartland or south-central Andes. For good overviews of the historical constitution of this region, see Brooke Larson, "Andean Communities, Political Cultures, and Markets: The Changing Contours of a Field," in *Ethnicity, Markets, and Migration in the Andes: At the Crossroads of History and*

Anthropology, ed. Brooke Larson and Olivia Harris (Durham, NC: Duke University Press, 1995), 5–53; Marie-Danielle Demélas, *La invención política: Bolivia, Ecuador, Perú en el siglo XIX* (Lima: Instituto Francés de Estudios Andinos and Instituto de Estudios Peruanos, 2003); and Xavier Albó et al., eds., *La integración surandina: Cinco siglos después* (Cuzco: Centro de Estudios Regionales Andinos "Bartolome de Las Casas," Corporación Norte Grande Taller de Estudios Andinos, Universidad Católica del Norte de Antofagasta, 1996).

3   Dennis O. Flynn and Arturo Giráldez, "Born with a 'Silver Spoon': The Origin of World Trade in 1571," *Journal of World History* 6:2 (1995): 201–221.

4   Carlos Sempat Assadourian, *El sistema de la economía colonial: Mercado interno, regiones y espacio económico* (Lima: Instituto de Estudios Peruanos, 1982).

5   Alfredo Ávila and John Tutino, "Becoming Mexico: The Conflictive Search for a North American Nation," in this volume. Tutino further distinguishes two zones in New Spain—a more indigenous Mesoamerica and the racially diverse and economically dynamic Spanish North America in *Making a New World: Founding Capitalism in the Bajío and Spanish North America* (Durham, NC: Duke University Press, 2011).

6   On the complexities of the links among indigenous tribute, communal governance, and national belonging, see Tristan Platt, *Estado boliviano y ayllu andino: Tierra y tributo en el Norte de Potosí* (Lima: Instituto de Estudios Peruanos, 1982); Marta Irurozqui Victoriano, *"A bala, piedra y palo": La construcción de la ciudadanía política en Bolivia, 1826–1952* (Sevilla: Diputación de Sevilla, 2000); Núria Sala i Vila, *Y se armó el tole tole: Tributo indígena y movimientos sociales en el Virreinato del Perú, 1790–1814* (Ayacucho: Instituto de Estudios Regionales José María Arguedas, 1996), 39, 164–176; and Christine Hünefeldt, *Lucha por la tierra y protesta indígena: Las comunidades indígenas del Perú entre Colonia y República, 1800–1830* (Bonn: Bonner Amerikanische Studien, 1982), 156–173.

7   Nils Jacobsen, *Mirages of Transition: The Peruvian Altiplano, 1780–1930* (Berkeley and Los Angeles: University of California Press, 1993), 47–48. Charles Arnade references a similar plan proposed by the Intendant of Potosí; Charles W. Arnade, *The Emergence of the Republic of Bolivia* (New York: Russell & Russell, 1957, 1970), 195.

8   Jordana Dym, "The Republic of Guatemala: Stitching Together a New Country," in this volume.

9   On concepts of patria, see Rossana Barragán, "Españoles patricios y españoles europeos: Conflictos intra-elites e identidades en la ciudad de La Paz en vísperas de la independencia 1770–1781," in *Entre la retórica y la insurgencia: Las ideas y los movimientos sociales en los Andes, siglo XVIII*, ed. Charles Walker (Cuzco: Centro de Estudios Regionales Andinos "Bartolomé de las Casas," 1996), 113–171; Marta Irurozqui, "De cómo el vecino hizo al ciudadano en Charcas y de cómo el ciudadano conservó al vecino en Bolivia, 1809–1830," in *Revolución, independencia y las nuevas naciones de América*, ed. Jaime E. Rodríguez (Madrid: Fundación MAPFRE TAVERA, 2005), 451–484; Ximena Medinaceli, "Elementos para imaginar una nación: El discurso del Aldeano," in *Bosquejo del estado en que se halla la riqueza nacional de*

Bolivia presentado al examen de la Nación por un Adleano hijo de ella, Año de 1830, ed. Ana María Lema and Rossana R. Barragán (La Paz: Plural Editores, Facultad de Humanidades y Ciencias de la Educación, Universidad Mayor de San Andrés, 1994), 149–155; and Javier F. Marion, "*Indios blancos*: Nascent Polities and Social Convergence in the Ayopaya Rebellion, Alto Perú (Bolivia), 1814–1821," *Colonial Latin American Historical Review* 15:4 (2006), 345–375.

10 Assadourian, *El sistema de la economía colonial.*

11 Peter J. Bakewell, *Miners of the Red Mountain* (Albuquerque: University of New Mexico Press, 1984); Jeffrey A. Cole, *The Potosí Mita, 1573–1700: Compulsory Indian Labor in the Andes* (Stanford, CA: Stanford University Press, 1985); Enrique Tandeter, *Coercion and Market: Silver Mining in Colonial Potosí, 1692–1826* (Albuquerque: University of New Mexico Press, 1993); and Ann Zulawski, *They Eat from Their Labor: Work and Social Change in Colonial Bolivia* (Pittsburgh: University of Pittsburgh Press, 1995). Several historians have demonstrated the ways in which gender relations were key to indigenous success in commerce (not to mention survival) within mining regions: Ann Zulawski, "Social Differentiation, Gender, and Ethnicity: Urban Indian Women in Colonial Bolivia, 1640–1725," *Latin American Research Review* 25:2 (1990): 93–113; Bianca Premo, "From the Pockets of Women: The Gendering of the Mita, Migration and Tribute in Colonial Chucuito, Peru," *The Americas* 57:1 (2000), 63–94; and Jane E. Mangan, *Trading Roles: Gender, Ethnicity, and the Urban Economy in Colonial Potosí* (Durham, NC: Duke University Press, 2005).

12 Although demand from China drove up silver prices between 1700 and 1750, Potosí's recovery did not begin until 1730 and peaked in 1780; Dennis O. Flynn and Arturo Giráldez, "Cycles of Silver: Global Economic Unity through the Mid-Eighteenth Century," *Journal of World History* 13:2 (2002), 391–427. Profitability also varied with the price of mercury and ultimately rested on the subsidy provided by the mitá labor draft; Tandeter, *Coercion and Market,* esp. 1–51, 115.

13 For production trends, see Richard L. Garner, "Long-Term Silver Mining Trends in Spanish America: A Comparative Analysis of Peru and Mexico," *American Historical Review* 93:4 (1988), 901–902. On mining in eighteenth-century Upper Peru, see Herbert Klein, *Bolivia: The Evolution of a Multi-Ethnic Community,* 2nd ed. (New York: Oxford University Press, 1992). For Lower Peru, see John Fisher, "Mining and the Peruvian Economy in the Late Colonial Period," in *The Economies of Mexico and Peru during the Late Colonial Period, 1760–1810,* ed. Nils Jacobsen and Hans-Jürgen Puhle (Berlin: Colloquium Verlag, 1986), 46–59. On Potosí, see Rose Marie Buechler, *The Mining Society of Potosi, 1776–1810* (Ann Arbor: Published for Dept. of Geography, Syracuse University, by University Microfilms International, 1981).

14 Enrique Tandeter, Vilma Milletich, María Matilde Ollier, and Beatríz Ruibal, "Indians in Late Colonial Markets: Sources and Numbers," in Larson and Harris, *Ethnicity, Markets, and Migration in the Andes,* 196–223.

15 Herbert S. Klein, *Haciendas and Ayllus: Rural Society in the Bolivian Andes in the Eighteenth and Nineteenth Centuries* (Stanford, CA: Stanford University Press,

1993), 90–99. Officials in Lima similarly noted that indigenous communities competed effectively with haciendas in Peru; Hünefeldt, *Lucha por la tierra y protesta indígena*, 137–138.

16 Platt, *Estado boliviano y ayllu andino*, 23–35; and María Luisa Soux, *El complejo proceso hacia la independencia de Charcas (1808–1826): Guerra, ciudadanía, conflictos locales y participación indígena en Oruro* (La Paz: Plural Editores; Lima: IFEA, Instituto Francés de Estudios Andinos, 2010), 44–56. Trade between Cochabamba and southern Peru declined in the nineteenth century; see Brooke Larson, *Colonialism and Agrarian Transformation in Bolivia: Cochabamba, 1550–1900* (Princeton, NJ: Princeton University Press, 1988); and Robert H. Jackson, *Regional Markets and Agrarian Transformation in Bolivia: Cochabamba, 1539–1960* (Albuquerque: University of New Mexico Press, 1994).

17 Tandeter et al., "Indians in Late Colonial Markets," 205. For studies of the production of wines and brandies in the region of Arequipa, see Kendall Brown, *Bourbons and Brandy: Imperial Reform in Eighteenth-Century Arequipa* (Albuquerque: University of New Mexico Press, 1980); and Prudence M. Rice, *Vintage Moquegua: History, Wine, and Archaeology on a Colonial Peruvian Periphery* (Austin: University of Texas Press, 2012).

18 On trade between Arequipa and both Cusco and Upper Peru, see Brown, *Bourbons and Brandy*, 73–102; and Alberto Flores Galindo, *Arequipa y el sur andino: Ensayo de historia regional (siglos XVIII–XX)* (Lima: Editorial Horizonte, 1977), 24–30.

19 Nils Jacobsen, "Livestock Complexes in Late Colonial Peru and New Spain: An Attempt at Comparison," in Jacobsen and Puhle, *The Economies of Mexico and Peru during the Late Colonial Period*, 113–142, especially 120.

20 Jacobsen, *Mirages of Transition*, 31–51.

21 Barragán, "Españoles patricios y españoles europeos," 117; and Sala i Vila, *Y se armó el tole tole*, 39.

22 David Cahill, *From Rebellion to Independence in the Andes: Soundings from Southern Peru, 1750–1830* (Amsterdam: Aksant, 2002), 45–48.

23 O'Phelan, *Un siglo de rebeliones anti-coloniales: Perú y Bolivia, 1700–1783* (Cuzco: CERA Bartolomé de las Casas, 1988), 175–187.

24 Ward Stavig, *The World of Túpac Amaru: Conflict, Community, and Identity in Colonial Peru* (Lincoln: University of Nebraska Press, 1999); and Sinclair Thomson, *We Alone Will Rule: Native Andean Politics in the Age of Insurgency* (Madison: University of Wisconsin Press, 2002).

25 Drawing the boundaries of eighteenth-century rebellion is complicated. Scarlett O'Phelan has proposed that the economic zone centered on providing Potosí with supplies (and, one could add, labor) and running through the highlands to Lima, gave rise to a zone of political consciousness and rebellion; Scarlett O'Phelan, *Rebellions and Revolts in Eighteenth-Century Peru and Upper Peru* (Köln: Böhlau, 1985). Steve J. Stern has argued for including the central highlands of Peru as an area of anticolonial resistance; Steven J. Stern, "The Age of Andean Insurrection, 1742–1782: A Reappraisal," in *Resistance, Rebellion, and Consciousness in the Andean Peasant World: 18th to 20th Centuries*, ed. Stern (Madison: University

of Wisconsin Press, 1987), 34–93. In a spatial analysis of rebellion limited to the region of Cuzco, Magnus Mörner and Efraín Trelles find a correlation between the attitudes of kurakas and communities toward Túpac Amaru based upon the old Inca divisions of Chinchasuyo (largely loyalist in 1780) and Kollasuyo (largely rebel in 1780); Magnus Mörner and Efraín Trelles, "A Test of Causal Interpretations of the Túpac Amaru Rebellion," in Stern, *Resistance, Rebellion, and Consciousness,* 94–109, especially 100–109.

26 O'Phelan, *Rebellions and Revolts in Eighteenth-Century Peru and Upper Peru;* David Cahill, "Taxonomy of a Colonial 'Riot': The Arequipa Disturbances of 1780," in *Reform and Insurrection in Bourbon New Granada and Peru,* ed. John R. Fisher, Allan J. Kuethe, and Anthony McFarlane (Baton Rouge: Louisiana State University Press, 1990), 255–291; and Sarah C. Chambers, *From Subjects to Citizens: Honor, Gender, and Politics in Arequipa, Peru, 1780–1854* (University Park: Pennsylvania State University Press, 1999), 17–20.

27 For the role of traders in various revolts, see O'Phelan, *Rebellions and Revolts in Eighteenth-Century Peru and Upper Peru.* For traders generally, see Luis Miguel Glave, *Trajinantes: Caminos indígenas en la sociedad colonial, siglos XVI/XVII* (Lima: Instituto de Apoyo Agrario, 1989).

28 On Túpac Amaru as a muleteer, see Mörner and Trelles, "A Test of Causal Interpretations of the Túpac Amaru Rebellion," 102; and Stavig, *The World of Túpac Amaru,* 157.

29 Charles F. Walker, *Smoldering Ashes: Cuzco and the Creation of Republican Peru, 1780–1840* (Durham, NC: Duke University Press, 1999), 25–28. On the role of Bastidas and other women, see Leon G. Campbell, "Women and the Great Rebellion in Peru, 1780–1783," *Americas* 42:2 (1985): 163–196; and Charles F. Walker, *The Tupac Amaru Rebellion* (Cambridge, MA: Belknap Press of Harvard University Press, 2014).

30 John H. Rowe, "The Incas under Spanish Colonial Institutions," *Hispanic American Historical Review* 37:2 (1957), 176 as quoted in Stavig, *The World of Túpac Amaru,* 206.

31 Stavig, *The World of Túpac Amaru,* 215, 221; and Cahill, *From Rebellion to Independence in the Andes,* 97.

32 In addition to the works cited in other notes, see Walker, *The Tupac Amaru Rebellion,* and Sergio Serulnikov, *Revolution in the Andes: The Age of Túpac Amaru,* trans. David Frye (Durham, NC: Duke University Press, 2013).

33 Documents about the rebellion were transcribed and published in Comisión Nacional del Sesquicentenario de la Independencia del Perú, *Colección documental de la independencia del Perú,* Vol. 2, *La Rebelión de Túpac Amaru* (Lima, 1971).

34 John Rowe, "El movimiento nacional inca del siglo XVIII," in *Túpac Amaru II—1780,* ed. Alberto Flores Galindo (Lima: Retablo de Pael Ediciones, 1976), 13–53; Thomas Cummins, "We Are the Other: Peruvian Portraits of Colonial Kurakacuna," in *Transatlantic Encounters: The History of Early Colonial Peru,* ed. Rolena Adorno and Kenneth Andrien (Berkeley: University of California Press, 1991), 203–231; and Alberto Flores Galindo, *Buscando un Inca* (Lima: Editorial

Horizonte, 1988), translated and published in English by Carlos Aguirre, Charles F. Walker, and Willie Hiatt as *In Search of an Inca: Identity and Utopia in the Andes* (Cambridge: Cambridge University Press, 2010).

35 See, for example, Túpac Amaru's "Edict to the Province of Chichas," in Stavig and Schmidt, *The Tupac Amaru and Catarista Rebellions*, 73–74.

36 Walker, *The Tupac Amaru Rebellion*, 86–108, 180–242.

37 See, for example, Leon G. Campbell, "Ideology and Factionalism during the Great Rebellion, 1780–1782," in Stern, *Resistance, Rebellion, and Consciousness*, 110–139. For a study of the kuraka class during this period, see David T. Garrett, *Shadows of Empire: The Indian Nobility of Cusco, 1750–1825* (Cambridge: Cambridge University Press, 2005).

38 Jan Szemiński, "Why Kill the Spaniard? New Perspectives on Andean Insurrectionary Ideology in the 18th Century," in Stern, *Resistance, Rebellion, and Consciousness*, 166–192.

39 Walker, *Smoldering Ashes*, 16–22, 51–54; quote on p. 17.

40 Thomson, *We Alone Will Rule*, especially 3–138.

41 Sergio Serulnikov, *Subverting Colonial Authority: Challenges to Spanish Rule in the Eighteenth-Century Southern Andes* (Durham, NC: Duke University Press, 2003), 220.

42 On Túpaj Katari, see Thomson, *We Alone Will Rule*, 180–231.

43 Nicholas Robins argues that the movement aimed at carrying out a genocide against non-Indians; Nicholas A. Robins, *Genocide and Millennialism in Upper Peru: The Great Rebellion of 1780–1782* (Westport, CT: Praeger, 2002).

44 Thomson, *We Alone Will Rule*, 276.

45 Carolyn Fick, "From Slave Colony to Black Nation: Haiti's Revolutionary Inversion," in this volume.

46 Sinclair Thomson, "Was There Race in Colonial Latin America?: Identifying Selves and Others in the Insurgent Andes," in *Histories of Race and Racism: The Andes and Mesoamerica from Colonial Times to the Present*, ed. Laura Gotkowitz (Durham, NC: Duke University Press, 2011), 85. On the rebellion in Oruro, see also Fernando Cajías de la Vega, *Oruro 1781: Sublevación de indios y rebelión Criolla*, 2 vols. (La Paz: Instituto de Estudios Bolivianos, 2005).

47 Thomson, "Was There Race in Colonial Latin America?," 79.

48 Garrett, *Shadows of Empire*, 211–256.

49 Leon G. Campbell, "The Army of Peru and the Túpac Amaru Revolt, 1780–1783," *Hispanic American Historical Review* 56:1 (1976), 31–57; and Mónica Ricketts, "The Rise of the Bourbon Military in Peru, 1768–1820," *Colonial Latin American Review* 21:3 (2012), 413–439.

50 Walker, *Smoldering Ashes*, 55–83; Thomson, *We Alone Will Rule*, 232–268; Chambers, *From Subjects to Citizens*, 31–37, 45–90; and Sala i Vila, *Y se armó el tole tole*. For the importance of the establishment of an Audiencia in Cusco as a forum for indigenous legal protest, see David Cahill and Scarlett O'Phelan, "Forging Their Own History: Indian Insurgency in the Southern Peruvian Sierra," *Bulletin of Latin American Research* 11:2 (1992), 125–167, especially 130–131.

51 On Ubalde and Aguilar, see Alberto Flores Galindo, "In Search of an Inca," in Stern, *Resistance, Rebellion, and Consciousness,* 193–210.

52 For an example of the "reluctant rebels" interpretation, see John Lynch, *The Spanish American Revolutions, 1808–1826,* 2nd ed. (New York: Norton, 1986). For some of the interpretive debates within Peru, see Alberto Flores Galindo, ed., *Independencia y revolución,* 2 vols. (Lima: Instituto Nacional de Cultura, 1987). For a refutation of the notion that there was little internal support for independence within Peru or Bolivia, see Scarlet O'Phelan Godoy, "El mito de la 'independencia concedida': Los programas políticos del siglo XVIII y del temprano XIX en el Perú y Alto Perú (1730–1814)," *Histórica* 9:2 (1985), 155–191.

53 Arnade, *The Emergence of the Republic of Bolivia;* René Danilo Arze Aguirre, *Participación popular en la independencia de Bolivia* (La Paz, Bolivia: Organización de los Estados Americanos, 1979); and Marion, "*Indios blancos.*" For a primary source narrative in which a midlevel patriot leader occasionally acknowledges the heroism of indigenous combatants, see José Santos Vargas, *Diario de un comandante de la independencia americana, 1814–1825* (Mexico: Siglo Veintiuno, 1982).

54 Soux, *El complejo proceso hacia la independencia de Charcas,* 230–240; quote on 234; and Marion, "*Indios blancos,*" 366–367.

55 Soux, *El complejo proceso hacia la independencia de Charcas,* 118–119; and Arze Aguirre, *Participación popular,* 160–161. According to Scarlett O'Phelan, members of the leadership included natives of Cusco and Arequipa as well as La Paz, Scarlett O'Phelan Godoy, "Santa Cruz y Gamarra: El proyecto de la confederación y el control político del sur andino," in *Guerra, región y nación: La Confederación Perú-Boliviana, 1836–1839,* ed. Carlos Donoso Rojas and Jaime Rosenblitt B. (Santiago: Dirección de Bibliotecas, Archivos y Museos, 2009), 17–38; here 21–22.

56 Arnade, *The Emergence of The Republic of Bolivia;* Arze Aguirre, *Participación popular;* Marion, "*Indios blancos*"; Vargas, *Diario de un comandante;* and Irurozqui, "De cómo el vecino hizo al ciudadano."

57 Marion, "*Indios blancos,*" 361–365.

58 Hünefeldt, *Lucha por la tierra y protesta indígena,* 174–187; and Sarah C. Chambers, "The Limits of a Pan-Ethnic Alliance in the Independence of Peru: The Huánuco Rebellion of 1812" (MA thesis, University of Wisconsin–Madison, 1986).

59 Ricketts, "The Rise of the Bourbon Military in Peru," 419.

60 Chambers, *From Subjects to Citizens,* 35–36.

61 Chambers, *From Subjects to Citizens,* 140; Walker, *Smoldering Ashes,* 92, and Natalia Sobrevilla Perea, *The Caudillo of the Andes: Andrés de Santa Cruz* (Cambridge: Cambridge University Press, 2011), 44–45. Núria Sala i Vila is currently researching elections held in Peru during the liberal period of 1820 to 1823.

62 Rafael Garófano and Juan Ramón de Páramo, *La constitución gaditana de 1812,* 2nd ed. (Cádiz: Diputación de Cádiz, 1987); for a translation of these articles into English, see Sarah C. Chambers and John Charles Chasteen, *Latin American Independence: An Anthology of Sources* (Indianapolis: Hackett, 2010), 97.

63 Tristan Platt, "Simón Bolívar, the Sun of Justice and the Amerindian Virgin: Andean Conceptions of the Patria in Nineteenth-Century Potosí," *Journal of Latin American*

Studies 25 (1993), 159–185. Víctor Peralta Ruiz and Marta Irurozqui Victoriano, *Por la concordia, la fusión y el unitarismo: Estado y caudillismo en Bolivia, 1825–1880* (Madrid: Consejo Superior de Investigaciones Científicas, 2000), 139–248, discuss the ways in which Spanish concepts of local belonging (*vecindad*) continued to shape understandings of citizenship (*ciudadanía*) into the nineteenth century. Langer, citing Platt, notes that for elites as well as Indians, notions of being American remained strong as compared to specific national identities; Erick D. Langer, "Bajo la sombra del Cerro Rico; Redes comerciales y el fracaso del nacionalismo económico en el Potosí del siglo XIX," *Revista Andina* 37 (2003), 77–91, here 84.

64 For an argument that indigenous peasants in villages around Cusco and Puno no longer envisioned an Inka restoration, see Cahill and O'Phelan, "Forging Their Own History."

65 On this rebellion, see Hünefeldt, *Lucha por la tierra y protesta indígena*, 41–53; and Walker, *Smoldering Ashes*, 97–105.

66 Walker, *Smoldering Ashes*, 111.

67 John R. Fisher, "The Royalist Regime in the Viceroyalty of Peru, 1820–1824," *Journal of Latin American Studies* 32 (2000): 52–84.

68 Walker, *Smoldering Ashes*, 121–123. One of Peru's leading historians and a native of Tacna mused that had the 1814 rebellion succeeded, the Peruvian nation would have had a "mestizo, indigenous, creole and provincial" identity; Jorge Basadre, *El azar en la historia y sus límites* (Lima: Ediciones PLV, 1973), 146.

69 Langer, "Bajo la sombra del Cerro Rico," 77–91; Antonio Mitre, "El monedero de los Andes: Región economica y moneda boliviana en el siglo XIX," *HISLA: Revista Latinoamericana de Historia Económica y Social* 8 (1986): 13–74; and José Deustua, *La minería peruana y la iniciación de la república, 1820–1840* (Lima: Instituto de Estudios Peruanos, 1986).

70 Jacobsen, *Mirages of Transition*, 57; Erick D. Langer and Viviana E. Conti, "Circuitos comerciales tradicionales y cambio económico en los Andes Centromeridionales (1830–1930)," *Desarrollo Económico* 31:121 (1991), 91–111; and Erick D. Langer, "Bringing the Economic Back In: Andean Indians and the Construction of the Nation-State in Nineteenth-Century Bolivia," *Journal of Latin American Studies* 41 (2009), 527–551.

71 José María Dalence, *Bosquejo estadístico de Bolivia* (1851; reprint; La Paz: Editorial Universidad Mayor de San Andrés, 1975), especially 23–24, 177–182, 201, 244–247, and 268–278. See also Iván Ramiro Jiménez, "Abundancia y carestía: La irrupción de las importaciones y la crisis del comercio interno hacia 1830," in Lema and Barragán, *Bosquejo del estado*, 157–173; and Tristan Platt, "Ethnic Calendars and Market Interventions among the *Ayllus* of Lipes during the Nineteenth Century," in Larson and Harris, *Ethnicity, Markets, and Migration in the Andes*, 259–296.

72 Mitre, "El monedero de los Andes."

73 Flores Galindo, *Arequipa y el sur andino*, 59–79; and Jacobsen, *Mirages of Transition*, 51–77. For later developments, see Manuel Burga and Wilson Reátegui, *Lanas y capital mercantil en el sur: La casa Ricketts, 1895–1935* (Lima: Instituto de Estudios Peruanos, 1981).

74　Víctor Peralta Ruiz, *En pos del tributo en el Cusco rural, 1826–1854* (Cuzco: CERA Bartolomé de las Casas, 1991); Erwin Grieshaber, "Survival of Indian Communities in Nineteenth-Century Bolivia: A Regional Comparison," *Journal of Latin American Studies* 12:2 (1980), 223–269; Jacobsen, *Mirages of Transition*, 121–132; Walker, *Smoldering Ashes*, 186–221.

75　Erick D. Langer, "Indigenous Independence in Spanish South America," in this volume.

76　Augusto Ramos Zambrano, *Fundación de Puno y otros ensayos históricos* (Arequipa: Instituto de Estudios Históricos Pukara, 2004), 45–48.

77　José Domingo Choquehuanca, *Ensayo de estadística completa de los ramos económico-políticos de la provincia de Azángaro en el Departamento de Puno de la República Peruana, del quinquenio contado desde 1825 hasta 1829 inclusive* (Lima: Imprenta de Manuel Corral, 1833), 29, 58–59.

78　For other cases from this region in which local elites imagined or even treated the indigenous population as citizens, see Cecilia Méndez, *The Plebeian Republic: The Huanta Rebellion and the Making of the Peruvian State, 1820–1850* (Durham, NC: Duke University Press, 2005); Chambers, *From Subjects to Citizens*; and Peralta Ruiz and Irurozqui Victoriano, *Por la concordia, la fusión y el unitarismo*.

79　Choquehuanca, *Ensayo de estadística*, 60.

80　Choquehuanca, *Ensayo de estadística*, 70. For a work that expresses more of a classical vision of liberalism with less local color, see José Domingo Choquehuanca, *Complemento al régimen representativo* (1845; reprint, Lima: Crédito Editorial, 1949). An anonymous contemporary of Choquehuanca from Bolivia similarly proposed development of the internal economy, but was more cautious in his assessment of the place of native Andeans in the nation; see Lema and Barragán, *Bosquejo del estado*.

81　Choquehuanca, *Ensayo de estadística*, 67.

82　Leonardo Altuve Carrillo, *Choquehuanca y su arenga a Bolívar* (Buenos Aires: Editorial Planeta, 1991), especially 341–346.

83　Paul Gootenberg, *Between Silver and Guano: Commercial Policy and the State in Postindependence Peru* (Princeton, NJ: Princeton University Press, 1989); and Gootenberg, "North-South: Trade Policy, Regionalisms, and *Caudillismo* in Post-Independence Peru," *Journal of Latin American Studies* 12:2 (1991), 273–308. On the distinct orientation of the northern Peruvian economy during the eighteenth century, see Susana Aldana Rivera, "Un norte diferente para la independencia peruana," in *El Siglo XIX: Bolivia y América Latina*, ed. Rossana Barragán, Dora Cajías, and Seemin Qayum (La Paz: Muela del Diablo Editores, 1997), 61–77.

84　Paul Gootenberg persuasively argues against an earlier dependency interpretation of guano, but it still left the South untouched; Gootenberg, *Imagining Development: Economic Ideas in Peru's "Fictitious Prosperity" of Guano, 1840–1880* (Berkeley and Los Angeles: University of California Press, 1993).

85　For the text of the independence declaration, see Peru, *Ministerio de Relaciones Exteriores, Colección de los tratados, convenciones capitulaciones, armisticios, y otros actos diplomáticos y políticos celebrados desde la independencia hasta el día, precedida de una introducción que comprende la época colonial,* vol. 2 (Lima: Imprenta del Estado, 1890), 154–158.

86 On the declaration of an independent Bolivia, see Sobrevilla Perea, *The Caudillo of the Andes,* 93; Arnade, *The Emergence of the Republic of Bolivia,* 195–198; and José Luís Roca, *Ni con Lima, ni con Buenos Aires: La formación de un estado nacional en Charcas* (La Paz: Plural Editores; and Lima: IFEA, 2007). On the underrepresentation of La Paz, with its large indigenous population, see Rossana Barragán, "Los elegidos: En torno a la representación territorial y la re-unión de los poderes en Bolivia entre 1825 y 1840," in *La mirada esquiva: Reflexiones históricas sobre la interacción del estado y la ciudadanía en los Andes (Bolivia, Ecuador y Perú), siglo xix,* ed. Marta Irurozqui Victoriano (Madrid: Consejo Superior de Investigaciones Científicas, 2005), 93–123.

87 On the formation of the confederation and the governance style and institutions implemented by Santa Cruz, see Sobrevilla Perea, *The Caudillo of the Andes,* 114–146; O'Phelan Godoy, "Santa Cruz y Gamarra"; Phillip Taylor Parkerson, *Andrés de Santa Cruz y la Confederación Perú-Boliviana, 1835–1839* (La Paz: Librería Editorial "Juventud," 1984); Cristóbal Aljovín de Losada, "A Break with the Past?: Santa Cruz and the Constitution," in *Political Culture in the Andes, 1750–1950,* ed. Nils Jacobsen and Cristóbal Aljovín de Losada (Durham, NC: Duke University Press, 2005), 96–115; Rossana Barragán, "The 'Spirit' of Bolivian Laws: Citizenship, Infamy and Patrichary," in *Honor, Status and Law in Modern Latin America,* ed. Sueann Caulfield, Sarah C. Chambers, and Lara Putnam (Durham, NC: Duke University Press, 2005), 66–86; Peralta Ruiz and Irurozqui Victoriano, *Por la concordia, la fusión y el unitarismo,* 109–135; and Jaime Rosenblitt Berdichesky, "El comercio tacneño y la Confederación Perú-Boliviana," in Donoso and Rosenblitt, *Guerra, región y nación,* 159–180. For the decrees of Santa Cruz in southern Peru, see Carlos Ortiz de Zevallos Paz-Soldán, ed., *Archivo Diplomático Peruano,* vol. 9: *Confederación Perú-Boliviana (1835–1839), part 1* (Lima: Ministerio de Relaciones Exteriores del Perú, 1972), 435–571; for the decree on Indians (Puno, May 9, 1809), 488–493.

88 Cecilia Méndez G., "Incas Sí, Indios No: Notes on Peruvian Creole Nationalism and Its Contemporary Crisis," *Journal of Latin American Studies* 28 (1996): 197–225.

89 Rossana Barragán, *Espacio urbano y dinámica étnica: La Paz en el siglo XIX* (La Paz: HISBOL, 1990), 41–47; for treaties, see Bolivia and José Rosendo Gutiérrez, *Colección de los tratado y convenciones celebrados por la República de Bolivia con los estados extranjeros* (Santiago: El Independiente, 1869).

90 Flores Galindo, *Arequipa y el sur andino,* 83–93; Langer, "Bringing the Economic Back In," 547–548; Mitre, "El monedero de los Andes," 39.

91 Klein, *Haciendas and Ayllus,* 112–159; Platt, *Estado boliviano y ayllu andino,* 36–72; Jacobsen, *Mirages of Transition,* 151–258; and Erick D. Langer and Robert H. Jackson, "Liberalism and the Land Question in Bolivia, 1825–1920," in *Liberals, the Church, and Indian Peasants: Corporate Lands and the Challenge of Reform in Nineteenth-Century Spanish America,* ed. Robert H. Jackson (Albuquerque: University of New Mexico Press, 1997), 171–192.

92 Melchor María Mercado, *Album de paisajes, tipos humanos y costumbres de Bolivia (1841–1869)* (Sucre: Archivo y Biblioteca Nacional de Bolivia, 1991), esp. plates on 160–177 and 185–188.

93 Justiniano Cavero Eguzquiza and Simón Martínez Izquierdo, *Geografía de los Estados Unidos Perú-Bolivianos o sea República de los Incas* (Lima, 1880); quote on xv. For an analysis of Inca imagery from independence through the War of the Pacific, see Teresa Gisbert, *Iconografía y Mitos Indígenas en el Arte* (La Paz: Gisbert y Cia. SA, 1980), 175–186.

94 Although witnesses to an indigenous rebellion in Puno as late as 1915 claimed there were aspirations to join with communities in Bolivia; O'Phelan Godoy, "Santa Cruz y Gamarra," 17–18. And Ollanta Humala, on his election as Peruvian president in 2011, spoke of aspirations to reunite Peru and Bolivia; "Humala Invites Morales to Consider the Re-unification of Peru and Bolivia," *MercoPress: South Atlantic News Agency* (Montevideo), June 22, 2011, http://en.mercopress.com, accessed June 22, 2015.

95 Although my interpretation of how nations emerged in Spanish America differs from that of Benedict Anderson, his conceptual framework is productive; Benedict Anderson, *Imagined Communities: Reflections on the Origin and Spread of Nationalism* (London: Verso, 1983).

10

INDIGENOUS INDEPENDENCE
IN SPANISH SOUTH AMERICA

ERICK D. LANGER

The independence of Latin America from 1810 to 1825 is one of the great political events of the modern era. All but a handful of the Iberian colonies broke
from their colonial rulers and established new nations. Other than Brazil (and
briefly Mexico), these new states became republics, as had the United States a
few decades earlier. This broad storyline, however, too often overshadows an
equally important and very complicated process by which indigenous peoples
claimed greater autonomy for many decades after independence. Many gained
considerable new autonomy within emerging nations; some found or increased
independence; and overall, native peoples often prospered after 1820 in ways
they had not been able to during long colonial centuries. Many who had never
been conquered by Europeans were able to take back lands lost in the eighteenth century. They, as well as native peoples who had lived within colonial
polities, remained engaged with the newly independent states as they had

before with the colonial empires—but many found new, more autonomous ways of engagement. This distinguishes the fifty years after independence from the colonial period and the era of national consolidation that followed after 1860. During this period, while new nations often struggled, many indigenous peoples enjoyed unprecedented independence.

In the second half of the nineteenth century, the window of opportunity closed as Spanish American elites[1] and the national states they ruled consolidated power and made alliances with outsiders to crush the autonomy gained by indigenous peoples during and in the decades after independence. The state-building processes that shaped Latin America in the second half of the nineteenth century brought the increasing subjugation and marginalization of native populations. This "third conquest" worsened conditions for indigenous people more than the late eighteenth-century consolidation of the colonial state (which Nancy Farriss calls the "second conquest").[2] The process of indigenous subjugation and marginalization has only recently begun to reverse; from the 1970s and accelerating into the early twenty-first century, indigenous peoples began to regain a share of political and economic power. The process has been slow and very uneven, as have the results for indigenous majorities.

This essay focuses on the era from late colonial times to the late 1860s, when indigenous peoples forged spaces in which they claimed increased political autonomy and relative economic prosperity. The picture is complicated, but the overarching trends are clear. Indigenous populations across the Americas exhibited many different characteristics and cannot be simply subsumed under the (artificial) category of "Indians."[3] Not only were there vast regional and national differences—the state did matter—but most indigenous populations were part of one of two general yet divergent categories: they were either peasants integrated into the colonial states, or peoples who resisted the hegemony of the Spanish or Portuguese, British or French Crowns and remained independent of the colonial (and later, national) states. The numbers of these independent peoples were small compared to the peasants living under colonial (mostly Spanish) rule in the eighteenth century, but the uncolonized controlled the majority of the territory of Latin America (and the Americas) until after 1860. Although we have much less documentation about these long-independent peoples, they matter for the importance of their own histories and cultures, and because like the indigenous peasants within the new republics, they profoundly affected the ways new nation-states became new countries.

This chapter argues, based on my own work within the new scholarly understanding of indigenous peoples from 1800 to 1870, that while political visionaries faced the complex conflicts of nation building, many indigenous peoples enjoyed unprecedented decades of power and prosperity. I concentrate on the Andean highlands and adjacent lowlands. As John Tutino argued for indigenous peasant communities within Mexico, this was a period of "decompression" in which the extractive colonial economies collapsed and state confiscatory powers weakened.[4] Meanwhile, along the frontiers the lack of formal militaries and infrastructure such as forts, missions, and roads meant that many indigenous peoples were able to liberate themselves from European or Spanish American hegemony or push back the frontiers and liberate territory that the Spanish had taken in the decades prior to independence.[5]

The scale of the Atlantic economy and the focus of documentation on the commercial sectors make it difficult to detail the changing levels of economic engagement and power at the regional, community, and household levels. Yet growing complaints of commercial difficulties and scarcities of profit among those who presumed to be powerful, and increasing evidence of independent production and commercial participation among long subordinate or marginal peoples, document new indigenous autonomies across the Andes and into nearby lowlands. These assertions of popular independence in times of struggles to create politically independent states paralleled the consolidations of "household production" that Carolyn Fick details for Saint Domingue as it became Haiti, and Alfredo Ávila and John Tutino show in the complicated process of Mexico's political development. The increased autonomy claimed by indigenous peoples (and former slaves in Haiti) differentiates the Andes and Mesoamerica (and the revolutionary plantation colony) from regions of the Americas, notably the United States, Cuba, and Brazil, where postindependence expansion of slavery consolidated power and increased coercions within plantation systems—and, in the United States and Brazil, increased pressures toward the displacement of nearby native peoples. In the case of the Andes, participation in the Atlantic economy continued during times of contested nation making, if at reduced levels, as Sarah Chambers emphasizes in chapter 9. And in that continuation, highland indigenous communities become increasingly important producers and interlocutors with the Atlantic economy and an incipient industrial capitalism, reinforcing the Andean ways of redistribution and reciprocity that Chambers also highlights. On the eastern frontiers, independent peoples took advantage of weakened and contested state powers in the long-colonized highlands to mix military power and trade relations to access goods—weapons, tools, cloth, and more—they did not produce. Only after 1860 did the equation change, as indigenous peoples were put under pressure by Spanish American elites and states that took advantage of deepening ties with North Atlantic capitalism to forge a new economic model and marginalize indigenous peoples.

Tightening the Screws: Empire and Indigenous Peoples before 1810
Indigenous peoples within and near Spain's empire faced a "second conquest"—
and sometimes a first—during the decades after 1750. Across the Andean highlands, indigenous peasants suffered from an intensifying *reparto de mercancías*,
in which the local officials called corregidores exacted rising surpluses through
monopoly sales of goods—backed by the officials' administrative and judicial
powers. Meanwhile Spanish authorities began to replace community officials
with outsiders, often mestizos, sometimes Spaniards, seeking greater control
over indigenous communities and their resources. Priests worked to squeeze
more monies from their indigenous charges, often leading to conflicts among
Church leaders, regime officials, and resistant communities. The successes of
these assertions of power and surplus extraction were uneven, but they were
especially resented in the Andean region, where the silver economy and thus
commercial opportunities were weaker than in New Spain.[6]

The increased pressures on and exploitation of the indigenous peasantry
came to a partial end by the 1780s, in the aftermath of the Great Rebellion in
the Southern Andes (1780–1784), which extended far beyond the rising famously led by Túpac Amaru. Three major movements emerged from Andean
communities, ranging from Potosí to Cuzco, with different motivations; all generated great violence; all were suppressed by Spanish forces hastily sent from
other regions of the viceroyalty. Many of these troops were mestizo or mulatto
militias recently organized as part of the Bourbon reforms that attempted to
impose the "second conquest."[7]

The defeat of the uprisings, the execution many leaders, and the punishments
meted out to participants and their communities blocked this first move toward
greater "Andean independence"—though not necessarily nation-making. Less
emphasized but also important, the Spanish Crown prohibited the repartos,
and by 1784 the office of corregidor was abolished, replaced by *intendentes* and
subdelegados who were prohibited from trading in their jurisdictions (with
only partial success). The new system—and the threat of another insurgency—
did alleviate the most resented exactions on the peasant population.[8] There
were gains taken in defeat.

Before and after the uprisings, both a cause of the revolts and a consequence
of the state's reforms afterward, Andean communities reconsidered and reorganized their internal leadership structures. Hereditary kurakas, the local nobility that often traced origins to pre-Inka times and had entrenched their status
as key intermediaries linking the Spanish and indigenous worlds during the late
sixteenth-century consolidation of the silver boom led by Potosí, lost ground
to commoners claiming leadership in the communities. At times, communities

ran the old kurakas (as well as non-Indian ones set up by Spanish authorities) out of town or even killed them, insisting that the *común* was to rule. After the Great Rebellion, led by kurakas such as Túpac Amaru—at times pressed by commoners against abusive kurakas—regime reforms accelerated the demise of the indigenous nobility. Annually elected *alcaldes de indios* replaced hereditary indigenous leaders in Andean communities.[9] The mix of rebellion and reform accelerated a new political culture among indigenous peasants in the Andes—a grassroots democracy that soon engaged the new, liberal winds that reverberated through the empire in the era of Cádiz.

The situation was different in the frontier areas east of the Andean heartland. There the Spanish Bourbon regime brought severe pressure on indigenous groups that had remained independent. They had not faced, or had fended off, the first conquest. Through the seventeenth century and into the eighteenth, the Spanish regime had remained mostly in the territories claimed in the sixteenth.[10] The revitalization of the Spanish state under Bourbons and the search for resources and revenues in a commercially dynamic and imperially competitive eighteenth century brought a more aggressive frontier policy. Military expeditions brought forts into long-uncolonized regions, followed by the establishment of missions under the Franciscans who aimed to incorporate, convert, and subordinate independent peoples. Scientific-military expeditions explored territories unknown to Crown officials. By the first decade of the nineteenth, the Spanish regime had expanded its reach into the lowland centers of indigenous resistance of South America: across the arid Chaco plains; pressing the southern borders of Chile past the Bío Bío River into Araucanía; and deep into the pampas of the Río de la Plata region. In Chile, intensified negotiations with the various native peoples south of the Bío Bío opened long-held indigenous territories to Spanish settlers. Independent peoples submitted to the frontier militias concentrated in new forts or lived around new missions set in regions where the European presence was new and intensifying. As David Weber argued, in the late colonial period the Spanish regime pressed a dynamic and successful (in Spanish terms) frontier policy based on a new conception of the Indian as "savage," supported by scientific explorations, militarization, and systematic trade with independent peoples.[11]

These policies and programs drove Spanish control beyond boundaries in place for over a century.[12] The only region of South America where the new Spanish aggressive policy did not work and where the Spanish did not gain initiative, territory, and influence was the jungle zone east of central Peru. There the Juan Santos Atahualpa rebellion expelled the Franciscan missions in the rough foothills east of the central Sierra in the 1740s.[13] But this was an exception.

MAP 10.1. Spanish imperial control in South America, ca. 1800

Across most frontier areas, the militarization through militias and professional troops, often followed by missions and sometimes by new Hispanic settlers, brought advances against independent indigenous peoples.

Regaining Power: Independence and Indigenous Peoples

The long struggles for independence set off after 1808 by Napoleon's assault on the imperial center in Spain and energized after 1810 by the participations offered and limited under Cádiz liberalism, brought new pressure on integrated indigenous populations across the Andes, as conflicts between autonomists and royalists became civil wars. Too often, interpretations of independence suggest that along the Andean mountain spine from the Audiencia de Quito (roughly present-day Ecuador) to the altiplano and high valleys ending south of Potosí, the dense settlements of long-colonized indigenous communities stood aside, in contrast to the assertive participations of so many in the Great Rebellion of the 1780s. It appears that Spanish Americans remained in charge during the wars that led to independence, and that indigenous peoples mostly served as transporters of goods and dependent auxiliaries, while often seeing their cattle and foodstuffs taken by troops on both sides. Yet indigenous men served in various armies and communities, backing one side or another based on local interests, conflicts, and opportunities. Many, likely a majority of integrated indigenous peoples, tried to keep their heads down and stay out of fighting among factions of people who had long aimed to rule them and claim their labor and surpluses. Some indigenous communities, as in Pasto, New Granada (today Colombia), backed the royalist cause after the Popayán governor decreased their tribute. They created a "popular royalism" that favored the commoners over the traditional powers, as some communities had farther south in the Great Rebellion.[14] When communities could negotiate participation on favorable terms, they might join the fray for a time; but as independence conflicts became generalized and violent, dealing with whatever army passed by became a strategy for survival.

A spate of urban movements across the Andes debated autonomy and loyalty in the aftermath of Napoleon's assault on imperial legitimacy in 1808. A patriot army sent from the city of Buenos Aires under Juan José Castelli entered Upper Peru (now Bolivia) but was defeated in 1811 at Huaqui, on the altiplano near Lake Titicaca. The *porteños* initially gained support in many indigenous communities along their march. Castelli proclaimed the end of tribute payments and denounced the "slavery" he imagined the Indians suffered, asserting that the Buenos Aires junta saw the Indians as "brothers."[15] Indigenous auxiliaries were instrumental in the Argentine army's victories in Suipacha, but Castelli's favor toward Indians turned many non-Indians against the "patriots." At the battle of Huaqui, the native auxiliaries who accompanied Castelli waited on the sidelines. With defeat at Huaqui, the porteño troops dispersed and began to sack the surrounding countryside and the Potosí treasury. The Indians of Sicasica refused to aid Castelli in his retreat. Other indigenous groups took advantage of the confusion to sack the city of La Paz, presumably controlled by "patriot" troops from Cochabamba.[16] The American Spaniards of La Paz made peace with the royalists and kept their peace until independence was declared.

Such urban adaptations for and against Cádiz liberalism sent conflict into the countryside. There Spanish American leaders seeking autonomy allied with indigenous villages to mount guerrilla campaigns against the loyalist forces. The most notable indigenous rebellion was the Pumacahua rising of 1814. Mateo García Pumacahua traced his lineage back to Inka kings; he had been a loyalist and a leading commander against Túpac Amaru in the 1780s. He became interim president of the Audiencia (the High Court and primary colonial authority in Cuzco). Feeling marginalized by loyalist authorities, in 1814 he joined a rebellion begun and led by Spanish Americans; Pumacahua became the main military commander and attracted many Indians to his rebel army. However, the rebellion was suppressed by well-armed Spanish troops and Indian auxiliaries in 1815 as Fernando VII reclaimed power and abrogated the Cádiz Constitution. Pumacahua was executed in the regional capital of Sicuani.[17]

Most of the guerrilla republiquetas were pacified by 1816. Overt combat between loyalists and groups seeking autonomy receded in the Andes until 1820, when Spanish liberals preparing to lead an expedition to fight the independence movement led by Simón Bolívar in Gran Colombia (modern Colombia and Venezuela) forced Ferdinand VII to reinstitute the Cádiz Constitution and its liberal precepts. That provided the opening for pro-independence armies to move north from Buenos Aires and Chile and south from Gran Colombia, to crush a still-loyal royalist Andean core. Bolívar and San Martín understood that only the "liberation" of the deeply indigenous Andean highland core, still ruled by powers loyal to Spain, could ensure political autonomy in their Caracas and Buenos Aires homelands.

The conflicts that led to independence in the Andes mixed civil wars among Spanish Americans and changing participation among indigenous leaders and communities as dynamics and opportunities evolved. Early events in Upper Peru revealed American Spaniards' ambivalence and indigenous communities' independence. In both Perus, elites feared that a revolution might become what they saw as a race war—that is, a rising of indigenous masses reminiscent of the

1780s. Spanish Americans had long benefited from the colonial system and in their dominance over the Indians, notably by receiving tribute and labor via the mitá and other means. Many native Andeans were leery of Spanish Americans and, after their initial enthusiasm for the Auxiliary Army from Buenos Aires, also of "foreigners" who promised much, but whose power and commitment to indigenous welfare proved tenuous. In the small republiquetas later formed to fight the royalists, Indians, mestizos, and Americans Spaniards mixed, but *españoles americanos* held most of the leadership.[18] In the regions that became Peru, many indigenous communities only mobilized in 1820, when the viceregal court faced a siege from porteño general San Martín's army from Chile and fled Lima seeking refuge in the ancient indigenous capital at Cuzco.[19] Even then, most native communities stood aside from the conflicts that created Peru and Bolivia.[20]

The situation was different on the frontiers. The wars that shook the Spanish empire and eventually led to independence had even more profound effects there. For independent peoples who did not recognize themselves as "Indians"— this was a Spanish term—these regions were not margins but homelands. For people who had remained free of Spanish rule, often while obtaining arms and other goods through raids and trades, the wars opened new times of real independence and economic expansion. And for many, the times of indigenous independence lasted long into the nineteenth century.

There were many and diverse reasons for the assertion of independent indigenous peoples along what the Spanish called *la frontera*. Many troops stationed at the frontier in the Bourbon military buildup left to fight on one side or the other in the independence wars (it was frontier troops, including the gauchos of the pampas and the *llaneros* of Venezuela and Colombia who backed San Martín and Bolívar). Royalist leaders knew that the most experienced troops manned the frontier forts; they repeatedly called them to defend the regime. Patriots recruited the same forces whenever they could. As wars persisted and widened within the core regions of the colonies, the officials saw higher priorities than funding frontier forts. As silver revenues fell and tribute payments dried up in the highland communities, governments could not support the forts. As troops and subsidies withdrew, indigenous peoples took over vast swaths of territory. In some regions, the mission system meant to contain and convert frontier ethnic groups collapsed when Spanish missionaries left, whether by force or fear. This occurred among once-thriving Franciscan missions among the Chiriguanos in the Andean foothills of eastern Upper Peru. In 1813, seventeen missions contained more than eighteen thousand Indians. By

1825, only two missions remained.[21] Similar processes weakened missions on the pampas and in the southern Chile.

Amid complex conflicts and adaptations along diverse frontiers, independent indigenous peoples recouped territories they had lost to Bourbon imperial offensives. Some independent Indians fought on the side of the patriots, including the Chiriguano cacique Cumbay. In 1813 he met porteño general Manuel Belgrano in Potosí to offer his warriors to the patriot leader.[22] The Pehuenche in Chile favored the royalists and collaborated with loyal officers to attack the recently established Chilean republic.[23] In turn, the Chilean patriot leader José Miguel Carrera had allied with the Ranquel Indians across the Andes to fight against patriot rivals.[24] Independent peoples took different sides during the wars; most aimed to promote their own independence; few developed an ideological predilection among Spanish Americans or Europeans, whose visions of Indians differed little and never included indigenous independence.

In sum, the wars in the early nineteenth century affected South American indigenous peoples differently. Peasants living under colonial Spanish rule suffered the depredations of warfare, losing livestock and supplies to passing armies. Many were forced to work for one side or the other as porters, spies, providing shelter and the like. Other indigenous peoples aimed to take their fates in their own hands, with limited success. The Pumacahua rebellion failed, in part because of the fear the earlier Great Rebellion in the 1780s still engendered among American Spaniards. At and beyond the frontier, independent peoples had different experiences. They quickly saw a lessening of the pressure of the late colonial state; in many regions they took back control over areas they had lost to Bourbon conquest. Some independent groups joined the wars, often on the side of the patriots. They helped create a military balance that favored their own independence—recouping lost territory and populations.

After Independence: Indigenous Power and Wealth

Once the wars were over, new and still contested Andean states relied more than ever on indigenous peoples and their tribute payments to sustain themselves. Other sources of income, notably mining revenues, diminished dramatically. The dependence of the new states in the Andes on tribute incomes led to a rebalancing of power between them, the indigenous communities within them, and the increasingly independent peoples on their margins. The new states did not have the capacity to put much pressure on indigenous groups, within or without, while many Spanish Americans looked to redefine the colonial pact in which indigenous groups held a predetermined subordinate

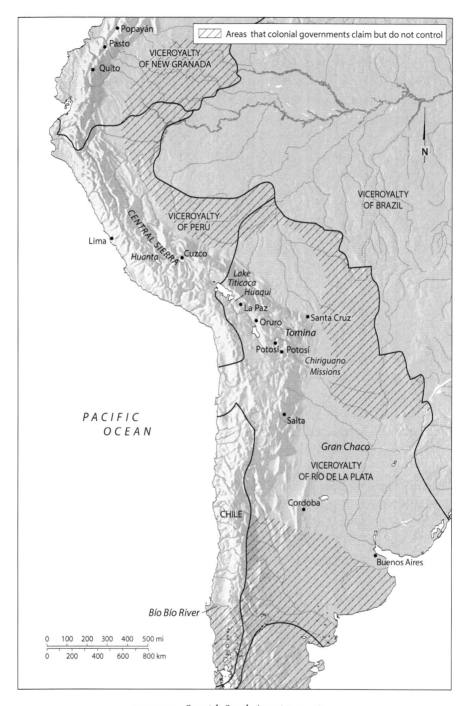

Popayán
Pasto
VICEROYALTY
OF NEW GRANADA
Quito

Areas that colonial governments claim but do not control

N

VICEROYALTY
OF BRAZIL

CENTRAL SIERRA
VICEROYALTY
OF PERU
Lima
Huanta Cuzco

Lake Titicaca
Huaqui
La Paz
Oruro   Santa Cruz
Tomina
Potosí Potosí
Chiriguano Missions

PACIFIC
OCEAN

Salta

Gran Chaco
VICEROYALTY
OF RÍO DE LA PLATA

Cordoba
CHILE

Buenos Aires

Bío Bío River

0   100   200   300   400   500 mi
0   200   400   600   800 km

MAP 10.2. Spanish South America, ca. 1820

position. This led to experiments in defining the nation as a multiethnic construct, attempts abandoned in the last quarter of the nineteenth century. Then indigenous peoples returned to subordinate positions; even worse, government policies deliberately marginalized them, or attempted to eliminate them completely, either physically (as happened along many frontiers), or as distinct peoples with their own institutions, cultures, and languages.

After Spanish rule ended and while nations were constructed and debated, the indigenous peoples integrated within the new states and the independent natives at their margins claimed real gains. The rising autonomy of indigenous peasants and communities within the nations led to greater prosperity and often higher standards of living because neither the state nor Spanish American landlords had the ability to extract as much surplus as during colonial times. In contrast to developments in Mexico, the new Andean governments reinstated the indigenous tribute, soon after abolishing it in the afterglow of independence. In Ecuador, Peru, and Bolivia, governments were desperately short of funds, as other revenue sources did not materialize.[25] They gave the renewed tribute different names, but the idea was the same—each Indian male between fifteen and fifty paid a tax in return for access to community land. That pact made explicit a relation implicit in the Spanish colonial order. It also made new states dependent on indigenous communities and gave their members, especially their men, a sense of entitlement to their lands. Across the Andes, the head tax endured at levels less than the colonial tribute. No government increased the amount of the head tax while the system remained in place. Presuming inflation over the nineteenth century, the head tax became a shrinking burden on each household—while solidifying rights to lands and autonomies in indigenous communities.[26]

Elsewhere in South America, tribute ended. In some, areas, tribute had counted for little and was abolished early in the republican era or shortly thereafter. In the regions that became Argentina, the only Indians to pay tribute lived as peasants in the far northwestern part of the federation's Andean provinces, and their contributions were insignificant to the national treasury. The Buenos Aires revolutionary government abolished tribute in 1811, before the invasion of Upper Peru.[27] In Colombia, the Congress of Cúcuta abolished Indian tribute in 1821; it lived on briefly as a "personal contribution," but largely disappeared by the end of the 1820s.[28]

Across the Andes, the basis for peasant organization, the república de indios, was strengthened as weak states relied on indigenous leaders to administer villages and collect tributes; the persistence of tribute fortified the village structures put in place to collect it. A few Spanish Americans became tribute collectors, now more a measure of integration into indigenous communities than an insertion of outside interference (as such attempts had become under Spanish rule). Arguably, postindependence Spanish South America was more republican and local governance stronger than in any period until the agrarian reforms of the twentieth century. It was a time of republican governance based in indigenous peasant villages, often invisible to Spanish American and mestizo townspeople, who suffered from caudillismo and ongoing political instability. The exception seems to have been Ecuador, where many highland Indian villages were controlled by Spanish American and mestizo landlords and officials.[29]

After independence, debate widened among Spanish Americans about whether Indians constituted citizens as other members of society did. Following the precedent of Cádiz, initial responses were yes: all citizens—no longer colonial subjects—should be equal.[30] When General José de San Martín invaded Lima with his Chilean and porteño troops, he decreed that all citizens should be called Peruvians; in the highlands this was taken to mean only Indians.[31] Simón Bolívar, in a famous 1824 decree that also followed Cádiz precedents, proclaimed that all Indian communities should be broken up and their lands distributed among their members. Lands not claimed by individual Indians would be sold by the state in public auction. A year later, Bolívar provided a formula for dividing the land, providing Indian caciques twice the land of ordinary community members, but also abolishing hereditary leadership (*cacicazgos*).[32] After Bolívar left and while facing fiscal penury and an indigenous majority demanding traditional roles and rights, the Bolivian state reversed these laws in the late 1820s. That reversal meant that integrated indigenous peoples in the Andes remained differentiated by the old "stain" of conquest and tributary subordination, though every country masked the fact by calling the tribute by different names, such as "personal contribution" (*contribución personal*). People thus marked as Indian still voted in national elections, but as the century wore on, literacy and landowning requirements increasingly excluded rural peoples, Indian or not. This did not affect village-level administration, which was subsumed under the Indian republics reinforced by the consolidation of their residents' separate status.[33] In sum—and in diverse local ways—indigenous peoples faced prejudice in the nations yet consolidated power and production in their communities.

Despite the equivocal and diminishing citizenship rights of Indian in national republics, their social rights remained intact or even expanded in their local communities—the heirs to colonial indigenous republics. We have little information on labor regimes in the early national decades. The information we have suggests a less oppressive hacienda regime; in some cases some land reforms effectively turned renters (*arrenderos*)[34] into smallholders. In others landlords gave haciendas to Indians, as happened in Tomina Province in southern Bolivia, where the priest Manuel Martín Santa Cruz in his 1857 testament donated his hacienda, Collpa Lupiara, to his Indian arrenderos.[35]

Similarly, we lack information on advanced pay and obligated rural labor on estates (too often called called debt peonage, implying domination that was rarely real) for the first few decades after independence. Still, Arnold Bauer has argued that postindependence labor relations were relatively favorable to the hacienda workers—a situation well documented across Mexico. Estate owners could not rely on weak states for police power to find or return workers who took proffered advances of goods and wages and then absconded. More revealing, why would employers offer pay in advance, given very weak enforcement mechanisms? The advances worked as enticements to labor, offered to men with lands and rights in entrenched communities. If they did not perform the work or repay, estates could rarely make their debtors pay in the decades of indigenous independence.[36] In Colombia, for example, Aline Helg shows that neither the state nor landlords could discipline labor in the mountainous and heavily forested Caribbean region, where people easily escaped and many villages were beyond the powers of governments or landlords.[37]

National state and landlord powers also weakened when indigenous leaders became local and regional authorities. Cecilia Méndez has shown that in the aftermath of the royalist rebellion in Huanta from 1825 to 1828, the indigenous peasant leaders Tadeo Choque and Antonio Abad Huachaca remained the regional authorities, the former as provincial governor, the latter as a justice of the peace. They fought for the heartland caudillo Andrés de Santa Cruz in the 1830s and until the ends of their lives remained the power brokers of their districts.[38]

Struggling national states without the resources and power to favor Spanish Americans and their commercial enterprises meant that indigenous peasants could engage in activities without governments or landlords being able (or at times even interested) to take the surplus. In the Andes, indigenous peasants controlled much of the food production and most of the transport sector, provisioning cities and mining centers as well as carrying minerals to the coast and imported goods into the highlands. Many traded in contraband silver, colluding with import/export merchants and, at times, with mine owners too. Informal alliance among indigenous muleteers and llama herders, merchants, and silver miners worked to keep the state weak so that all could avoid taxes.[39] No wonder the definition of the Andean states was vague and contested for decades, as Sarah Chambers shows. Many Spanish American elites and indigenous communities did not see defined boundaries or stable powers as in their best interests.

Andean peasant communities joined in extensive commerce, supplying cities with foodstuffs and locally made textiles, along with forage, fuel, and wood (though the difficulty of getting at the municipal records has hindered a full analysis of its importance). Until the late nineteenth century, indigenous communities held the vast majority of arable land, making their predominance of food production a certainty. Tristan Platt has documented that northern Potosí communities produced the wheat that supplied much of the Bolivian highlands. Municipal police records provide evidence of the amount of foodstuffs that indigenous traders sold in nineteenth-century cities such as Oruro and Potosí.[40]

Outside the control of the new states—though not outside their imagined boundaries—still-independent peoples joined in important commerce often tied to international trade; with no state authority to record it, their commerce remains unmeasured. Most significant was the cattle trade in the South American pampas. Kristine Jones details how the raiding economies of the Mapuche and other peoples of the Southern Cone as well as the Comanche and Apache who ruled between Mexico and the United States became enterprises important to the world economy. They competed directly and successfully with Spanish Americans for the resources of their regions.[41] Such raiding economies made possible the rise of proto-states such as Calfucará, an alliance of Araucanian and Pampas Indians who dominated the salt licks of the Salinas Grandes where the cattle herds taken from the pampas had to pass on their way west to Chile.[42]

The commercial opportunities claimed by independent Indians were tied to the weakness of the new republics.[43] The frontier military balance shifted to favor independent Indians—an advantage that endured to the 1870s. The new states facing difficulties financing activities in their core regions and wracked by internecine conflict drew frontier-hardened militias to help rule their heartland cores—often to little avail. Some leaders tried to bring independent Indians into the fight, but at their peril. Such independent peoples brought independent agendas, sometimes launching campaigns against their "allies" and often raiding for their own advantage, debilitating national frontiers even more. In only one case is it clear that the engagement of independent indigenous warriors brought gains to Spanish Americans: Juan Manuel de Rosas, the governor of Buenos Aires, allied himself with Calfucará and other caciques to fight the Voroganos allied with the Carrera brothers in disputes over rule of the Argentine Confederation in 1830. To succeed, Rosas had to pay his Indian allies thousands of horses and cattle, along with expensive sugar and tobacco.[44]

The balance of power favoring independent Indians led to uneasy relations with frontier towns and villages, and large landlords too. Alliances shifted constantly as political realities changed, reflecting rivalries on both sides of the frontier. In central Argentina, along the eastern frontier of Peru, and in southeastern Bolivia fights among political factions, different jurisdictions, and indigenous peoples with their own allies and enemies led to raids and conflicts in which indigenous groups might ally with Spanish American states or factions to launch strikes against indigenous groups or Spanish American towns linked to their political opponents. Violence was endemic across frontier regions, affecting every political and social unit from national and indigenous federation leaders all the way down to the household level. Baretta and Markoff long ago detected enduring violence on cattle frontiers in Latin America; this analysis suggests that the violence as was as much about political power as about cattle.[45]

In these decades of independence, indigenous groups leveraged superior powers of violence to gain access to goods they otherwise would not have had. Landlords and local officials paid goods to keep Indians at bay. In Argentina, provincial governments paid *indios amigos* what they called *vicios*, goods such as tobacco and sugar, horses and cattle, to compensate their service as buffers to other, hostile Indians. Many leaders of powerful groups on the pampas and in Patagonia maintained constant written communication with provincial governors. Some maintained embassies in provincial capitals, creating state-like relations with their provincial peers.[46] In Bolivia, landlords and departmental governors paid Chiriguanos to remain allies—tribute Spanish Americans paid to Indians. Still, independent Indians often switched allegiances, leading Spanish Americans to accuse them of treachery—as if indigenous peoples could not have their own strategic, diplomatic, and economic interests. Much of the frustration came as Spanish Americans saw that they were the weaker party— the payers of tribute. They could only hope that independent Indians would become dependent on them for goods they could not produce themselves: firearms, sugar, and fine cloth. As there were usually multiple suppliers, alliances remained fragile and raids continued.[47]

The decades from the 1820s to the 1860s, or even the 1880s (depending on the region) saw indigenous peoples claim lives more independent and often more well off than during late colonial times. The peasants and communities that had been integrated into the Spanish polity after the conquest were rarely integrated fully as citizens within national states after independence. But they managed quite well without much interference from state authorities. As landed villagers provided most of the foodstuffs to the towns and villages throughout the Andes, peasants clung to the tributary regime—a small

FIGURE 10.1. Indigenous independence—imagining the threat after its end

burden exchanged for great local autonomy. Weak states continued to support the communities, reinforcing local self-rule and the landholding essential to villagers, regional economies, and state revenues. Local patriarchal democracies continued within villages entrenched in rights long ago granted to them as *repúblicas de indios*.

Spanish American landlords had little access to capital during the postindependence period of weak markets; they could not rely on weak and contested states to force labor or the repayment of advances. So supposedly powerful elites pressed favors and advances to keep men on the job, even guaranteeing credit at local shops.[48] At and beyond the frontiers, independent raids by indigenous peoples that Spanish Americans insisted on calling "Indians"—presuming their subordination while the latter repeatedly demonstrated their power—brought constantly shifting alliances, wars, and trades, and even the payment of tributes by Spaniards to Indians. Political turbulence was everywhere, in national heartlands, along frontiers, and beyond. So too was unprecedented indigenous independence: in communities denied full citizenship, but guaranteed lands and local autonomies; among independent peoples who would not recognize that they should live as Indians, docile and dependent.

Indigenous and Popular Independence across the Americas

Indigenous independence reached far beyond the Andean highlands and nearby lowlands during the decades after 1810. In the Mesoamerican regions of central and southern Mexico, former indigenous republics lost legal sanction and faced attempts to privatize their lands, yet decades of national commercial troubles and political instability allowed many communities to consolidate control of production for sustenance and local markets.[49] In the once commercially rich Bajío, a decade of insurgency took down the silver economy and enabled indigenous and mixed-race peoples, long without rights to indigenous republics, to take control of local production while prejudicing the commercial foundations of the nation.[50] And beyond the frontiers of a once expansive New Spain, a Comanche empire built in a century of war and trade with Spanish North America used mobile cavalries to mount assertive raids and active trades and emerge as the dominant power on the high plains west of the Mississippi from 1810 and 1850.[51]

Assertions of indigenous independence after 1810 are most notable in and near the Andes and New Spain, once the core regions of Spain's American empire. The fall of the empire and the collapse of the silver economies weakened regime powers and cut entrepreneurial opportunities, opening spaces in which indigenous communities and other popular groups pressed claims to independence within struggling new nations. The fall of Spain's empire and the silver economies also undermined the Spanish American nations' abilities to press power beyond their borders, enabling Comanche, Mapuche, and other independent peoples' new assertions of power.

Assertions of indigenous and popular independence extended beyond the regions once pivotal to the silver economies. In the western highlands of Guatemala, Maya communities grounded in indigenous republics and entrenched on the land made themselves central to the struggles that created a Guatemala nation separate from the imagined Central American Federation.[52] In lowland Yucatán, a region famously beyond the dynamism of New Spain's silver economy, communities pressed their interests after 1821—culminating in a devastating war for Maya independence (too long mislabeled a caste war) in the 1840s that threatened the capital at Mérida and enabled thousands to live in true independence for decades.[53] Far to the south, in the interior headwaters of the Río de la Plata system, Guaraní peoples long dealing with Jesuit missions (until the 1767 expulsion) in lands contested by Spanish and Portuguese frontiersmen became the foundation of a Guaraní-speaking Paraguay after 1810, turning inward against participation in Atlantic trade.[54]

While popular assertions of independence were most widespread and successful across Spain's former domains, they were important in the Atlantic slave societies, too. That former slaves ruled Haiti is often noted as a hemispheric exception; that ex-slaves there shaped the second American nation by taking the land for family production is less often noted and makes Haitian independence less exceptional. Autonomy on the land was a key goal and a widespread reality across the hemisphere in the age of independence. And Haitians' success helped inspire parallel risings by slaves seeking their definitions of freedom and independence across Atlantic America. Near Richmond, Virginia, the conspiracy known as Gabriel's Rebellion developed in 1800 while the Haitian Revolution continued. The plot was revealed to authorities; the conspirators arrested and executed—yet the threat alone led national politicians to resolve an emerging political crisis, preserving national unity and the emerging economy of cotton and slavery.[55] The 1812 Aponte rebellion challenged slavery in Cuba in the year the Cádiz Constitution proclaimed liberties for American Spaniards and indigenous peoples too, but not people of African ancestry.[56] Slaves rose in British Demerara in 1823 and in Bahia, Brazil, in 1835.[57] Conspiracies rumored and real were everywhere where slavery continued.[58] When the United States fell into civil war over slavery in 1860, slaves quickly looked to their own interests in a conflict they could not control.[59] Amid that struggle, slaves in Dutch Guyana rose against their bondage.[60]

Many people of African ancestry bound to labor as slaves pursued independence across the Americas. After Haiti, however, they found little success. Did the reconsolidation of slave-based export economies (beyond Haiti) after 1800 provide economic resources, sustain state powers, and contain slaves' assertions? The contrast with the widespread collapse of silver, enduring political instability, and the meaningful turn to indigenous independence in Spanish America seems clear.

Key exceptions to indigenous independence during the first half of the nineteenth century confirm that comparative understanding. Where expanding slave-based production for export sustained early commercial prosperity, funded political stability, and drove expansion into interiors to further export production, notably in the U.S. South, indigenous peoples faced war and displacement. Andrew Jackson's campaigns and the forced removal of the Cherokee to Oklahoma are the most famous of the assaults that make the contrast clear.[61] In Brazil's south-central interior, indigenous peoples faced pressures culminating in war just before the arrival of the Portuguese court in 1808. The contested shift to political independence that led to the Brazilian empire brought brief times of relief that soon became a contested indigenous independence as coffee plantations worked with slave labor expanded into natives' homeland.[62]

In the making of new countries across the Americas, complexity and divergence were everywhere. Still, revealing patterns emerge: where commercial economies struggled and state-making proved long and contested, indigenous peoples claimed meaningful independence; where slavery and export prosperity persisted, slaves sought "independence" on the model of Haiti, yet found little success; where cotton and slavery drove into indigenous lands, slavery expanded and native peoples faced death and displacement. Only in Haiti did the laboring subjects of colonial prosperity claim enduring independence. They inspired many others—and set fear spreading among those who still aimed to profit from slavery. For their self-liberating efforts, Haitians gained lives of autonomous poverty on the land, faced military rulers at home, and lived excluded from the world of commercial nations—the only world that mattered among those who ruled across the Atlantic and the Americas in the nineteenth century.

While political visionaries struggled to create states that would allow political independence to a few across the Americas, indigenous peoples, slaves of African ancestry, and diverse others pressed their own visions of independence. For them, access to land, community rights, family production, and cultural autonomy were often more important than state powers. The latter, after all, were often mobilized against popular groups pressing their versions of independence. During decades when state building was contested and commercial economies struggled, indigenous and popular independence was a clear goal and a widely lived reality—in Haiti, across Spanish America, and in continental interiors never subjected to colonial rule. It rarely survived the expansion of export economies and the consolidations of state power that marked the Americas after 1870.

Notes

1 The term they identified themselves with was *españoles americanos*, in distinction to indios or mestizos. In later times, scholars have called them creoles (criollos), but this is not what they called themselves, at least not in the Andes. For an essay on the use of *españoles americanos* in the south-central Andes, see Tristan Platt, "Historias unidas, memorias escindidas: Las empresas mineras de los hermanos Ortiz y la construcción de las élites nacionales, Salta y Potosí 1800–1880," in *Dos décadas de investigación en historia económica comparada en América Latina: Homenaje a Carlos Sempat Assadourian*, ed. Margaret Menegus (Mexico City: Colegio de México, 1999), 285–362.

2 Nancy Farriss, *Maya Society under Colonial Rule: The Collective Enterprise of Survival* (Princeton, NJ: Princeton University Press, 1984), 355–388.

3 There is a huge literature on the meaning of "Indian," the evolution of the term, and the uses of the word. See for example Robert F. Berkhofer Jr., *The White Man's Indian: Images of the American Indian from Columbus to the Present* (New York: Random House, 1978); for Latin America, see for example the recent works of Rebecca Earle, *The Return of the Native: Indians and Myth-Making in Spanish America, 1810–1930* (Durham, NC: Duke University Press, 2007), and James F. Brooks, *Captives and Cousins: Slavery, Kinship, and Community in the Southwest Borderlands* (Chapel Hill: University of North Carolina Press, 2002).

4 See John Tutino, *From Insurrection to Revolution in Mexico: Social Bases of Agrarian Violence, 1750–1940* (Princeton, NJ: Princeton University Press, 1986), chap. 6.

5 This was not the case for the Portuguese. The continuity in the state under the Braganza dynasty even after independence helped enable the Brazilian empire to maintain its frontiers and even expand, to the detriment of independent groups. See Hal Langfur, *The Forbidden Lands: Colonial Identity, Frontier Violence, and the Persistence of Brazil's Eastern Indians, 1750–1830* (Stanford, CA: Stanford University Press, 2006).

6 Farriss, *Maya Society under Colonial Rule*. For an overview of the effects of the *reparto*, see Karen Spalding, "Exploitation as an Economic System: The State and the Extraction of Surplus in Colonial Peru," in *The Inca and Aztec States 1400–1800: Anthropology and History*, ed. George A. Collier, Renato I. Rosaldo, and John D. Wirth (New York: Academic Press, 1982), 322–344, and Scarlett O'Phelan Godoy, *Un siglo de rebeliones anticoloniales: Perú y Bolivia 1700–1783* (Cuzco: Centro de Estudios Rurales Andinos Bartolomé de las Casas, 1988); for the replacement of indigenous community leaders, see Sergio Serulnikov, *Subverting Colonial Authority: Challenges to Spanish Rule in Eighteenth-Century Southern Andes* (Durham, NC: Duke University Press, 2003). For the conflict between priests and late colonial authorities, Nicholas A. Robins, *Priest-Indian Conflict in Upper Peru: The Generation of Rebellion, 1750–1780* (Syracuse: Syracuse University Press, 2007).

7 See Leon G. Campbell, *The Military and Society in Colonial Peru, 1750–1810* (Philadelphia: American Philosophical Society, 1978). The most complete up-to-date analyses of the revolt are Charles F. Walker, *The Tupac Amaru Rebellion* (Cambridge, MA: Belknap Press, 2014), and Sergio Serulnikov, *Revolution in the Andes: The Age of Túpac Amaru* (Durham, NC: Duke University Press, 2013). Also see the essay by Sarah Chambers for more detail on the revolts.

8 For the best overview of the aftermath of the Great Rebellion, see Charles F. Walker, *Smoldering Ashes: Cuzco and the Creation of Republican Peru, 1780–1840* (Durham, NC: Duke University Press, 1999), 55–83. However, Walker does not deal adequately with the issue of the alleviation of the tax burden on Andean peasants.

9 See S. Elizabeth Penry, "The Rey Común: Indigenous Political Discourse in Eighteenth-Century Alto Perú," in *The Collective and the Public in Latin America: Cultural Identities and Political Order*, ed. Luis Roniger and Tamar Herzog (Brighton: Sussex Academic Press, 2000), 219–237. For an overview of this change, see Scarlett O'Phelan Godoy, *Kurakas sin sucesiones: Del cacique al alcalde de indios.*

Perú y Bolivia 1750–1835 (Cuzco: Centro de Estudios Rurales Andinos Bartolomé de las Casas, 1997).

10 This does not mean that the Spanish (and the Portuguese) hadn't explored virtually all of the Americas by the sixteenth century; other than some slave raiding— especially the *bandeiras* of the Portuguese—the boundaries established by the end of the sixteenth century between the colonial states and the independent Indians remained remarkably stable. They largely paralleled the limits of peasant econo- mies the Spanish had conquered, with some expansion especially into northern Mexico because of the silver to be had there. In the case of Brazil, the discovery of diamonds and gold in the Minas Gerais region in the late seventeenth century brought about similar expansion of Portuguese control.

11 The literature on late colonial frontier activities is too vast to recite here. For some suggestive work, see David J. Weber, *Bárbaros: Spaniards and Their Savages in the Age of Enlightenment* (New Haven, CT: Yale University Press, 2005); Richard W. Slatta, "Spanish Colonial Military Strategy and Ideology," in *Contested Grounds: Compara- tive Frontiers on the Northern and Southern Edges of the Spanish Empire*, ed. Donna J. Guy and Thomas E. Sheridan (Tucson: University of Arizona Press, 1998), 83–96.

12 Weber, *Bárbaros*. As Pekka Hämäläinen points out for the northern reaches of Spanish America, the Spanish entered into an alliance with the Comanche to contain the Apaches. The situation there was more complicated than might appear from Spanish records. See Hämäläinen, *The Comanche Empire* (New Haven, CT: Yale University Press, 2008), chap. 3.

13 There are many books on the Juan Santos Atahualpa rebellion, though few in the recent past. For a summary of the significance of the rebellion, see Steve J. Stern, "The Age of Andean Insurrection, 1742–1782: A Reappraisal," in *Resistance, Rebellion, and Consciousness in the Andean Peasant World 18th to 20th Centuries*, ed. Steve J. Stern (Madison: University of Wisconsin Press, 1987), 34–93. For a study of the subsequent period, see Nuria Sala i Vila, *Selva y Andes: Ayacucho (1780–1929). His- toria de una región en la encrucijada* (Madrid: Consejo Superior de Investigaciones Científicas, Instituto de Historia, 2001).

14 See Marcela Echeverri, "Popular Royalists, Empire, and Politics in Southwestern New Granada, 1809–1819," *Hispanic American Historical Review* 91:2 (2011), 237–269.

15 "Proclama de Castelli a los indios del virreinato de Perú," as cited in René Danilo Arze Aguirre, *Participación popular en la independencia de Bolivia* (La Paz: Fun- dación Cultural Quipus, 1987), 145.

16 "Proclama de Castelli a los indios del virreinato de Perú," 148–151.

17 Walker, *Smoldering Ashes*, 97–14.

18 There is an increasing literature on the small guerrilla movements in Upper Peru and an analysis of the ethnic composition of these movements. See for example Javier Marion, "*Indios Blancos*: Nascent Polities and Social Convergence in Bolivia's Ayopaya Rebellion, 1814–1821," *Colonial Latin American Historical Review* 15:4 (2006). For the classic account of the republiquetas, see Charles W. Arnade, *La dramática insurgencia de Bolivia* (La Paz: Editorial Juventud, 1972), 47–72.

19 See Ezequiel Beltrán Gallardo, *Las guerrillas de Yauyos en la emancipación del Perú 1820–1824* (Lima: Editores Técnicos, 1977).

20 The best discussion of this issue is José Luis Roca, *Ni con Lima ni con Buenos Aires: La formación de un Estado nacional en Charcas* (Lima: Instituto Francés de Estudios Andinos/Plural, 2007).

21 See Alejandro M. Corrado, *El Colegio Franciscano de Tarija y sus misiones*, 2nd ed., vol. 2 (Tarija: Editorial Offset Franciscana, 1990), 288–292, and Erick D. Langer, *Expecting Pears from an Elm Tree: Franciscan Missions on the Chiriguano Frontier in the Heart of South America, 1830–1949* (Durham, NC: Duke University Press, 2009), 50.

22 For an analysis of this encounter, see Thierry Saignes, *Historia del pueblo chiriguano*, coord. Isabelle Combès (La Paz: Instituto Francés de Estudios Andinos, 2007), 117–122.

23 Pilar Herr, "Indian-Spanish Relations on Chile's Southern Frontier, 1819–1832," in Langer, *Indians, State and Frontier*, unpublished ms.

24 Benjamín Vicuña Mackenna, *El ostracismo de los Carreras* (Santiago: Imprenta del Ferrocarril, 1857), 329–350.

25 See Mark van Aken, "The Lingering Death of Indian Tribute in Ecuador," *Hispanic American Historical Review* 61:3 (1981), 429–459; Víctor Peralta Ruíz, *En pos del tributo: Burocracia estatal, élite regional y comunidades indígenas en el Cusco rural, 1826–1854* (Cuzco: Centro de Estudios Regionales Andinos Bartolomé de Las Casas, 1991); and Erick D. Langer, "El liberalismo y la abolición de la comunidad indígena en Bolivia en el siglo XIX," *Historia y Cultura* 14 (1988), 59–95. A good summary of the Andes as a whole is Brooke Larson, *Trials of Nation Making: Liberalism, Race, and Ethnicity in the Andes, 1810–1910* (Cambridge: Cambridge University Press, 2004).

26 We need studies on prices in nineteenth-century Latin America to prove this point.

27 See David Bushnell, *Reform and Reaction in the Platine Provinces, 1810–1852* (Gainesville: University Presses of Florida, 1983), 9–11.

28 David Bushnell, *The Santander Regime in Gran Colombia* (Westport, CT: Greenwood, 1970), 175–176. Also see Larson, *Trials of Nation Making*, 71–102. My thanks to Marcela Echeverri, who helped me understand the complexities of Indian tribute in Colombia.

29 Andrés Guerrero, "The Administration of Dominated Populations under a Regime of Customary Citizenship: The Case of Postcolonial Ecuador," in *After Spanish Rule: Postcolonial Predicaments of the Americas*, ed. Mark Thurner and Andrés Guerrero (Durham, NC: Duke University Press, 2003), 272–309, and Erin O'Connor, *Gender, Indian, Nation: The Contradictions of Making Ecuador, 1830–1925* (Tucson: University of Arizona Press, 2007).

30 In fact, this is what the 1812 Cádiz Constitution posited, but Ferdinand VII reneged on it when he returned to power in 1816.

31 Mark Thurner, *From Two Republics to One Divided: Contradictions of Postcolonial Nationmaking in Andean Peru* (Durham, NC: Duke University Press, 1997), 24.

32 José Flores Moncayo, *Legislación boliviana del indio* (La Paz: n.p., 1953), 23–39. In this, Bolívar followed the ideas of the 1812 Constitution of Cádiz, which defined all citizens born in Spanish territories as Spanish citizens. For Cádiz, see the essay by Roberto Breña.

33 For the Andes, see Thurner, *From Two Republics*; Marta Irurozqui, *"A bala, piedra y palo": La construcción de la ciudadanía política en Bolivia, 1826–1952* (Seville: Diputación de Sevilla, 2000), and Larson, *Trials of Nation Making*.

34 "Arrendero" is a category that implied paying rent in money, goods, and services to the landlord in return for the use of a plot of land and a small house.

35 Notaría de Padilla (Chuquisaca, Bolivia), 1882, fs. 176–179.

36 Arnold J. Bauer, "Rural Workers in Spanish America: Problems of Peonage and Oppression," *Hispanic American Historical Review* 59:1 (1979), 34–63. It is possible that the concept of debt peonage only began in the 1840s as an invention of U.S. imperialists who wanted to equate labor conditions in Mexico with slavery in the United States, thus justifying the U.S. invasion of Mexico and the taking of half its territory. See Shelley Streeby, *American Sensations: Class, Empire, and the Production of Popular Culture* (Berkeley: University of California Press, 2002), esp. 189–213.

37 Aline Helg, *Liberty and Equality in Caribbean Colombia, 1770–1835* (Chapel Hill: University of North Carolina Press, 2004).

38 Cecilia Méndez, *The Plebeian Republic: The Huanta Rebellion and the Making of the Peruvian State, 1820–1850* (Durham, NC: Duke University Press, 2005).

39 See Erick D. Langer, "Bringing the Economic Back In: Andean Indians and the Construction of the Nation-State in Nineteenth-Century Bolivia," *Journal of Latin American Studies* 41:3 (2009), 527–551.

40 Tristan Platt, *Estado tributario y librecambio en Potosí (siglo XIX): Mercado indígena, proyecto proteccionista y lucha de ideologías monetarias* (La Paz: Instituto de Historia Social Boliviana, 1986). These records exist in the municipal archives as well as fragments in the police records of the Archivo Nacional de Bolivia (Sucre) in Tribunal Nacional de Cuentas.

41 Kristine L. Jones, "Comparative Raiding Economies: North and South," in Guy and Sheridan, *Contested Ground*, 97–114. For the Comanche, see Hämäläinen, *Comanche Empire*.

42 See Kristine L. Jones, "Calfucará and Namuncurá: Nation Builders on the Pampas," in *The Human Tradition in Latin America: The Nineteenth Century*, ed. Judith Ewell and William H. Beezley (Wilmington, DE: Scholarly Resources, 1989), 175–186. Also see Julio Vezub, *Valentín Saygüeque y la "Gobernación indígena de las Manzanas": Poder y etnicidad en la Patagonia Septentrional (1860–1881)* (Buenos Aires: Prometeo Libros, 2009), and Silvia Ratto, *Indios y cristianos: Entre la guerra y la paz en las fronteras* (Buenos Aires: Sudamericana, 2007). What is still missing, of course, is an analysis of what happened to the cattle on the western side of the Andes. Did the hides end up in the ballast tanks of whalers who called on ports in southern Chile?

43 Here there is a marked distinction with imperial Brazil, which did not suffer from this weakness.

44 See Daniel Villar, Juan Francisco Jiménez, and Silvia Mabel Ratto, *Conflicto, poder y justicia en la frontera bonaerense 1818–1832* (Bahía Blanca: Universidad Nacional del Sur, 2003). For the military balance of power on nineteenth-century frontiers, see Langer, "The Eastern Andean Frontier (Bolivia and Argentina) and Latin American Frontiers: Comparative Contexts (19th and 20th Centuries)," *The Americas*, 59:1 (July 2002), 33–63.

45 Silvio R. Duncan Baretta and John Markoff, "Civilization and Barbarism: Cattle Frontiers in Latin America," *Comparative Studies in Society and History* 20:4 (1978), 587–620. For eastern Peru, see Sala i Vila, *Selva y Andes*. Also see Erick D. Langer, "La violencia cotidiana en la frontera: Conflictos interétnicos en el Chaco boliviano," *Sociedades en movimiento: Los pueblos indígenas de América latina en el siglo XIX*, comp. Raúl J. Mandrini and Carlos D. Paz (Tandil, Argentina: IEHS, 2007), 19–32.

46 See Vezub, *Valentín Saygüeque*. Geraldine Davies is working on a dissertation on these relations and has found more correspondence of the type that Vezub found.

47 There is an increasing literature on these relations. See for example Silvia Ratto, "El 'negocio pacífico de los indios': La frontera bonaerense durante el gobierno de Rosas," *Siglo XIX: Revista de Historia* 15 (1994), 25–47; and Erick D. Langer, "Foreign Cloth in the Lowland Frontier: Commerce and Consumption of Textiles in Bolivia, 1830–1930," in *The Allure of the Foreign: The Role of Imports in Post-Colonial Latin America*, ed. Benjamin S. Orlove (Ann Arbor: University of Michigan Press, 1997), 93–112.

48 See for example Erick D. Langer and Gina Hames, "Commerce and Credit on the Periphery: Tarija Merchants, 1830–1914," *Hispanic American Historical Review* 74:2 (May 1994), 285–316.

49 John Tutino argued this long ago in *From Insurrection to Revolution in Mexico*.

50 See John Tutino, "The Revolution in Mexican Independence: Insurgency and the Renegotiation of Property, Production, and Patriarchy in the Bajío, 1800–1855," *Hispanic American Historical Review* 78:3 (1998), 367–418.

51 The key study is Hämäläinen, *Comanche Empire*.

52 This is detailed by Jordana Dym in chapter 7.

53 In her classic study *Maya Society under Colonial Rule*, Nancy Farriss emphasized that enduring Maya community and cultural autonomies were constructed in a context of marginal Spanish commercial development. On the 1840s Maya War for Independence, the classic study remains Nelson Reed, *The Caste War of Yucatán* (Stanford, CA: Stanford University Press, 1964). Studies taking regional politics and community interests into greater account began with Terry Rugeley, *Yucatan's Maya Peasantry and the Origins of the Caste War* (Austin: University of Texas Press, 1996).

54 See Julia Sarreal, *The Guaraní and Their Missions: A Socioeconomic History* (Stanford, CA: Stanford University Press, 2014), and Thomas Whigham, *The Politics of River Trade: Tradition and Development in the Upper Plata, 1780–1870* (Albuquerque: University of New Mexico Press, 1991).

55 Douglas Egerton, *Gabriel's Rebellion: The Virginia Slave Conspiracies of 1800 and 1802* (Chapel Hill: University of North Carolina Press, 1993); on the politics

of 1800, see James Horn, Sue Ellen Lewis, and Peter Onuf, eds., *The Revolution of 1800: Democracy, Race, and the New Republic* (Charlottesville: University of Virginia Press, 2002).

56 Matt Childs, *The 1812 Aponte Rebellion in Cuba and the Struggle against Atlantic Slavery* (Chapel Hill: University of North Carolina Press, 2006).

57 See Emilia Viotti da Costa, *Crowns of Glory, Tears of Blood: The Demerara Slave Rebellion of 1823* (New York: Oxford University Press, 1994), and João Reis, *Slave Rebellion in Brazil: The Muslim Uprising of 1835 in Bahia* (Baltimore: Johns Hopkins University Press, 1995).

58 For example, Robert Paquette, *Sugar Is Made with Blood: The Conspiracy of La Escalera and the Conflict between Empires over Slavery in Cuba* (Middletown, CT: Wesleyan University Press, 1988).

59 That the conflict was ultimately about slavery is detailed in Chandra Manning, *What This Cruel War Was Over: Soldiers, Slavery, and the Civil War* (New York: Knopf, 2008). Manning explores slaves turn to self-liberation during the war in *Troubled Refuge: Struggling for Freedom in the Civil War* (New York: Knopf, 2016).

60 Marjoleine Kors is writing a major analysis of this conflict.

61 Among many studies, see two books by William McLaughlin: *Cherokee Renascence in the New Republic* (Princeton, NJ: Princeton University Press, 1992), which details the rise of Cherokee independence in times of national uncertainty, and *After the Trail of Tears: The Cherokee's Struggle for Sovereignty, 1839–1880* (Chapel Hill: University of North Carolina Press, 1994), which emphasizes the search for indigenous independence in the face of a forced removal.

62 Langfur, *The Forbidden Lands.*

CONSOLIDATING DIVERGENCE

The Americas and the World after 1850

ERICK D. LANGER AND JOHN TUTINO

After a century of conflict and transformation the diverse new countries of the Americas began to consolidate around 1870. Polities stabilized. The United States held together after the Civil War; Brazil became a republic in 1889; Cuba a nation in 1895. The many nations of Spanish America settled into new boundaries and found a new political calm notable in the shadow of the preceding decades of conflict. Economies accelerated in the entrenched world of industrial capitalism. The United States—at least its industrial Northeast—joined in industrial leadership. The rest of the Americas found new dynamism as commodity exporters: old silver regions turned to new crops and minerals to supply the industrial cores; long marginal areas found roles in the global economy; and the old Atlantic exporters carried on as they faced the end of slavery.

The mid-nineteenth century, however, was not without conflicts, contradictions, and new divergences. A series of wars proved pivotal to the end of slavery, the end of indigenous independence, and the consolidation of states sustained by export economies. First and most transforming was the War for North America of 1846–1848. That conflict brought Texas with lands for the expansion of cotton and slavery and California with gold mines that stimulated western settlement into the republican union. It left Mexico with half its territorial claims, continuing commercial difficulties, political instability—and enduring indigenous autonomies. And it began the demise of Comanche power.[1] The challenge of incorporating Mexican and indigenous territories into the United States reopened the question of the expansion of slavery, leading to the deadly civil war of 1860–1865 that ended slavery, preserved the Union, and enabled a continental expansion driven by northern industries, commercial farming across the Midwest and West (as railroads, barbed wire, and repeating rifles ended Comanche and other indigenous independence), and mining and grazing across the far West—while a once-dynamic South struggled to produce cotton without slavery (or rights for ex-slaves).

The end of the U.S. Civil War coincided with the War of the Triple Alliance (better, the War against Paraguay) of 1864–1870. A Brazilian empire still grounded in coffee and slavery allied with Uruguayan and Argentine republics rising as suppliers of wool, livestock, and wheat to industrial Britain to attack Paraguay—a nation of Guaraní independence, language, and culture all but closed to world trade. Britain backed its allied suppliers in a conflict that destroyed the Guaraní peoples and their independence, forcing the interior of South America open to trade.[2] While that conflict raged, a multiracial alliance in Cuba rose in 1868 to challenge Spanish rule and slavery in a war that lasted a decade; Spanish rule survived to oversee a process that ended slavery in 1886. Cuba began to make sugar without slaves, and soon without Spain, as the war of 1895–1898 led to independence under U.S. hegemony.[3]

Meanwhile, in the shadow of the destructive U.S. Civil War and while the Ten Years War challenging slavery continued in Cuba, Brazilian military officers returning from what proved a difficult war against Guaraní Paraguay began to question slavery. They resisted service as slave chasers, enabling decades in which northeastern planters facing declining sugar markets sold slaves to southern planters expanding coffee production, creating an empire with a free North and a slave South. Slaves increasingly ran away and resisted; northern states and southern cities ended slavery, allowing them to recruit runaways (many they had recently sold away) as free workers. Slavery fell in Brazil in 1888, followed a year later by the collapse of the empire that had sustained it.[4]

As the nineteenth century approached its end, slavery finally ended as a major support of export production in the Americas. The fall of slavery coincided with the consolidation of republics: in the United States after 1865, in Brazil after 1889, in Cuba from 1895. Yet former slaves faced exclusions everywhere: all the former slave societies recruited growing numbers of immigrants to sustain urban and rural production. As Haitians had faced beginning in 1804, the emancipation of slaves led to marginalization of ex-slaves and their descendants. After a long conflictive era of making new countries, former Atlantic slave societies found different roles in the world of industrial capitalism that expanded rapidly after 1870: Haitians remained committed to family production and excluded from global trades; Brazilians continued to produce increasing amounts of coffee, leading world production without slaves; Cubans continued to supply U.S. markets with sugar, ruled by U.S. investors who brought prejudices against Afro-Cubans and limits to Cuba's republican independence.[5]

The United States, by contrast, soared to continental hegemony after 1870. An urbanizing Northeast saw its industries begin to compete in global markets; the South provided cotton raised by ex-slave sharecroppers facing Jim Crow exclusions; farmers across the Mississippi basin and beyond gained mechanized ways of production in new markets ruled by powerful rail and commercial trusts that provoked populist discontent; and regions taken from Mexico and cleared of Comanche and other native peoples boomed with a mix of mining, commercial grazing, and irrigated agriculture as Anglo-American entrepreneurs promoted a transformation of the Spanish North American economy by mixing European settlers and Mexican workers. The rise of the United States to global importance in the world of industrial capitalism came with enduring internal contradictions.[6]

Meanwhile, the core regions of Spanish America—once home to great indigenous states; then from 1550 to 1810 the center of silver economies pivotal to global trades—after 1870 consolidated national republics built on new export economies that enabled the subordination of the indigenous peoples that had found unprecedented (and often unrecognized) independence after 1810. New countries became oligarchic republics shaped by liberal land rules, the triumph of export-import flows fueling an industrial capitalism centered along a North Atlantic axis, and political exclusions that kept power and prosperity among elite Spanish Americans and immigrant allies who brought capital and ties to global markets.

The diverse national outcomes are well known. Peru found wool and guano as exports to fund state consolidation and constrain indigenous communities—processes furthered when copper from Cerro de Pasco brought added export revenues and state powers.[7] Bolivia found export revenues in tin in the late nineteenth century—and used them to subordinate assertive Aymara and others on the eastern frontiers.[8] Chile stabilized early, thanks to the earnings of feeding gold-rush California and despite an active indigenous frontier to the south; it later flourished with nitrate exports (in large part in coastal zones taken from Peru and Bolivia in the War of the Pacific, 1879–1884); it consolidated its liberal, oligarchic, export republic with late nineteenth-century copper sales.[9] Struggling republics from Colombia and Venezuela through Central America to Guatemala found coffee the way to revenues in world trade; they strengthened state powers—and pressed against mixed populations and native communities that often faced attacks on lands and demands for labor that brought new subordinations.[10]

Mexico lived parallel yet different developments after 1870: liberals in power pressed to privatize indigenous community lands, promote foreign investment, and stimulate exports while limiting political participations. Silver finally regained the heights of earlier times in the 1870s—as the United States and Germany joined Britain on the gold standard, ensuring that the value of silver plummeted. Still, politics stabilized while vanilla exports rose in the 1860s, coffee in the 1880s, henequen (supplying twine to mechanizing agriculture in the United States) in the 1890s, and copper and petroleum (supplying U.S. industry) around 1900.[11] The diversity of exports made Mexico different, as did its internal industrialization—rare outside the United States in the nineteenth-century Americas. Textile industries founded in the 1830s survived and expanded to serve national markets. More notably, Monterrey—long a small northeastern town suddenly near the U.S. border after the war of the 1840s—gained capital by facilitating exports of slave-grown Confederate cotton to British and northern U.S. mills during the Civil War. It used the capital and entrepreneurial skills generated then, and its rise as a rail junction in the 1880s, to build textile, beer, glass, and iron industries serving Mexican markets from the 1890s—soon joined by Guggenheim-owned smelters processing silver ore for export to the United States.[12]

A glance might suggest that Mexico had emerged from the collapse of silver, political conflicts, indigenous autonomies, international wars, and territorial losses to build a republic and an economy set to prosper in the world of industrial capitalism. It was the only American nation outside the United States to combine industry and agriculture for local markets and exports, along with rising mineral and energy sectors. But Mexican industries came late; they remained constrained to supplying limited national markets. As in most of Spanish America, in Mexico commodity exports drove prosperity that favored a few and excluded the many (except as poor producers and poorly paid workers) to sustain an oligarchic republic of deepening inequities.

Everywhere in the Americas, the consolidation of nations shaped by concentrating prosperity and widening exclusions came with the promotion among the powerful of new theories of racial hierarchy in which people of European ancestry were proclaimed inherently superior, legitimating the subordination and marginalization of all non-Europeans, whether of indigenous, African, or mixed ancestry. Racial exclusions and discriminations might vary from the sharp black-white lines drawn in the United States, to the gradations of color accepted in Brazil and the Caribbean, to the diverse anti-indigenous visions that formed across Spanish America—with greater or lesser openness to mixed peoples. Still, "scientific" exclusions proliferated as republics consolidated in the late nineteenth century.[13]

By 1900, the old European empires were gone (except for a few Caribbean remnants). Slavery too had finally vanished in the Americas as a sanctioned way of production for profit. Such celebrated triumphs, however, came with economies that still profited the few and marginalized the many—whether once independent indigenous peoples or recently freed slaves. And in the expansion of socially exclusionary export economies serving an industrial capitalism that concentrated production and power in northwestern Europe and the northeastern United States, the people of the republics consolidating across the Americas shared much with others around the world.

In the United States, the industries, railroads, mine operators, oil developers, and the commercial interests that integrated an urbanizing Northeast and Midwest with a still agro-pastoral South and West (and western mines) all boomed—except in recurrent years of collapse. Sharecroppers descended from slaves grew the cotton that sustained northern industries—and faced racial exclusion. Also excluded were the surviving natives forced into reservations to make their lands available for commercial expansion, the Mexicans still present or newly arrived who laid tracks, built dams and irrigation systems, worked mines, and picked crops. Less excluded but clearly prejudiced were the many farmers, often of European immigrant ancestry, who lived with climate and market uncertainties that led to mounting debts while railroads and commodities traders profited from their produce. Also prejudiced were the newly arrived immigrants crushed into urban slums or dispersed in mill towns across the Northeast, struggling to find work at more than poverty wages while the industries they sustained drove continental expansion and global trades. Viewed as a single nation—the United States was on the rise. Viewed as a continental empire, while industries and cities rose in the Northeast bringing profit to some, prosperity to many, and lives of difficult labor to too many, people across the rest of the nation faced export economies that concentrated wealth and prejudiced producers—freed slaves, Mexicans, Native Americans, and many workers and farmers of European ancestry, too. One only need read populist political rhetoric to know that many Euro-Americans living during westward expansion believed they faced exploitations around 1900.

While a rising United States prospered from exclusions within and Latin American nations forged oligarchic republics grounded in export economies and social subordinations, the late nineteenth century saw a new expansion of European empires. People across Africa and the Middle East, South and Southeast Asia, faced armies empowered by the same technologies that subordinated independent Amerindians. Made dependent on European rulers, newly colonized regions were drawn into the same world of industrial capitalism that shaped countries across the Americas. They too supplied commodities to industrial centers—and bought industrial products. And European imperial rule came sanctioned by the same "scientific" racisms that legitimated New World exclusions. "Native" peoples everywhere lost lands, lived exploitations, and faced denigration as workers often imagined as lazy and requiring coercion.[14]

The second generation European empires of the late nineteenth century did not replicate the early global polities that integrated the first world economy after 1500. The first empires faced slow transport and communications capacities; their military powers were limited and easily replicated (note the resistant power of New World nomads once they gained horses and firearms). The result was the polycentric first world economy in which Potosí and the Bajío could be more important than Madrid or Seville, Bahia and Rio de Janeiro more important than Lisbon, Saint Domingue as important as Paris.

The second wave of European empires used new industrial technologies of transport and communication and newly deadly weapons to draw a wider world of others into the economy of capitalist concentration: China and South Asia, once key industrial regions of the polycentric world economy; an Islamic world that had led the world in trade and technology before 1400; African kingdoms that engaged in diverse trades before focusing on supplying slaves. After 1870, all but China were drawn into empires; all including China were pressed to supply commodities and cheap labor and buy industrial products. Capitalists and empire builders everywhere justified their powers and others' subordination as grounded in "inherent" racial differences.

Latin American republics and African, Islamic, and Asian imperial subjects became essential peripheries in the world of concentrated industrial capitalism around 1900. Yet that world would not last. And the American republics that had emerged from the new countries formed in the conflictive transformations of 1750 to 1850 found that, as republics, they faced better chances than many recently colonized regions in the new era of national assertion and global transformation that began in 1910.

The challenge to the global industrial capitalism only consolidated after 1870 came quickly. Mexico—perhaps the most promising and polarized of the Spanish American republics—collapsed in revolution in 1910. In 1914, Britain and Germany, industrial powers competing for global hegemony, faced off in a deadly Great War. The United States joined to turn the tide in Britain's favor while Russia exploded in a revolution that challenged capitalism—but not industrialization. While victorious Anglo-Americans worked to restore industrial capitalism, Mexico and the Soviet Union began contrasting projects of national development, the former capitalist, the latter socialist. Global industrial capitalism collapsed in the Depression of the 1930s, turning the Americas and the world toward a search for "national development."

People across the hemisphere dreamed that the benefits of industrialism, long concentrated in Britain, northwestern Europe, and the northeastern United States, could be brought home to benefit everyone. There were possibilities in large nations like Mexico, which had a strong industrial start, and in Argentina and Brazil, which had limited starts but ample and diverse resources. Elsewhere, the dream often proved an illusion. But for decades, while the industrial powers faced depression and wars hot and cold, American republics turned to promising and sometimes promoting shared welfare among their diverse peoples. In the same era, the peoples of the second colonial empires were first drawn into their rulers' wars and then turned to anticolonial campaigns that ended imperial rule between 1945 and 1970; they left deep divisions, entrenched exclusions, and insurmountable challenges of national development, especially if equity was a goal.

Throughout the twentieth century, Spanish America's indigenous peoples pressed rights to fair, prosperous, and often-autonomous inclusion within nations. The Mexican revolution was revolutionary because villagers led by Emiliano Zapata fought for rights to land and self-rule long grounded in indigenous republics and recently lost under liberal reforms. They lost the war but won the land, forcing a new regime claiming to be revolutionary (while seeking national capitalist development) to return land to communities. Later, major agrarian reforms occurred in Bolivia in 1953 and in Peru in the late 1960s, giving land to rural workers who had labored on the haciendas. The Mexican example, however uneven in application and outcomes, became a beacon for indigenous peoples and rural villagers across the Americas—resonating in movements for indigenous rights from Chiapas to Ecuador and beyond in the late twentieth century.[15]

Broad promises of national development with egalitarian inclusions in the United States helped movements for African American, women's, Mexican American, and others' rights to flourish in the face of enduring resistance during decades of war, depression, war, cold war, and colonial adventures. Parallel movements rose across the Caribbean and in Brazil, too—and in the diverse societies across the globe that remained divided by racist legacies as they emerged from the last colonial empires.

The new countries that emerged from the first colonial empires across the Americas lived histories laden with conflict and contradiction, promise and challenge. The empires that organized the first global economy from 1500 to 1810 offered subordinating inclusions to indigenous peoples who survived the disease-driven depopulation that shaped the sixteenth century, especially in the Spanish domains that forged the silver economies that drove global trades for centuries. The same empires forced millions of enslaved Africans to labor in the spaces vacated by that depopulation, especially in Atlantic plantations that sent sugar, tobacco, and other goods to Europe.

The century of conflict that took down the first colonial empires across the Americas, created new countries, and spurred industrial capitalism led first to contested nations and indigenous independence across Spanish America; stronger nations (and an enduring colony) built on expanding slavery in the United States, Brazil, and Cuba; and an isolated nation of poverty in revolutionary Haiti. Contradictions were everywhere—as were promises of liberation and openings to autonomy. The global consolidation of industrial capitalism after 1870 brought export economies, oligarchic republics, and subordinated (and often expropriated) indigenous peoples across Spanish America. It brought the end of slavery in the United States, Cuba, and Brazil—and kept former slaves marginal and often excluded. Haitians found little change or gain. Then the turn to national development after 1910 opened possibilities (always limited and often contested) for indigenous communities, excluded racial groups, and women across the hemisphere and around the world—in times marked by global wars and depressions, national revolutions and anticolonial movements. There have been real gains—and obvious limits.

As promises of national development give way a globalization often presented as a utopian opportunity, centuries of history of conflict and contradiction, opportunity and uncertainty—and changing divergences—across the Americas and the world suggest that those seeking just inclusions and shared prosperity should keep one eye on the promise and another on the enduring potential for constraints, conflicts, and contradictions. Dynamic cities and growing industries now spread across the globe. Yet concentrations of power, production, and prosperity mix everywhere with exclusions, poverty, and marginality. Before 1850, slavery forced millions of Africans to migrate to labor; now millions around the world seek to migrate in search of distant opportunities—while powerful states work to limit their mobility. Coercions remain, sometimes forcing people to labor, often pressing them to stay home—or in the shadows—to face marginality. Meanwhile, indigenous peoples in the Andes, across the Americas, and around the world again press for autonomies that might enable them to participate with real benefits. Historic challenges persist—in new globalizing formulations of production and power, participation and resistance. The once new countries of the nineteenth-century Americas face continuing challenges—shared by many newer countries across the globe.

Notes

1 See Pekka Hämäläinen, *The Comanche Empire* (New Haven, CT: Yale University Press, 2008), and Brian DeLay, *War of a Thousand Deserts: Indian Raids and the U.S.-Mexican War* (New Haven, CT: Yale University Press, 2008).

2 On Paraguay and the war, see Thomas Wigham, *The Politics of River Trade: Tradition and Development in the Upper Plata, 1870–1970* (Albuquerque: University of New Mexico Press, 1991), and E. Bradford Burns, *The Poverty of Progress: Latin America in the Nineteenth Century* (Berkeley: University of California Press, 1983).

3 See Ada Ferrer, *Insurgent Cuba: Race, Nation, and Revolution, 1868–1898* (Chapel Hill: University of North Carolina Press, 1999), and Gillian McGillivray, *Blazing Cane: Sugar Communities, Class, and State Formation in Cuba, 1868–1959* (Durham, NC: Duke University Press, 2009).

4 See Emilia Viotti da Costa, *The Brazilian Empire: Myths and Histories* (Chapel Hill: University of North Carolina Press, 2000); Robert Conrad, *The Destruction of Brazilian Slavery, 1850–1888* (Berkeley: University of California Press, 1973); and Robert Brent Toplin, *The Abolition of Slavery in Brazil* (Boston: Atheneum, 1972).

5 On Cuba and the United States, see Louis Pérez, *On Becoming Cuban: Identity, Nationality, and Culture* (Chapel Hill: University of North Carolina Press, 1999).

6 See Eric Foner, *Reconstruction: America's Unfinished Revolution* (New York: Harper, 2002); Monica Prasad, *The Land of Too Much: American Abundance and the Paradox of Poverty* (Cambridge, MA: Harvard University Press, 2013); Michael Kazin, *The Populist Persuasion: An American History* (Ithaca, NY: Cornell University Press, 1998); and Katherine Benton-Cohen, *Borderline Americans: Racial Division and Labor War in the Arizona Borderlands* (Cambridge, MA: Harvard University Press, 2009).

7 See Paul Gootenberg, *Between Silver and Guano: Commercial Policy and the State in Postindependence Peru* (Princeton, NJ: Princeton University Press, 1989); Nils Jacobsen, *Mirages of Transition: The Peruvian Altiplano, 1780–1930* (Berkeley: University of California Press, 1993); and Florencia Mallon, *The Defense of Community in the*

Peru's Central Highlands: Peasant Struggle and Capitalist Transition, 1860–1940 (Princeton, NJ: Princeton University Press, 1983).

8   See Erick Langer, *Economic Change and Rural Resistance in Southern Bolivia, 1880–1930* (Stanford, CA: Stanford University Press, 1989) and *Expecting Pears from an Elm Tree*; see also Laura Gotkowitz, *A Revolution for Our Rights: Indigenous Struggles for Land and Justice in Bolivia, 1880–1952* (Durham, NC: Duke University Press, 2008).

9   Harold Blakemore, *British Nitrates and Chilean Politics, 1886–96* (Cambridge: Cambridge University Press, 1974), and Thomas Klubock, *Contested Communities: Class, Gender, and Politics in Chile's El Teniente Copper Mine, 1904–1951* (Durham, NC: Duke University Press, 1998).

10 Marco Palacios, *Coffee in Colombia: An Economic, Social, and Political History, 1850–1970* (Cambridge: Cambridge University Press, 2002); William Roseberry, *Coffee and Capitalism in the Venezuelan Andes* (Austin: University of Texas Press, 1984); and Robert Williams, *States and Social Evolution: Coffee and the Rise of National Governments in Central America* (Chapel Hill: University of North Carolina Press, 1994).

11 On vanilla, Emilio Kourí, *A Pueblo Divided: Business, Property, and Community in Papantla, Mexico* (Stanford, CA: Stanford University Press, 2004); on coffee, Heather Fowler Salamini, *Working Women, Entrepreneurs, and the Mexican Revolution: The Coffee Culture of Córdoba, Veracruz* (Lincoln: University of Nebraska Press, 2013); on henequen, Allen Wells and Gilbert Joseph, *Summer of Discontent, Seasons of Upheaval: Elite Politics and Rural Insurgency in Yucatán, 1876–1915* (Stanford, CA: Stanford University Press, 1996); on oil, Jonathan Brown, *Oil and Revolution in Mexico* (Berkeley: University of California Press, 1993).

12 On textiles, Aurora Gomez-Galvariatto, *Industry and Revolution: Social and Economic Change in the Orizaba Valley, Mexico* (Cambridge, MA: Harvard University Press, 2013); on Monterrey, Rodolfo Fernández, "Revolution and the Industrial City: Violence and Capitalism in Monterrey, Mexico, 1880–1920" (PhD diss., Georgetown University, 2014).

13 Brooke Larson, *Trials of Nation Making: Liberalism, Race, and Ethnicity in the Andes, 1810–1910* (New York: Cambridge University Press, 2004); Nancy Stepan, *The Hour of Eugenics: Race, Gender, and Nation in Latin America* (Ithaca, NY: Cornell University Press, 1991); Marisol de la Cadena, *Indigenous Mestizos: The Politics of Race and Culture in Cuzco, Peru, 1919–1991* (Durham, NC: Duke University Press, 2000).

14 C. A. Bayly, *The Birth of the Modern World, 1780–1914* (Oxford: Wiley-Blackwell, 2003).

15 See Lynn Stephen, *Zapata Lives! Histories and Cultural Politics in Southern Mexico* (Berkeley: University of California Press, 2002), and Waskar Ari, *Earth Politics: Religion, Decolonization, and Bolivia's Indigenous Intellectuals* (Durham, NC: Duke University Press, 2014).

ALFREDO ÁVILA is Research Professor at the Institute of Historical Research at the National Autonomous University of Mexico. He is author of *En nombre de la nación* and *Para la libertad: Los republicanos en tiempos del imperio, 1821–23*. He is working on a history of early experiments with liberalism in Spanish American countries.

———

ROBERTO BREÑA is Research Professor in the Center for International Studies of the Colegio de México. His books include *El primer liberalismo español y los precesos de emancipación de América, 1808–1824* and *El imperio de las circunstancias: Las independencies hispanoamericanas y la revolución liberal española*.

———

SARAH CHAMBERS is Professor of History at the University of Minnesota, Twin Cities. She is author of *From Subjects to Citizens: Honor, Gender, and Politics in Arequipa, Peru, 1780–1854* and *Families in War and Peace: Chile from Colony to Nation*. She continues to study women and gender in the formation of American nations.

———

JORDANA DYM is Professor of History at Skidmore College. She is author of *From Sovereign Villages to Nation States: City, State, and Federation in Central America, 1759–1839*, and coeditor of *Politics, Economy, and Society in Bourbon Central America, 1759–1821* and *Mapping Latin America: A Cartographic Reader*.

———

CAROLYN FICK serves as Associate Professor of History at Concordia University, Montreal. Her book *The Making of Haiti: The Saint Domingue Revolution from Below* opened the recent rethinking of that movement from the perspective the slaves that took arms to free themselves and found a black nation.

————

ERICK LANGER is Professor of History and International Affairs at Georgetown University. His books include *Economic Change and Rural Resistance in Southern Bolivia, 1880–1930* and *Expecting Pears from an Elm Tree: Franciscan Missions on the Chiriguano Frontier in the Heart of South America, 1830–1949.*

————

ADAM ROTHMAN is Professor of History at Georgetown University. He is author of *Slave Country: American Expansion and the Origins of the Deep South* and *Beyond Freedom's Reach: A Kidnapping in the Twilight of Slavery* and is currently working on a general history of emancipation in the United States.

————

DAVID SARTORIUS is Associate Professor of History at the University of Maryland, College Park. He is author of *Race, Loyalty, and the Ends of Empire in Spanish Cuba.* He is currently working on politics and sexuality in Cuban slave society.

————

KIRSTEN SCHULTZ is Associate Professor of History at Seton Hall University. Her book *Tropical Versailles: Empire, Monarchy, and the Portuguese Court in Rio de Janeiro, 1808–1821* is a key study of transatlantic power. She is now completing a new analysis of governance in eighteenth-century Brazil.

————

JOHN TUTINO is Professor of History and International Affairs, and Director of the Americas Initiative, at Georgetown University. He is author of *From Insurrection to Revolution in Mexico: Social Bases of Agrarian Violence, 1750–1940* and *Making a New World: Founding Capitalism in the Bajío and Spanish North America.*

Barbeyrac, 82

Baretta, Silvio R. Duncan, 365

Barrundia, José Francisco, 304, 306

Barrundia Zepeda, Juan, 292–93

Basques, 282, 293

Bastidas, Micaela, 324

Battle of Ayacucho (1824), 91

Battle of New Orleans (1815), 116

Battle of San Jacinto (1836), 265

Battle of the Alamo (1836), 265

Bauer, Arnold, 363

Beckert, Sven, 5, 55

Belgrano, Manuel, 359

Bentham, Jeremy, 179

Bill of Rights, 115

Blackburn, Robin, 3, 4

Black Hawk War (1832), 119

Bolívar, Simón, 17, 51, 168, 192, 318–19, 331, 362

Bolivia, 3, 10, 17, 58, 318–19, *324*, 365; agrarian reforms, 382; confederation with Peru, 332–38; exports, 378–79; map, *337*

Bourbon dynasty, 85, 236, 237, 241, 251–52, 280, 282–83, 284, 321, 323

Boxer, Charles, 204

Boyer, Jean-Pierre, 163, 164, 166–67

Bravo, Nicolás, 257–58, 267

Brazil: coffee trade, 9, 14, 54, 182, 201–2, 221, 368, 377; constitutionalism, 214; as Empire, 202–3, 210, 223–24; free trade, 211; in global economy, 204–10, 218, 220; gold trade, 39–40, 42, 205–7; independence, 8, 13–14, 54, 201, 211–22; indigenous labor appropriation, 207–8; indigenous marginalization, 223, 368; *juntas de fazenda*, 208; maps, *206, 217*; Portuguese court in, 8–9, 201–2, 220; Portuguese monarchy in, 47, 51, 212, 243; as Republic, 224; slave trade, 2, 6, 9, 14, 39–40, 46, 52–54, 182–83, 202, 203, 207, 208–9, 212, 218–22, *221*, 377; sovereignty, 212–17, 222–24; sugar trade, 38, 40, 52; tobacco trade, 204

Britain: on Brazilian independence, 218, 219; industrial revolution, 5, 7, 12, 16, 31–32; investment in Mexico, 258–59; world economy, domination of, 43–45, 62, 212, 258

Brown, John, 125

Buenos Aires, 58–59, 87–88, 90, 318, 321, 322

Burnet, David, 265

Bustamante, Anastasio, 260, 261, 262

Bustamante, Carlos María de, 247, 250

Bustamante, José de, 285

Byron, Lord, 77

cacao trade, 40, 289

caciques. See kurakas

Cádiz Constitution (1812), 7, 9, 73, 77, 87; goal of, 89; implementation in Spanish America, 89–93, 185, 187–91, 192, 213, 247, 248, 249, 252, 285–86, 290–91, 330–31; intellectual sources of, 81–87; Preliminary Discourse, 85–86

Cádiz liberalism, 11–12, 15, 17, 51, 74–87, 247–52; Catholicism as sole religion, 80; Church reaction to, 81; intellectual sources of, 81–87; main protagonists, 78; Spanish America and, 87–98, 285, 288; tenets, 79–80

Calfucará, 364

Calhoun, John, 120–21

California: gold rush, 61–62, 121; as U.S. state, 269, 377

Calleja, Félix, 246, 249–50, 251

Campomanes, Pedro Rodríiguez, 179

Canada, 112–13

Caracas, 87–88, 90

Carlos III, 81, 83, 282

Carlos IV, 76, 81, 83, 242, 243

Carrera, José Miguel, 359

Carrera, Rafael, 299–300, *301*, 303–5, 306

Casáus y Torres, Ramón, 302

Catholicism, 80, 81, 235, 257

cattle trade, 364

Cherokee Constitution (1827), 119

Chiapas, 286, 288–89

Chile, 17, 58, 92, 319, 336, 379

China: demand for silver, 42–43, 44–45, 48, 234, 317; demise of, 10; as economic power, 5, 25, 381; opium trade, 48–49; porcelain trade, 25; silk trade, 25; trade routes, 29, 31

cholera epidemic, 265–66, 299

Choque, Tadeo, 363

Choquehuanca, José Domingo, 333–34

Christophe, Henri, 146, 156, 159, 160–62

citizenship: of indigenous populations, 79, 89, 330; to patriot army fighters, 335; of people of African descent, 330; popular sovereignty and, 167, 288; post-abolition, 147, 153, 158, 162, 164, 167. *See also* specific countries

Civil War, U.S. (1861–1864), 2, 10, 12, 14, 62, 121–29, *128*, 269, 368, 377

cochineal trade, 16, 36–37, 60, 281, 292, 294, 297

Frank, Andre Gunder, 27
French constitutional thought, 81, 82, 83–84
French National Convention, 145
French Revolutionary Wars (1792–1815), 8, 96, 115
Fuente, Alejandro de la, 182, 190
Fuentes Franco, Andrés, 303
Fuentes y Guzmán, Francisco Antonio, 278–79
Fugitive Slave Clause, 115
Fugitive Slave Law (1850), 125
Furtado, Francisco Xavier de Mendonça, 207–8
fur trade, 33

Galbaud, Thomas, 145
Galdíz, Pedro, 187
Galindo, Juan, 295
Gálvez, Mariano, 295, 296–98, 303, 306
Gamarra, Agustín, 329–30, 331, 332, 336
García Paláez, Antonio, 300–301
Garrison, William Lloyd, 124–25
Gazeta de Guatemala (newspaper), 282
Gettysburg Address (1863), 127
Godoy, Manuel, 74, 78, 83, 242, 243
gold standard, 379
gold trade, 26, 27–28, 33, 42, 49; California gold rush, 61–62, 121; costs and infrastructure, 205–7; slavery in, 204–5
Goman, Jean-Baptiste, 163
Gómez Farías, Valentín, 262, 263, 264–65, 266
Gómez Pedraza, Manuel, 260
Goya, Francisco, 74
Goyeneche, José Manuel, 329–30
Granada, Nicaragua, 285
Granados, Luis Fernando, 6
grana trade. *See* cochineal trade
Gran Colombia, Federation of, 168, 279, 357
Grand Anse, Haiti, 163
Great Depression (1929–1939), 62
Great Rebellion in the Southern Andes (1780–1784), 353, 354
Great Sioux War (1876), 120
Grito de Dolores, 245–46
Grotius, 82
Guanajuato, 36, 37
guano exports, 58, 335, 378
Guaraní peoples, 59, 367, 377
Guatemala (country), 286; borders, 294, 295, 296; cochineal trade, 292, 294, 297; coffee trade, 297, 306; conservative regime, 301–5; continuities and ruptures, 306–7; federation challenges, 293–95; foreign residents, 298–99; immigrants, 303; indigenous majorities in, 3, 16; indigenous rights, 291–92; indigo trade, 284–85, 291, 292, 294, 297; as indivisible, 303–4; literacy, 302; Livingston Codes, 297; map, 294, 296; rebellions, 304–5, 306; sovereignty, 306–7; state formation, 290–93, 297, 306; state to republic, 300–303; taxation, 299–300
Guatemala (Kingdom), 10, 15–16, 60, 278, 286; citizenship, 286, 287–88; divided districts in, 279–84, 283, 286, 288; independence, cusp of, 284–88; independence, fissures of, 288–90; indigenous rights, 287; map, 283
Guatemala City, Guatemala, 280, 281, 282, 285, 291, 304
Guerra, François-Xavier, 76, 95
Guerrero, Vicente, 244, 251, 252–53, 260–62
Guridi y Alcocer, José Miguel, 245
Gusmão, Alexandre de, 207
Gutiérrez Estrada, José María, 266–67

Habsburg dynasty, 39, 84–85, 204, 280
Haiti, 2, 164; citizenship, 147, 153, 158, 162, 164, 167; coffee trade, 161, 165, 169; as divided, 160–62; freedom in, 146–47; independence, 148–57, 168, 368, 369; land distribution, 162–67; map, 166; peasant empowerment, 163–67; plantation citizenship, 147–48; plantation economy, 5, 49, 143, 157, 163, 168–69; plantation structure, 149–50, 153–55, 159, 160–61; poverty in, 6; slavery in, 3, 14; trade relations, 148–49, 155. *See also* Saint Domingue
Haitian Revolution (1791–1804), 4, 8, 11, 12–13, 45–46, 51–52, 96; background, 142–45; sugar trade, demise of, 168–69
Hamilton, Alexander, 49, 107–9, 110, 115
Hamnett, Brian, 92
Harpers Ferry Raid (1859), 125
Hartford Convention (1814), 116
Havana, Cuba: British seizure of, 42, 208; economic expansion, 179–80, 182, 294; shipbuilding, 37
head taxes, 258, 323, 333, 361. *See also* tribute payments
Helg, Aline, 363
Herrarte, José Mariano, 303
Herrera, José Joaquín de, 267
Hidalgo, Miguel, 47–48, 88, 245–46

Hispaniola, 139, 152. *See also* Haiti; Saint Domingue

historic nationalism (*nacionalismo histórico*), 81, 84–88

Honduras, 16, 286, 293

House of Braganza, 204

Houston, Samuel, 265

Huachaca, Antonio Abad, 363

Humboldt, Alexander von, 234

imperialism, 8

Inca/Inka peoples, 30, 33–35, 316–17

India, 5, 11, 41, 42, 44

indigenous populations: appropriation of labor, 207–10; appropriation of land from, 6, 17, 362; arable land of, 364; citizenship, 79, 89, 362; colonized vs. uncolonized, 351; cultural assimilation, 307; diseases from Europe, 26, 39, 234; displacement of, 1–2, 119–20; on frontier, independence of, 358–59; grassroots democracy, 354; hacienda regimes, 362–63; head taxes, 258, 323, 333, 361; independence, 17–18, 268, 350–69, *366*; inversions, 55–63; local politics, 239–40, 336; marginalization of, 223, 361, 380; post-independence, 359–66; second conquest of, 351, 353–56; self-rule, 8, 237, 280–81; stereotyped conceptions of, 354; third conquest of, 351; tribute payments, 89, 237, 246, 254, 284, 287, 318, 323–26, 329, 330–31, 333–34, 359, 361–62, 369; weak republics and, 364–66. *See also* specific countries; specific peoples

indigo trade, 16, 40, 60, 284–85, 291, 292, 294, 297

industrial capitalism: consolidation of, 382, 383; rise of, 3, 4–5, 6, 7, 12, 376; U.S. transition to, 122–23, 129

Infiesta, Ramón, 185, 186

Inka. *See* Inca/Inka peoples

Inquisition, abolition of, 80

intendentes, 353

Iturbide, Agustín de, 51, 60, 252–55, 288

Iturrigaray, José de, 243, 245

Jackson, Andrew, 116, 119

Jamaica, 39

Jefferson, Thomas, 49–50, 115–16, 117, 155–56

Jesuit missions, 38, 208, 367

João, King, 8, 14, 51, 211, 213, 219

Johnson, Lyman, 59

Johnson, Samuel, 111

Jones, Kristine, 364

José I, 207

Jovellanos, 84–85

Juárez, Benito, 270–71

Juarros, Domingo, 278–79, 281, 282, 285

Juguetillo, El (journal), 247

Junta Americana, 246

Junta Central, 76, 87

Junta de Reformas de Ultramar, 191

Junta Nacional Americana, 248

juntas de fazenda, 208

Katari, Tomás, 326

Katari, Tupaj. *See* Apasa, Julián

Knight, Franklin, 179

kurakas, 33, 35, 318, 327–28, 329, 353–54, 362

ladinos, 16, 281, 284, 289, 291, 298, 300, 307

Langfur, Hal, 210, 223

Langley, Lester, 3–4

La Parra, Emilio, 83

Larrazábal, Antonio, 300–301

Latin America: commodity production in, 168; impoverishment, 183–84; independence, 48, 52, 177, 381–82; indigenous independence, 350–69; military-authoritarian rule in, 51; monarchies in, 162. *See also* Americas; specific countries

Laurens, Henry, 112

Leclerc, Charles Victor-Emmanuel, 155, 156

Leo XII, 258

liberalism, Hispanic, 7, 79, 81. *See also* Cádiz liberalism

Lin, Man-Houng, 48

Lincoln, Abraham, 109, 125, 126–28

Livingston Codes, 297

Los Altos, Guatemala, 288, 289, 299, 300, 303, 304–5, 306

Louisiana, 39, 118–19

Louisiana Purchase (1803), 8, 116, 117–18

Louis XVI, 46, 142

Lynch, John, 3

Machado, Gerardo, 185

maize production, 30

Manchester, Alan, 212

Manifest Destiny, 120

Manifesto de los Persas, 93

Mantúfar, Lorenzo, 295

Mapuche peoples, 364